Texas Science • Texas Science • Texas Science • Texas Science • Texas Science • Texas Science • Texas Science • Texas

Interactive SCIENCE™

Go to PearsonTexas.com to learn science through videos, labs, online activities, and more!

PEARSON Texas.com

Glenview, Illinois • Boston, Massachusetts • Chandler, Arizona • Hoboken, New Jersey

You are an author!

My Photo

You are one of the authors of this book. You can write in this book! You can take notes in this book! You can draw in it too! This book will be yours to keep.

Fill in the information below to tell about yourself. Then write your autobiography. An autobiography tells about you and the kinds of things you like to do.

Name ....

School ....

City or Town ....

Autobiography ....

....

....

....

Acknowledgments appear on pages EM24–EM26, which constitute an extension of this copyright page.

ON THE COVER
A pack of gray wolves is often just one family: a male, a female, and their offspring.

PEARSON

Softcover: ISBN-13: 978-0-328-80752-9
ISBN-10: 0-328-80752-4
9 18

Hardcover: ISBN-13: 978-0-328-80331-6
ISBN-10: 0-328-80331-6
5 6 7 8 9 10 V011 18 17 16 15 14

Program Authors

DON BUCKLEY, M.Sc.
Director of Technology & Innovation,
The School at Columbia University, New York, New York
Don Buckley has transformed learning spaces, textbooks, and media resources so that they work for students and teachers. He has advanced degrees from leading European universities, is a former industrial chemist, published photographer, and former consultant to MOMA's Education Department. He also teaches a graduate course at Columbia Teacher's College in Educational Technology and directs the Technology and Innovation program at the school. He is passionate about travel, architecture, design, change, the future, and innovation.

ZIPPORAH MILLER, M.A.Ed.
Associate Executive Director for Professional Development Programs and Conferences, National Science Teachers Association, Arlington, Virginia
Mrs. Miller is currently the associate executive director for professional development programs and conferences at NSTA. She provides professional development and e-learning opportunities to science educators nationwide. She is a former K–12 science supervisor and STEM coordinator for the Prince George's County Public School District in Maryland. During her tenure there, she served as teacher, STEM coordinator, principal, and administrator. Mrs. Miller is passionate about providing quality educational opportunities to all students.

MICHAEL J. PADILLA, Ph.D.
Eugene P. Moore School of Education, Clemson University, Clemson, South Carolina
A former middle school teacher and a leader in middle school science education, Dr. Michael Padilla has served as president of the National Science Teachers Association and as a writer of the 1996 National Science Education Standards. He is a professor of science education at Clemson University. As lead author of the *Science Explorer* series, Dr. Padilla has inspired the team in developing a program that promotes student inquiry and meets the needs of today's students.

KATHRYN THORNTON, Ph.D.
Professor, Mechanical & Aerospace Engineering, University of Virginia, Charlottesville, Virginia
Selected by NASA in May 1984, Dr. Kathryn Thornton is a veteran of four space flights. She has logged more than 975 hours in space, including more than 21 hours of extravehicular activity. As an author on the *Scott Foresman Science* series, Dr. Thornton's enthusiasm for science has inspired teachers around the globe.

MICHAEL E. WYSESSION, Ph.D.
Associate Professor of Earth and Planetary Science, Washington University, St. Louis, Missouri
An author on more than 50 scientific publications, Dr. Wysession was awarded the prestigious Packard Foundation Fellowship and Presidential Faculty Fellowship for his research in geophysics. Dr. Wysession is an expert on Earth's inner structure and has mapped various regions of Earth using seismic tomography. He is known internationally for his work in geoscience education and research, and was an author of the Next Generation Science Standards.

Planet Diary Author

JACK HANKIN
Science/Mathematics Teacher, The Hilldale School, Daly City, California
Founder, Planet Diary Web site
Mr. Hankin is the creator and writer of Planet Diary, a science current events Web site. Mr. Hankin is passionate about bringing science news and environmental awareness into classrooms.

Activities Author

KAREN L. OSTLUND, Ph.D.
President-Elect, National Science Teachers Association, Arlington, Virginia
Dr. Ostlund has over 40 years of experience teaching at the elementary, middle school, and university levels. She was Director of WINGS Online (Welcoming Interns and Novices with Guidance and Support) and the Director of the UTeach / Dell Center for New Teacher Success with the UTeach program in the College of Natural Sciences at the University of Texas at Austin. She also served as Director of the Center for Science Education at the University of Texas at Arlington, as President of the Council of Elementary Science International, and as a member of the Board of Directors of the National Science Teachers Association. As an author of Scott Foresman Science, Dr. Ostlund was instrumental in developing inquiry activities.

ELL Consultant

JIM CUMMINS, Ph.D.
Professor and Canada Research Chair, Curriculum, Teaching and Learning Department at the University of Toronto
Dr. Cummins's research focuses on literacy development in multilingual schools and the role technology plays in learning across the curriculum. *Interactive Science* incorporates research-based principles for integrating language with the teaching of academic content based on Dr. Cummins's work.

Program Consultants

WILLIAM BROZO, Ph.D.
Professor of Literacy,
Graduate School of Education,
George Mason University,
Fairfax, Virginia
Dr. Brozo is the author of numerous articles and books on literacy development. He coauthors a column in *The Reading Teacher* and serves on the editorial review board of the *Journal of Adolescent & Adult Literacy.*

KRISTI ZENCHAK, M.S.
Biology Instructor,
Oakton Community College,
Des Plaines, Illinois
Kristi Zenchak helps elementary teachers incorporate science, technology, engineering, and math activities into the classroom. STEM activities that produce viable solutions to real-world problems not only motivate students but also prepare students for future STEM careers. Ms. Zenchak helps elementary teachers understand the basic science concepts and provides STEM activities that are easy to implement in the classroom.

Content Reviewers

Brian Ancell, Assistant Professor
Department of Geosciences
Texas Tech University
Lubbock, Texas

D. Brent Burt, Professor
Department of Biology
Stephen F. Austin State University
Nacogdoches, Texas

Gerald B. Cleaver, Ph.D.
Department of Physics
Baylor University
Waco, Texas

David Lamp
Associate Professor of Physics/Education
Texas Tech University
Lubbock, Texas

Dr. Richard H. Langley
Department of Chemistry
Stephen F. Austin State University
Nacogdoches, Texas

Heidi Marcum
Department of Environmental Science
Baylor University
Waco, Texas

Emilia Morosan
Rice University
Houston, Texas

Aaron S. Yoshinobu, Ph.D
Associate Professor
Department of Geosciences
Texas Tech University
Lubbock, Texas

Built for Texas

Texas Interactive Science covers 100% of the Texas Essential Knowledge and Skills for Science. Built on feedback from Texas educators, *Texas Interactive Science* focuses on what is important to Texas teachers and students, and creates a personal, relevant, and engaging classroom experience.

Pearson would like to extend a special thank you to all of the teachers from across the state of Texas who helped guide the development of this program.

Unit A
Science, Engineering and Technology

This scientist is recording observations about the animal. Scientists use detailed observations to draw conclusions and construct reasonable explanations.

STEM Project
Go online to find the project for this chapter. You will build a three-dimensional model of a tent.

The Nature of Science

PEARSON Texas.com

Unit B
Physical Science

An object's density, compared to water's density, determines if it will float or sink in water.

STEM Project

Go online to find the project for this chapter. You will design, build, and fly a kite.

Properties of Matter

PEARSON Texas.com

Unit B
Physical Science

Forms and Uses of Energy

These kids are using energy to swing. The energy of motion is one kind of energy.

STEM Project
Go online to find the project for this chapter. You will design a "greener" lighting plan that saves energy.

PEARSON Texas.com

Unit B
Physical Science

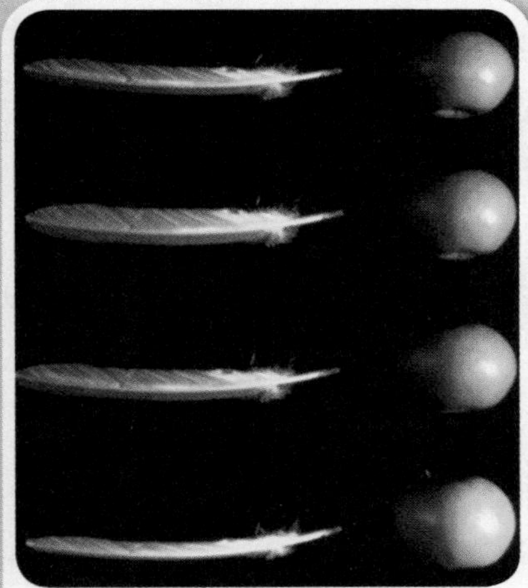

Gravity is a force that pulls objects toward Earth's center. It works on both the feather and the apple, causing them both to fall.

STEM Project

Go online to find the project for this chapter. You will design a bridge and test its strength.

Forces and Their Effects

PEARSON Texas.com

Unit C
Earth Science

This canyon, found in Big Bend National Park in West Texas, was formed by the Rio Grande. The flowing river eroded away rock to create these steep walls.

STEM Project

Go online to find the project for this chapter. You will design a container that will reduce the materials used to package cereal.

Earth's Surface

PEARSON Texas.com

Water is in the air all around us. We can't see it because it is a gas. The water in the air froze on this man's beard.

STEM Project
Go online to find the project for this chapter. You will design, build, and test a wind vane.

The Water Cycle, Weather, and Climate

PEARSON Texas.com

Unit C
Earth Science

Earth's rotation on its axis causes the cycle of day and night, as well as the apparent motion of the sun across the sky.

Earth and Space

PEARSON Texas.com

These animals in Texas depend on each other to survive. Cattle egrets eat insects cattle scare with their movement. The birds have food and the cattle have fewer pests!

STEM Project
Go online to find the project for this chapter. You will design, build, and test a multi-layered water filter.

Ecosystems

PEARSON Texas.com

Unit D
Life Science

A Texas Horned Lizard has several adaptations that help it survive, including blowing up like a spiky balloon and squirting blood from its eyes!

STEM Project

Go online to find the project for this chapter. You will design a device that will automatically water an indoor plant.

Growth and Survival

PEARSON Texas.com

Videos that bring Science to life!

Go to **PEARSON Texas.com** to watch exciting Untamed Science videos!

The Untamed Science team has created a unique video for every chapter in this book!

PEARSON Texas.com

Engage with the Page!

Untamed Science videos make learning science fun at the beginning of every chapter.

This is your book. You can write in it. Connect and interact as you read the Texas Interactive Science write-in student edition.

WHAT is this?
Texas
Chapter 9
Growth and Survival
Lesson 1 What are some physical structures in living things?
Lesson 2 How do adaptations help organisms survive?
Lesson 3 What are the life cycles of some animals?
How do living organisms adapt and survive?

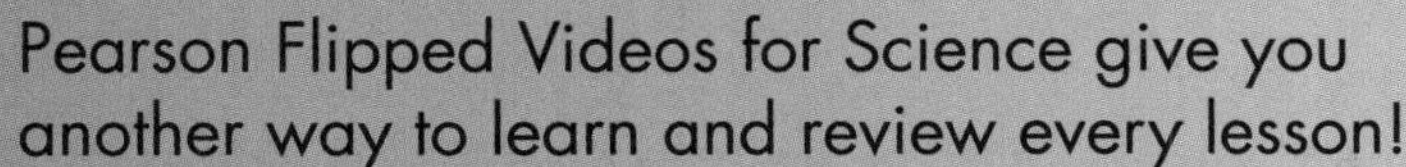

Pearson Flipped Videos for Science give you another way to learn and review every lesson!

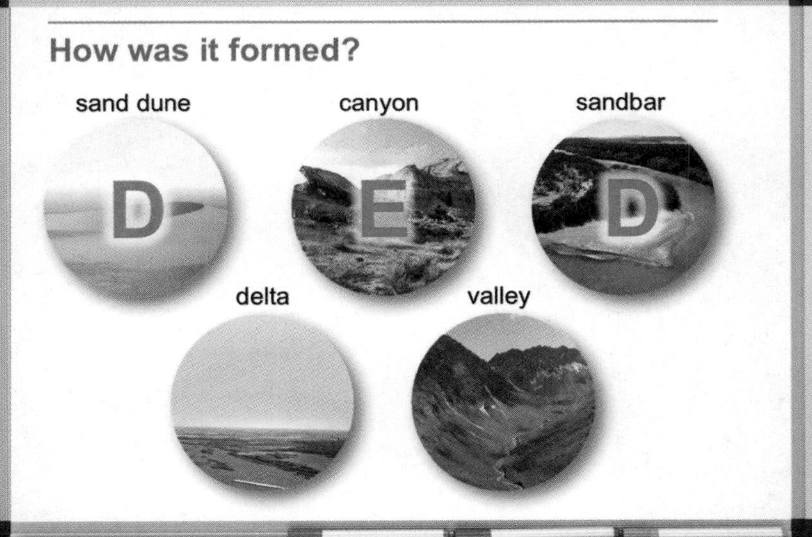

Get active with science with whiteboard-ready activities.

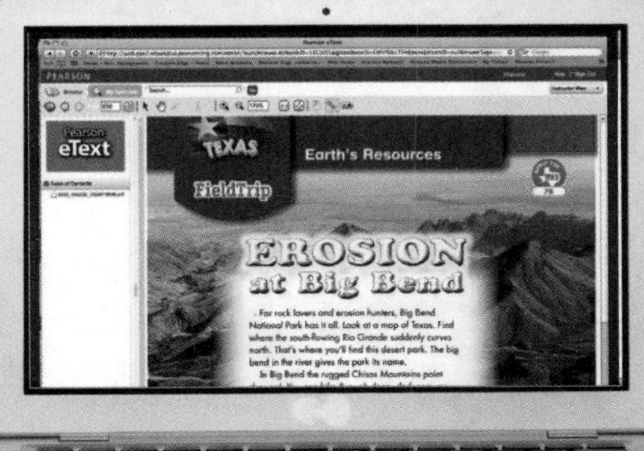

Access all print program resources in English or Spanish at PEARSONTexas.com.

Connect what you do to what you read and see.

Be a Scientist!

Engage with science through hands-on activities in each lesson! With easy-to-find materials, these activities can be conducted in the classroom or at home!

Start Each Chapter

Lab zone **Inquiry Warm-Up**

TEKS 10A, 1A, 2A, 2B, 2C, 2D, 2F, 2G

How can temperature affect seed growth?

Materials
seeds (basil, pinto bean)
2 clear plastic cups
2 wet paper towels

Texas Safety LAB RULES
If any water spills, notify your teacher immediately. Wash your hands thoroughly upon completing the activity.

1. Choose one type of seed to test. Use the cups and towels to grow the seeds.
2. Put one cup in a refrigerator. Put the other cup in a dark place in your classroom.
3. **Predict** how temperature will affect the seeds.
4. **Collect Data** Create a table to organize, examine, and evaluate your observations. Use a computer, if possible.

Inquiry Skill
You can **collect data** by drawing what you observe.

Seed Observations

Temperature	Type of Seed				
	Day 1	Day 2	Day 3	Day 4	Day 5
Cold					
Room temperature					

Explain Your Results

5. Compare your results with those of other groups. How did the seeds respond to temperature? **Infer** how this response might help a pinto-bean plant respond to changing seasons.

416

Lab zone **Quick Lab**

TEKS 10A, 1A, 2A, 2C, 2D, 2E, 2F, 3C

Which bird beak can crush seeds?

Materials
glue
craft sticks
2 clothespins
4 pieces of straw

Texas Safety LAB RULES
Keep your work area clean. If any glue spills, notify your teacher immediately.

1. **Make a Model** of a heron's beak. Glue 2 craft sticks to a clothespin. Use the other clothespin as a model of a cardinal's beak. Use pieces of a straw as models of seeds.
2. Use the heron's beak. Pick up a seed. Does the beak crush the seed? Try 5 times. **Record.**
3. Repeat with the cardinal's beak. Record.

Explain Your Results

4. **Draw a Conclusion** Which bird crushes seeds?
5. There are many seeds in a cardinal's environment. There are many fish, insects, and small animals in a heron's environment. **Infer** how the structure of each bird's beak helps the bird survive in its environment.

419

Start Each Lesson

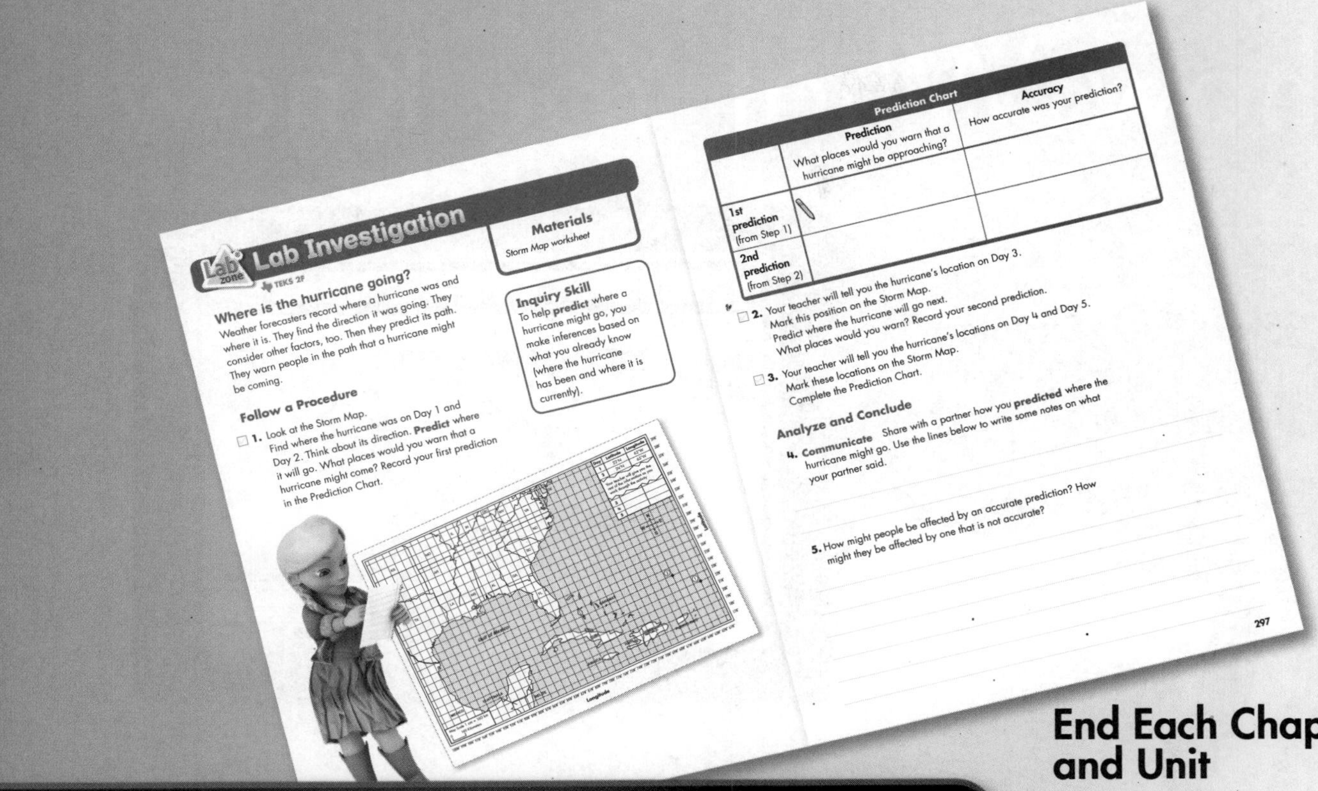

Lab Investigation

TEKS 2F

Where is the hurricane going?

Weather forecasters record where a hurricane was and where it is. They find the direction it was going. They consider other factors, too. Then they predict its path. They warn people in the path that a hurricane might be coming.

Materials
Storm Map worksheet

Inquiry Skill
To help **predict** where a hurricane might go, you make inferences based on what you already know (where the hurricane has been and where it is currently).

Follow a Procedure

☐ **1.** Look at the Storm Map. Find where the hurricane was on Day 1 and Day 2. Think about its direction. **Predict** where it will go. What places would you warn that a hurricane might come? Record your first prediction in the Prediction Chart.

Prediction Chart

	Prediction What places would you warn that a hurricane might be approaching?	Accuracy How accurate was your prediction?
1st prediction (from Step 1)		
2nd prediction (from Step 2)		

☐ **2.** Your teacher will tell you the hurricane's location on Day 3. Mark this position on the Storm Map. Predict where the hurricane will go next. What places would you warn? Record your second prediction.

☐ **3.** Your teacher will tell you the hurricane's locations on Day 4 and Day 5. Mark these locations on the Storm Map. Complete the Prediction Chart.

Analyze and Conclude

4. Communicate Share with a partner how you **predicted** where the hurricane might go. Use the lines below to write some notes on what your partner said.

5. How might people be affected by an accurate prediction? How might they be affected by one that is not accurate?

297

End Each Chapter and Unit

At PEARSONTexas.com go online and conduct labs virtually! No goggles and no mess.

Have Fun!

Show What You Know!

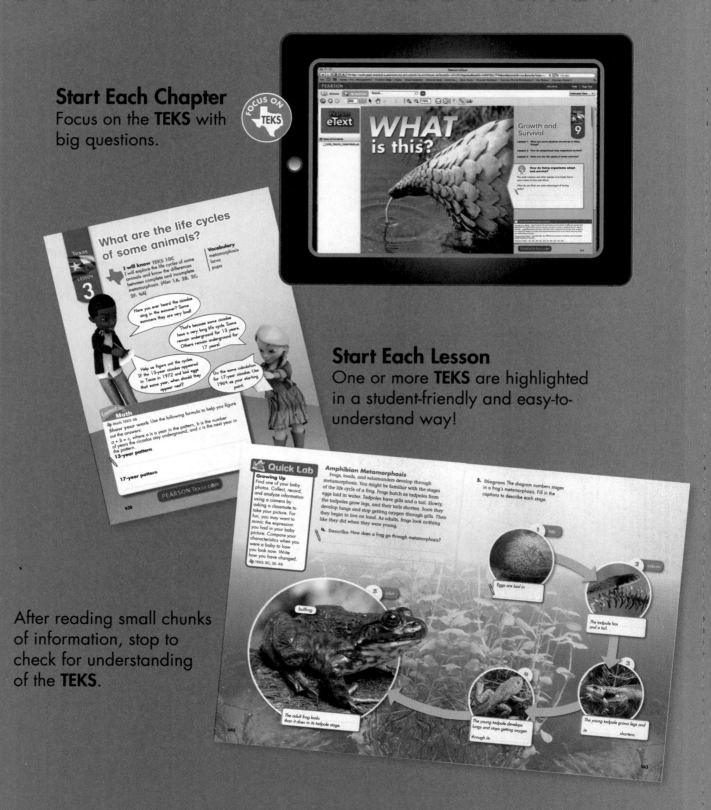

Start Each Chapter
Focus on the **TEKS** with big questions.

Focus on TEKS

Pearson eText

WHAT is this?

Growth and Survival 9

What are the life cycles of some animals?

I will know TEKS 10C I will explore the life cycles of some animals and know the differences between complete and incomplete metamorphosis. (Also 1A, 2B, 2C 2F, 4A)

Vocabulary
metamorphosis
larva
pupa

Have you ever heard the cicadas sing in the summer? Some summers they are very loud!

That's because some cicadas have a very long life cycle. Some remain underground for 13 years. Others remain underground for 17 years!

Help us figure out the cycles. If the 13-year cicadas appeared in Texas in 1972 and laid eggs that same year, when should they appear next?

Do the same calculation for 17-year cicadas. Use 1964 as your starting point.

Start Each Lesson
One or more **TEKS** are highlighted in a student-friendly and easy-to-understand way!

Quick Lab

Amphibian Metamorphosis

After reading small chunks of information, stop to check for understanding of the **TEKS**.

Apply content to new situations from Texas and beyond.

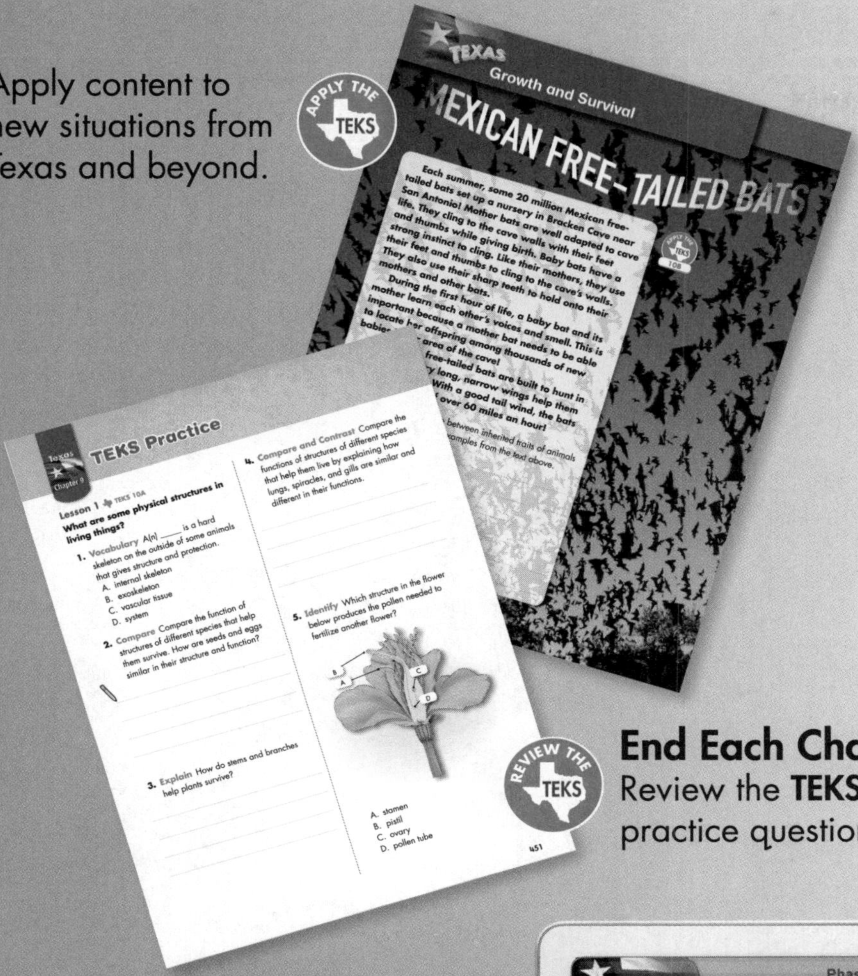

End Each Chapter
Review the **TEKS** with practice questions.

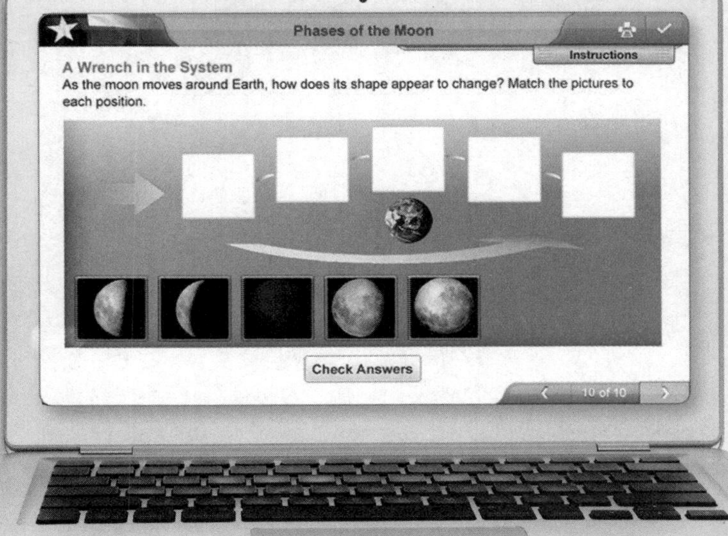

See what you already know.

Check what you know at the end of each lesson and chapter.

Get More Practice on skills and/or content, based on your performance.

Predict your exam readiness with unit-level benchmark assessments.

Get extra practice instantly online!

Track Your Learning Online.

Texas

Unit A

Science, Engineering, and Technology

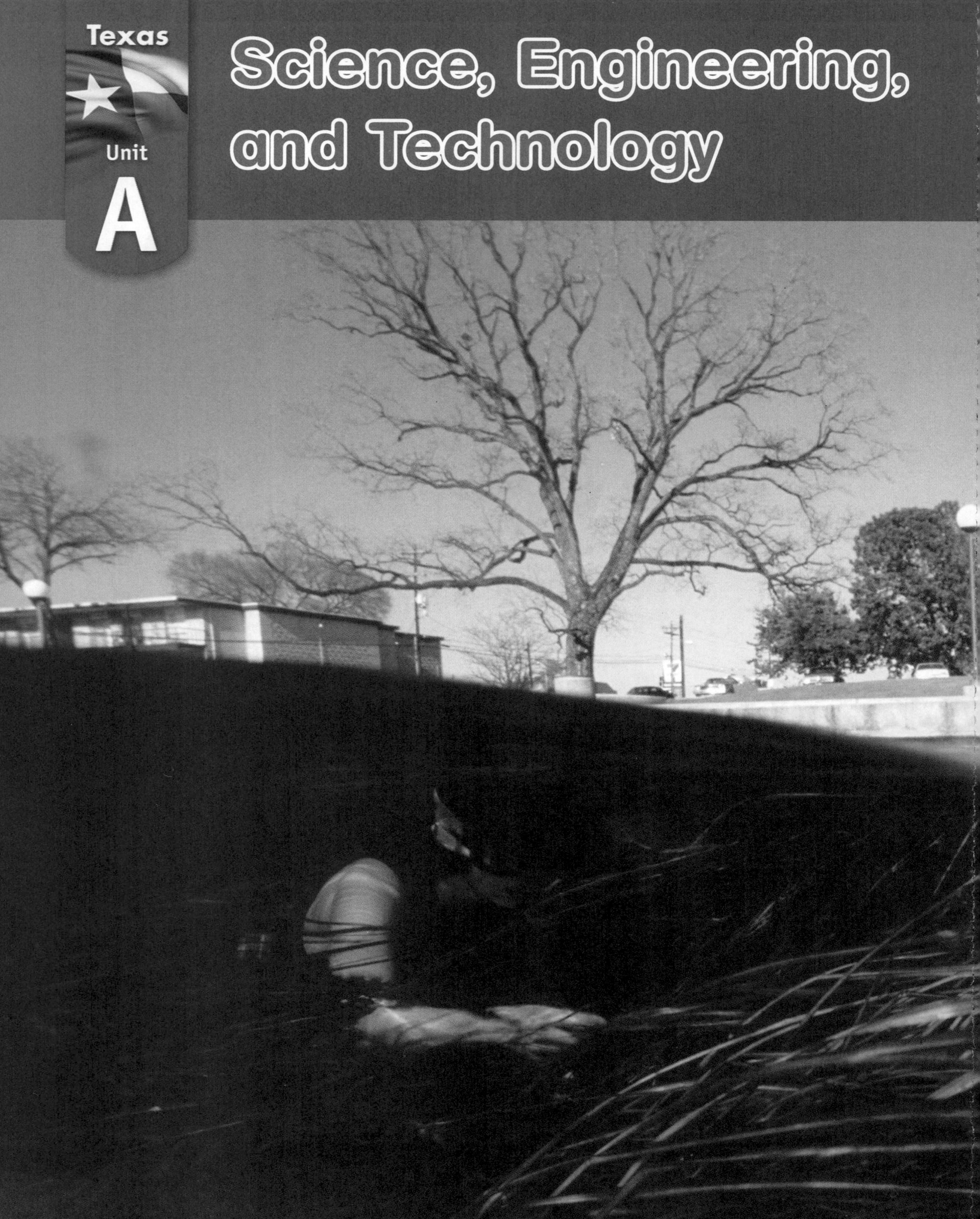

Texas Essential Knowledge and Skills

Process TEKS

Scientific Investigation and Reasoning: 2A, 2B, 2C, 2D, 4A

Additional Process TEKS

1A, 2E, 2F, 2G, 3A, 3C, 3D, 4B

What is she trying to DISCOVER?

Texas

Chapter 1

The Nature of Science

How do scientists ask questions and find answers?

Scientists use a variety of skills and tools to discover new things about the world around them.

How is this young scientist using tools to learn more about her world?

....

....

Texas Essential Knowledge and Skills

Process TEKS: 2A Describe, plan, and implement simple experimental investigations testing one variable. **2B** Ask well-defined questions, formulate testable hypotheses, and select and use appropriate equipment and technology. **2C** Collect information by detailed observations and accurate measuring. **2D** Analyze and interpret information to construct reasonable explanations from direct (observable) and indirect (inferred) evidence. **4A** Collect, record, and analyze information using tools, including calculators, microscopes, cameras, computers, hand lenses, metric rulers, Celsius thermometers, prisms, mirrors, pan balances, triple beam balances, spring scales, graduated cylinders, beakers, hot plates, meter sticks, magnets, collecting nets, and notebooks; timing devices, including clocks and stopwatches; and materials to support observations of habitats or organisms such as terrariums and aquariums.

Additional Process TEKS: 1A, 2E, 2F, 2G, 3A, 3C, 3D, 4B

PEARSON Texas.com

Lab zone® Inquiry Warm-Up

TEKS 2B

What questions do scientists ask?

Scientists ask questions about objects, organisms, and events. Good scientific questions can be answered by making observations and measurements.

☐ **1.** Work in a group. Cut apart the questions.
Classify the questions into 2 piles.
Pile 1 Good Scientific Questions

Pile 2 Not Good Scientific Questions

☐ **2.** Discuss how you made each sorting decision.

Materials

Scientific or Not? worksheet
scissors

Texas Safety
LAB RULES

Handle sharp items carefully.

Inquiry Skill

You **classify** when you sort things into groups.

Explain Your Results

3. Draw a Conclusion
Pick one question from Pile 1. Letter of question: ____
Explain why it is a good scientific question.

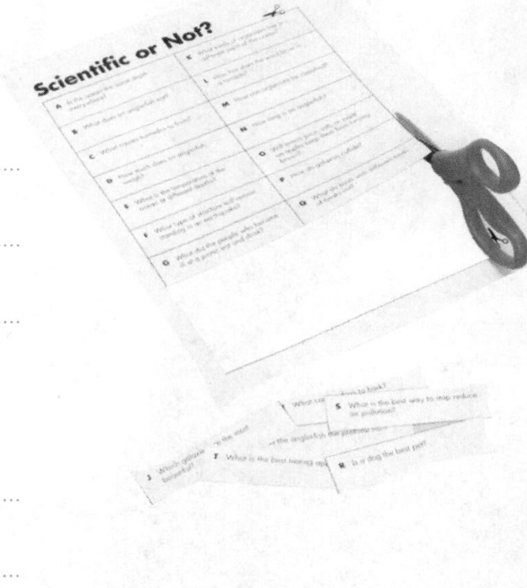

4. Pick one question from Pile 2. Letter of question: ____
Explain why it is not a good scientific question.

5. Pick another question from Pile 2. Letter of question: ____
Rewrite it to make it into a good scientific question.
Then explain why it is a good scientific question.

Focus on Text Features

You will practice the reading strategy of using **text features**. Text features, such as headings, highlighting, pictures, and captions, give you clues about what you will read.

heading

picture of a pencil

A **caption** tells specific information about a picture.

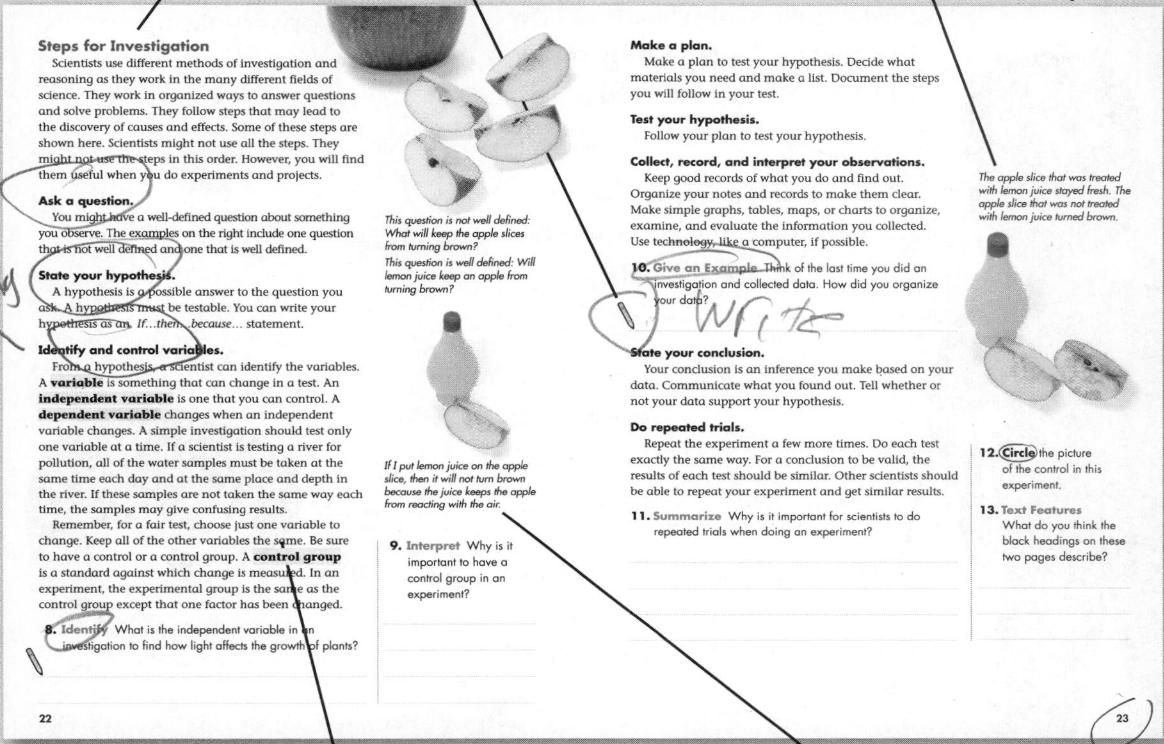

Steps for Investigation

Scientists use different methods of investigation and reasoning as they work in the many different fields of science. They work in organized ways to answer questions and solve problems. They follow steps that may lead to the discovery of causes and effects. Some of these steps are shown here. Scientists might not use all the steps. They might not use the steps in this order. However, you will find them useful when you do experiments and projects.

Ask a question.

You might have a well-defined question about something you observe. The examples on the right include one question that is not well defined and one that is well defined.

State your hypothesis.

A hypothesis is a possible answer to the question you ask. A hypothesis must be testable. You can write your hypothesis as an *If... then... because...* statement.

Identify and control variables.

From a hypothesis, a scientist can identify the variables. A **variable** is something that can change in a test. An **independent variable** is one that you can control. A **dependent variable** changes when an independent variable changes. A simple investigation should test only one variable at a time. If a scientist is testing a river for pollution, all of the water samples must be taken at the same time each day and at the same place and depth in the river. If these samples are not taken the same way each time, the samples may give confusing results.

Remember, for a fair test, choose just one variable to change. Keep all of the other variables the same. Be sure to have a control or a control group. A **control group** is a standard against which change is measured. In an experiment, the experimental group is the same as the control group except that one factor has been changed.

8. Identify What is the independent variable in an investigation to find how light affects the growth of plants?

This question is not well defined: What will keep the apple slices from turning brown?
This question is well defined: Will lemon juice keep an apple from turning brown?

If I put lemon juice on the apple slice, then it will not turn brown because the juice keeps the apple from reacting with the air.

9. Interpret Why is it important to have a control group in an experiment?

22

Make a plan.

Make a plan to test your hypothesis. Decide what materials you need and make a list. Document the steps you will follow in your test.

Test your hypothesis.

Follow your plan to test your hypothesis.

Collect, record, and interpret your observations.

Keep good records of what you do and find out. Organize your notes and records to make them clear. Make simple graphs, tables, maps, or charts to organize, examine, and evaluate the information you collected. Use technology, like a computer, if possible.

10. Give an Example Think of the last time you did an investigation and collected data. How did you organize your data?

State your conclusion.

Your conclusion is an inference you make based on your data. Communicate what you found out. Tell whether or not your data support your hypothesis.

Do repeated trials.

Repeat the experiment a few more times. Do each test exactly the same way. For a conclusion to be valid, the results of each test should be similar. Other scientists should be able to repeat your experiment and get similar results.

11. Summarize Why is it important for scientists to do repeated trials when doing an experiment?

The apple slice that was treated with lemon juice stayed fresh. The apple slice that was not treated with lemon juice turned brown.

12. Circle the picture of the control in this experiment.

13. Text Features What do you think the black headings on these two pages describe?

23

yellow highlight

A **picture** shows something you will read about.

Practice It!

Read the text features in the chart below. Find the text features in the textbook pages shown above. Write a clue that each one gives you about the content.

Text Feature	Clue
picture of a pencil	
yellow highlight	
heading	

Texas
LESSON
1

What do scientists do?

I will know TEKS 2B, 2C
I will know how to ask questions and make hypotheses for scientific investigations. I will know how to collect information by making observations. (Also **1A**)

Vocabulary
research
hypothesis
observation

We are going to Austin next week. My mom wants to see the bats.

What does Austin, Texas have to do with bats?

The largest urban bat colony in North America is under the Congress Street Bridge in Austin.

Does the bridge cross a river or does it cross a lake?

Connect to
Social Studies

Use a map Use a map of Austin, Texas to find the Congress Street Bridge. Describe its location. Identify which body of water the bridge crosses. **Social Studies TEKS 6A**

PEARSON Texas.com

Lab zone® Quick Lab

TEKS 1A

Is it safe?

Materials

pencil

☐ **1.** Read the following sentences. Write the word *safe* on the line if the statement demonstrates safe practices for classroom and outdoor investigations. If the sentence does not demonstrate safe practices, write the word *unsafe* on the line.

Texas Safety LAB RULES

Read the science activity thoroughly and understand its purpose before you begin.

☐ **2.** Cindy put her hair in a ponytail before she began the science activity.

....

☐ **3.** Julio started the science activity and put his goggles on when he started using science tools.

....

☐ **4.** Maria decided to wear her new flip-flops on the day her class was doing an outdoor science activity.

....

Explain Your Results

5. Communicate Explain why you must follow safe practices during classroom and outdoor activities.

....

....

....

6. Analyze and Interpret What should you do if you see someone following unsafe practices during an investigation?

....

....

Problems, Decisions, and New Ideas

How deep is the ocean? What creatures live in its depths? The world around us is filled with things that are still unknown. To better understand the world, scientists first define a problem and then try to find answers.

1. **Ask Questions** What questions might a scientist ask about the ocean?

Well-Defined Questions
The Flower Garden Banks National Marine Sanctuary is located off the coast of Texas. The sanctuary was created because scientists feared that the creatures that lived there would be harmed or killed. Scientists ask many well-defined questions about this area.

How far off the coast of Texas is this sanctuary? The sanctuary is located about 175 km southeast of Galveston, Texas.

What creatures live in the sanctuary? The Flower Garden Banks sanctuary includes creatures such as brain and star corals, manta rays, sea turtles, whale sharks, and a variety of fish.

Scientific investigation begins with a well-defined question. A well-defined question is a question that can be tested and answered by conducting some type of investigation. Almost every part of your life has been improved in some way by science or by something that science made possible. Science can help you get the information you need to make good decisions too. Should you snack on a banana or a soda? What can you do to avoid catching a cold? Scientists can help answer questions, solve problems, and form new ideas through the use of scientific processes.

2. Explain What is a well-defined question?

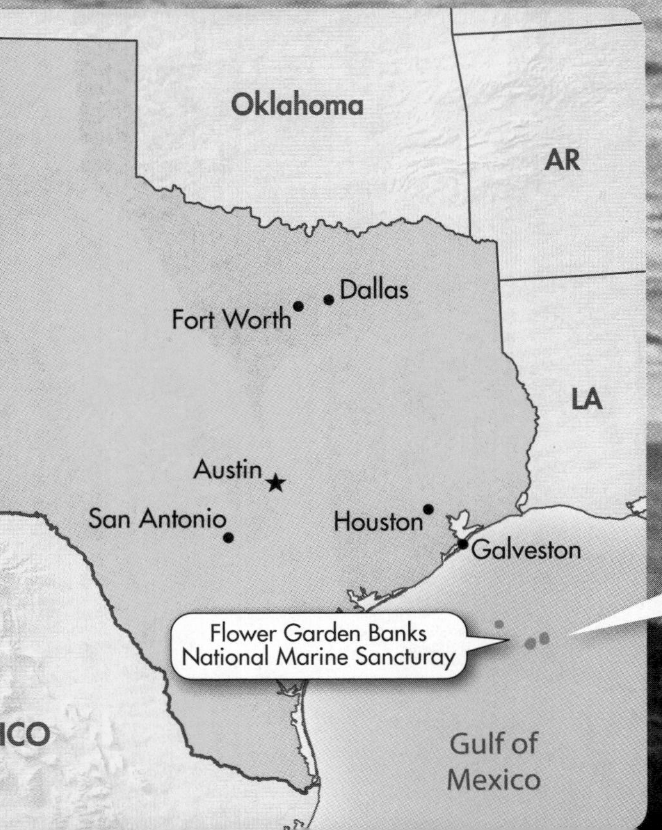

What is the total area of the sanctuary? The sanctuary is made up of three areas: the Stetson Bank, the West Flower Garden Bank, and the East Flower Garden Bank. The total area of the three banks is about 150 square kilometers.

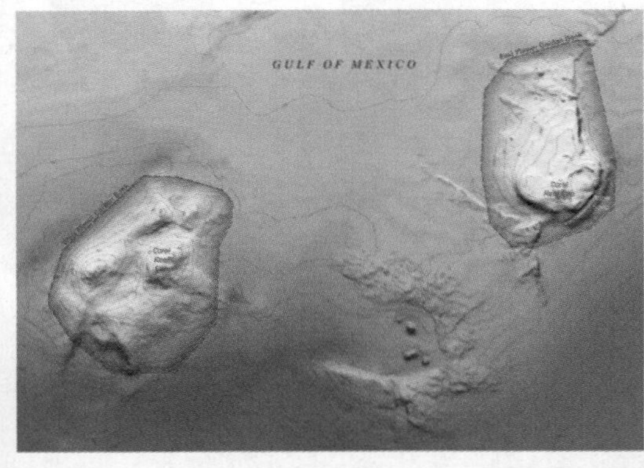

Scientific Research and Knowledge

After scientists define a problem, they begin their investigation with research. To **research**, scientists study a variety of appropriate reference materials. The reference materials they use need to be sources of information that scientists have agreed upon. Scientists cannot draw valid conclusions from information that cannot be verified by other scientists. For example, a scientist researching ocean water cannot simply find information from a random Internet source and use it in an investigation. The source must be reliable, and the information must have been reviewed and verified by other scientists.

Examples of appropriate reference materials may include books and scientific journals. Scientists may use articles in the scientific journals to do their research. These articles are written by scientists and reviewed by other scientists before they are published. Many of these journals can be found in libraries and on the Internet. Sometimes, information even from reliable sources can change. New findings might cause scientists to rethink old ideas.

3. Analyze The scientists below found information on the Internet in a blog. Could they use this information to answer a scientific problem they have defined? Explain your answer.

Make Hypotheses

Scientists use a problem they have defined and research from appropriate sources to form a hypothesis. A **hypothesis** is a statement of what you think will happen during an investigation. It is often written in the form of an *if... then... because* statement. Scientists use experience and what they have found in their research to predict what they think will be a solution to the problem.

Look at the picture above. One example of a hypothesis that scientist might have made is, *If the level of water pollution increases, then the population of manatees will decrease because the plants they eat cannot live in highly polluted water.*

4. **Compose** You have read one possible hypothesis about manatees. Write an example of a different hypothesis the scientist could have formed.

A Bright Invention
Through research and careful observation, scientists often find solutions to everyday problems. Think about your community. Define a pollution problem that affects it. What are some ideas you can think of to solve this problem? Share your ideas with others.

Make Observations

Scientists use many skills and processes to find answers to problems. One of these is making observations. An **observation** is something you find out about objects, events, or living things by using your senses. Scientists make observations very carefully. In this way, they can be sure that the information they gather is reliable. Scientists often use tools, such as thermometers, to extend their senses. Scientists are also good at organizing their observations. When scientists have collected their information, they analyze and interpret it to draw conclusions. They also share their findings with other scientists, who can then see if their own results are similar.

For example, scientists may have observed that a group of sea turtles returns to the same beach every year to lay eggs. The scientists want to find out what causes the turtles to return and where they go between the yearly beach visits. Scientists used identification tags and radio transmitters to observe that a sea turtle might travel thousands of kilometers in one year and return to the same beach.

5. Analyze The scientist below is observing a sea turtle. What well-defined question might the scientist ask, and how might she find answers to the question?

Draw Conclusions

Scientists use their observations to draw conclusions. When they draw a conclusion, they analyze and interpret the information they learned through their observations. For example, a scientist may observe that some populations of birds that eat certain fish are decreasing. The scientist may then observe that the fish have been dying. By testing the properties of soil samples from the riverbed, the scientist may be able to observe qualities of the soil, such as the presence of pollution. By analyzing and interpreting this information, the scientist might conclude that pollution in the river is causing the living things there to be unhealthy and to die or move away.

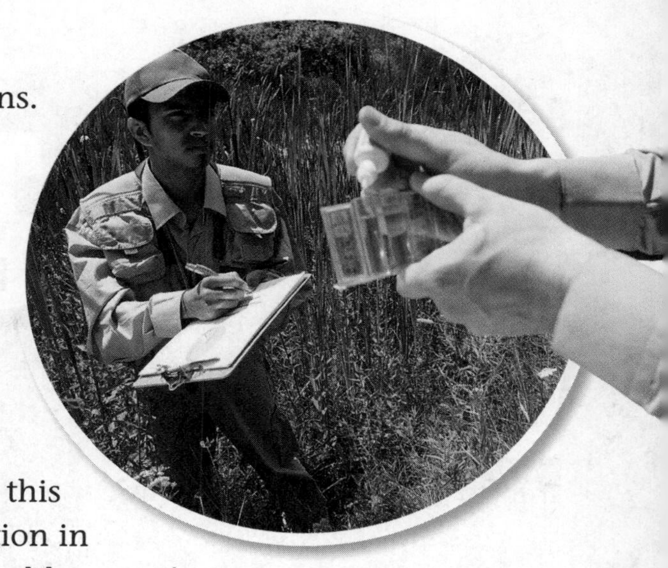

These scientists are testing for pollution.

6. **Describe** Tell how scientific testing helps scientists draw conclusions.

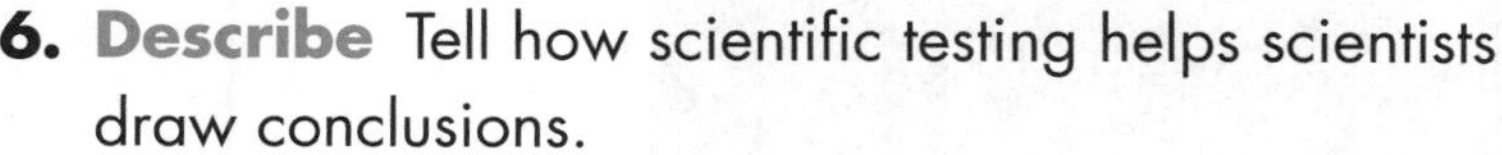

got it?

7. **Explain** What are four things that scientists do?

8. **Explain** How can people solve problems?

9. **Draw Conclusions** Why should you use a variety of sources when you do research for an investigation?

Stop! I need help with

Wait! I have a question about

Go! Now I know

Nature of Science

The McDonald Observatory

The McDonald Observatory is located in the Davis Mountains in West Texas. The clear night sky and distance from city lights makes the location an ideal place for studying the nighttime sky.

The Hobby-Eberly Telescope (HET) is one of several telescopes at the McDonald Observatory. Scientists use the telescope to search for new planets and to study stars and distant galaxies. The telescope helps scientists search for planets and study stars by analyzing light from the distant objects.

The Hobby-Eberly Telescope is not like most telescopes. Rather than one large mirror, the HET has 91 mirrors that gather light. Each mirror is only one meter wide and weighs about 250 pounds! Using many small mirrors made the telescope cheaper to build. The telescope is positioned so that it can track a specific object in the sky for up to 2.5 hours. Scientists track a series of objects each night. This gives more scientists the opportunity to gather data from the nighttime sky.

Explain Why might it be an advantage to scientists to have a telescope that studied more than one object each night?

STEM

Science in Your Backyard

BEST Robotics Competition

TEKS 3D

Do you like robots? Do you like to build things? Do you like a challenge? If the answer to all of these questions is yes, someday soon you might find yourself participating in the BEST Robotics Competition! BEST stands for "Boosting Engineering Science and Technology." Each year, middle school and high school teams compete to build winning robots.

Each student team is given the same box of materials. The box contains a special "micro-energy chain" to help power the robot. Other items include such things as plywood, PVC pipes, threaded rods, screws, piano wire, and a bicycle inner tube. Teams have six weeks to use the materials to design and build a robot. The robot must be able to perform a series of three-minute tasks.

Designing and building the robots provides students with many advantages. Students learn the design process in a hands-on way. They learn to analyze and solve problems. They also learn what engineers do. This helps students develop the skills needed for future employment.

The day of the competition, the robots are pitted against one another in rounds of tasks. The best-performing robots move to the next round of competition. Eventually one robot in each division is crowned the winner!

Identify Underline sentences that describe the advantages to students of designing and building the robots.

How do scientists investigate?

I will know **TEKS 2A, 2B**
I will know different methods of investigation and the steps for scientific investigations. I will know how to ask well-defined questions for scientific investigations. (Also **1A**, **2C**, **2D**, **2E**, **2F**, **2G**, **3C**, **4A**)

Vocabulary
experiment
model
variable
independent variable
dependent variable
control group
procedures

I read that scientists are investigating how to make electric cars travel even farther on one charge.

That would be a great improvement. Have they published any results?

One model they tested costs $3.67 to recharge. It costs about 2 cents per kilometer to drive.

Can you help me find out how far that electric car can travel on one charge?

Show your work To find out the number of kilometers the electric car can travel on one charge, first convert the $3.67 to 367 cents. Then you divide 367 by 2. **Math TEKS 3E, 7**

PEARSON Texas.com

Quick Lab

TEKS 1A, 2A, 2C, 4A

Which method keeps bread freshest?

1. Put 2 slices of bread on a plate. **Observe** with a hand lens. **Record.** Cover 1 slice with waxed paper.

2. Put another slice in a paper bag. Close the bag. Put another slice in a plastic bag. Seal the bag.

3. Wait 5 days. Observe the slices with a hand lens. Record your observations on the chart.

Materials

4 slices of bread
paper plate
hand lens
waxed paper
paper bag
plastic bag

Texas Safety LAB RULES

Never eat or drink in the lab area.

Bread Observations

	Waxed Paper	Plastic Bag	Paper Bag	Uncovered Slice
Day 5				

Explain Your Results

4. **Interpret Data** Compare the freshness of the bread slices after 5 days.

5. **Infer** How could you combine methods to keep bread fresh longer?

Scientific Investigation

Scientific investigation usually begins with an observation. For example, someone observes that cars with a certain shape are more fuel-efficient. Scientists then ask a question about this observation. To answer their question, scientists collect data. One important way to find reliable answers is to do an experiment. An **experiment** is the use of scientific investigation and reasoning to test your hypothesis. Remember that a hypothesis is a statement of what you think will happen in an investigation.

1. **Explain** What is the purpose of an experiment?

There is no single way to find answers in science. The methods used by a biologist to study living things may be different from those used by an astronomer to study stars. For both types of scientists, however, it is important to observe, collect information, test ideas, make predictions, and share their findings with other scientists who can disagree with those findings or confirm them.

However, it is not always possible to manipulate variables in a way that can answer scientific questions. Sometimes you have to design an investigation to test a hypothesis without doing a controlled experiment. In addition to controlled experiments, three types of investigations that scientist use are models, surveys, and sampling. These often help scientists test hypotheses.

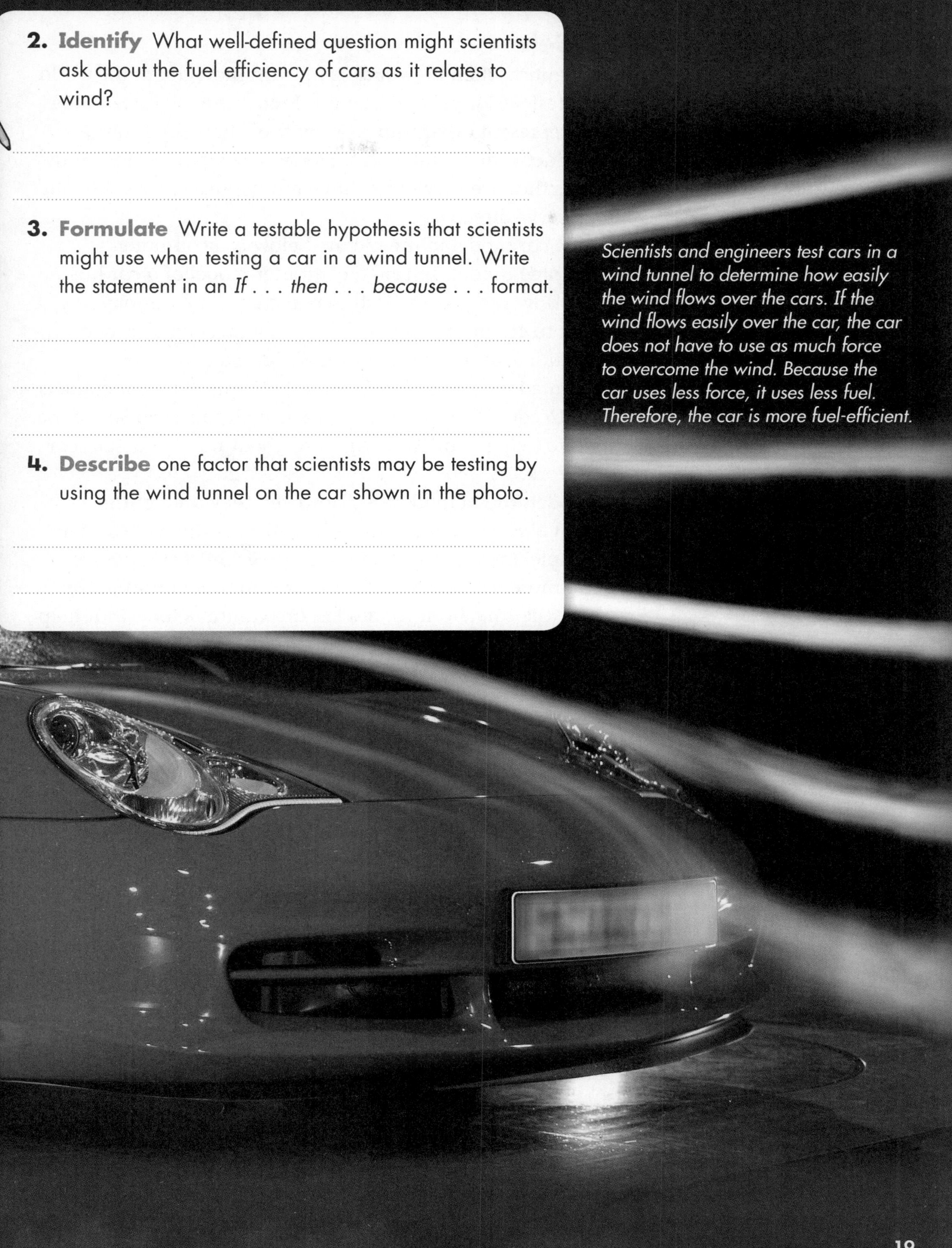

2. **Identify** What well-defined question might scientists ask about the fuel efficiency of cars as it relates to wind?

3. **Formulate** Write a testable hypothesis that scientists might use when testing a car in a wind tunnel. Write the statement in an *If . . . then . . . because . . .* format.

4. **Describe** one factor that scientists may be testing by using the wind tunnel on the car shown in the photo.

Scientists and engineers test cars in a wind tunnel to determine how easily the wind flows over the cars. If the wind flows easily over the car, the car does not have to use as much force to overcome the wind. Because the car uses less force, it uses less fuel. Therefore, the car is more fuel-efficient.

Quick Lab

Falling Water

Carefully make a hole 2 cm from the top of a cup. Make an identical hole 5 cm below the first one. Hold your fingers over the holes. Fill the cup with water. Predict what will happen when you let go. Try it. Hold the cup high over a sink or tub. Observe. Try it again. State your conclusion.

TEKS 2C, 2D, 2F

Models

Scientists often use **models** to learn more about the world or to test designs and materials. Models are objects or ideas that represent other things. They show how something is constructed or how it works. Models are often used to study things that are very large, have many parts, or are difficult to observe directly.

The car model in the picture below is a computer-generated model. Testing a computer model of a car has some advantages over testing real cars. For example, it is easier to control parts of the experiment, such as driving conditions, in a computer model. Once a computer-generated model car has been tested virtually, a machine is used to carve the car out of clay. The physical model can be used to help scientists learn more about how an actual car will work.

Models are helpful tools. However, they are not the actual objects. Testing different models or the real car, for example, may give different results. Scientists may have to do more research and testing to find more information about the cars. Even so, models are valuable tools that help scientists understand the world around them.

5. Give an Example What is another advantage of using a computer-generated model of a car?

These models help scientists study cars.

Surveys and Sampling

Scientists do investigations in many different fields of science. Sometimes the best way for a scientist to investigate is by using a survey. Surveys can be questionnaires that are given to a number of people whose answers are recorded and then analyzed. Sometimes people are interviewed in person or on the phone. For example, if a number of people became ill at a picnic, doctors would want to know what each person ate and drank. They would also want to know who got sick and who did not. The answers will help them find the source of the illness.

Scientists also use sampling to collect data. Scientists examine random individuals from a population. For example, doctors may examine a few people from the picnic and see how healthy they are. Doctors can then generalize their results to all the people at the picnic. This may also help the doctors find the source of the illness.

6. Evaluate Write one question that the doctor could be asking the patients in the picture below in his survey.

7. CHALLENGE How could a scientist use sampling to investigate the health of the deer population in a forest preserve?

Steps for Investigation

Scientists use different methods of investigation and reasoning as they work in the many different fields of science. They work in organized ways to answer questions and solve problems. They follow steps that may lead to the discovery of causes and effects. Some of these steps are shown here. Scientists might not use all the steps. They might not use the steps in this order. However, you will find them useful when you do experiments and projects.

Ask a question.

You might have a well-defined question about something you observe. The examples on the right include one question that is not well defined and one that is well defined.

This question is not well defined: What will keep the apple slices from turning brown?

This question is well defined: Will lemon juice keep an apple from turning brown?

State your hypothesis.

A hypothesis is a possible answer to the question you ask. A hypothesis must be testable. You can write your hypothesis as an *If...then...because...* statement.

If I put lemon juice on the apple slice, then it will not turn brown because the juice keeps the apple from reacting with the air.

Identify and control variables.

From a hypothesis, a scientist can identify the variables. A **variable** is something that can change in a test. An **independent variable** is one that you can control. A **dependent variable** changes when an independent variable changes. A simple investigation should test only one variable at a time. If a scientist is testing a river for pollution, all of the water samples must be taken at the same time each day and at the same place and depth in the river. If these samples are not taken the same way each time, the samples may give confusing results.

Remember, for a fair test, choose just one variable to change. Keep all of the other variables the same. Be sure to have a control or a control group. A **control group** is a standard against which change is measured. In an experiment, the experimental group is the same as the control group except that one factor has been changed.

8. Identify What is the independent variable in an investigation to find how light affects the growth of plants?

9. Interpret Why is it important to have a control group in an experiment?

Make a plan.

Make a plan to test your hypothesis. Decide what materials you need and make a list. Document the steps you will follow in your test.

Test your hypothesis.

Follow your plan to test your hypothesis.

Collect, record, and interpret your observations.

Keep good records of what you do and find out. Organize your notes and records to make them clear. Make simple graphs, tables, maps, or charts to organize, examine, and evaluate the information you collected. Use technology, like a computer, if possible.

10. Give an Example Think of the last time you did an investigation and collected data. How did you organize your data?

The apple slice that was treated with lemon juice stayed fresh. The apple slice that was not treated with lemon juice turned brown.

Communicate your conclusion.

Your conclusion is an inference you make based on your data. It tells whether or not your data support your hypothesis. When you are confident that your conclusion is valid, you can communicate it to others in written form or in verbal form.

Do repeated trials.

Repeat the experiment a few more times. Do each test exactly the same way. For a conclusion to be valid, the results of each test should be similar. Other scientists should be able to repeat your experiment and get similar results.

11. Summarize Why is it important for scientists to do repeated trials when doing an experiment?

12. Circle the picture of the control in this experiment.

13. Text Features What do you think the black headings on these two pages describe?

Document Procedures

Meaningful scientific results come from experiments that can be replicated. In order for a scientific experiment to be replicated, the procedures must be thoroughly explained, or documented. **Procedures** are step-by-step instructions for completing a task.

Procedures are important when experimenting but also when doing things such as making certain foods or playing games.

A recipe is a type of procedure.

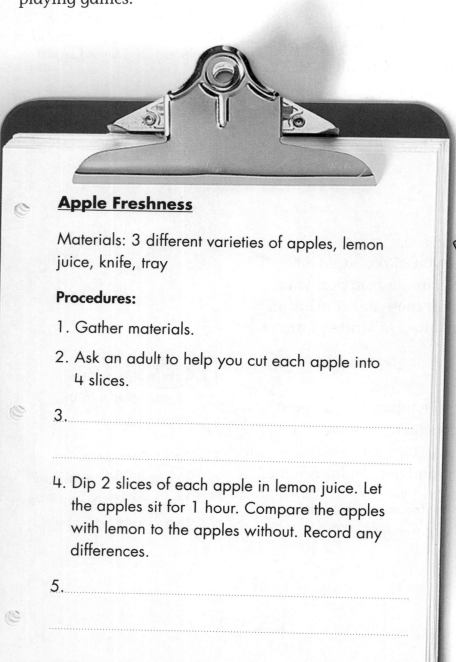

Apple Freshness

Materials: 3 different varieties of apples, lemon juice, knife, tray

Procedures:

1. Gather materials.
2. Ask an adult to help you cut each apple into 4 slices.
3. ....

....

4. Dip 2 slices of each apple in lemon juice. Let the apples sit for 1 hour. Compare the apples with lemon to the apples without. Record any differences.
5. ....

....

....

14. CHALLENGE Read the procedure for apple freshness. Fill in the missing procedures. What might happen if one step was missing?

....

....

....

....

....

....

....

When you design an experiment, it is important to write your procedures so that someone who reads them can follow them and repeat your experiment. If you leave out details, your procedure may not be followed exactly. The experiment may then give unintended results. This means the original experiment was not repeated and the conclusion may be different.

15. Evaluate Look at the procedures for the Apple Freshness experiment again. What might you change about the procedures to make it easier for others to follow?

got it?

16. Explain Why would a scientist use a model in an investigation? Write two reasons.

17. Describe What are some ways you can use to investigate different types of questions?

Stop! I need help with

Wait! I have a question about

Go! Now I know

How do scientists collect and interpret data?

I will know TEKS 4A
I will know how to select and use tools to collect and interpret data. (Also 1A, 2B, 2C, 2D, 2F, 2G, 3A, 4B)

Vocabulary
data
inference

Math TEKS 9C

Scientists collect information over long periods of time. They use this information to make predictions. The monthly temperature averages shown in the graph below were calculated after collecting information for several years. Answer the questions below using the graph.

Which month has the highest average temperature?

Which two months have the lowest average temperatures?

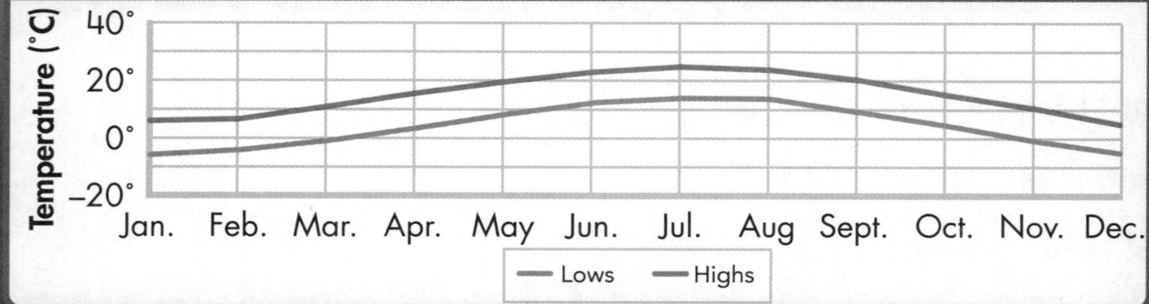

PEARSON Texas.com

Quick Lab

TEKS 1A, 2B, 2C, 2F, 4A

Why do scientists use thermometers?

1. **Record** the air temperature of the room.
2. Pour room-temperature water into Cup A. Pour warm water into Cup B. Pour slightly warm water into Cup C.
3. Feel the water in each. Record *cool, warm,* or *neither.* **Measure** the temperatures in °C and °F. Record.

Comparing Temperatures

	Temperature		
	Feels (warm, cool, neither)	°C	°F
Cup A (room-temperature water)			
Cup B (warm water)			
Cup C (slightly warm water)			

Explain Your Results

4. **Interpret Data** Compare how warm the water felt with your **measurements.**

5. **Draw a Conclusion** Discuss why scientists use thermometers to **collect** temperature **data.**

Materials

room-temperature water
3 plastic cups, labeled A, B, and C
warm water
slightly warm water
thermometer

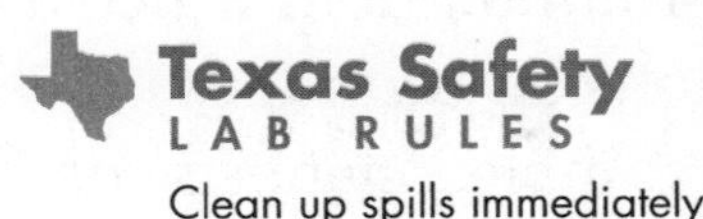

Clean up spills immediately.

Data Collecting

Tornadoes can be very dangerous. In a tornado, winds can gust to more than 160 kilometers per hour (100 miles per hour), lift up objects, and cause very serious damage. What makes a tornado form? Scientists have done a great deal of research to try to understand the cause of tornadoes, but there is still a lot to learn in order to predict when tornadoes will happen.

In order for scientists to be able to predict tornadoes more successfully, they need to collect large amounts of data. **Data** are information from which a conclusion can be drawn or a prediction can be made.

For example, scientists can collect data about the air temperature before a tornado forms. These data can be connected to information they already know about other weather patterns during that time. It is important that each type of data be collected consistently and recorded in a useful way. Scientists can find relationships among data and possibly make predictions about how a tornado forms.

1. **Decide** Suppose you collect data about the type of weather your town has been experiencing. Can you use the data to draw conclusions about all other areas in the state? Explain.

2. Circle what scientists need to do to predict tornadoes.

SMART-RADARS This truck is hauling a mobile Doppler radar called SMART RADAR. The Doppler radar can be moved to the location of a severe storm, such as a tornado, and collect data while the storm is in progress.

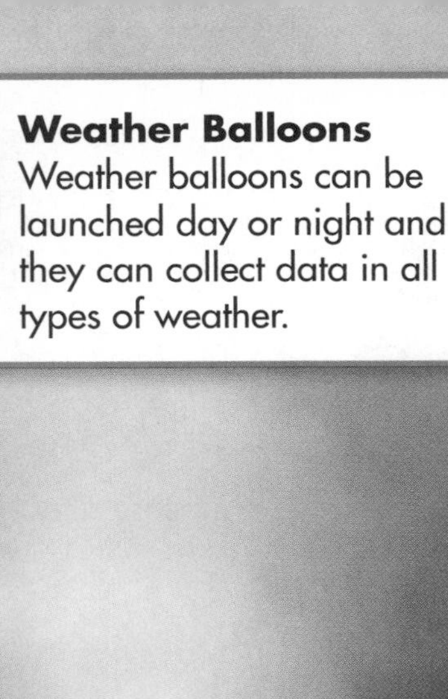

Weather Balloons
Weather balloons can be launched day or night and they can collect data in all types of weather.

Mobile Mesonet Vehicles These cars are equipped with rooftop weather stations that can collect weather data. These cars are driven to positions near tornadoes to study the airflow around the tornadoes.

Mobile X-Band
The mobile X-Band radar also is used to collect weather data. This radar can be used to collect data about small objects, such as water droplets forming clouds.

Scientific Tools

You use many different tools to collect, record, and analyze information. The tool you use depends upon the task you want to perform.

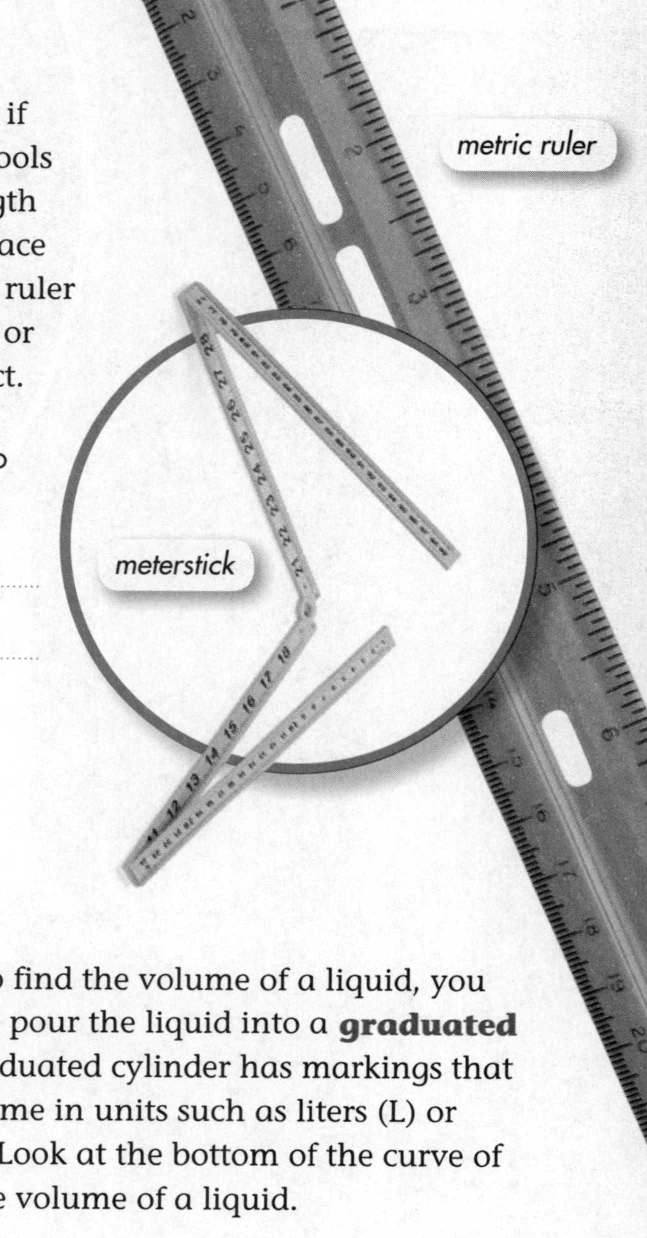

You may use a **metric ruler** or a **meterstick** if you want to measure length and distance. Both tools have marks that show centimeters. To collect length information using a metric ruler or meterstick, place one end of the object above the zero mark on the ruler or meterstick. Then read the number on the ruler or meterstick that is below the other end of the object.

1. Analyze Why is the meterstick the better tool to use to measure the length of a room?

....

....

graduated cylinder

60 mL mark

If you want to find the volume of a liquid, you use a **beaker** to pour the liquid into a **graduated cylinder**. A graduated cylinder has markings that tell you the volume in units such as liters (L) or milliliters (mL). Look at the bottom of the curve of liquid to find the volume of a liquid.

2. Infer Why should you look at a graduated cylinder at eye level when reading the measurement?

....

....

To find the mass of an object, you use a **pan balance** or a **triple-beam balance**. To use a pan balance, place the object in one pan. Then add gram cubes to the other pan until both pans balance. The total mass of the gram cubes equals the mass of the object. To use a triple-beam balance, slide the riders along the beams until the pointer rests at zero. Then add up the values marked by the riders.

3. Apply Collect information using tools. Use a pan balance to find the mass of a book.

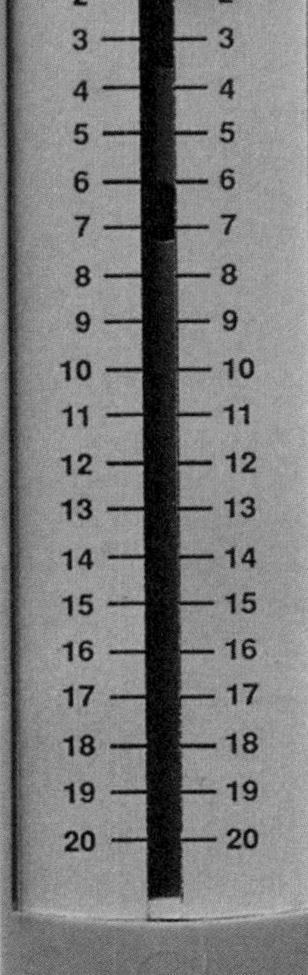

spring scale

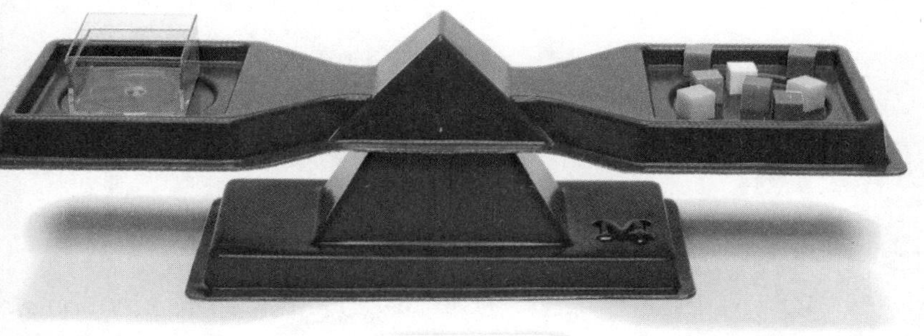

pan balance

You use a **spring scale** to measure weight and other forces. Place the object to be measured on the hook. Read the number on the scale to find the object's weight in newtons (N).

You can analyze information using a spring scale by comparing the weights of different objects.

4. Compare Tell how you would measure the mass of a toy. Then tell how you would find its weight.

stopwatch

You often need to use timing devices when conducting experiments. To use a **stopwatch**, push a button to mark exactly when you start and stop timing a process. A stopwatch might report time in minutes, seconds, and parts of a second, such as milliseconds (ms).

A **clock** is another timing device, but you have to note the exact start time to get a precise measurement. A clock may show time only in hours and minutes.

5. Contrast How is operating a stopwatch different from using a clock?

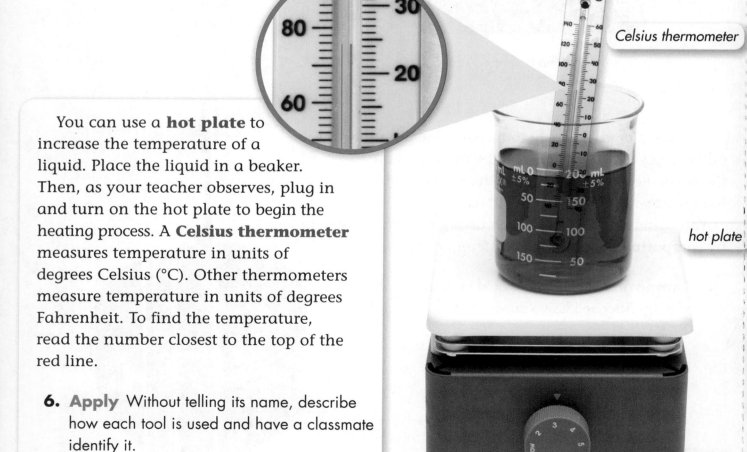

Celsius thermometer

hot plate

You can use a **hot plate** to increase the temperature of a liquid. Place the liquid in a beaker. Then, as your teacher observes, plug in and turn on the hot plate to begin the heating process. A **Celsius thermometer** measures temperature in units of degrees Celsius (°C). Other thermometers measure temperature in units of degrees Fahrenheit. To find the temperature, read the number closest to the top of the red line.

6. Apply Without telling its name, describe how each tool is used and have a classmate identify it.

A **hand lens** can make an object appear larger. The lens helps you see the small details of the object. To observe an object with a hand lens, hold the lens close to your eye. Then bring the object toward the lens until you can see the details clearly.

You use a **microscope** to observe objects that are too small for you to see using only your eyes. To use a microscope, place a thin piece of the object on a glass slide. Attach the slide to the stage. Then move the mirror so light from a lamp is reflected onto the bottom of the stage. Look through the top lens while you slowly turn the knob until you see the image clearly.

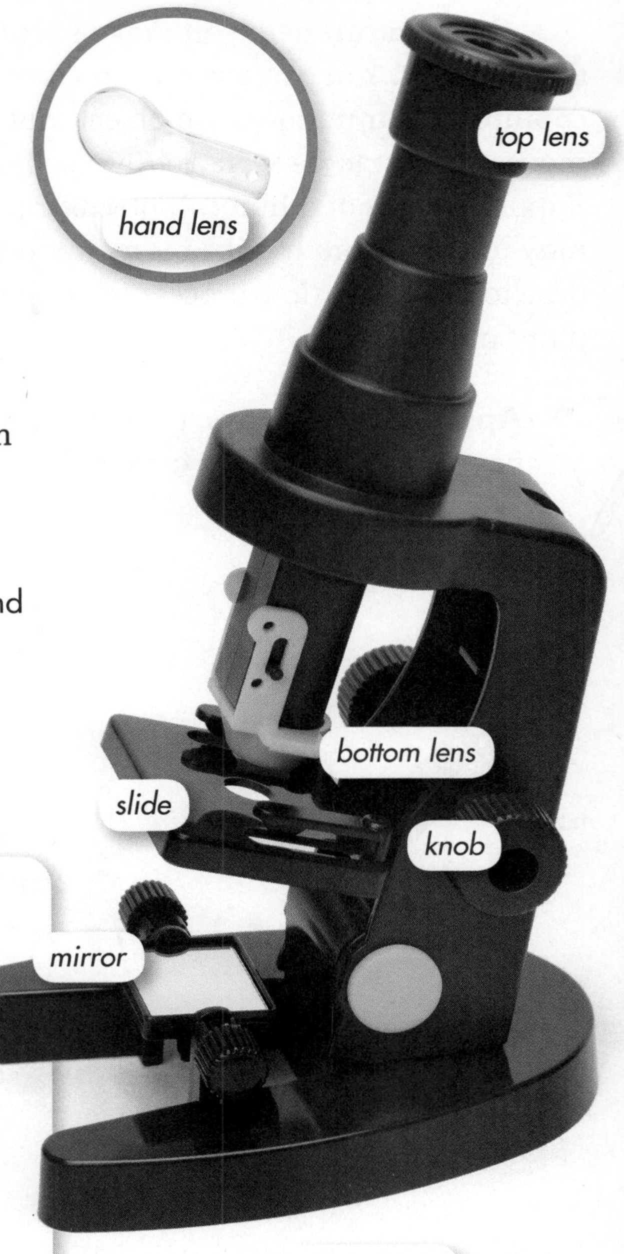

7. Compare and Contrast How are a hand lens and a microscope similar? How are they different?

....

....

Light reflecting off a **mirror** can help you observe images. Some mirrors can make an image appear larger or smaller than the object.

You can collect information using mirrors. For example, drivers use rear-view mirrors to collect information about the cars behind them. Dentists use small mirrors to collect information about the health of their patients' teeth.

A glass **prism** bends light. White light is a mixture of colors. When you shine a white light through a prism, the colors bend at different angles and separate.

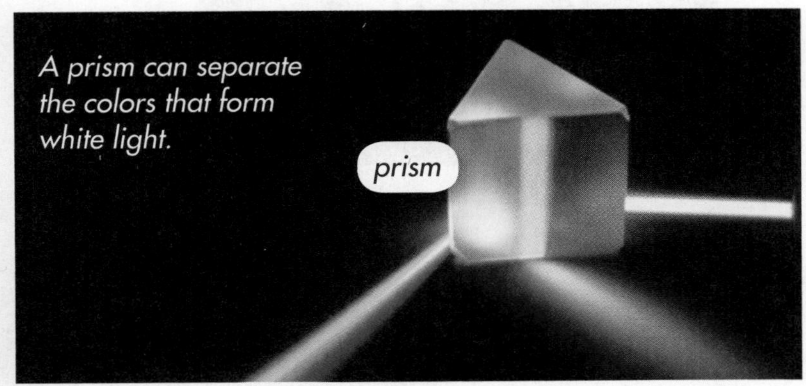

A prism can separate the colors that form white light.

8. Analyze How can a prism help you analyze the properties of colors?

....

....

....

....

A **camera** can help you make scientific observations. You can use certain cameras to capture a clear image of an object that moves too fast to be seen clearly, such as the flapping wings of a hummingbird. You also may use a camera to take many images over time to observe a slow process, such as a plant growing.

9. Apply How might you use a camera to study how storm waves affect a beach?

camera

magnet

Magnets pull on objects made of certain metals such as iron. To find out if an object contains such a metal, hold the magnet near it. If the object contains the metal, it will move toward the magnet, or the magnet will move toward the object.

terrarium

Aquariums and **terrariums** provide habitats for organisms so that you can observe them. An aquarium is a container filled with water. Freshwater or saltwater plants and animals may live in it. A terrarium is not filled with water. Terrariums may contain dry-land plants and small animals, such as insects, reptiles, or amphibians.

10. Apply In which habitat would an angel fish live?

aquarium

You might use a **collecting net** to gather insects or other small organisms so that you can observe them. Collecting nets are useful because they can capture an animal without harming it.

collecting net

calculator

As you collect measurements and other data, you can enter the numbers on a **calculator**. Then you can do operations such as addition and multiplication easier and faster than you could with paper and pencil.

11. Apply Write a set of directions for adding 3 + 6 + 10 on a calculator.

You can use a **computer** to collect information. A computer also can help you find patterns in your data. Then you can show those patterns in charts, tables, and graphs that you make on the computer.

computer

Using a **notebook** helps you keep track of your observations and measurements. Your notes can include observations, experimental processes, and data.

12. Apply Use a magnet to test five classroom objects for iron metal. Record your results in a notebook.

Safety

Scientists know they must work safely when doing experiments. You need to be careful when doing science investigations in a classroom or outdoors. It is important to keep yourself and other people safe. Care must be taken to make sure all living organisms, including plants and animals, are handled properly.

Follow these safety rules.

13. Explain Why might it be important to ask questions after your teacher gives instructions?

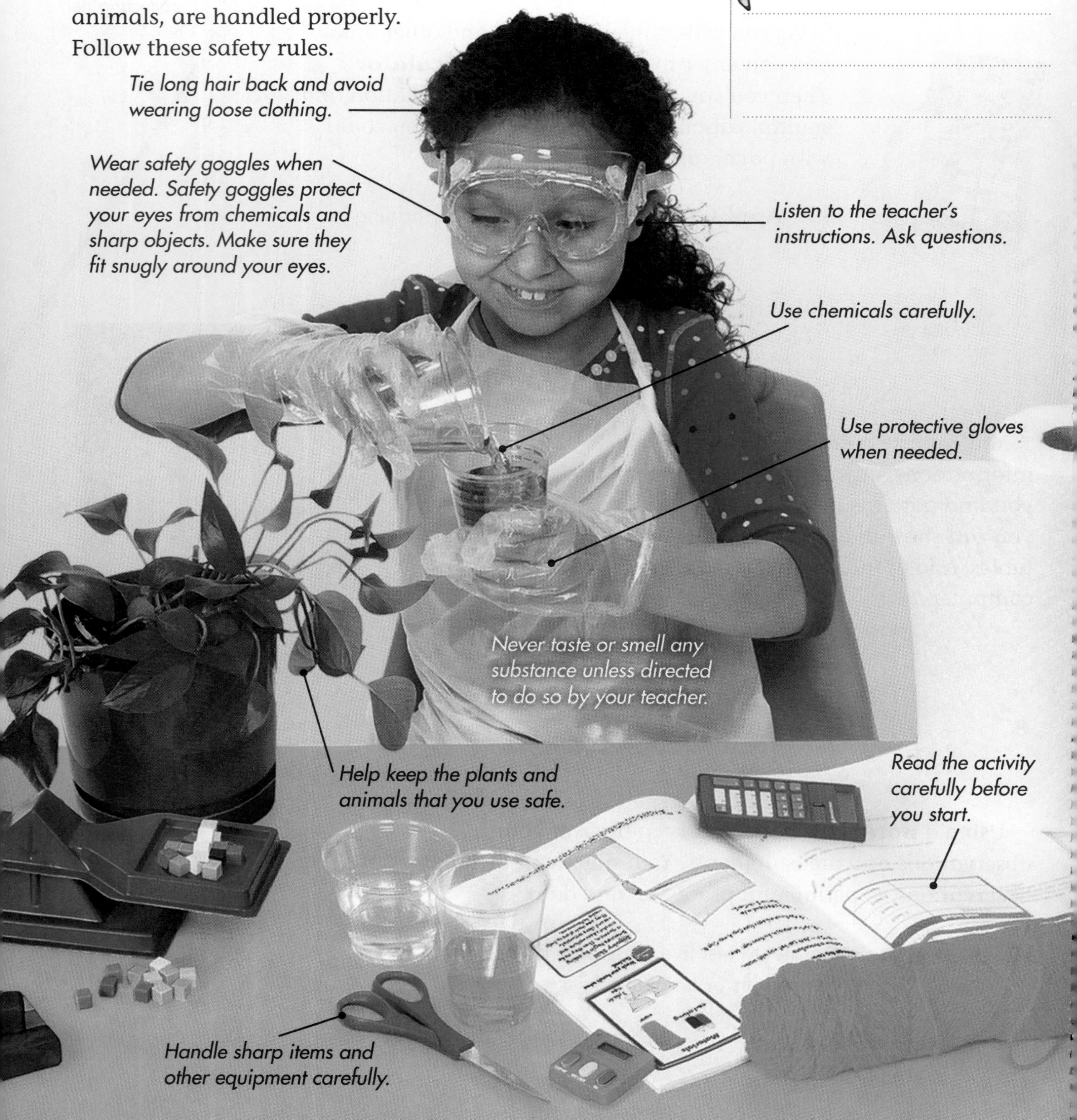

Tie long hair back and avoid wearing loose clothing.

Wear safety goggles when needed. Safety goggles protect your eyes from chemicals and sharp objects. Make sure they fit snugly around your eyes.

Listen to the teacher's instructions. Ask questions.

Use chemicals carefully.

Use protective gloves when needed.

Never taste or smell any substance unless directed to do so by your teacher.

Help keep the plants and animals that you use safe.

Read the activity carefully before you start.

Handle sharp items and other equipment carefully.

Organize Data

When scientists make observations, they must organize, examine, and evaluate their data. Organizing data helps scientists recognize patterns. Scientists often use technology, like a computer, to organize their data in tables, graphs, charts, and maps.

Tables and Graphs

One way that scientists organize data is by using a table. Look at the table below. It shows that scientists have collected data on the frequency of tornadoes in various states and have organized the information.

Once the information has been organized into a table, it may be displayed in a graph, such as the bar graph below. Graphs can help scientists see mathematical relationships in their data. The information in both the table and the graph is the same, but it is shown in different ways.

Number of Tornadoes This Year for Selected States

State	Number of Tornadoes	Land Description
Florida	55	flat
Indiana	22	flat
Louisiana	27	flat
New York	7	hilly
Oregon	2	hilly

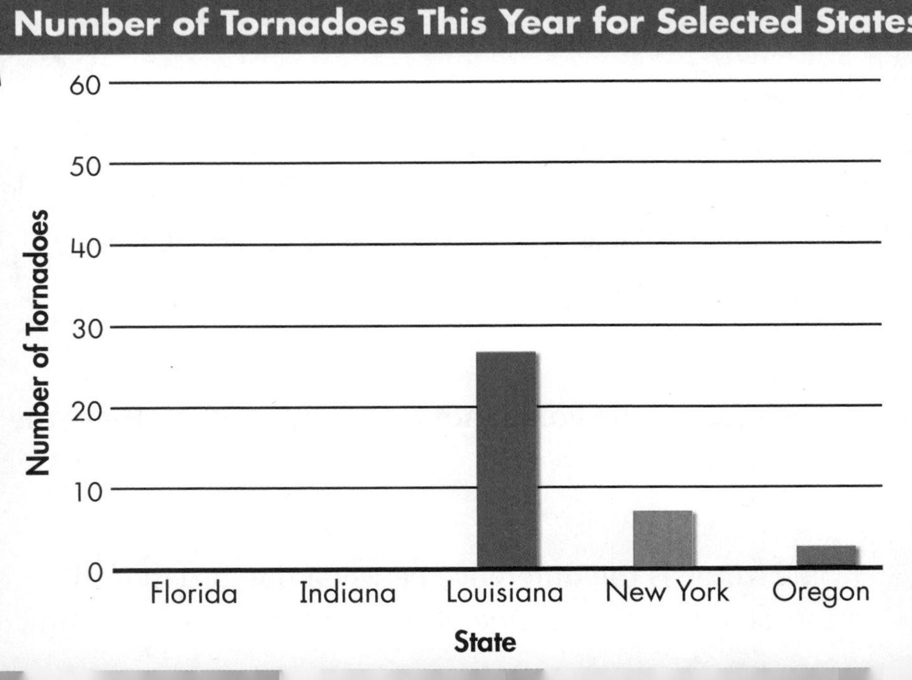

14. Compute Use data in the table to complete the bar graph.

15. Infer Based on the table and graph, what might land descriptions tell you about tornadoes and where they are most likely to occur?

Estimate and Measure
Estimate the length, width, or height of an object in your classroom. Then collect information using tools by measuring the object with a meterstick or metric ruler. Make a chart to record your data. Do this with 5 objects in the room. Compare. Did your estimates get more accurate with practice?
TEKS 4A

16. Calculate Look at the table on the previous page. What is the median number of tornadoes for the five states in the table and graph? What is the mean?

Interpret Data

When scientists interpret data, they look at the information they have collected by using tools safely to observe, measure, and estimate. Then they try to find patterns in that data. Patterns may help them construct explanations or make predictions. Weather forecasts are predictions that may help people better prepare for severe storms.

Scientists use values such as the mean, median, mode, and range when they interpret data. These values can help scientists determine the quality and usefulness of data. This analysis may help scientists decide whether they have enough information or whether they should collect more data.

Mean

The mean is the average. You find the mean by adding the data together and then dividing by the number of data. Rainfall measurements were taken daily for one week and the following data were obtained:

0 mm, 4 mm, 15 mm, 7 mm, 20 mm, 3 mm, 0 mm

mean = sum of data ÷ number of data

Step 1: Find the sum.

$0 + 4 + 15 + 7 + 20 + 3 + 0 = 49$

Step 2: Divide the sum by the number of data to find the mean.

$49 \div 7 = 7$

The mean of the data is 7 mm.

Median

The median is in the middle. Half of the data are lower than the median and half are higher. Put the data in order:

0 mm, 0 mm, 3 mm, 4 mm, 7 mm, 15 mm, 20 mm

The median of the data is 4 mm.

Mode

The mode is the value that occurs most often. Here, the mode is 0 mm.

Range

The range is the difference between the largest and smallest values. The range of the data is 20 – 0 = 20 mm.

Make Inferences

Science deals with observations and facts. Imagine that you hear a dog barking in the distance. This is a scientific observation because anyone listening to and looking at the dog would agree that the dog is barking. Data and observations are facts. For example, the statement *Dogs bark* is a fact.

Scientific observations are different from opinions. An opinion is a personal belief and is not always based on facts. An example of an opinion in this case would be *The dog is a bad dog.* A scientist uses facts and observations to draw conclusions and make inferences. An **inference** is a conclusion based on observations. An example of an inference is *The dog is barking because it sees a rabbit.* In science, for a conclusion to be valid, it must be based on observations and sound reasoning, not on opinion.

17. Infer Look at this picture of a dog. Write a statement that is an observation. Write a statement that is an inference.

got it?

18. Determine You are finding the mass of a rock. You place the rock in one pan of a pan balance. You add mass cubes to the other pan. How do you know when to stop adding mass cubes?

19. How are data used in science?

Stop! I need help with

Wait! I have a question about

Go! Now I know

How do scientists support their conclusions?

I will know TEKS 2A, 2D
I will know how to do investigations. I will know how to analyze and interpret information and draw conclusions.
(Also 1A, 2C, 2E, 2F, 4A)

Vocabulary
evidence

Connect to Math

Math TEKS 7

Some of the dinosaur tracks at Dinosaur Valley State Park near Glen Rose, Texas are 15 to 25 inches long. Scientists study tracks like these to reach conclusions. For example, they believe that the tracks were made by an *Acrocanthosaurus*.

To see how large these footprints are, take a large sheet of paper and draw a line that is 15 inches long. Then draw another line that is 25 inches long. Compare the length of your foot to the length of the lines that you drew. Are these footprints longer than your footprints? What conclusion does this evidence support?

PEARSON Texas.com

Quick Lab

TEKS 1A, 2A, 2C, 2E, 4A

Which towel absorbs the most water?

Materials

graduated cylinder
water
plastic cup
3 sheets each of 3 different brands of paper towel

1. Pour 100 mL of water into a cup. **Measure** carefully. Wad up one Brand A towel. Dip it completely into the cup and remove it. Measure and **record** the water left in the cup.

2. Repeat twice using the same brand of towel.

3. Repeat Steps 1 and 2 using each of the other brands.

Paper Towel Testing

Trial	Water Left in Cup (mL)		
	Brand A	Brand B	Brand C
1			
2			
3			
Total			

Clean up spills immediately.

Explain Your Results

4. **Draw a Conclusion** Which towel absorbed the most?

5. How did carrying out repeated trials help you trust your conclusions?

For each trial, dip your towel the same way.

Draw and Defend Conclusions

After analyzing the information that has been collected, scientists draw conclusions about what they have discovered by interpreting their data. Scientists defend those conclusions by using the observations they made during their investigations. Sometimes, different conclusions can be drawn from the same set of data. Other scientists may question the methods that the scientists used to draw their conclusions, and the evidence from the investigations must be reviewed, analyzed, evaluated, and critiqued using evidence, logical reasoning, and experimental and observational testing. Scientists examine all sides of the evidence when reviewing other scientists' explanations.

For example, the behavior of some types of birds is not well known. Scientists must continue to collect and interpret data in order to understand the different behavior of the birds, such as their migration patterns, diet, and shelter preferences. Scientists have drawn conclusions about these bird behaviors, but the scientists' conclusions must be defended with appropriate scientific observations.

1. Give an Example What is one way a scientist may defend a conclusion? **Underline** a statement in the text to support your answer.

Scientists collect and interpret information about the prairie chickens in an effort to save them from disappearing from Earth.

Bison and cattle live on the refuge too. Their grazing causes the grass to grow in clumps. The prairie chicken chicks use the spaces between the clumps as pathways.

2. Analyze Use the scientists' observations to explain if grazing animals help or harm prairie chickens.

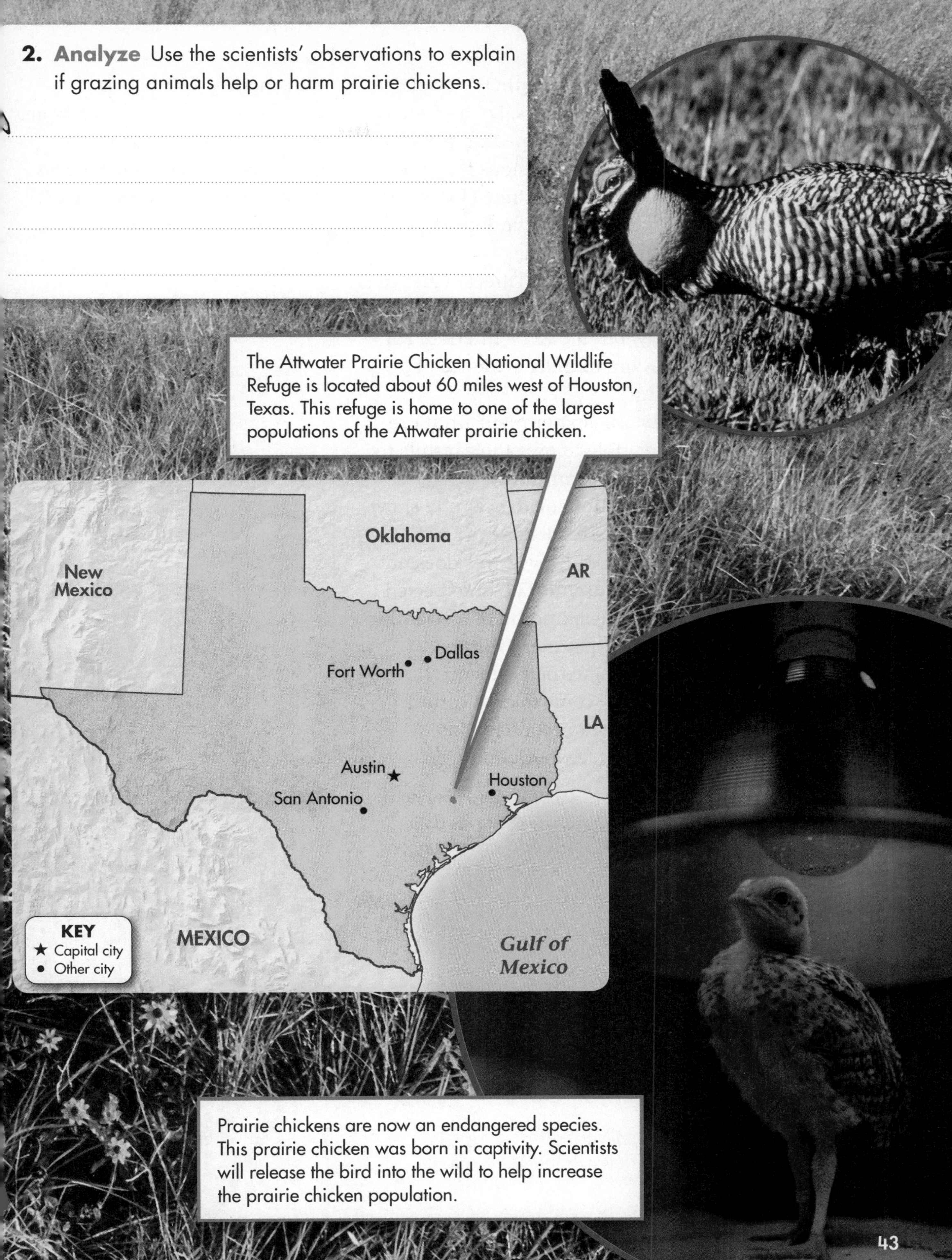

The Attwater Prairie Chicken National Wildlife Refuge is located about 60 miles west of Houston, Texas. This refuge is home to one of the largest populations of the Attwater prairie chicken.

Prairie chickens are now an endangered species. This prairie chicken was born in captivity. Scientists will release the bird into the wild to help increase the prairie chicken population.

Evidence

One way for scientists to ensure that their work is valid is to share their results with others. Each of their investigations must be replicable, or repeatable, by other scientists. In addition, the conclusions that the scientists drew about their experiments must be based on evidence. **Evidence** is a set of observations that make you believe that something is true.

Evidence might be direct or indirect. Direct evidence is observable, such as the color of a rock. Indirect evidence cannot be observed directly, but it can be inferred. For example, tall ocean waves are indirect evidence of a high wind speed.

When scientists have testable experiments that are based on evidence, they are able to give their results to other members of the scientific community.

During a scientific investigation, evidence may show results that are unexpected. The evidence may not support a scientist's hypothesis. However, this does not mean the experiment was not useful. The unexpected findings can lead to a new understanding of a scientific concept or cause scientists to experiment further.

Sometimes, scientists may misinterpret evidence from an investigation. They may come to an incorrect conclusion. This is why it is important for scientists to communicate with and accept feedback from one another.

3. Justify This scientist is testing a sample of ice from Antarctica. Do you think other scientists will be able to replicate this experiment? Why or why not?

Quick Lab

Coin Flip Scientists gather evidence to make valid conclusions. How often do you think a coin will come up heads? Flip a coin ten times. How often did it come up heads? Have your partner repeat your experiment. Did the results change? Draw a conclusion and explain it.

TEKS 2C, 2D, 2F

This scientist may be able to use his data as evidence to support his hypothesis.

Review and Retest

Scientists must describe exactly what they did in an experiment and how they did it. This allows other scientists working in the same field to replicate the experiment to see if the results are the same. They may also ask questions about the experiment and point out problems.

In science, communication is important. Scientists must describe their procedures and report their findings honestly. They must answer questions. Although some variation in results is acceptable, the results from different scientists should be similar. If results are not consistent, then the experiment must be done again.

4. List two things these scientists may be talking about. **Underline** a statement in the text that supports your answer.

got it?

5. Interpret You want to find where a wooden stud is behind a wall so you know where to hang a heavy picture. You tap on the wall in different places and listen for a change in sound. Are you using direct or indirect evidence? Explain.

6. Evaluate Why is it important that scientists' conclusions be based on evidence?

Stop! I need help with

Wait! I have a question about

Go! Now I know

Lab Investigation

TEKS 1A, 2A, 2C, 3A

How does a banana slice change over time?

As you carry out this investigation, practice the inquiry skills you have learned.

Materials

3 banana slices
3 plastic cups
plastic spoon

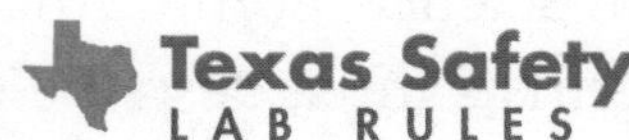

Texas Safety LAB RULES

Wash your hands thoroughly upon completing the activity.

Follow a Procedure

- ☐ **1.** Place a whole banana slice in a cup.
- ☐ **2.** Use a spoon to cut another banana slice into 4 pieces. Place the pieces in a second cup.
- ☐ **3.** Put another banana slice into a third cup. Mash this slice with a spoon.

Inquiry Skill

Scientists begin by asking a question. Then they make careful observations and record data accurately. They use their data to help make **inferences.**

☐ **4. Observe** the slices when you place them in the cup and each hour for 3 hours.
Record your observations in the chart.

Changes to Banana Slices over Time

Time	Observations		
	Whole Slice	Cut-Up Slice	Mashed Slice
When placed in cup			
After 1 hour			
After 2 hours			
After 3 hours			

Analyze and Conclude

5. Communicate Examine your data.
Identify a simple pattern you **observed.**

....

....

6. Make an **inference** to explain about the pattern you identified.

....

....

7. How can investigating cut bananas help scientists learn about other fruits?

....

....

....

MY PLANET DIARY

TEKS 3D

Deep in the ocean lies a world that is almost completely unexplored by humans.

Scientists have discovered animals, such as the giant tubeworm, that live in extreme conditions 2,600 meters below the ocean's surface. That far below the surface there is extremely high pressure and not very much oxygen or light. Structures called hydrothermal vents are near volcanoes and release very hot water. The water temperature can be more than 400°C!

Giant tubeworms can grow to be up to 2.5 meters long and 10 centimeters wide. They do not have mouths. Instead, giant tubeworms absorb nutrients made by tiny bacteria that live inside of them!

hydrothermal vents

giant tubeworms

What might a scientist do to find out how giant tubeworms interact with their environment?

Vocabulary Smart Cards

research
hypothesis
observation
experiment
model
variable
independent variable
dependent variable
control group
procedure
data
inference
evidence

Play a Game!

Cut out the Vocabulary Smart Cards.

Work with a partner. Choose a card.

Say one word you can think of that is related to that vocabulary word in some way. It might be an example.

Have your partner guess the word. How many clues did it take to guess the correct word?

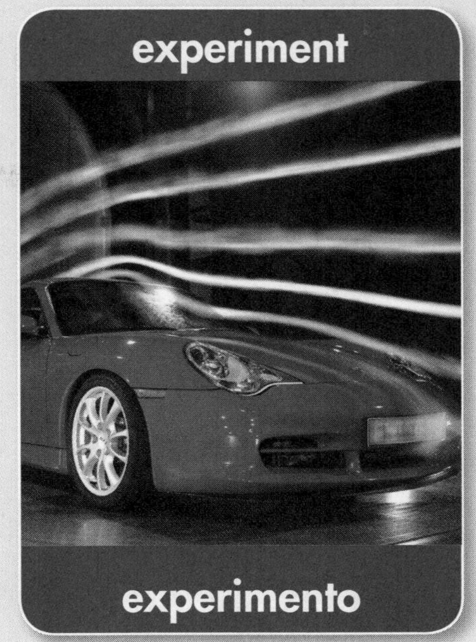

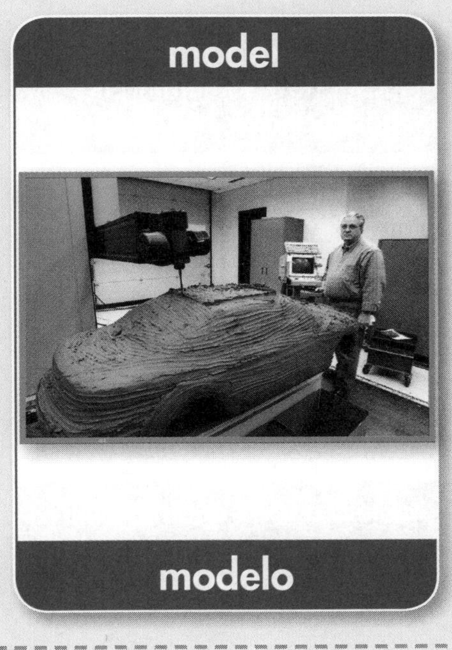

Interactive Vocabulary

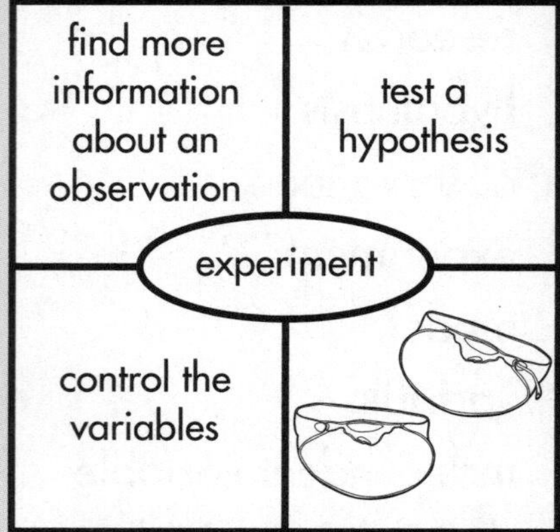

Make a Word Square!

Choose a vocabulary word and write it in the center of the square. Fill in the squares with related ideas, such as a definition, a characteristic, an example, or something that is not an example.

study of a variety of reference materials about a subject

Give an example of something you have researched.

estudio de una variedad de materiales de referencia sobre un tema

the use of scientific investigation and reasoning to test a hypothesis

Write three related words.

uso de investigación y razonamiento científicos para poner a prueba una hipótesis

statement of what you think will happen during an investigation

Write three related words.

enunciado de lo que crees que ocurrirá en una investigación

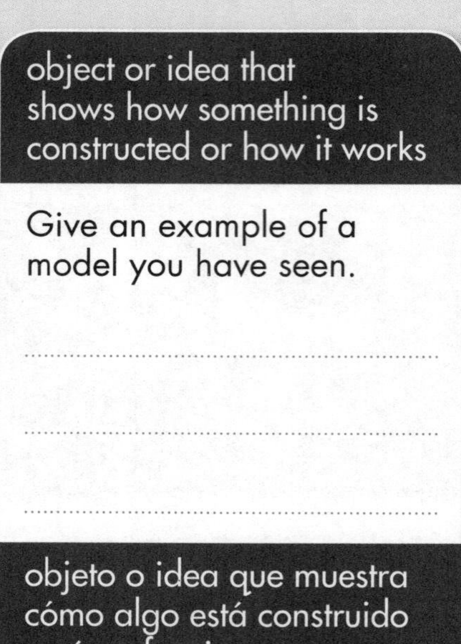

object or idea that shows how something is constructed or how it works

Give an example of a model you have seen.

objeto o idea que muestra cómo algo está construido o cómo funciona

something you find out about objects, events, or living things using your senses

Write a sentence using this term.

algo que descubres con tus sentidos sobre los objetos, sucesos o seres vivos

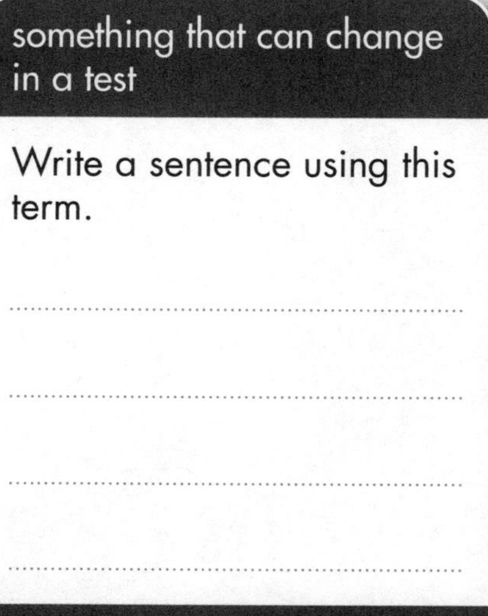

something that can change in a test

Write a sentence using this term.

algo que puede cambiar durante una prueba

evidence

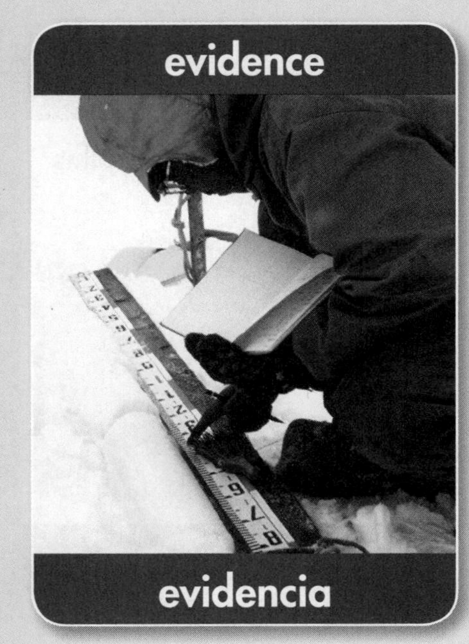

evidencia

procedure

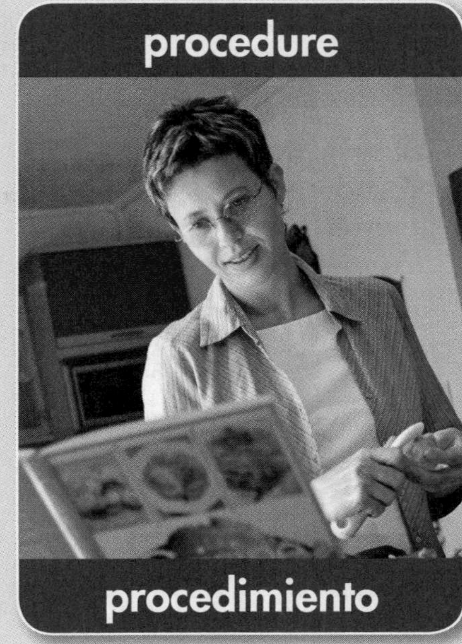

procedimiento

independent variable

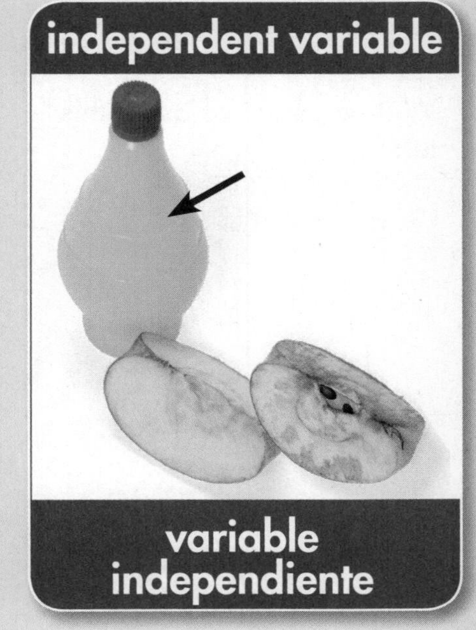

variable independiente

data

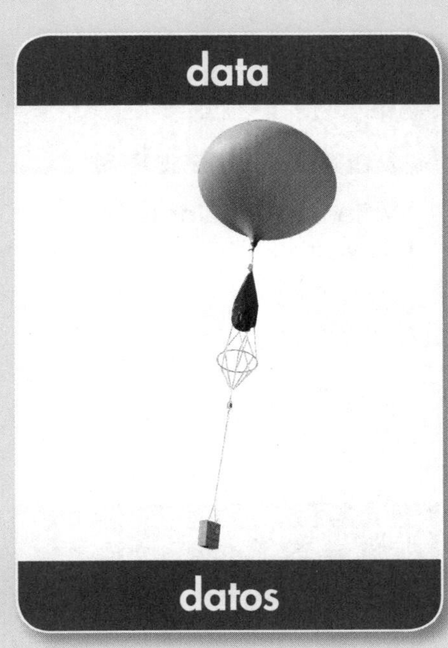

datos

dependent variable

variable dependiente

inference

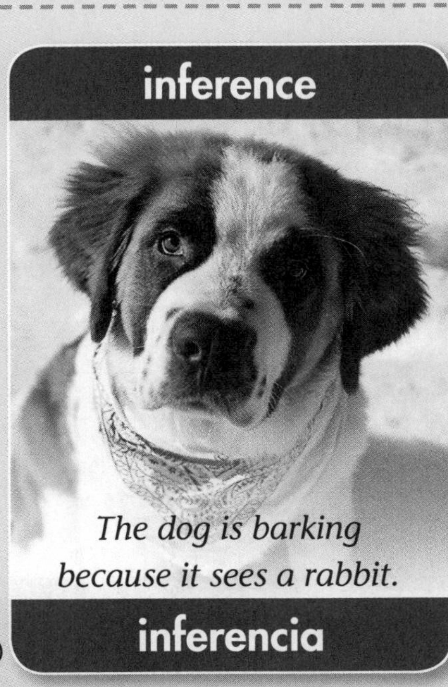
The dog is barking because it sees a rabbit.

inferencia

control group

grupo de control

the variable that you control

Write a sentence using this term.

variable que tú controlas

step-by-step instructions for completing a task

Give an example of a procedure you have followed.

instrucciones paso por paso para realizar una tarea

observations that make you believe something is true

Write a sentence using this word.

observaciones que te hacen creer que algo es cierto

the variable that changes when the independent variable changes

What was the dependent variable in your experiment?

variable que cambia cuando la variable independiente cambia

information from which a conclusion can be drawn or a prediction can be made

Write the singular form of this word.

información de la cual se puede sacar una conclusión o hacer una predicción

a standard against which change is measured

Write a sentence using this term.

estándar que se usa para medir un cambio

a conclusion based on observations

Use any form of this word in a sentence.

conclusión basada en observaciones

TEKS Practice

Lesson 1 TEKS 2B, 2C

What do scientists do?

1. **Vocabulary** An observation is something you find out about objects, events, or living things by using your ________.
   A. senses
   B. research
   C. hypothesis
   D. conclusion

2. **Analyze** Which of the following is a detailed observation?
   A. The rock is red.
   B. The rock is pretty.
   C. The rock was formed by extreme heat and pressure.
   D. The rock has wide bands of red and thinner bands of orange.

3. **Recognize** At the beginning of an investigation, you write the following statement. *If I cover the plant with plastic wrap, water will appear on the inside because the plant gives off water vapor.* What is this statement?
   A. a conclusion
   B. a hypothesis
   C. a measurement
   D. a control group

Lesson 2 TEKS 2A, 2B

How do scientists investigate?

4. **Write About It** Why is it important for scientists to write well-defined questions?

5. **Recognize** You are testing to see if music helps plants grow better. You divide the plants into four groups.

Plant Groups

Group	Music Type
A	jazz
B	classical
C	rock
D	none

   How many variables are you testing?
   A. 1
   B. 2
   C. 3
   D. 4

6. **Plan** When you are setting up an experiment to test one variable, which group must be included in the experiment?

TEKS Practice

Lesson 2 TEKS 2A, 2B

How do scientists investigate?

7. **Describe** a simple investigation that tests one variable.

8. **Write About It** Write a well-defined question that could be tested.

Lesson 3 TEKS 2B, 4A

How do scientists collect and interpret data?

9. **Identify** Jose is conducting an experiment. He needs to measure the mass of a rock. Which tool should he use?

A. prism
B. balance
C. meterstick
D. graduated cylinder

10. **Recognize** What does this tool measure?

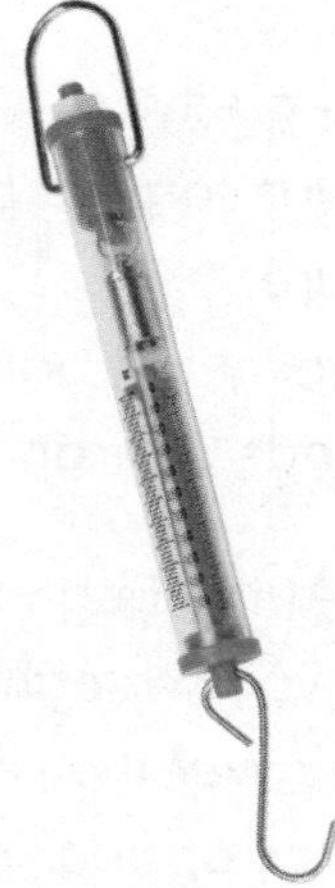

11. **Identify** You watch your neighbors as they leave their apartment building. They have suitcases with them. They all get into the car and drive away. You think they are going on vacation. Is your thought a fact or an inference? Explain.

TEKS Practice

Lesson 4 TEKS 2A, 2D

How do scientists support their conclusions?

12. Explain When scientists perform their one-variable investigations, how do they use evidence?

13. Analyze You are testing to see if adding fertilizer helps a plant grow. The table below shows your data.

Plant Groups

Group	Fertilizer Added (g)	Amount of Growth (cm)
Control	none	2.3
A	1	3.5
B	2	2.9
C	3	0 (plant died)

What reasonable explanation can you make from this observable evidence?

Chapter 1

Lesson 1 What do scientists do?
In Lesson 1, you learned that scientists ask questions and write testable hypotheses. They collect information by making detailed observations. Scientists also make reasonable explanations from observations.

Process TEKS: 2B, 2C, 2D

Lesson 2 How do scientists investigate?
In Lesson 2, you learned that scientists ask well-defined questions and use different methods for investigations. Investigations test one variable.

Process TEKS: 2A, 2B

Lesson 3 How do scientists collect and interpret data?
In Lesson 3, you learned that scientists collect data using the appropriate tools and technology.

Process TEKS: 4A

Lesson 4 How do scientists support their conclusions?
In Lesson 4, you learned that scientists collect evidence. Then they analyze and interpret their evidence and draw conclusions.

Process TEKS: 2A, 2D

★ TEKS Practice: Chapter Review

Read each question and circle the best answer.

1 Devin observes bees buzzing around his garden. What is one well-defined question Devin could investigate about bees?

A Which flowers taste best to bees?

B Why don't bees stay on one flower very long?

C Do bees use color to choose which flowers to visit?

D Do bees know they will die if they sting a person?

2 The table shows how much water is used by a family each time one of them performs an ordinary activity.

Family Water Use per Activity

Activity	Water Used (L)
Taking shower	50–77
Taking bath	96–116
Washing hands	4–8
Flushing toilet	19–27
Brushing teeth	19–39
Washing dishes by hand	20–77
Washing dishes in automatic dishwasher	27–58

Based on evidence in the table, what can you infer about water use by the family?

F The longer an activity lasts, the more water is used for that activity.

G Each activity uses a different amount of water from one time to the next.

H Washing dishes by hand saves water compared with using a dishwasher.

J The data could be added up to show a family's total daily water use.

3 Madison wants to see whether wool acts as a heat insulator. She fills two jars of the same size with the same amount of hot water. Both water samples have the same starting temperature. Madison places a thermometer in each jar and covers one jar with an old wool sock. The thermometer sticks out of a hole in the sock. For 10 minutes Madison measures the temperature of the water every 2 minutes. Which table will allow Madison to record all her data?

A

Time (min)	Temperature without Sock (°C)	Temperature with Sock (°C)
0		
10		

B

Temperature without Sock (°C)	Temperature with Sock (°C)

C

Time (min)	Temperature without Sock (°C)	Temperature with Sock (°C)
0		
2		
4		
6		
8		
10		

D

Time (min)	Temperature with Sock (°C)
0	
2	
4	
6	
8	
10	

4 A valid conclusion is based on evidence that —

F others agree with

G confirms a hypothesis

H is very precise

J is interpreted correctly

5 The drawing shows a model of Earth.

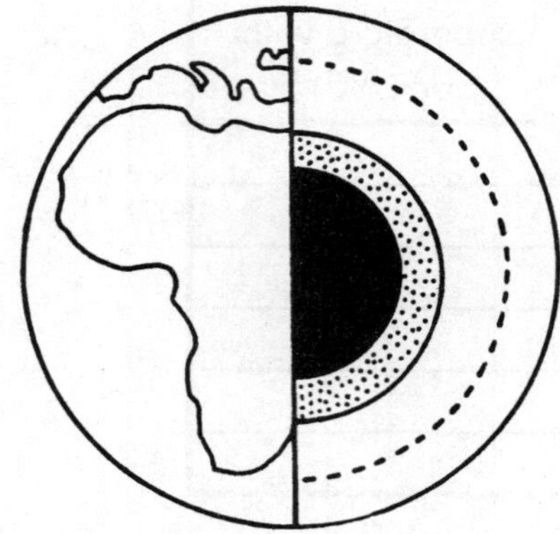

What does this model show that you cannot see for yourself?

A A view of Earth's place in space

B A view of Earth's inner layers

C A view of Earth's total size

D A view of how Earth formed

6 Two groups investigate how many marbles a toy boat can hold before it sinks. Each group follows the same procedure, using the same boat. The table shows their results.

Number of Marbles That Sink a Toy Boat

	Group 1	Group 2
Number of marbles	13	9

What should the two groups do to make their results more reliable?

F Choose the data that makes more sense.

G Run more trials.

H Use different marbles.

J None of the above

7 Alexis wants to investigate shadows. Her materials include a wooden block, a flashlight, and a white wall. The picture shows how Alexis sets up her materials.

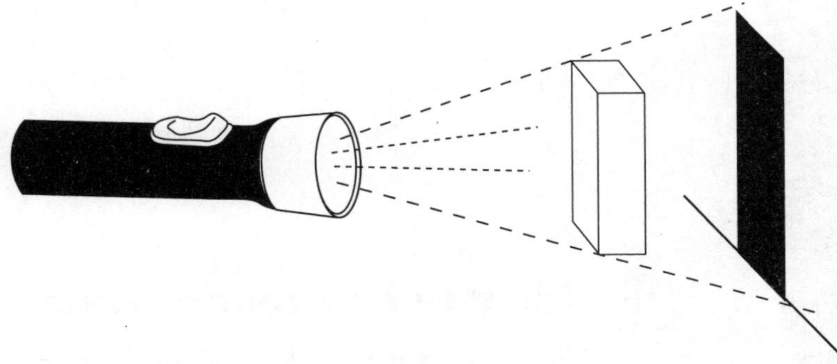

Alexis watches the size of the shadow as she moves the flashlight closer to the wooden block. What is the independent variable in her experiment?

A The position of the light source

B The size of the light source

C The size of the wooden block's shadow

D The position of the block

If you have trouble with . . .							
Question	1	2	3	4	5	6	7
See chapter (lesson)	1 (1)	1 (3)	1 (3)	1 (3, 4)	1 (2)	1 (2)	1 (2)
TEKS	2B	2D	2G	2D, 3A	3C	2E	2A

Lab zone® Open-Ended Inquiry

TEKS 2B, 2F, 2G

Materials

computer
graphing software
table-generating software

Inquiry Skill

Before beginning an experiment, ask a **well-defined question** and **formulate a testable hypothesis.** A good hypothesis will guide you as you carry out the experiment.

What is our favorite fruit?

Samantha likes fruit, but she dislikes the fruits that are served in the cafeteria. She believes that students would eat more fruit at lunch if they were offered fruits that they like. She decided to use a survey to find out which fruit her classmates liked best.

Ask a question.

☐ **1.** Ask a **well-defined question** for your experiment. Write your question on the line below.

....

....

State a hypothesis.

☐ **2. Formulate a testable hypothesis** by completing the sentence.

....

....

....

Identify and control variables.

☐ **3.** Some surveys do not have a dependent variable and an independent variable like a traditional experiment does. A survey contains a question or a group of questions. A survey often is used to get other people's opinion on a subject. After a selected group of people answers the question or questions, the answers are examined.

Write the question for your survey that you plan to ask your classmates.

....

....

Design your test.

☐ **4.** Describe how you will do your survey. Be sure to make a list of the four fruits that you plan to use on your survey.

Collect and record your data.

☐ **5.** Construct an appropriate table using technology to organize your data. Use a computer to construct a table of your survey responses. Your table might look like the one below. Make sure that you include a title.

Grade 5 Favorite Fruits

Fruit	Number of Students
apple	4
orange	6
strawberries	12
banana	8

Interpret your data.

☐ **6.** Construct a simple graph using technology to examine information. Use your table and a computer to construct a bar graph like the one below. Make sure that you give it a title and label the *x*-axis and the *y*-axis. Examine your data and write your conclusions below.

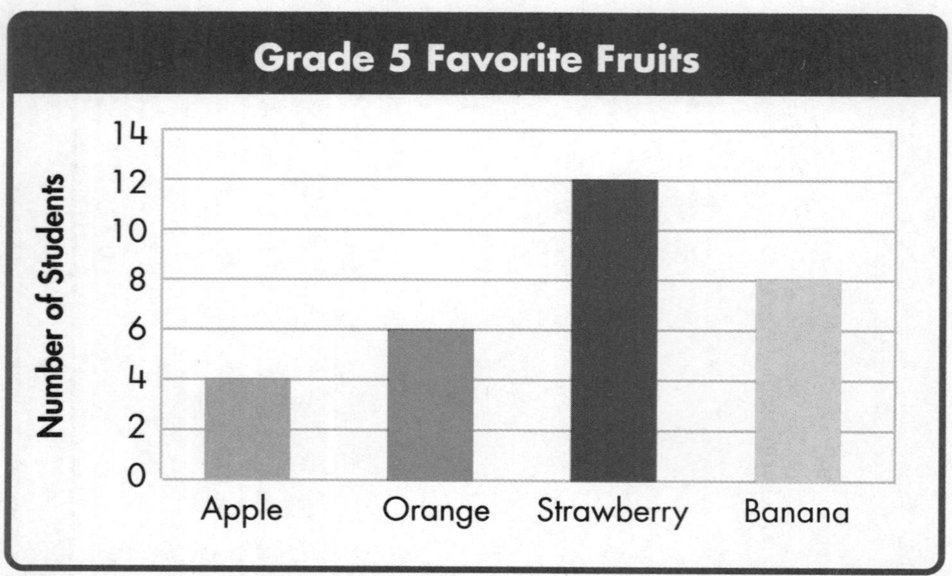

☑ **7.** Look at your graph closely. Which fruit was the favorite for the entire classroom?

State your conclusion.

8. Communicate your conclusion. Compare your hypothesis with your results.

Physical Science

Texas Essential Knowledge and Skills

Content TEKS

Matter and Energy: 5A, 5B, 5C, 5D
Force, Motion, and Energy: 6A, 6B, 6C, 6D

Process TEKS

1A, 1B, 2A, 2B, 2C, 2D, 2E, 2F, 2G, 3A, 3B, 3C, 3D, 4A, 4B

What makes up these GIANT crystals?

Texas

Chapter 2

Properties of Matter

How are weight and volume affected when objects are combined?

You see small crystals, such as sugar or salt, every day. But have you ever seen crystals like these? These giant crystals are in a cave in the Chihuahuan Desert.

This cave was once filled with water that had minerals dissolved in it. How do you think the crystals formed?

Texas Essential Knowledge and Skills

Readiness TEKS: 5A Classify matter based on physical properties, including mass, magnetism, physical state (solid, liquid, and gas), relative density (sinking and floating), solubility in water, and the ability to conduct or insulate thermal energy or electric energy.

Supporting TEKS: 5B Identify the boiling and freezing/melting points of water on the Celsius scale. **5C** Demonstrate that some mixtures maintain physical properties of their ingredients such as iron fillings and sand. **5D** Identify changes that can occur in the physical properties of the ingredients of solutions such as dissolving salt in water or adding lemon juice to water.

Process TEKS: 1A, 2C, 2D, 3C, 3D, 4A, 4B

PEARSON Texas.com

Lab zone® Inquiry Warm-Up

TEKS 5A, 1A, 3C

What are the particles in matter like?

Make a model to illustrate what you think particles might be like in a solid, liquid, and gas. In this chapter you will learn what scientists have discovered.

☐ **1.** Draw a balloon, a cup, and a block.

☐ **2.** Think about the particles in a gas, liquid, and solid.

☐ **3.** Draw or develop a model that represents how something works or looks that cannot be seen. Make a model to show what a solid, liquid, and gas might look like. Use the pasta to represent the particles.

Explain Your Results

4. How do you think the particles in your model are different from those that make up matter?

Materials

paper
pasta

Demonstrate safe practices as described in the *Texas Safety Standards* during classroom investigations. Never drink or eat in the lab area.

Inquiry Skill

Making a model can help you understand what something might look like.

Focus on Compare and Contrast

You will practice the reading strategy of **compare and contrast** in this chapter. Comparing and contrasting information can help you learn about the relationships between words and ideas. When you compare, you find how two words or ideas are alike. When you contrast, you find how the words or ideas are different.

Ice on a Lake

A lake is filled with liquid water during the summer. During a cold winter, the water changes. If the temperature drops below the freezing temperature of water, the liquid water starts to freeze and becomes ice. A thin layer of solid ice forms on top of the water. The longer the air temperature stays cold and the colder it gets, the thicker the ice becomes. But no matter how thick it gets, the ice still floats on the water. Unlike other substances, water becomes less dense when it becomes a solid. Despite the differences, liquid water and ice are two forms of water.

Practice It!

Read the paragraph and look for ways liquid water and ice are alike and different. Compare and contrast water and ice by filling in the Venn diagram below. Write words or phrases that describe liquid water in one circle. Write words or phrases that describe ice in the other circle. Write words that describe how they are the same in the section in the middle where the circles overlap.

liquid water **both** **ice**

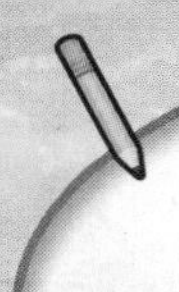

Texas

LESSON

1

How can matter be described?

I will know TEKS 5A
I will know how to classify matter based on physical properties, including mass, magnetism, and density. (Also **2C**, **4A**)

Vocabulary
mass
volume
density
magnetism

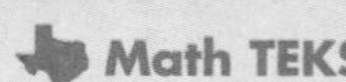

Connect to Math

Math TEKS 3A

The huge Balanced Rock at Big Bend National Park is a dramatic sight. How would you describe this object? There are many ways to measure and describe the things around us. These descriptions help us to classify and categorize things. You can use objects with a known measurement to help estimate and compare objects.

If a person with a mass of 50 kg stood next to a rock and a stick that was 1 meter in length, estimate these physical properties of the rock:

If you estimate that the rock is twice as tall as the length of the stick, how tall is the rock?

....

If you estimate that the rock is 3 times as wide as the length of the stick, how wide is the rock?

....

If the boulder has a mass that is 25 times that of the person, then the boulder has a mass of

.... kg.

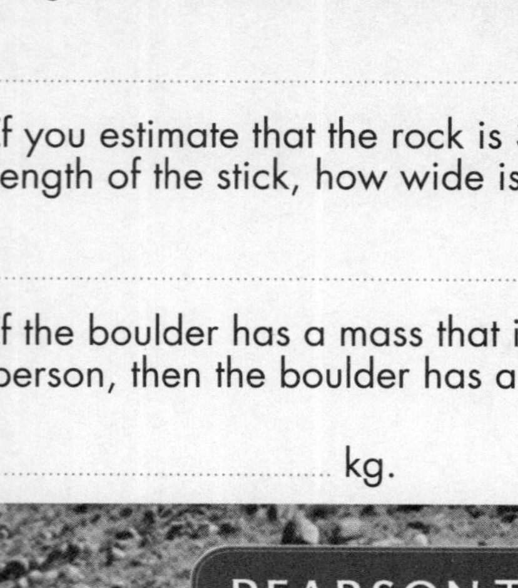

PEARSON Texas.com

Quick Lab

TEKS 5A, 2C, 4A

How can magnetism help you to classify matter?

Materials

magnet
copper wire, 5 cm
aluminum foil, 5 cm square
iron nail or rod, about 5 cm
5 steel paper clips

Texas Safety LAB RULES

Be careful with sharp objects.

1. Roll the aluminum foil to form a 5 cm rod.
2. Collect information using tools, including magnets. Bring the north pole of the magnet close to the iron rod. **Observe.** Repeat with the aluminum foil and the copper wire. What do you observe?
3. Repeat Step 2 using the south pole of the magnet instead of the north pole. What do you observe?
4. While holding the magnet against one end of the iron nail, bring the other end of the nail close to a paper clip. What do you observe? Repeat this step using the foil and the wire. Record all your observations in the table below.
5. **Classify** Classify matter based on the physical property of magnetism by labeling each metal as magnetic or non-magnetic.

Metal	Attracted by N. Pole	Attracted by S. Pole	Transmits Magnetism	Type of Metal
Iron				
Aluminum				
Copper				

Explain Your Results

6. **Infer** Suppose you found a metal that was attracted by the south pole of a magnet. What other properties is this metal likely to have?

1. **Classify** Explain how you might take measurements of a balloon to prove that air has mass and takes up space.

Matter

Like ice, water, and air, you are made of matter. All living and nonliving things are made of matter. Matter is anything that has mass and takes up space. Mass is the amount of matter in an object. Matter includes the food we eat, our homes, our furniture, the sun, the moon, and this book.

Some matter is easy to see and understand. A baseball bat might be made of wood. You can see the wood material and feel its texture and mass. It takes up space. What about air? Is air matter? You usually cannot see air, but you know that you can blow air into a balloon. The air will fill the balloon. The full balloon shows you that air has mass and takes up space.

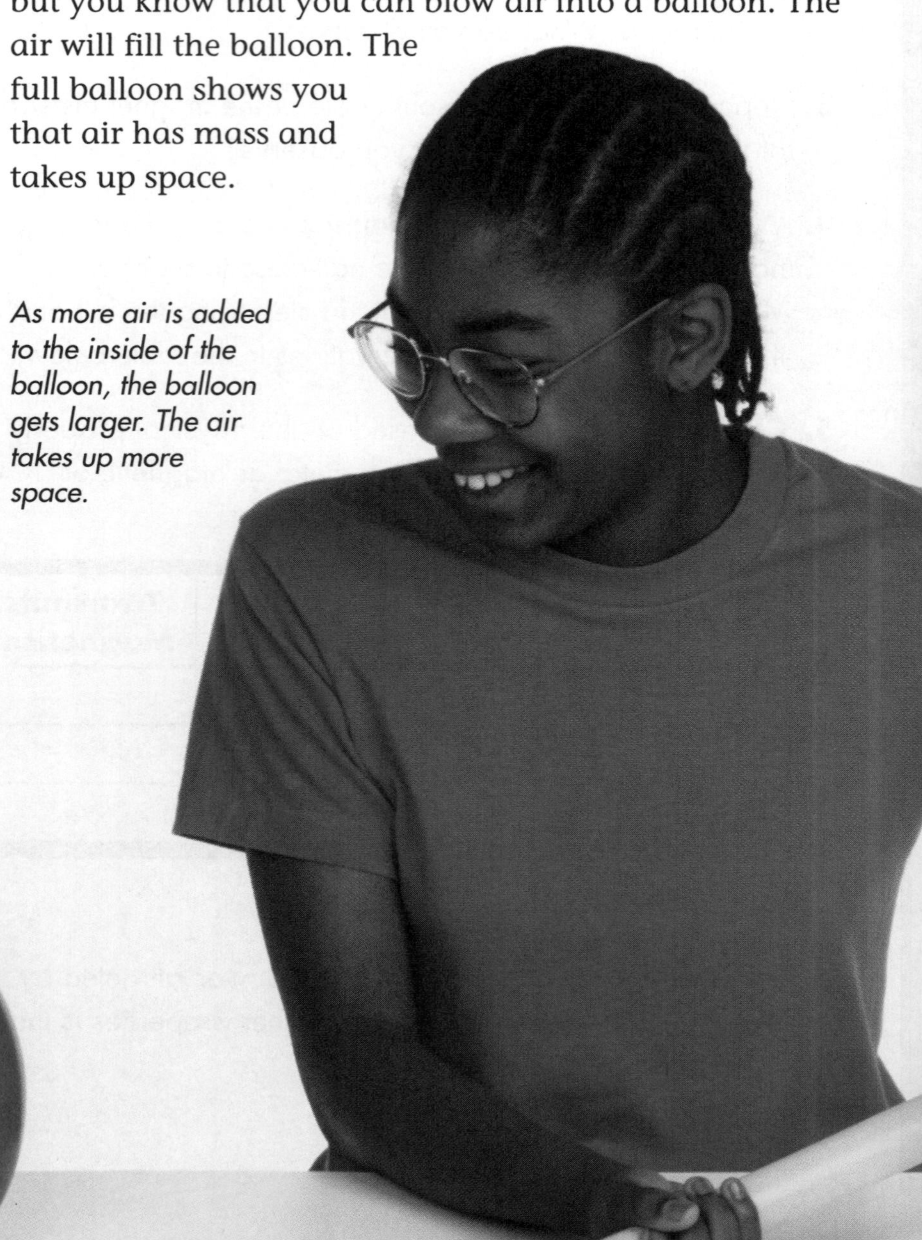

As more air is added to the inside of the balloon, the balloon gets larger. The air takes up more space.

A large sand sculpture is made of matter. It takes up a lot of space. It has a large mass. But if you look at it closely, you will see that it is made of tiny sand grains. A sand grain is also made of matter. It is gritty and tan colored, like the sculpture. But unlike the sculpture, a sand grain has a small mass and it does not take up a lot of space. All matter is made of tiny parts.

These sand grains are small particles. They are easy to see under a microscope. They are made of even smaller particles, too small to see with a regular microscope.

All matter can be described in terms of physical properties. How is a football different from a baseball? How is a cup of water different from a cup of dirt? The way you could describe these different things is based on their physical properties. Most physical properties can be observed and described.

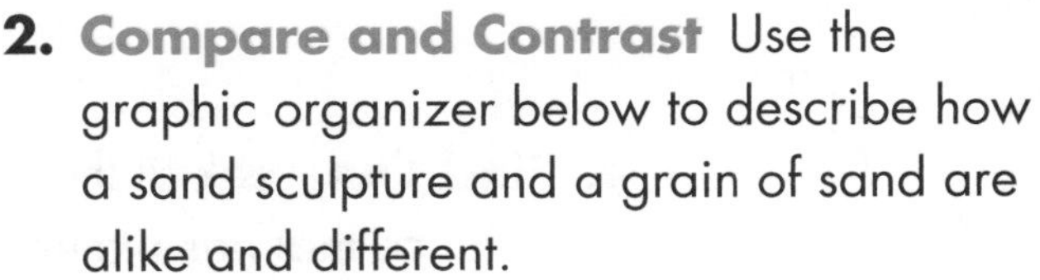

2. Compare and Contrast Use the graphic organizer below to describe how a sand sculpture and a grain of sand are alike and different.

Sand Sculpture | **Grain of Sand**

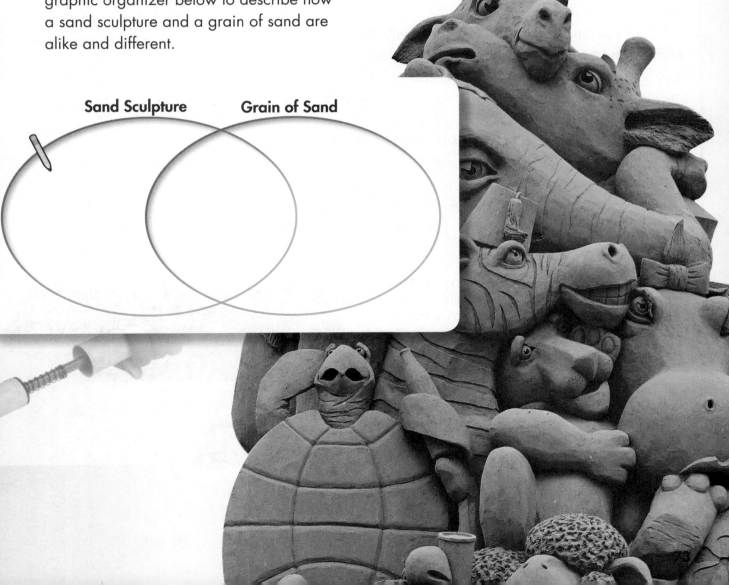

Mass

The amount of matter in a solid, liquid, or gas is called its **mass**. Mass is measured by using a balance, often using units of grams or kilograms.

Often the weight of an object is confused with its mass. Mass and weight are related, but they are not the same thing. An object's mass is the same everywhere. An object's weight can vary. For example, in a place with low gravity, such as the moon, an object will weigh less than it does on Earth. However, on Earth's surface gravity has more or less the same strength everywhere. Therefore, weight gives us a fair idea of the mass of an object. To classify objects by their mass, we can just compare their weights on Earth.

Another way to classify objects by their mass is by comparing how much force is needed to move the object. For example, if you were to push two different objects, the object with less mass would move farther or faster with the same push.

A more accurate way to classify objects by their mass is to measure their mass using a pan balance. To find the mass of a solid, such as a toy car, you place the object on one side of a pan balance. On the other side, you place objects of known mass, such as gram cubes. When the two sides balance each other, the total mass of all the known masses equals the mass of the object.

You can also use the pan balance to compare the mass of objects. If you place a different object on each side of the balance, the pan of the balance holding the most mass will be lower.

3. **Classify** matter based on the physical property of mass. If you have three different objects, what are two ways you could use a pan balance to classify them by their mass?

4. **Find Out** Look at the balance that has water. Count the cubes. What is the mass of the water inside the container?

The empty container on the left has a mass of 8 g. We know this because it takes 8 cubes to balance it. Each cube has a mass of 1 g.

Now the container has water. More cubes are needed to balance the extra mass. These extra cubes match the mass of the water.

Volume

The amount of space an object takes up is its **volume.** Volume can be measured in milliliters (mL).

You can use a graduated cylinder to find the volume of a liquid. You just pour the liquid into the cylinder and read the volume off the scale, at the surface.

Solids also have volume. If you put liquid in a graduated cylinder and let a solid object sink in the liquid, the solid takes up some space. The liquid that was in that space is forced to go up. The change in the height of the liquid column tells you the volume of the solid.

Gases have volume. In fact, a small mass of gas can fill a large volume. You can measure the volume of a gas using an upside-down, partially submerged graduated cylinder filled with water. If you blow air into the cylinder with a straw, the bubbles will push some water out. The volume of water pushed out is the same as the volume of the gas.

5. Identify Circle the milliliters on the graduated cylinder that allow you to determine the volume of the toy car.

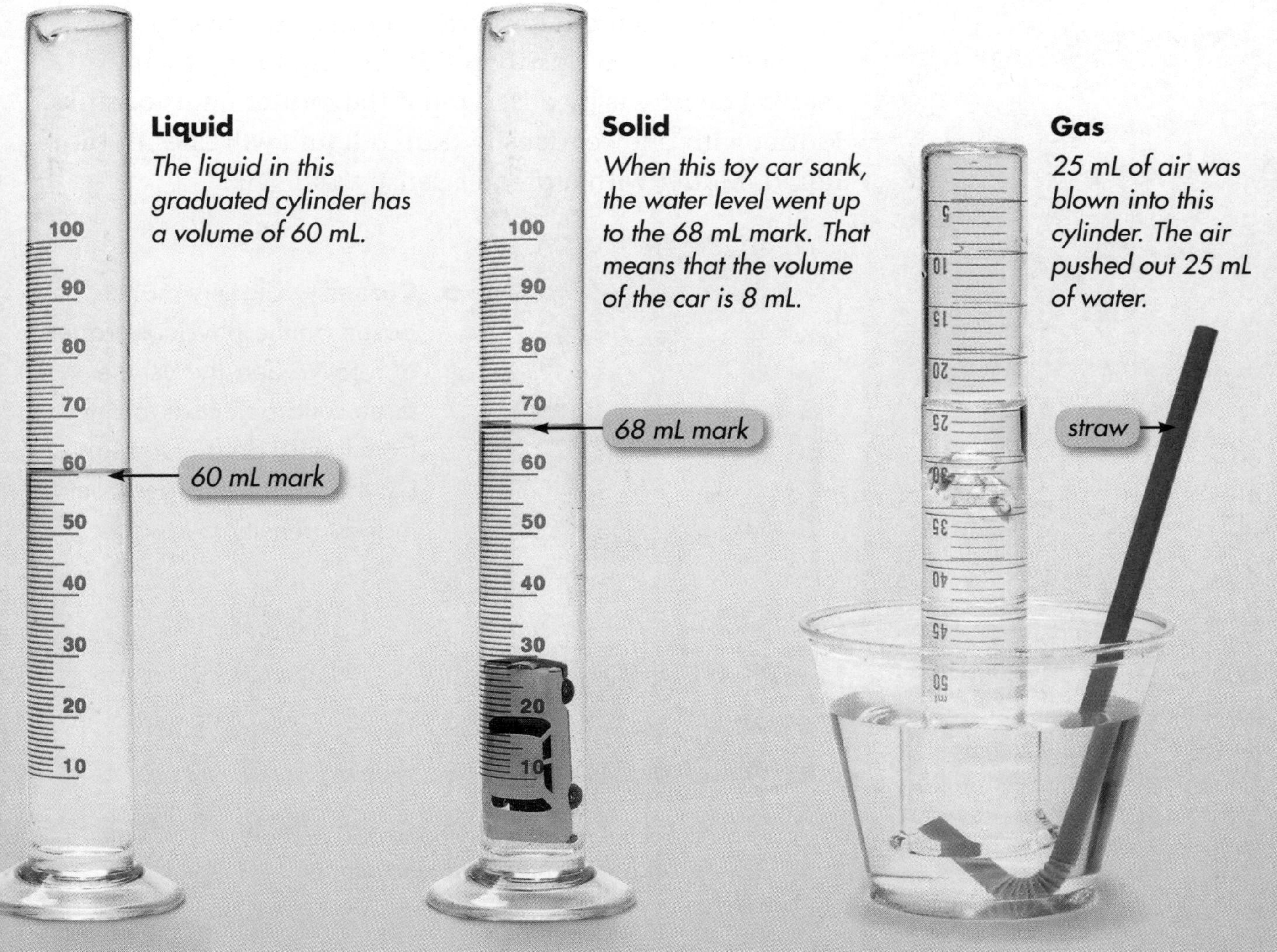

Liquid
The liquid in this graduated cylinder has a volume of 60 mL.

Solid
When this toy car sank, the water level went up to the 68 mL mark. That means that the volume of the car is 8 mL.

Gas
25 mL of air was blown into this cylinder. The air pushed out 25 mL of water.

Density

Another physical property of matter is density. **Density** is the amount of matter in a given volume. The density of a solid object can be calculated by dividing the object's mass by its volume. The density of a liquid is found the same way.

Each solid and liquid has a specific density. Because of this, density can be used to identify matter. It can also be used to classify matter by its relative density, or how the densities of different kinds of matter compare to each other.

You can think about differences in density by imagining two objects that are the same size but made from different materials. For example, a bowling ball is made of heavy material. Even though it is almost the same size as a basketball, you could not throw it high enough to go through a basketball hoop. The bowling ball has a greater density than the basketball. Now, imagine a ball made of cork that is the size of a bowling ball. You could classify the cork ball as having a lower density than a bowling ball.

Another way to classify solids and liquids by their relative density is by observing if the matter floats or sinks. Matter with a lower density than a liquid will float in that liquid. Matter with a greater density will sink.

7. Infer A boat floats on top of water. An anchor works by sinking to the bottom. The density of water is 1 gram per cubic centimeter. What do you know about the density of the boat and the density of the anchor?

6. Classify Classify matter based on the physical property of relative density. List the three solid objects in order from lowest density to highest. List the liquids in order from highest density to lowest.

Each liquid (corn syrup, water, and oil) and object has a different density.

Magnetism

Some substances have the property to pull on or attract certain metals. This property is called **magnetism**. The metals that are attracted include iron, cobalt, nickel, and gadolinium. When you place a magnetic substance near iron or one of the other metals, the two objects pull toward each other with a strong force. Magnetic substances do not attract wood, plastic, paper, or other objects that do not contain these metals.

8. Identify Is this rock magnetic? How do you know?

got it?

9. Classify You find three different rocks while exploring the Rio Grande valley with friends. You are asked to classify the rocks using the physical property of mass. Describe what tool you would use and how you would use it.

10. Explain What is the connection between an object's density and its ability to float or sink?

Stop! I need help with

Wait! I have a question about

Go! Now I know

STEM
Science • Technology
Engineering • Math

How Much Do You Weigh in Space?

TEKS 3D

A person's weight is a pull between their body and Earth. As astronauts move away from Earth, this pull weakens and their weight becomes less.

Imagine that you are a NASA engineer in Houston preparing a space launch to the moon and back. Since an astronaut weighs less on the moon, taking off from the moon to return to Earth will use up less fuel. However, the mass of an astronaut does not change. This mass affects how quickly the spacecraft can speed up or slow down without injuring the astronaut. Even in complete weightlessness, these safety limits must be observed.

Now imagine that you're an astronaut traveling to Jupiter. Your weight on Jupiter is based on how much Jupiter's gravity pulls on your body. Since Jupiter has more mass than Earth, it has more gravity and your weight is more. You can calculate your weight on Jupiter by multiplying your Earth weight by 2.4.

______ x 2.4 = [weight on Jupiter]

What would your weight be on Jupiter?

Infer How do you think your weight would change if you were able to visit a planet that had more mass than Jupiter? Explain your answer.

WHAT FLOATS YOUR BOAT?

You know that boats float on the water. Other objects float too. Can you predict which objects might float and which might sink?

For this experiment, you will need to fill a bucket with water. Next, collect five small objects from around your house or yard that will fit into the bucket.

List them in your science notebook. Next to each one, predict whether it will float or sink in the bucket of water.

After you have made your predictions, test each one by dropping it in the water. Did your object sink or float? Write down the results in your science notebook. How often were you right? How many times were you wrong? Which object surprised you the most?

Infer What property is important in determining if an object sinks or floats in water?

What are solids, liquids, and gases?

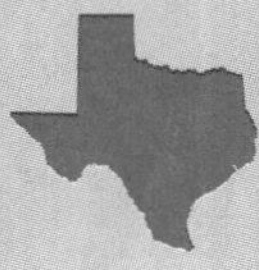

I will know TEKS 5A, 5B
I will know how to classify matter based on its physical state as a solid, liquid, or a gas. I will know the boiling point, freezing point, and melting point of water in Celsius degrees. (Also **1A**, **2C**, **2D**, **4A**)

Vocabulary
solid
liquid
gas
melting point
boiling point

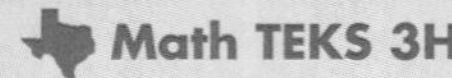

Math

STEM

Math TEKS 3H

Making the ice to cover a rink for a hockey team such as the Dallas Stars is a complicated task. The 45,000 to 57,000 liters of water is put down slowly in layers. The first layer is only about $\frac{1}{32}$ of an inch thick. When that freezes, another layer of about $\frac{1}{32}$ of an inch goes on top of it. The third layer is about $\frac{1}{16}$ of an inch. The last 8 to 10 layers flood the floor and freeze one at a time. Finally, the ice is 1 inch thick and play can begin! Compare the layers of ice by converting the fractions to common denominators.

What is the largest denominator in the fractions? ....

Convert $\frac{1}{16}$ of an inch to this denominator: ....

What is the total of the first three layers using this denominator? Show your work.

....

What fraction of the inch of ice makes up the last 8 to 10 layers? Show your work.

....

Quick Lab

TEKS 5B, 1A, 2C, 2D, 4A

How can water change state?

1. Fill the cup with crushed ice.
2. Collect information using tools, including Celsius thermometers. Place the thermometer in the cup of ice. Hold the cup to keep it from tipping. Wait 30 seconds. Read the temperature.
3. Record the temperature. Remove the thermometer.
4. Put one of the pieces of ice in your hand. Observe what happens.
5. Put the cup in a warm place.
6. When the ice starts to melt, read and record the temperature.

Explain Your Results

7. **Infer** What caused the ice to change from a solid to a liquid?

8. **Compare and Contrast** Analyze information using tools, including Celsius thermometers. How do the temperatures of the solid ice and the melting ice compare?

Materials

beaker, foam cup, or other container

crushed ice

Celsius thermometer

Be sure to return lab equipment to its proper location.

States of Matter

Water has three forms. Water is a solid when it is frozen as ice. Water is a liquid in the ocean. In the air, water can be a gas. Solid, liquid, and gas are the most familiar states, or phases, of matter.

The state of water, or of any material, is due to the motion and arrangement of its particles. The particles are always moving, but they move different amounts in different states. Think of the different locations that you might move in. In a large park, you might be able to run quickly in many directions. There is a lot of space for you to move. In the classroom, you might be able to walk up and down the aisles and around the front or back of the room. On a crowded bus you might not be able to move much at all.

1. **Compare and Contrast** Look at the picture. How are the solid butter and liquid oil alike and different?

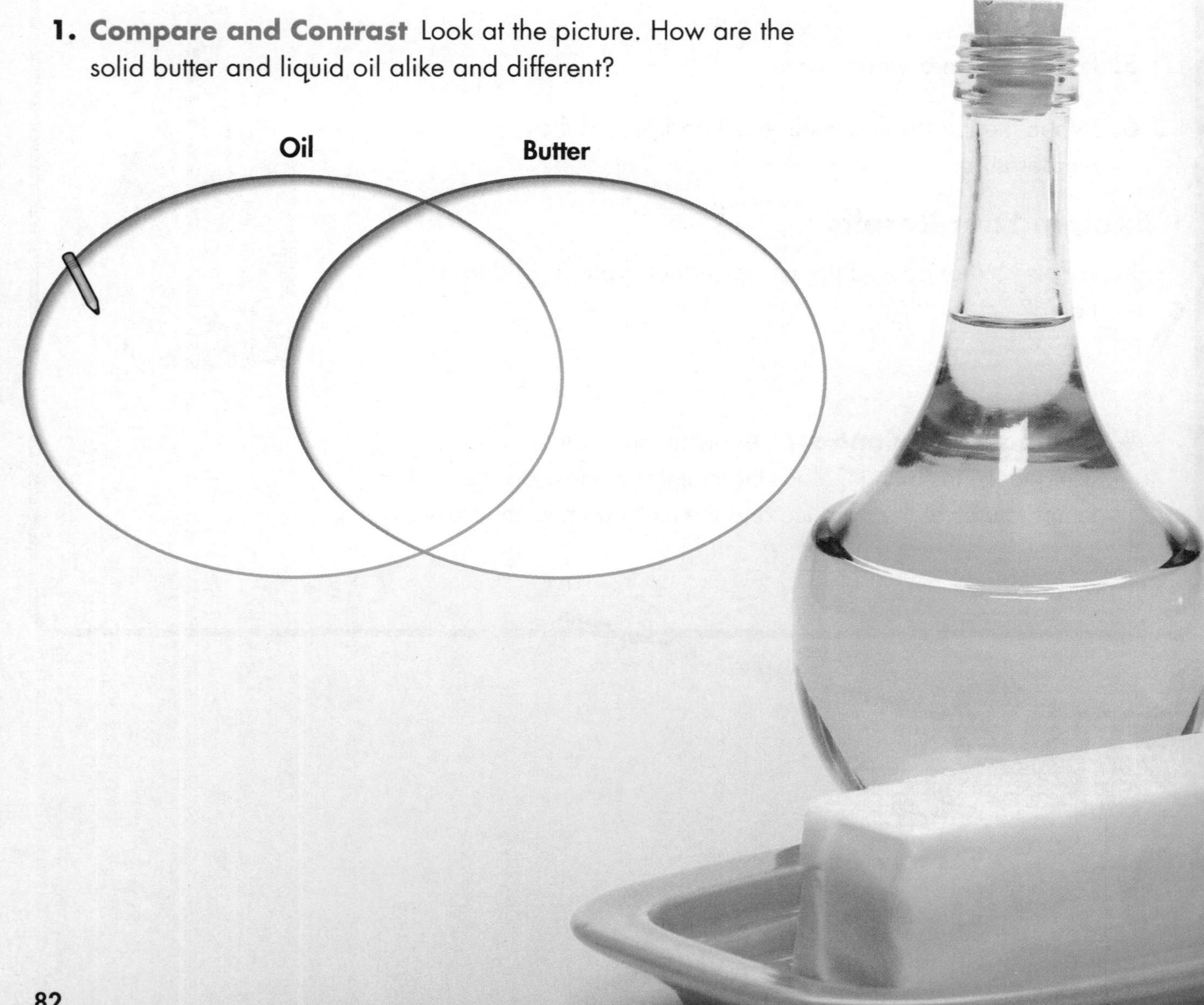

Most materials around you are solids, liquids, or gases. If the motion of their particles changes, their state of matter can change. For example, cooking oil is a liquid. Butter is a solid when it is cold, but butter can also turn to liquid if it is heated.

In each instance, the butter is still the same material, whether it is liquid or solid. The change in state comes from adding or taking away energy.

2. **Draw Conclusions** What would happen to the state of the liquid butter if you put it in a refrigerator?

3. **Explain** What happens to the motion of the particles of butter when it is cooled?

Solids

A substance that has a definite shape and volume is classified as a **solid**. Volume is the amount of space an object takes up. The particles of a solid are very close together. For the most part they stay in the same place. They do not slide easily past each other. However, they vibrate in place.

Liquids

A substance that has a definite volume but no definite shape is classified as a **liquid**. The particles of a liquid can move by gliding past each other. A liquid can take the shape of its container. Forces hold liquid particles together, so a liquid keeps a definite volume.

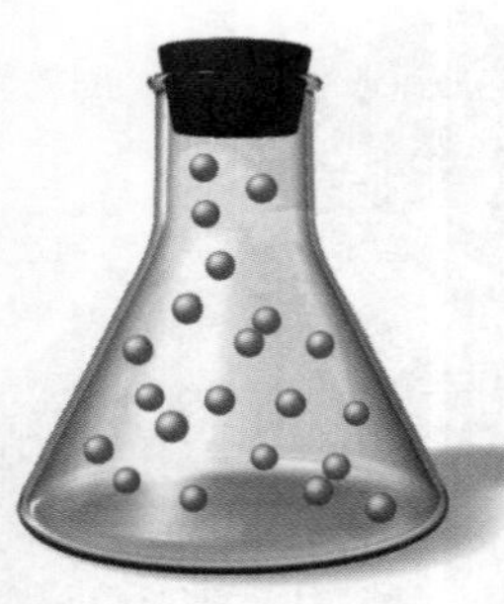

Gases

A substance without a definite volume or shape is classified as a **gas**. The particles of a gas are far apart compared to the particles of solids and liquids. A gas can be squeezed into a smaller volume. Gas particles only affect one another when they collide as they move. If a gas is placed in an empty container, its particles will spread out evenly. The gas will fill all the space and take the shape of that container.

4. Classify List the states of matter in a table. Then write if each state has a definite volume and a definite shape.

State of Matter	Definite shape?	Definite volume?

Freezing and Melting

As liquids get colder, their particles slow down. At some point they stop gliding past each other and can only vibrate in place. The liquid becomes a solid. The temperature at which a material changes between solid and liquid states has two names. It is called the freezing point when a liquid turns into a solid. It is called the **melting point** when a solid turns into a liquid. Therefore, the melting point and the freezing point are the same temperature. This temperature is often just referred to as the melting point.

Each material has its own melting point. Therefore, the melting point can be used to help identify a material. The melting point and freezing point of water is 0 degrees Celsius.

Some materials are more useful in their solid state than in their liquid state. For example, lead is a metal that is dense. Solid lead is used to weigh down or sink fishing hooks.

This lead fishing sinker is solid metal. It keeps its shape and volume.

The melting point of lead is 327°C. At this temperature, solid lead becomes liquid and can be poured into molds to give it any shape we want.

5. Compare What is the difference between the melting point and freezing point of a substance?

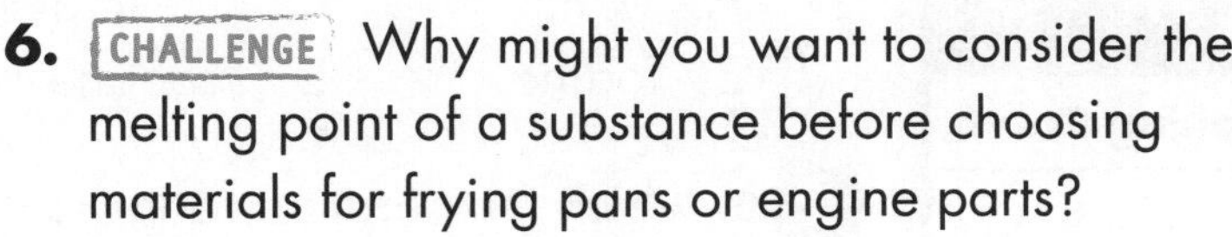

6. CHALLENGE Why might you want to consider the melting point of a substance before choosing materials for frying pans or engine parts?

7. Recognize What two things can happen to water at 0 degrees Celsius?

Lab zone Quick Lab

Wandering Ice

Place an ice cube on a dish and set it in a place where it will not be disturbed. Observe how long it takes for the ice cube to melt. Observe how long it takes for the water to evaporate. TEKS 2C

Evaporation and Condensation

Evaporation takes place when particles leave a liquid and become a gas. Particles evaporate from a liquid when they are at the surface of the liquid and are moving upward with enough speed. This is how rain puddles and the water in wet clothes evaporate.

If the temperature of a liquid is high enough, particles will change to a gas not only at the surface, but also throughout the liquid. As gas particles move quickly upward through a liquid, bubbles of gas form under the surface of the liquid. The **boiling point** of a liquid is the temperature at which this occurs. Air pressure affects this temperature. For example, at the normal air pressure at sea level, the boiling point of water is 100°C. On a high mountain it may be several degrees lower. Boiling points are usually given for sea-level conditions. This makes comparisons fair.

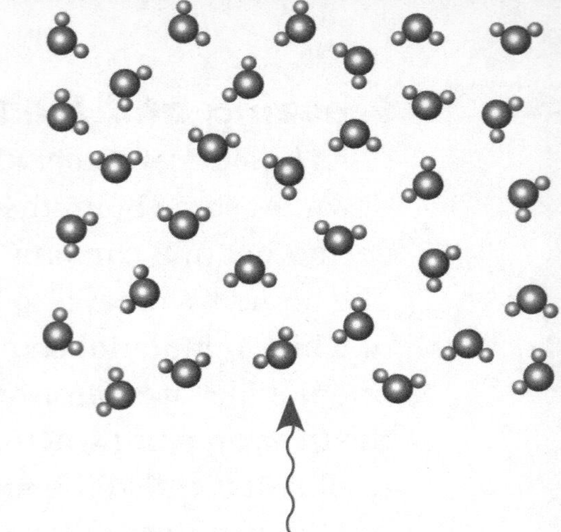

Molecules of water evaporate from the clothes as they dry. In water vapor, the molecules of water are far apart.

Connect to **Math**

Math TEKS 9A

Ranges

The chart shows the temperatures at which 5 different substances change form.

Boiling Points (°C)

Liquid	Boiling Point
Water	100°C
Acetic acid (found in vinegar)	118°C
Chlorine	–34°C
Propane	–42°C
Iodine	185°C

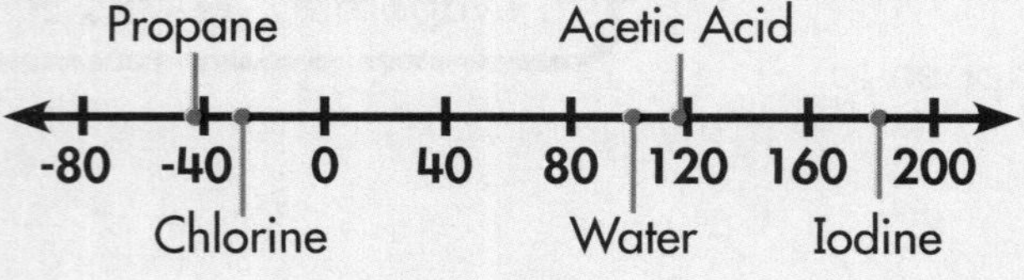

1. Which liquid has the highest boiling point?
   A. Water
   B. Iodine
   C. Acetic acid
   D. Propane

2. In which temperature range is the greatest gap between boiling points?
   F. 185°C to 100°C
   G. –34°C to –42°C
   H. 118°C to –42°C
   I. 100°C to –34°C

3. CHALLENGE Choose a common substance, such as ammonia or rubbing alcohol. Research its boiling point, and add this information to the chart. Plot the new data point on the number line.

8. Identify A pan of water is on a hot plate at sea level. The temperature of the water is 80 degrees Celsius. How many more degrees does the temperature need to increase before the water boils? Explain.

When a gas cools down, the gas particles slow down and turn into a liquid. This process is called condensation. You might see condensation occurring on a bathroom mirror. The mirror is covered with a thin film of wet, liquid water. This water forms as the gas water vapor in the air hits the surface of the mirror and cools.

Find the water on the grass. It didn't rain, so how did the water get there? It came from the air! As the temperatures cooled in early morning, the water vapor in the air cooled and became liquid water on the grass.

got it? TEKS 5A, 5B

10. Identify Identify the freezing and melting point of water on the Celsius scale.

11. Classify Classify matter based on physical properties by writing the physical state of helium, diamonds, and rubbing alcohol.

Stop! I need help with

Wait! I have a question about

Go! Now I know

Texas

LESSON

3

What are mixtures and solutions?

I will know TEKS 5A, 5C, 5D
I will know how to classify matter based on its solubility in water. I will know that some mixtures keep the physical properties of their ingredients. I will know that changes can occur in the physical properties of the ingredients in a solution.
(Also **1A, 4A, 4B**)

Vocabulary
mixture
solution
solubility

What are you having for breakfast?

I am having orange juice and corn flakes with raisins, strawberries, and milk added to it.

That sounds good, but I like a different mixture of fruits in my cereal.

How much fruit do you like in your cereal?

Connect to **Math**

Show your work If your cereal contains 27 grams of corn flakes and 9 grams of blueberries, what fraction of the cereal is corn flakes? What fraction is made up of blueberries? To calculate the fraction of each part, use the grams of one part as the numerator and the total grams as the denominator. Then simplify the fractions so that their denominators are as small as possible. **Math TEKS 1A**

Corn flakes .... = ...

Blueberries .... = ...

PEARSON Texas.com

Quick Lab

TEKS 5A, 1A, 4A, 4B

Which solid will dissolve?

Materials

safety goggles
hand lens
4 plastic cups
masking tape
spoon
sand
salt
water

1. Collect information using tools, including hand lenses. Use a hand lens to **observe** the sand and salt.
2. Put 1 spoonful of sand into both Cup A and Cup B. Put 1 spoonful of salt into both Cup C and Cup D.
3. Fill each cup halfway with water. Stir only Cup A and Cup C. Observe.

Wear safety goggles. Never eat or drink in the lab area.

Explain Your Results

4. What properties did you **observe** that would help you to classify the substances?

5. **Identify** the substance that dissolved. What helped it dissolve? Which substance did not dissolve?

Mixtures

A **mixture** is made by placing different materials together. Although the mixture itself has specific properties, each part in some mixtures maintains its own physical properties. For example, a salad is a mixture. There are different types of salads, each with its own description and characteristics. The salad is made by cutting and putting vegetables together to create a mixture. However, the different vegetables in the salad do not change their flavors or colors. Most foods that you eat are mixtures of different ingredients.

What are some other common mixtures that you see in your daily life? The soil outside your house is likely a mixture of different types of tiny rocks and other materials. You or someone you know may set out birdseed for birds to eat. The birdseed is a mixture of different types of seeds.

The bowl of fruit is a mixture. It contains several different parts.

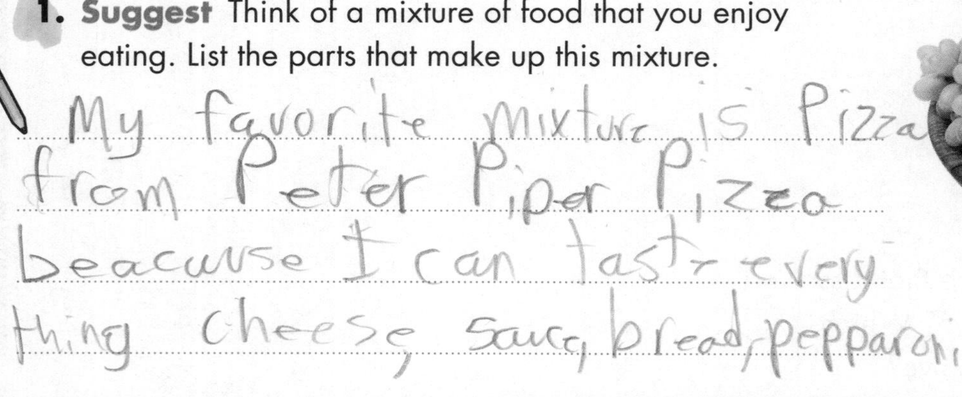

1. **Suggest** Think of a mixture of food that you enjoy eating. List the parts that make up this mixture.

My favorite mixture is Pizza from Peter Piper Pizza beacuse I can tast every thing cheese, sauce, bread, pepparoni

2. **Support** Why is the bowl of beads to the left not a mixture?

There is just 1 kind of item

Different ingredients of some mixtures can be separated from the rest of a mixture. This separation is possible because each ingredient maintains its physical properties. For example, suppose that your favorite breakfast is a mixture of cereal and raisins. You could easily separate out the raisins with a spoon to eat them first. The parts of a mixture may be combined in different amounts. The bowl of cereal you eat today could have more raisins than the one you ate yesterday.

3. **Explain** How could you prove that the ingredients in the mixtures shown maintain their physical properties?

You can separate
You can taste each one sepratly
You can see them each one
sepretly but togethetho

Mixed-Up Foods
Find two different mixtures you eat at home. What are the parts of the mixtures? Tell whether you would ever eat any of the parts separately. TEKS 5C

Separating Mixtures

You can use the physical properties of a substance to separate it from a mixture. The materials in a simple mixture can be separated because they have different physical properties. For example, a magnet can separate iron filings from sand. This separation happens because iron has the property of being attracted by magnets. Sand does not have that property. A screen filter can be used to separate a mixture of pebbles and sand. The smaller particles go through the screen but the pebbles do not. Sometimes you can sort the parts of a mixture by hand.

4. Classify Complete the chart below. Draw a mixture in the first row. Write how to separate the iron filings and sand and the items in the new mixture.

Mixture			
How Can You Separate?	Pour through a strainer.		

5. CHALLENGE Suppose you had a mixture of sand and small, hollow beads. How might you separate the mixture?

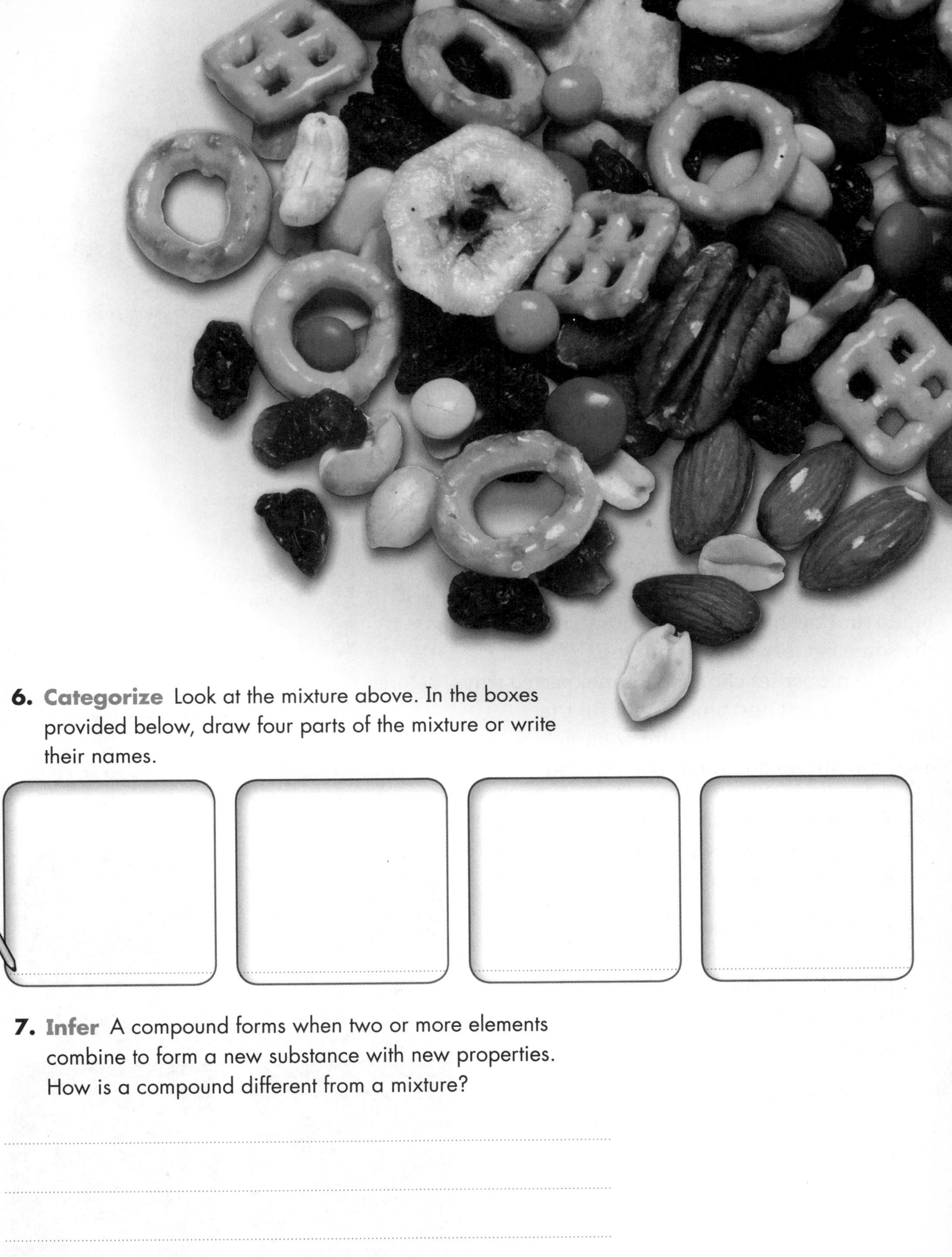

6. Categorize Look at the mixture above. In the boxes provided below, draw four parts of the mixture or write their names.

7. Infer A compound forms when two or more elements combine to form a new substance with new properties. How is a compound different from a mixture?

Solutions

A mixture in which the substances are spread out evenly and do not settle is called a **solution**. In a solution, the substance that is dissolved is called the solute. The substance in which the solute is being dissolved is called the solvent. In a solution of sugar and water, the solute is sugar and the solvent is water. Water is sometimes called a "universal solvent" because it can dissolve many substances. When a solid dissolves, the individual particles separate from the solid and spread evenly throughout the liquid.

These crystals dissolve easily in water.

Solutions can be made by dissolving a solid or a gas in a liquid. Solutions also can also be made by combining two liquids and even two solids.

When you mix two different substances in a solution, some of their properties can change. For example, the red liquid shown is no longer red after it is mixed with the blue liquid. The solution is purple, a color that is a blend of blue and red.

Other properties of the two liquids are added when the liquids are mixed. For example, to find the mass of the purple mixture you can add the masses of the red liquid and the blue liquid. Notice that the total mass is the same before and after mixing.

Some properties changed in unexpected ways. Before mixing, the red and blue liquids fill the bottle. After mixing, the total volume is reduced, even though no liquid has been spilled!

As the volume of the liquid decreases during mixing, the level of the liquid drops.

unmixed liquid

mixed liquid

The mass stays the same.

8. Compare and Contrast Draw what you think the mixture of the purple solid and water will look like after stirring.

9. Identify the changes that have occurred in the physical properties of the two ingredients of this solution.

....

....

....

This toy has a colorless liquid floating on a blue-colored liquid. The colorless liquid and the plastic figures will not dissolve in the blue liquid. They are insoluble *in it.*

Solubility

Many materials can make solutions with water. You can dissolve more of some materials than others in the same amount of water. Some materials will not dissolve in water at all. This describes a material's **solubility** in water. Different substances can have different solubility in other solvents.

10. CHALLENGE The plastic figures in the picture are insoluble in the blue liquid. What else can you tell about their solubility?

....

....

....

got it? TEKS 5C, 5D

11. Demonstrate Explain how you might go about proving that a mixture of peanuts, walnuts, and pecans still maintains the properties of the original ingredients you mixed together.

....

....

....

12. Identify Describe the changes that occur to water and salt after you mix them together in a solution.

....

....

Stop! I need help with ....

Wait! I have a question about ....

Go! Now I know ....

Lab Investigation

TEKS 5A, 5C, 1A, 4A, 4B

What are some ways to separate a mixture?

The ingredients in a mixture can be separated out of the mixture by their physical properties. Demonstrate that some mixtures maintain the physical properties of their ingredients.

Materials

4 plastic cups
spoon
salt
sand
3 metal marbles
warm water
graduated cylinder
pencil
coffee filter
rubber band
foil

Follow a Procedure

1. Label the 4 cups *A, B, C,* and *D.* In Cup A place 1 spoonful of salt, 2 spoonfuls of sand, 3 marbles, and 100 mL of water.
2. Carefully make 4 holes in the bottom of Cup B by pushing a pencil through the bottom of the cup from the inside.
3. Hold Cup B over Cup C. All at once, pour the mixture from Cup A into Cup B. Move Cup B around to clean the marbles. **Record** the part of the mixture that was removed by straining.

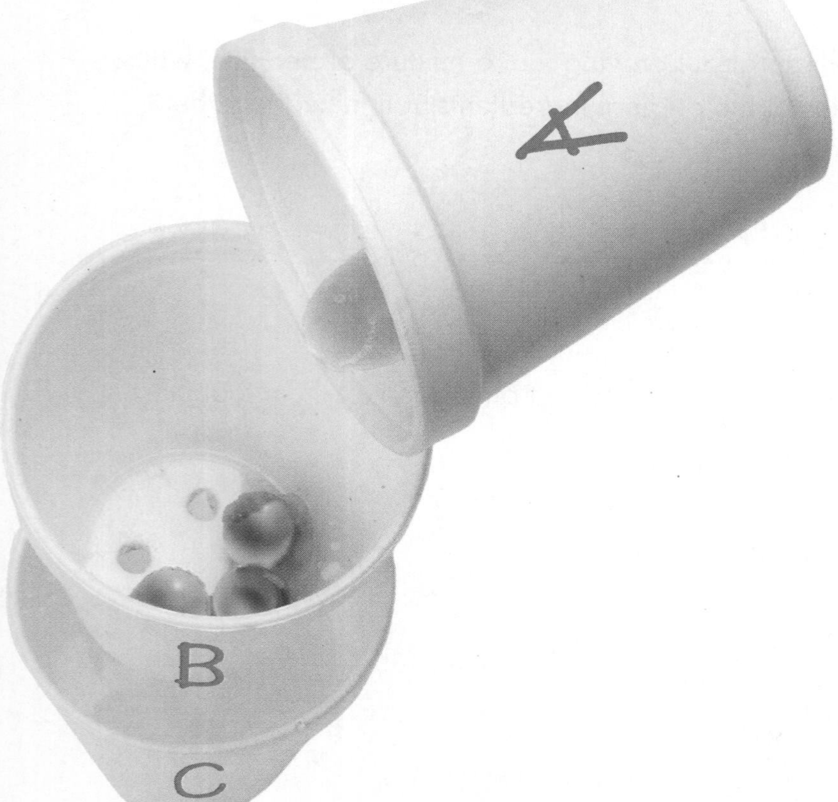

Texas Safety
LAB RULES

Demonstrate the use of safety equipment as described in the *Texas Safety Standards* during classroom investigations. Wear safety goggles.

Inquiry Skill

Scientists record data on charts and use the data to help **make inferences.**

Results of Separation		
Separating Method	**Part Removed**	**Part Not Removed**
Straining		
Filtering		
Evaporation		

☑ **4.** Put a coffee filter in Cup D. Slowly pour the mixture from Cup C into Cup D. Record the part of the mixture that was removed by filtering.

☑ **5.** Remove the filter. Use the spoon to drip 2 drops of the liquid onto the foil. Let the liquid evaporate. Record the results.

Use a rubber band to fasten the filter to the cup.

Analyze and Conclude

6. Communicate Name a property you used to separate parts of the mixture.

....

7. Infer Describe another mixture. How could the properties of matter help you separate it into its parts?

....

....

....

TEXAS my planet Diary

TEKS 5A, 3D

What if we could have all of the electricity we ever needed without any pollution? Engineers at the Solar Energy Lab at the University of Texas at Austin have mapped the surface of the state to determine that Texas ranks first in the United States in the amount of solar energy available.

How can we harness this energy? We use solar panels to capture the sun's energy and convert it to electricity. These solar panels change the energy using semiconductors, or materials that conduct less electricity than conductors but more than insulators. It cannot be classified as a regular conductor or insulator. Semiconductors produce electrical currents when exposed to sunlight.

As engineers develop better solar panels with more efficient semiconductors, more energy will be available using only the sun as a source. Perhaps you will see the day when energy is so abundant that you do not need to worry about turning off the lights in your house.

Solar panels use materials that conduct electricity and capture energy from sunlight.

Why do you think a regular conductor would still be needed in a solar panel?

....

....

Vocabulary Smart Cards

mass
volume
density
magnetism
solid
liquid
gas
melting point
boiling point
mixture
solution
solubility

Play a Game!

Cut out the Vocabulary Smart Cards.

Work with a partner.

Player 1 chooses a Vocabulary Smart Card.

Say as many words as you can think of that describe that vocabulary word to Player 2.

Player 2 guesses the word.

magnetism

magnetismo

mass

masa

solid

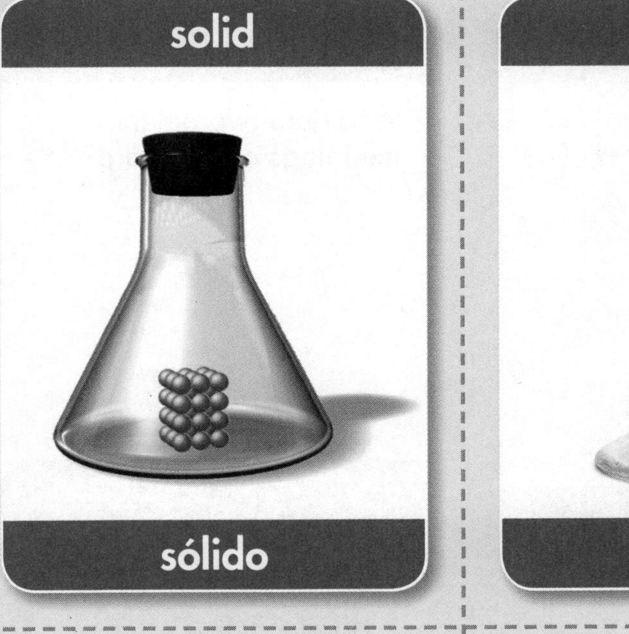

sólido

volume

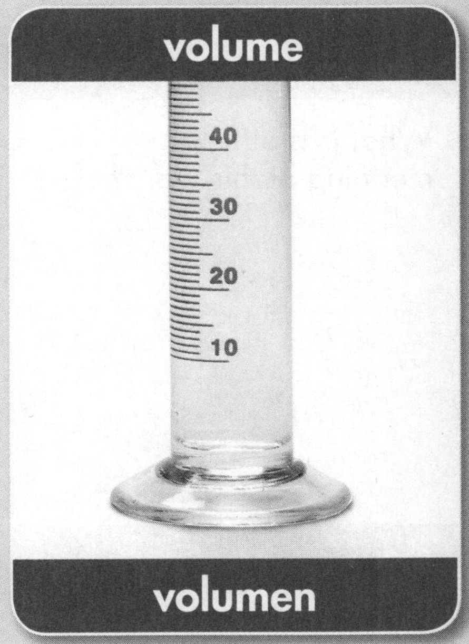

volumen

liquid

líquido

density

densidad

the amount of matter in a solid, liquid, or gas

Write a sentence using this word.

cantidad de materia que tiene un sólido, líquido o gas

the ability of an object to attract certain metal objects

Draw an example of this word.

capacidad de un objeto de atraer ciertos objetos de metal

the amount of space an object takes up

What is a different meaning of this word?

el espacio que ocupa un objeto

a substance that has a definite shape and volume

What are two other meanings of this word?

sustancia que tiene una forma y un volumen definidos

the mass of an object divided by its volume

Write a sentence using this word.

masa de un objeto dividida por su volumen

a substance that has a definite volume but no definite shape

Draw an example.

sustancia que tiene un volumen definido pero no una forma definida

Interactive Vocabulary

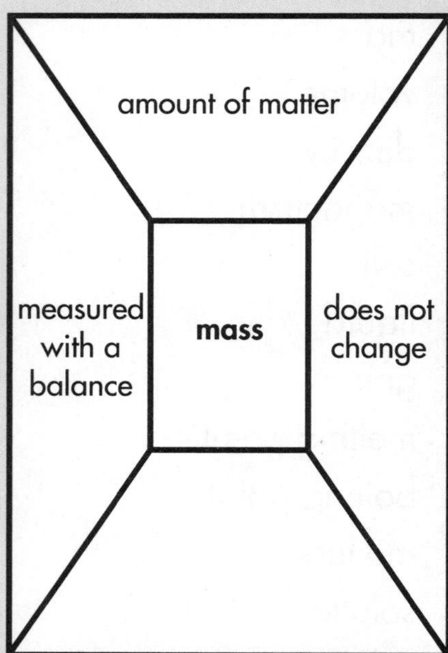

Make a Word Frame!

Choose a vocabulary word and write it in the center of the frame. Write or draw details about the vocabulary word in the spaces around it.

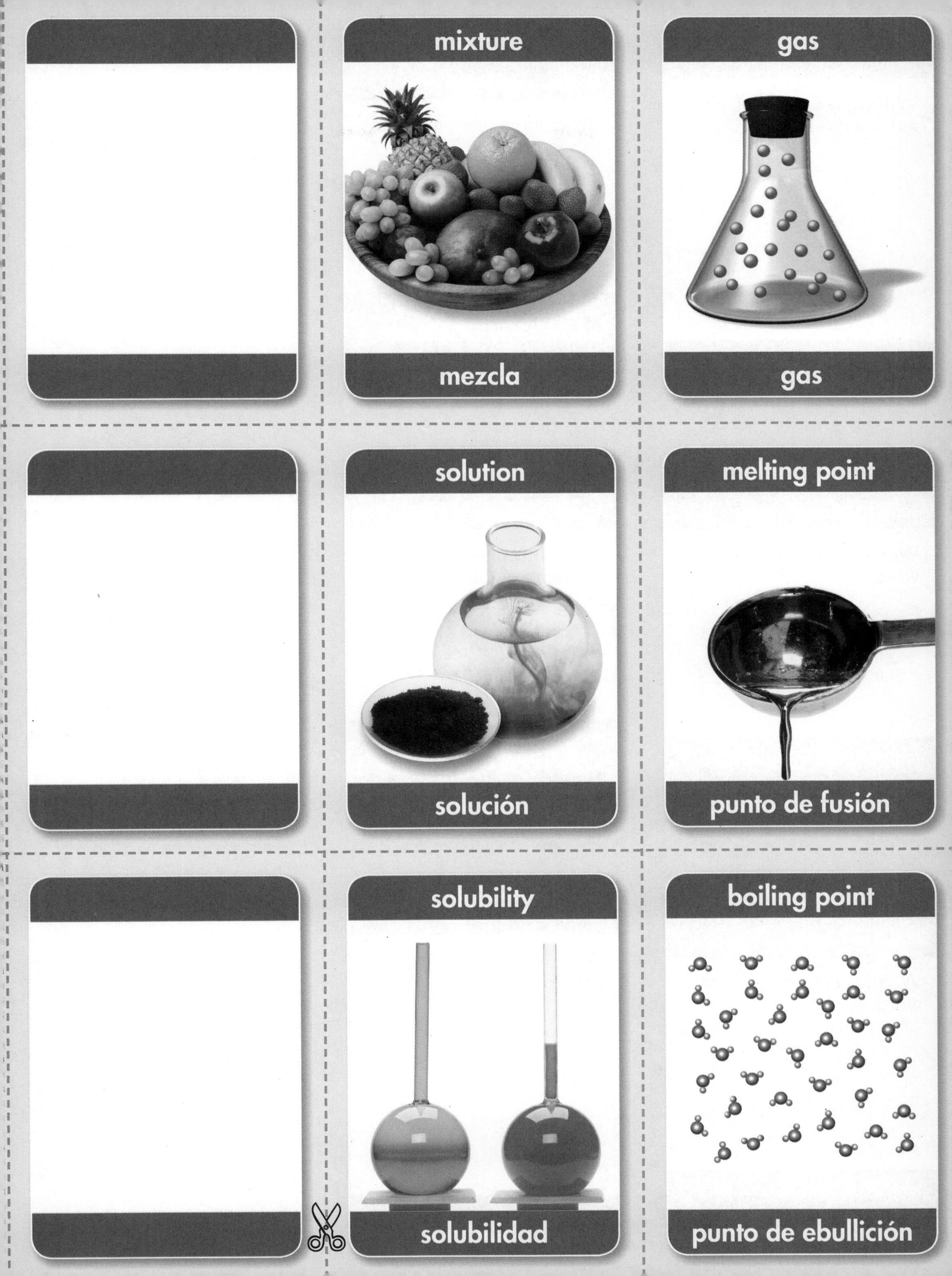
mixture
mezcla
gas
gas
solution
solución
melting point
punto de fusión
solubility
solubilidad
boiling point
punto de ebullición

a substance without a definite volume or shape

Write an example of this word.

sustancia que no tiene ni volumen ni forma definidos

different materials placed together, but each material keeps its own properties

Write three other forms of this word.

unión de materiales diferentes en la cual cada material mantiene sus propiedades

the temperature at which a substance changes from a solid to a liquid

Write a sentence using this word.

temperatura a la cual una sustancia cambia de sólido a líquido

a mixture in which substances are spread out evenly and will not settle

What is a different meaning of this word?

mezcla en la cual una sustancia se dispersa de manera uniforme en otra sustancia y no se asienta

the temperature at which a substance changes from a liquid to a gas

Write a sentence using this word.

temperatura a la cual una sustancia cambia de líquido a gas

ability of one substance to dissolve in another

Write a sentence using this word.

capacidad de una sustancia de disolverse en otra

Texas
Chapter 2

TEKS Practice

Lesson 1 TEKS 4A, 5A

How can matter be described?

1. **Analyze** Analyze information using pan balances. You put one object in the left pan of a pan balance. You put another object in the right pan. How can you tell which object has more mass?

2. **Vocabulary** The amount of matter an object has is its __________.
   A. weight
   B. volume
   C. size
   D. mass

3. **Predict** Which of the following items would be attracted to a magnet?
   A. water
   B. glass
   C. iron
   D. wood

4. **Predict** You have two liquids with different densities. The liquids don't mix. What will happen when you pour the liquids into a graduated cylinder?

5. **Do the Math!** Calculate the density of an object with a mass of 50 grams and a volume of 5 cubic centimeters. Write the density as the amount of grams in one cubic centimeter.

6. **Classify** An object will sink or float in water based on its relative __________.
   A. mass
   B. density
   C. volume
   D. size

TEKS Practice

Lesson 2 TEKS 5A, 5B

What are solids, liquids, and gases?

7. Compare and Contrast Write one way water and ice are the same and one way they are different.

8. Identify Water has a melting point of 0 degrees Celsius. Its freezing point is __________.

A. 0 degrees Celsius
B. below 0 degrees Celsius
C. above 0 degrees Celsius
D. 32 degrees Celsius

9. Identify Identify the boiling point of water at sea level on the Celsius scale.

A. 0 degrees Celsius
B. 32 degrees Celsius
C. 100 degrees Celsius
D. 212 degrees Celsius

10. Classify Which physical properties describe a solid?

A. definite volume, definite shape
B. definite volume, no definite shape
C. no definite volume, no definite shape

11. Classify Which physical properties describe a gas?

A. definite volume, definite shape
B. definite volume, no definite shape
C. no definite volume, no definite shape

12. Classify How can you change the shape of a liquid?

Lesson 3 TEKS 5A, 5C, 5D

What are mixtures and solutions?

13. Vocabulary A mixture of iron filings and sand can be separated because they ________.

A. maintain their properties
B change physical properties
C. form a solution
D. change their state of matter

14. Identify You add a tablespoon of salt crystals to water. After stirring, the salt crystals ________.

A. were destroyed
B. changed to a gas
C. dissolved into a solution
D. were removed

15. Classify Use your previous experience to classify matter based on its solubility in water. Classify shampoo, candle wax, butter, and honey as soluble or insoluble in water.

Chapter 2

Lesson 1 How can matter be described?
In Lesson 1, you learned how to analyze information using a pan balance. You learned how to classify matter based on physical properties, including mass, magnetism, volume, and relative density (sinking and floating).
Readiness TEKS 5A, Process TEKS 4A

Lesson 2 What are solids, liquids, and gases?
In Lesson 2, you learned how to classify matter based on physical properties, such as solid, liquid, or gas. You learned the boiling point, freezing point and melting point of water in degrees Celsius.
Readiness TEKS 5A, Supporting TEKS 5B

Lesson 3 What are mixtures and solutions?
In Lesson 3, you learned how to classify matter based on its solubility in water. You learned that some mixtures keep the physical properties of their ingredients but that changes can occur in the physical properties of the ingredients in a solution.
Readiness TEKS 5A, Supporting TEKS 5C, 5D

★ TEKS Practice: Chapter Review

Read each question and circle the best answer.

1 Katie places a rock in a graduated cylinder that holds about 22 mL of water. The rock sinks to the bottom of the cylinder, as shown.

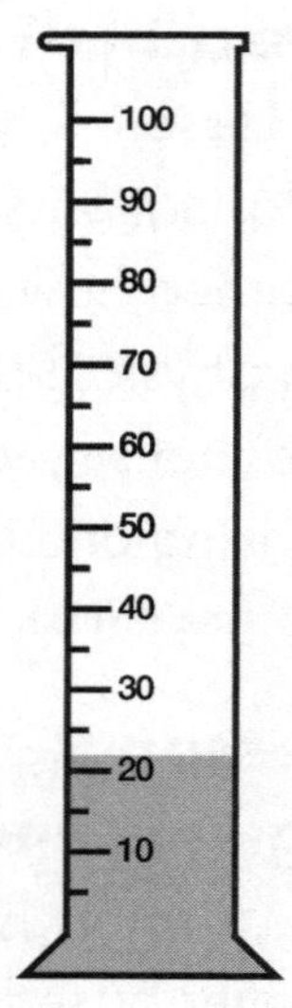

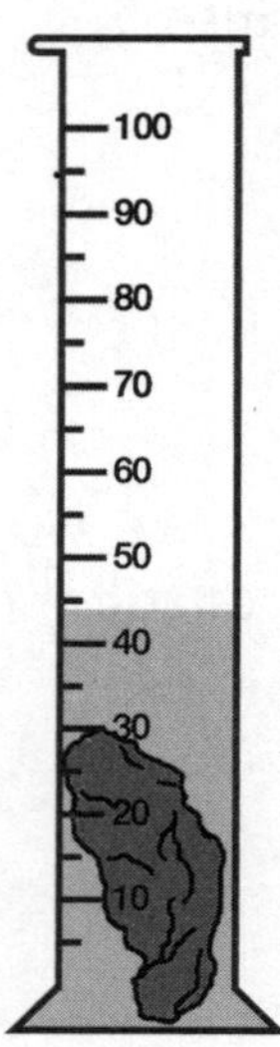

What can Katie conclude about the rock?

A The rock has less mass than the water.

B The rock has about the same mass as the water.

C The rock has a greater volume than the water.

D The rock has about the same volume as the water.

2 Many activities in the science classroom require students to wear goggles. During which activity is it most important that you wear goggles?

F Stretching a balloon over the top of a bottle

G Finding the mass of a marshmallow

H Measuring the length of your finger

J Putting a spoonful of sand into water

3 Marisol wants to model the arrangement of the particles that make up an ice cube and the particles that make up liquid water. She finds the diagrams below in a library book.

States of a Substance

Diagram A Diagram B Diagram C

What is the best way for her to use these diagrams to model the particles of an ice cube and water?

A Use diagram A to model the ice cube and diagram B to model the water

B Use diagram A to model the ice cube and diagram C to model the water

C Use diagram B to model the ice cube and diagram A to model the water

D Use diagram B to model the ice cube and diagram C to model the water

---

4 The melting point of water is 0°C. Its boiling point is 100°C. The thermometers show the temperature of four samples of water.

Thermometer Readings (°C)

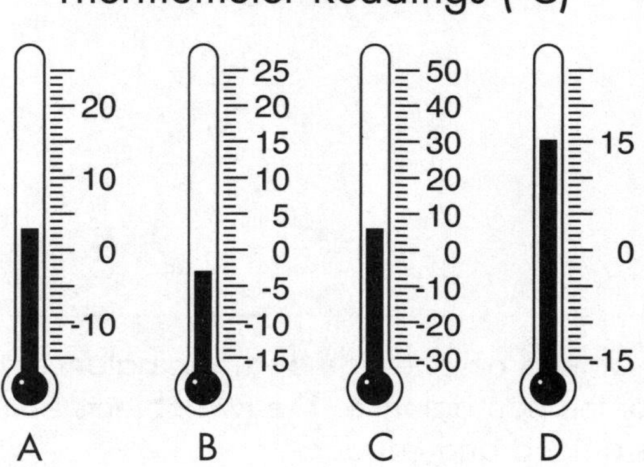

Which statement is true?

F Only sample B is solid.

G All four samples are liquid.

H Only samples A and C are liquid.

J None of these

5 A mixture contains salt, sand, water, iron filings, and marbles. Ernesto carries out the following investigation to separate the parts of the mixture:

Step 1: Pour the mixture through a screen with large holes.
Step 2: Pass a magnet through the mixture.
Step 3: Pour the mixture through a screen with very small holes.
Step 4: Heat the mixture to evaporate the liquid.

Which part of the mixture is removed during step 3?

A Salt

B Sand

C Marbles

D Iron filings

6 Microballoons are tiny, hollow glass spheres filled with air. They are often no wider than a human hair. In fact, they are so small that they look like bits of powder. People who make boats, surfboards, and model airplanes often add microballoons to the glues they use. The right mixture of glue and microballoons is as strong as glue when it dries. But it is also lightweight. The mixture of glue and microballoons can hold parts together tightly without weighing them down. Which material keeps the mixture light enough to help a boat or surfboard float in water?

F Air

G Glass

H Glue

J Hair

7 Matt places a small piece of lead on one side of a pan balance. He places a larger piece of copper on the other side of the pan balance. The two objects balance each other. What can he conclude about the pieces of lead and copper?

A The lead has a greater mass than the copper.

B The copper and the lead have the same mass.

C The copper has a greater mass than the lead.

D The copper and the lead have the same volume.

★ TEKS Practice: Cumulative Review

8 Emily buys a feeder for the birds in her yard. She wonders how much food the birds eat in one week. What information will give Emily the most accurate way to measure this?

F The number of bags of birdseed used in one week

G The number of scoops of birdseed needed to fill the feeder and the number of times the feeder must be filled in one week

H The kind of food the birds eat when they come to the feeder

J The grams of birdseed the feeder holds when full and the number of times it must be filled in a week

9 Deepak investigates the temperature in his classroom. First, he estimates how warm the room feels. Next, he records the temperature in three spots around the room and calculates an average reading. Finally, his teacher reads a thermostat to report the actual temperature. The chart shows data from the investigation.

Estimated Temperature (°C)	Thermometer Reading (°C)	Thermostat Temperature (°C)
26	Reading 1: 25	25
	Reading 2: 26	
	Reading 3: 27	
	Average: 26	

What is the best way to tell that Deepak's measurements are accurate?

A They match the estimate.

B They were almost the same when repeated.

C They are close to the actual value.

D They were measured using the correct tool.

If you have trouble with . . .									
Question	1	2	3	4	5	6	7	8	9
See chapter (lesson)	2 (1)	2 (3)	2 (2)	2 (2)	2 (3)	2 (3)	2 (1)	1 (3)	1 (3)
TEKS	5A	5D	5A	5B	5C	5C	5A	2C	4A

Where is the ENERGY?

Texas

Chapter 3

Forms and Uses of Energy

How can the amount of stored energy affect motion?

These drummers are playing traditional music. The dancer's steps require strength and coordination.

Where do you think the dancer gets his energy? How do you know he has energy?

....

....

....

Texas Essential Knowledge and Skills

Readiness TEKS: 6A Explore the uses of energy, including mechanical, light, thermal, electrical, and sound energy. **6B** Demonstrate that the flow of electricity in circuits requires a complete path through which an electric current can pass and can produce light, heat, and sound. **6C** Demonstrate that light travels in a straight line until it strikes an object or travels through one medium to another and demonstrate that light can be reflected such as the use of mirrors or other shiny surfaces and refracted such as the appearance of an object when observed through water.
Process TEKS: 1A, 2A, 2B, 2C, 2D, 2F, 3A, 3D, 4A, 4B

PEARSON Texas.com

Lab zone® Inquiry Warm-Up

TEKS 6A, 2A, 2C, 2D, 2F, 4A

How can the amount of stored energy affect motion?

☐ **1. Observe** Turn the winder on the toy 2 turns. Release. Collect information using a clock or stopwatch by timing. How long the toy stays in motion. Record.

☐ **2.** Repeat 3 times, but use a different number of turns each time.

Materials

timer, stopwatch, or clock with a second hand

windup toy

Inquiry Skill

You **communicate** when you explain your observations.

Stored Energy and Motion

Number of Turns	Time Toy Stayed in Motion (seconds)

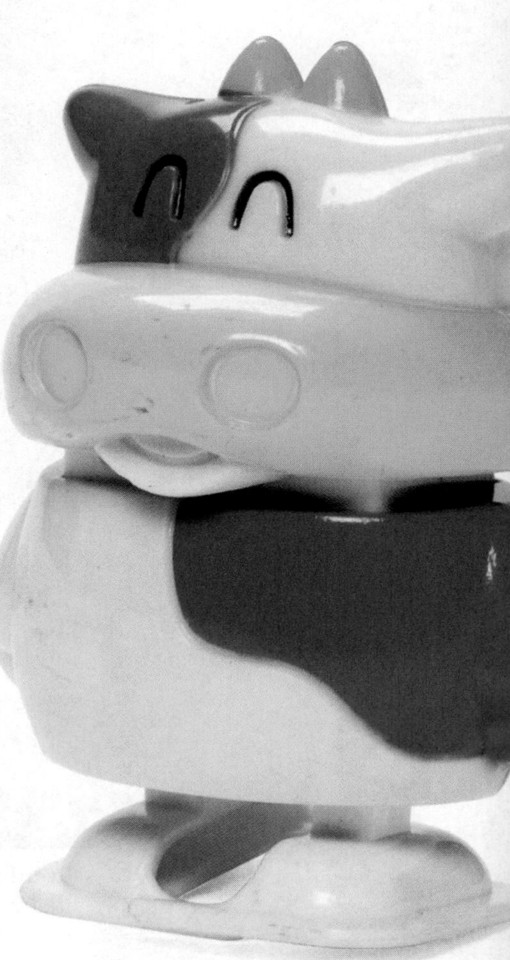

Explain Your Results

3. Communicate Explain how the number of turns affected the time the toy stayed in motion.

4. How did you change stored energy into motion?

Connect to Reading

Focus on Draw Conclusions

You will practice the reading strategy **draw conclusions.** A good reader can put together facts to build a new idea, or a conclusion. Learning to draw conclusions can help you evaluate what you read and observe.

Ultrasound is the use of sound energy to create images of the internal structures of the body. By sending sound waves into the body, doctors can safely visualize organs including the heart, liver, and kidneys, and can diagnose diseases. Ultrasound is often used to record the development of a fetus during pregnancy. It can be used to clean teeth, break up kidney stones, and stimulate bone growth.

Practice It!

Use the graphic organizer. List facts from the paragraph above and draw a conclusion.

Fact

Conclusion

What is energy and how is it used?

I will know TEKS 6A
I will know how to classify matter based on how it conducts or insulates thermal or electric energy. I will know what energy is. I will know how it can be used.
(Also **1A**, **2C**, **2D**, **3A**, **4A**, **5A**)

Vocabulary
energy
kinetic energy
potential energy

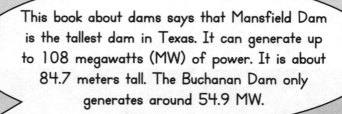

This book about dams says that Mansfield Dam is the tallest dam in Texas. It can generate up to 108 megawatts (MW) of power. It is about 84.7 meters tall. The Buchanan Dam only generates around 54.9 MW.

I see that the Buchanan Dam is only 44.3 meters tall and the Starcke Dam is only 30.1 meters tall.

That must mean that the tallest dam produces the most power.

Connect to Math **STEM**

How much taller is the Mansfield Dam than the Buchanan Dam and the Starcke Dam? **Math TEKS 3K**

Quick Lab

 TEKS 6A, 1A, 2C, 2D, 3A, 4A

How can you increase a marble's energy?

Energy can be stored in objects. The position of an object can affect the energy it has. We can see the effects of this energy when it changes into another form.

Materials

3 books
grooved ruler
small plastic container
meter stick
tape
marble

Texas Safety LAB RULES

Identify potential safety hazards and know which precautions to take.
Do not throw marbles; roll them.
Pick up marbles after each trial.
Avoid stepping on marbles.

1. Place one book on the floor and prop the ruler against the book and the floor. Place the container about 4 inches from the end of the ruler on the floor. Mark the position of the container with a small piece of tape.

2. Roll the marble down the groove of the ruler to move the container. Measure the distance from the tape where the container started to where it moved, and **record** that distance in the chart.

Number of Books	Distance Container Moves
1	
2	
3	

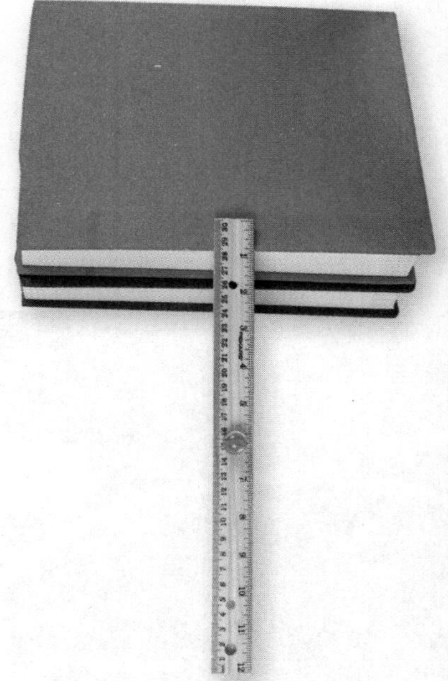

3. Repeat the experiment using two stacked books and again using three books.

4. **Communicate** How many books produced the farthest movement of the container?

5. **Interpret** What caused the marble to gain energy? Interpret your information to construct a reasonable explanation from indirect evidence.

Energy

Turn on a light switch. Rub your hands together to warm them. Roll a pencil across your desk. You are using energy! **Energy** is the ability to do work or cause a change. Whenever the position, the chemical structure, or the look of something changes, energy is required. You use energy when you move, look at something, hear a sound, talk, get warm, or turn on any electrical item. Energy comes in many forms, and we use them all the time.

1. **Ask Questions** Besides homes, what are other major energy consumers in the United States?

Commercial Commerce accounts for around 19% of the use of energy. You see this energy in use when you visit lit and heated buildings, like your school and stores.

Residential Residential or home use of energy accounts for 23% of all energy use in the United States. In your home, you need electricity to power appliances, video games, televisions, and lights. You might also use natural gas, a fuel, as energy to heat your home, dry clothes, and cook food.

According to the U.S. Energy Information Administration, Texas consumes and produces more energy than any other state. This is due in a large part to Texas's high population and its growing economy.

2. **Explore** Choose one sector of energy consumption in the United States. Explain how it relates to you.

Industrial Industry accounts for around 31% of the United States' total energy consumption. Factories make the products we use. A large percentage of industry is dedicated to the production of even more energy, such as electricity, or fuels such as gas, coal, and oil.

Transportation Transportation accounts for around 28% of our energy use. You use this energy whenever you take a bus, train, or car.

Forms of Energy

Energy cannot be made or destroyed. It is transferred from form to form. Energy also moves from one object to another. Energy can exist in many forms. Here are some common forms of energy.

Electrical energy is caused by the movement of electrically charged particles. When you use the toaster, you are using electrical energy. Electricity flows through devices to power them. Metals are good conductors of electricity.

3. Describe Give an example of something that uses electrical energy in your home.

....

Thermal energy is energy due to randomly moving particles that make up matter. You can feel the flow of thermal energy as heat. As food cooks, pots and pans conduct thermal energy to the food because they are made of metal, which is a good conductor of thermal energy. The thermal energy causes changes in the food as the food cooks. Thermal energy is also used when ore is processed with heat to produce iron and steel.

Sound energy is the energy of vibrations carried by air, water, or other matter. You use sound energy when your alarm clock wakes you up, or when you listen to your favorite music. Ultra-high sound energy is used to create images of soft tissue such as lungs, hearts and kidneys. Sound energy creates vibrations so it can also be used to clean things.

Kinetic energy is the energy of motion. Anything moving, like a moving swing or a hurricane, has this kind of energy. Kinetic energy is used in transportation such as cars or trains. Every movement you make uses kinetic energy.

4. **Describe** Give an example of something that has kinetic energy in school.

Light energy travels as waves and can move through empty space. Some light energy comes from the sun and travels to Earth. These sunflowers use this light energy to help make their own food.

Potential energy is energy that is stored in an object. An object's potential energy can be released as other forms of energy. For example, when a truck burns fuel, the potential energy in gasoline is released as sound, heat, and motion.

5. **Conclude** **Circle** the names of the forms of energy in use when you turn on a fan in your home.

Energy Everywhere

Kinetic and potential energy are forms of mechanical energy. The mechanical energy of an object may be all potential, all kinetic, or a bit of both.

6. Label Explore the uses of mechanical energy by finding as many examples of kinetic and potential energy as you can in the scene. Label the scene using the key below. For the kinetic energy labels, add a phrase to state how it is being used. For example, the bus uses kinetic energy to transport people.

K = kinetic **P** = potential

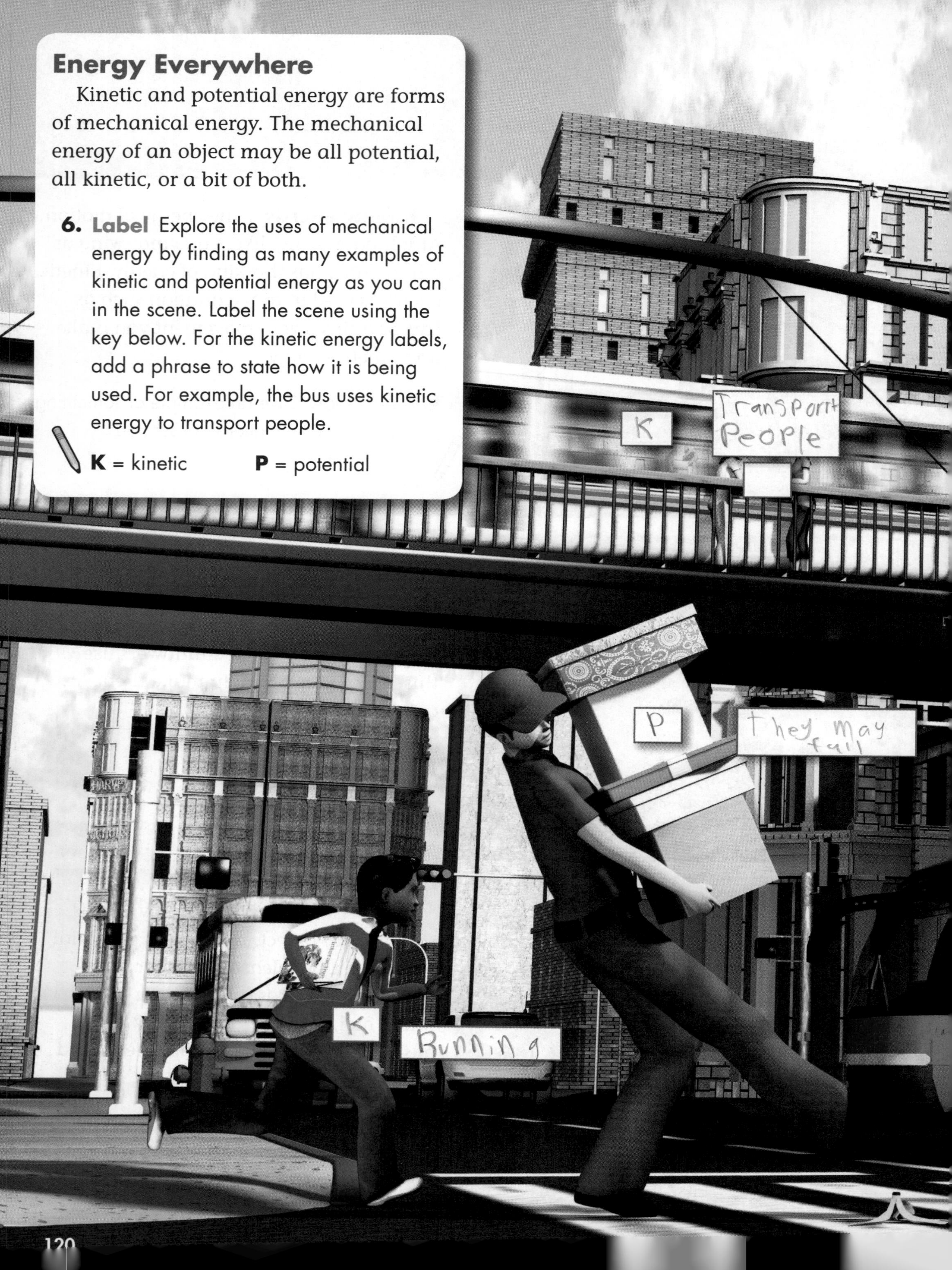

K
Cleaning Windows
STOP
32
K
Walking
Café
rant

Thermal Energy

Thermal energy is due to the movement of particles. The faster the motion of the particles, the more thermal energy they have. Slow-moving particles have less thermal energy. You feel thermal energy in the form of heat. Heat is the energy that is transferred from one object to another object with less thermal energy. Heat always goes from a warmer object to a cooler object.

Thermal energy is very important. It cooks your food, keeps you warm, and helps to clean clothes and dishes. It can also be transformed into light, as you see in candles, campfires, and light bulbs.

7. **Observe** Explore the uses of thermal energy by looking around you and naming all the things you see that generate thermal energy.

Stove light bulb
labtop micro wave

Quick Lab

Heat It Up Collect and analyze information using tools, including beakers and hot plates. Working with your teacher, pour 200 mL of water in a beaker and place it on a hot plate. Place a thermometer in the water and warm it up until the temperature is 50°C. Remove the beaker from the hot plate and place it on a safe surface. Record the temperature of the water again after 5, 10, and 15 minutes. Use a clock to measure the time intervals. Describe what happens to the temperature as time goes by.

TEKS 2C, 4A

Thermal conductivity is the transfer of thermal energy as heat from one material to another. This occurs when substances differ in temperature. Solids and liquids tend to be better conductors of heat than gases. Solids and liquids have very little space between particles, while gases have a great deal of space between particles. The more space there is between particles, the less likely that they will collide and transfer energy.

Metals are excellent conductors of thermal energy, which is why most cooking pots and pans are made of metal. Materials such as rubber and cloth are poor conductors of heat. They are used in clothes to keep you warm because they prevent your body heat from leaving.

got it? TEKS 5A

8. Identify Name some examples of materials that are good conductors of both thermal and electrical energy.

9. Classify Classify matter based on the ability to conduct or insulate thermal energy or electrical energy. Which of these items are good thermal conductors? Sort the items in the list by writing each one in the correct column of the table.

- wood
- steel
- plastic
- air
- rubber
- glass
- copper

Good Thermal Conductors	Poor Thermal Conductors

Stop! I need help with

Wait! I have a question about

Go! Now I know

Texas

LESSON 2

What is sound energy and how is it used?

I will know TEKS 6A
I will know what sound energy is.
I will know how it can be used.
(Also 1A, 2D, 2F, 4B)

Vocabulary
vibration

Connect to Social Studies

Social Studies TEKS 21A

Music is one of the best uses of sound energy. Texas is known for having some of the best music festivals in the United States. Consider the sound energy created at such a festival. The musicians and their instruments create sound energy, and technology makes the sound loud so that crowds can hear it. The crowds generate their own sound energy.

Think about your favorite musical performer or group. What musical instruments do they use to make their sound?

PEARSON Texas.com

Quick Lab

TEKS 6A, 1A, 2D, 2F, 2G, 4B

What makes sound change?

Materials

string
plastic 2 L bottle with cap
marker
funnel
pitcher of water

If any water spills, notify your teacher immediately.

Follow a Procedure

1. Tie one end of a string around the neck of a bottle. Tie the other end to a marker.
2. Use a funnel. Fill the bottle about $\frac{1}{3}$ full with water. Screw the cap tightly onto bottle.
3. Hang the bottle from the string.
4. **Observe** What happens when you pluck the string?
5. Make changes to the experiment, such as how much water is in the bottle, how hard you pluck the string, or how long the string is. Create a table to record your predictions and observations on how the sound changes. Use a computer, if possible. Include these changes as your row headings: add water, subtract water, pluck gently, pluck hard, shorten string.

Hold the marker on the table.

Pluck the string here.

Almost touching the floor.

Analyze and Conclude

6. **Predict** What will happen to the sound if you take most of the water out of the bottle? Test your prediction. Use multiple trials.
7. **Infer** Look for a pattern. How does the length of the string affect the pitch? Propose an explanation.
8. **Observe** How did the energy change when you plucked the string gently and then hard?

Sound

Sound is a wave of vibrations that spreads from its source. A **vibration** is the back-and-forth motion of an object. As sound waves travel through a material, such as air, the molecules in the material vibrate in a regular pattern. The molecules bump into each other, passing this pattern on to other molecules. Sound is used by many organisms to communicate.

Your vocal cords vibrate when you talk or sing. Vocal cords make the particles in the air around them vibrate. These vibrations travel outward through the air as sound waves. The sound waves travel in all directions. Even someone behind the girl can hear her singing.

1. Compare and Contrast How are your vocal cords and the strings on a guitar alike and different?

....

....

....

Uses of Sound Energy in Industry

People who work in industry can use sound energy to clean machinery. One engine even uses sound to run. Engineers also work to minimize the sound of the products they make, such as cars, fans, and lawn mowers. Sound that is too loud can be harmful, so factories have to reduce the volume around the machines.

Uses of Sound Energy in Music

Musicians use sound energy in different ways. They make sound vibrations on drums by striking them. They blow into clarinets to cause the reeds to vibrate. They produce sound vibrations on guitars by plucking or rubbing wires.

2. Infer The girl is playing a guitar. How could she stop the sound after she plucks the string?

....

....

....

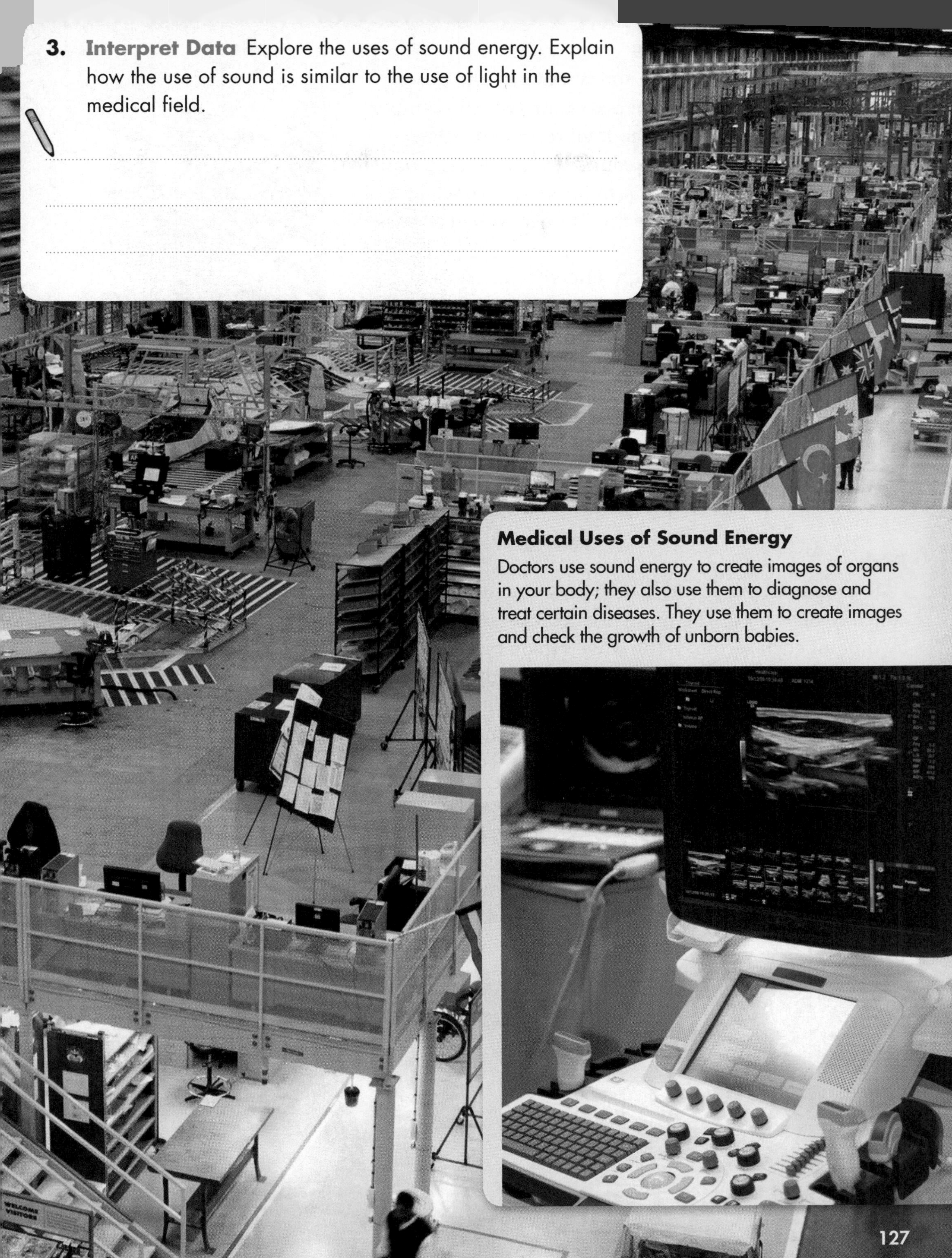

3. **Interpret Data** Explore the uses of sound energy. Explain how the use of sound is similar to the use of light in the medical field.

Medical Uses of Sound Energy

Doctors use sound energy to create images of organs in your body; they also use them to diagnose and treat certain diseases. They use them to create images and check the growth of unborn babies.

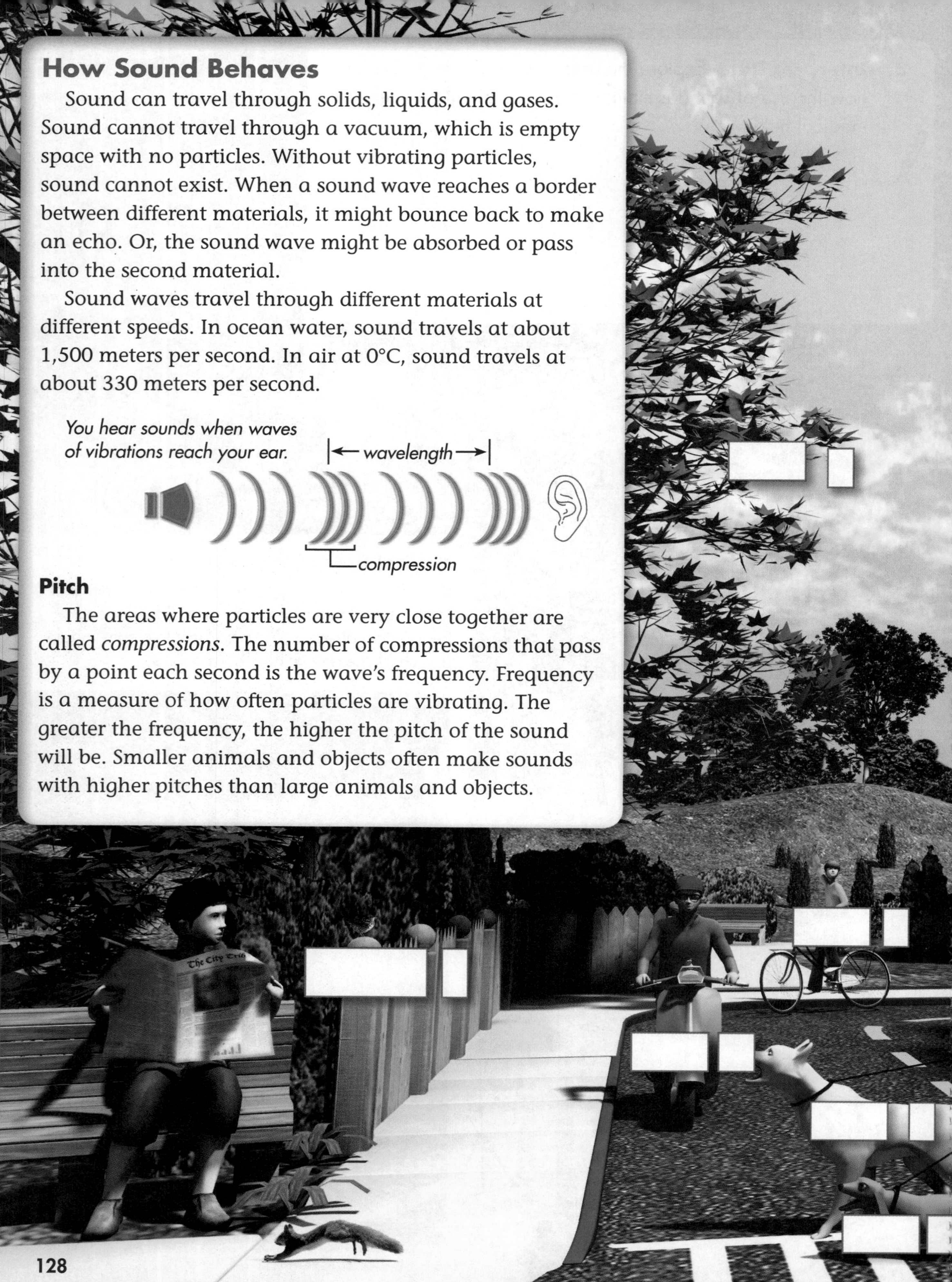

How Sound Behaves

Sound can travel through solids, liquids, and gases. Sound cannot travel through a vacuum, which is empty space with no particles. Without vibrating particles, sound cannot exist. When a sound wave reaches a border between different materials, it might bounce back to make an echo. Or, the sound wave might be absorbed or pass into the second material.

Sound waves travel through different materials at different speeds. In ocean water, sound travels at about 1,500 meters per second. In air at 0°C, sound travels at about 330 meters per second.

You hear sounds when waves of vibrations reach your ear.

Pitch

The areas where particles are very close together are called *compressions*. The number of compressions that pass by a point each second is the wave's frequency. Frequency is a measure of how often particles are vibrating. The greater the frequency, the higher the pitch of the sound will be. Smaller animals and objects often make sounds with higher pitches than large animals and objects.

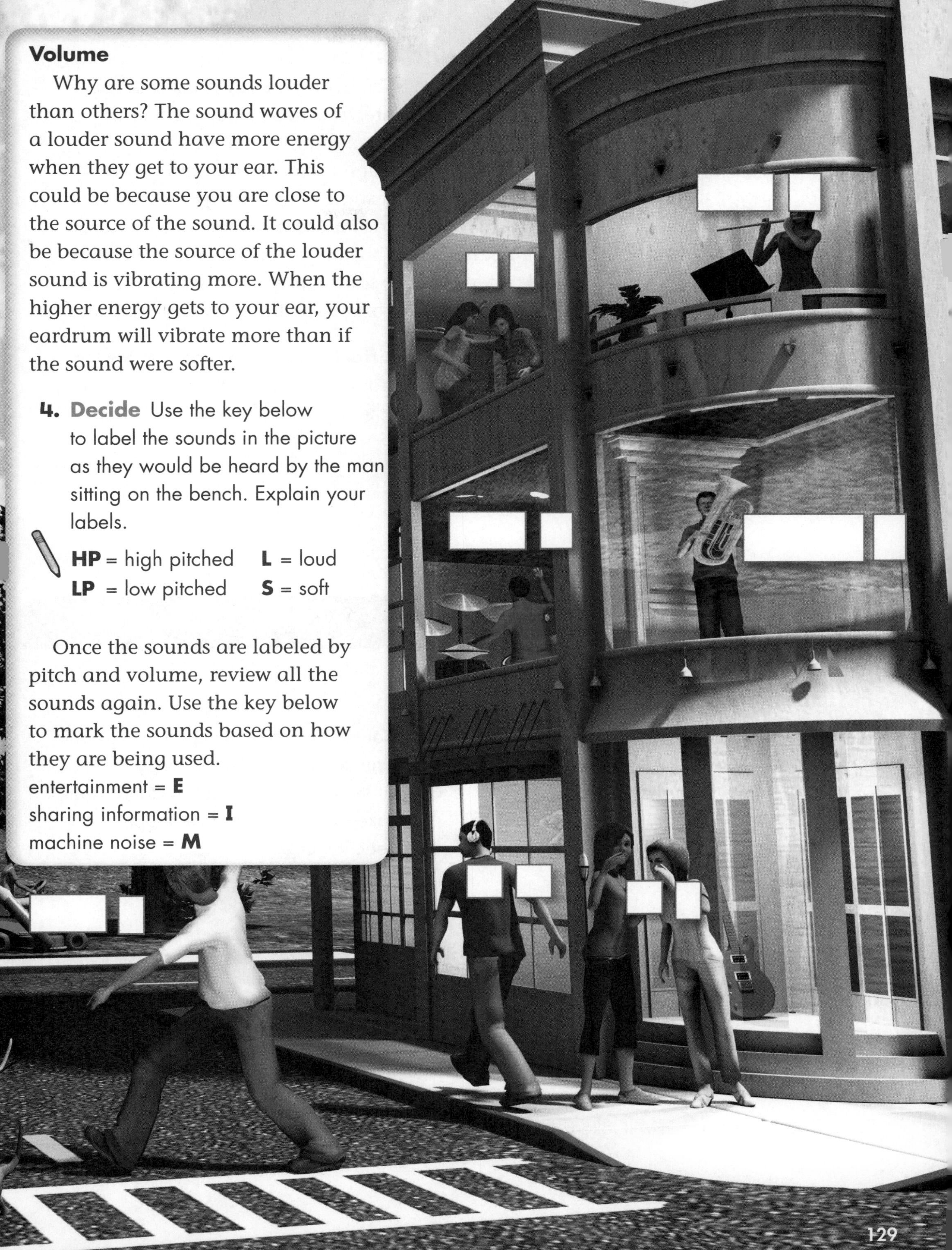

Volume

Why are some sounds louder than others? The sound waves of a louder sound have more energy when they get to your ear. This could be because you are close to the source of the sound. It could also be because the source of the louder sound is vibrating more. When the higher energy gets to your ear, your eardrum will vibrate more than if the sound were softer.

4. **Decide** Use the key below to label the sounds in the picture as they would be heard by the man sitting on the bench. Explain your labels.

HP = high pitched **L** = loud
LP = low pitched **S** = soft

Once the sounds are labeled by pitch and volume, review all the sounds again. Use the key below to mark the sounds based on how they are being used.
entertainment = **E**
sharing information = **I**
machine noise = **M**

Sound and Energy Transfer

For a sound to be heard, energy must first cause an object to vibrate. Vibrating objects transmit, or send off, energy as sound waves in air. The energy is transferred through the air as the sound waves move. Eventually, some of the energy reaches your ear, and your eardrum absorbs some of the energy. Your eardrum will begin to vibrate, and vibrations are interpreted as sound in your brain. In this way, the energy of the original vibrations passes to you.

Energy from this vibrating tuning fork is being transferred to the liquid.

5. Cause and Effect Look at the picture to the left. What effects does this energy transfer have on the liquid and on the tuning fork?

Connect to **Math**

Math TEKS 3A, 3C

Estimating Time

The speed of sound in air at 20°C is about 340 $\frac{m}{s}$. If you know how far away an object is, you can estimate the time it takes for its sound to reach your ear. Just divide the distance by the speed of sound.

Example

You are standing 705 m away from a soccer player when she kicks the ball. Estimate to the nearest second how long it will take for the sound of the kick to reach your ear.

705 is close to 700.
340 is close to 350.

Since 700 ÷ 350 is 2, it will take about 2 s.

You watch the beginning of a volcanic eruption from 3,370 m away. Estimate to the nearest second how long it will take for the sound of the eruption to reach your ear.

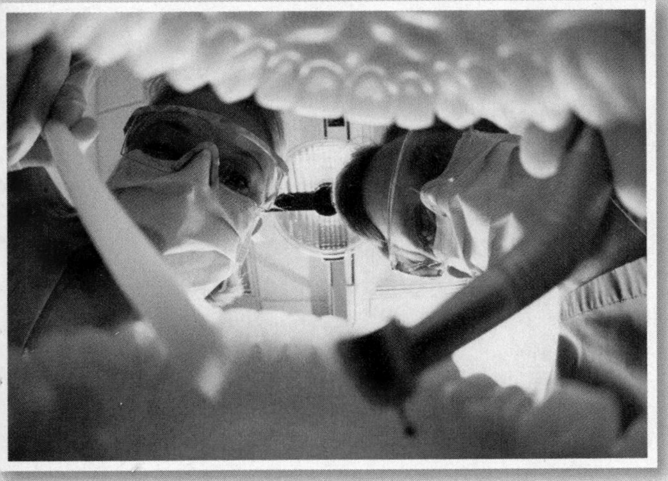

Sound can deliver energy for tooth cleaning. The sound vibrations of the instrument shake the dental plaque loose as a stream of water rinses it out.

6. **Infer** Without a water stream in the picture above, the cleaning tip might overheat. Why do you think this happens?

The String Phone
Work with a partner. Punch a small hole in the bottom of each of two cups. Cut a piece of string about six meters long. Thread it through the cups. So the string cannot come out, knot it inside each cup. Hold the cups so the string is taut. Talk into one cup while a partner holds the other cup over one ear. Take turns talking and listening. **TEKS 6A**

got it?

7. **Explain** Why is the pitch of a thick guitar string lower than the pitch of a thin string?

8. **Understand** Why c[illegible] so[illegible]d not travel through a vacuum?

Stop! I need help with

Wait! I have a question about

Go! Now I know

What is light energy and how is it used?

I will know TEKS 6A, 6B
I will know what light energy is.
I will know how it can be used.
I will know how light travels. I will know that it can be reflected or refracted.
(Also **1A, 2C, 2D, 4A, 6C**)

Vocabulary
transparent
translucent
opaque
reflection
refraction

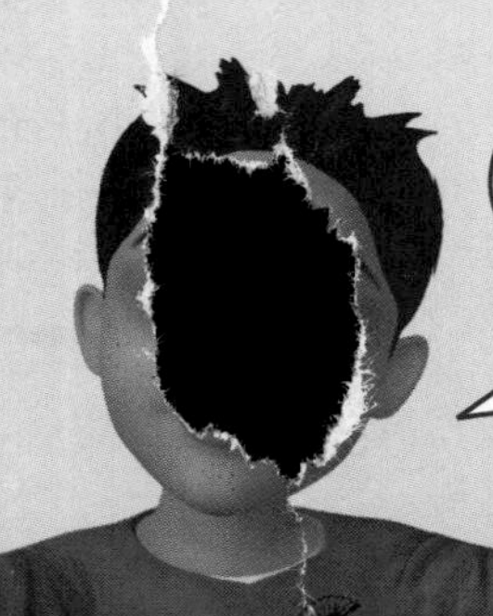

Hey, my father let me use his refracting telescope. I wanted to get a better look at the moon.
I read about telescopes while I was writing a report on Galileo. He used a refracting telescope over 400 years ago. This type of telescope uses lenses to refract light and magnify the image, making it seem larger.

Connect to Math

Math TEKS 7

There are two sets of binoculars at the lab. One has a magnification of 10x (ten times), and the other magnifies 20x. Suppose a bird is 12 meters away and appears 5 millimeters tall. How big would the bird appear to the viewer using each of the binoculars?

Show your work To find the new size, multiply the bird's size by the magnification number. To convert that measurement to centimeters, divide by 10.

PEARSON Texas.com

Quick Lab

TEKS 6C, 1A, 2C, 2D

How does light travel?

Materials

ruler
pencil
4 sheets of card stock paper
hole punch
modeling clay
flashlight

1. **Make a Model**
   - Use the ruler and pencil to draw lines from corner to corner of each of three pieces of paper.
   - Use the hole punch to create a hole where the lines cross each other in the middle of the paper.
   - Place all 4 cards parallel to each other with the modeling clay holding up the cards. (See diagram.)
2. **Observe** Use the flashlight to shine light through the first hole. What do you see on the blank card?

Texas Safety
LAB RULES
Return laboratory equipment to its proper location.

Now demonstrate that light travels in a straight line until it strikes an object. Move the card closest to the blank card so that the holes no longer line up. What do you see?

Explain Your Results

3. **Communicate** Explain what occurs in this setup.

4. **Interpret** Interpret your information to construct a reasonable explanation of how light travels from direct evidence.

How Light Travels

Light can pass through some materials and not others. **Transparent** materials let nearly all light pass through them. Glass and air are examples. **Translucent** materials allow some light to pass through, but not all. Waxed paper and most lampshades are translucent. **Opaque** materials do not let any light pass through. Wood and metal are examples of opaque materials.

Light can travel in a vacuum. A vacuum is empty space with no matter in it. When light travels in a vacuum it moves in a straight line. Light also moves in a straight line when it travels within the same transparent material. When light hits the boundary between two different materials, it may change direction.

1. **Classify** Name two things that are transparent and two that are opaque.

....

....

....

....

Opaque materials
An opaque material does not let light shine through. This opaque bowl prevents us from seeing the bottom part of the orange.

opaque

Translucent materials
Block glass windows and stained glass windows such as these are translucent; light comes through, but not completely. You cannot see clearly what is on the other side of the window, but you can see some light.

2. Draw Conclusions Suppose you have three types of curtains made of the following: clear plastic, sheet of metal, and light cloth. Order these curtains according to how much light they would let through. Which would you use to prevent anyone outside from looking into your window? Why?

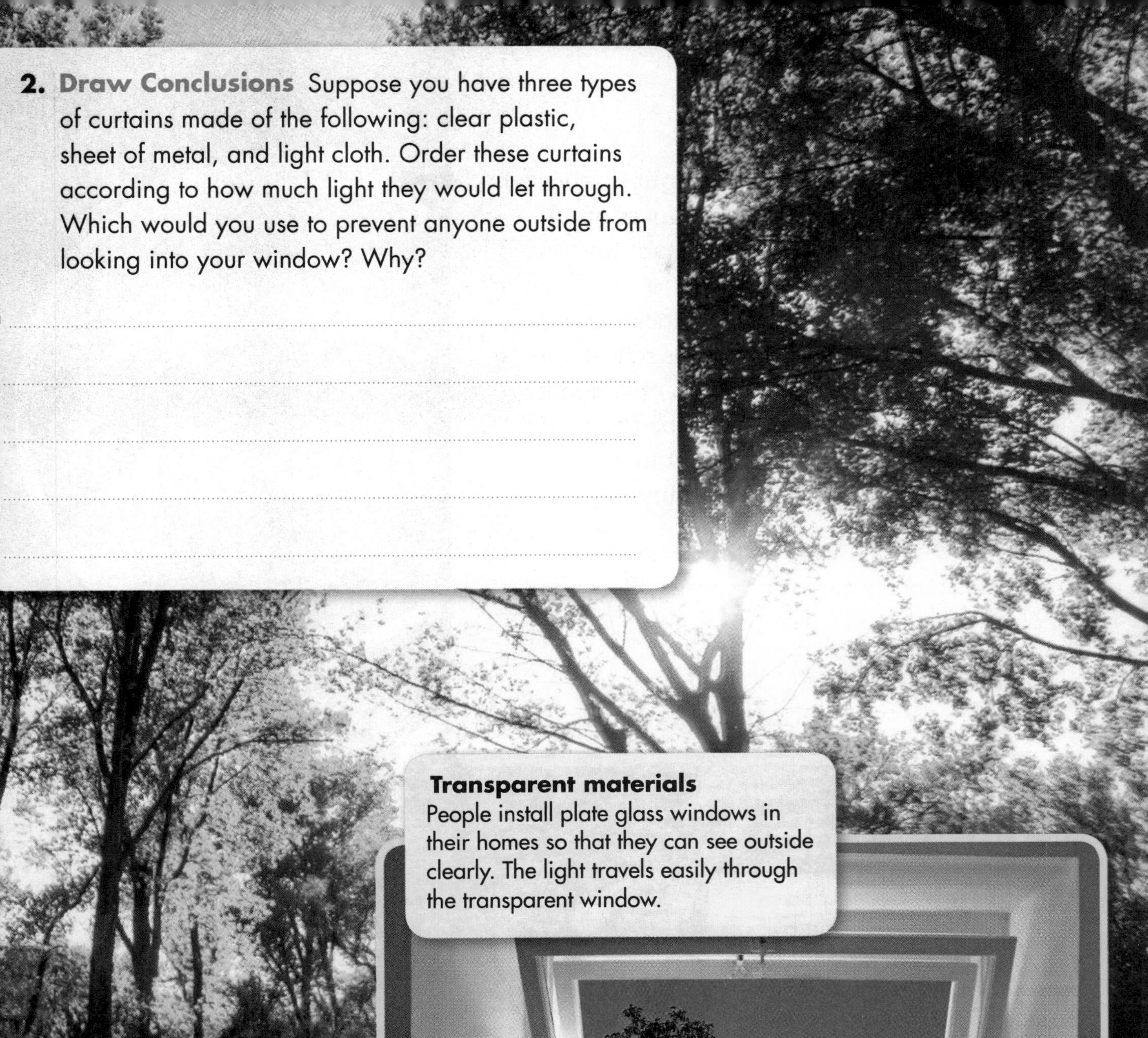

Transparent materials
People install plate glass windows in their homes so that they can see outside clearly. The light travels easily through the transparent window.

Light from the sun does not pass through these trees. This creates a pattern of shadows on the ground.

Light Changes Direction

Reflection

When light hits an object, some light is reflected. **Reflection** happens when light bounces off an object. The light still moves in a straight line but goes in a different direction.

All materials reflect some light. Black surfaces reflect very little light. White surfaces reflect a large amount of light. Mirror images form on smooth surfaces, such as polished metal or the still water of a pond. These surfaces reflect light in a very regular way, forming clear reflected images.

3. Compare and Contrast Look at the books in your classroom to see which covers reflect more light. What do you notice?

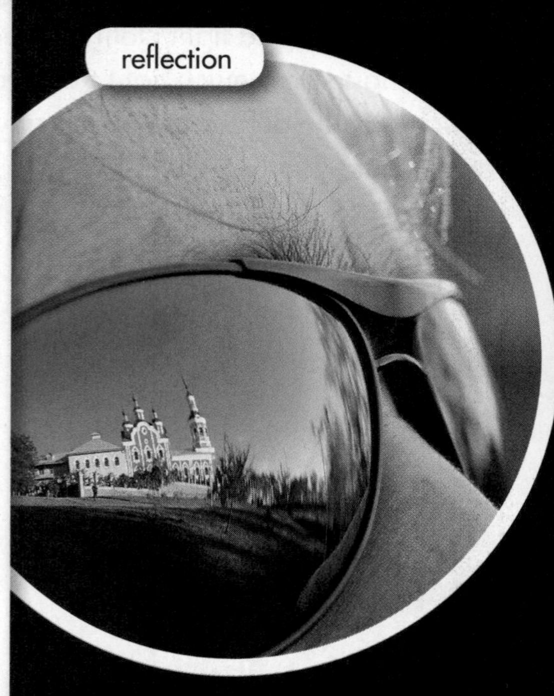

Quick Lab

Path of Light Collect and analyze information using a mirror. Draw a line down the center of a small mirror and on a piece of paper. Prop the mirror up on its edge in front of the paper. Align the line of the paper with that of the mirror. Hold a flashlight on the perpendicular, and aim it at the line on the mirror. Demonstrate that light can be reflected. Observe the path of the light. Now hold the flashlight a little to the left of the perpendicular. Draw a line on the paper to show the path of the light toward and away from the mirror. Repeat with the flashlight farther to the left. What do you notice about the path of the light?

TEKS 4A, 6C

Light reflects off a mirror.

Refraction

Light can bend when it enters a new material at an angle different from 90 degrees. This is because light travels at different speeds in different materials. As one side of the light wave slows down when it enters the new material, the other side is still going fast and the wave bends. For example, light bends when it goes from air to water. This bending is called **refraction**.

In order to refract light, materials have to be transparent.

A lens is a polished piece of glass with curved surfaces that makes things look larger or smaller when you look through the lens. Lenses do this by refracting the light. Microscopes, telescopes, cameras, and prescription glasses have lenses. Their lenses refract light in different ways and for different purposes. Scientists and optometrists have learned how to create lenses that magnify faraway stars and tiny microscopic animals, and improve the eyesight of humans.

4. Classify Look around the classroom. Which objects reflect and which refract? Fill out the table below with your findings.

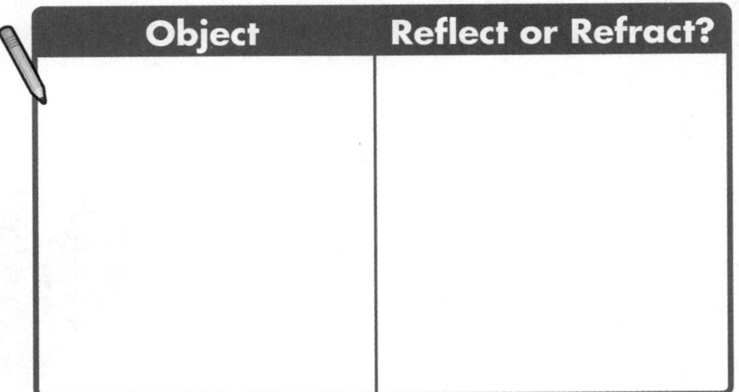

Object	Reflect or Refract?

Light is refracted by a lens.

refraction

Gamma radiation can kill cancer cells.

X rays show the shape of this skull.

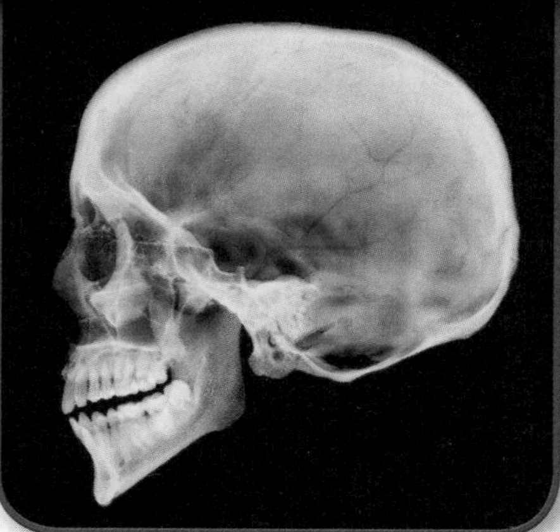

Flowers look very different under ultraviolet light.

Light Waves and Color

Like sound, light travels in waves that have certain wavelengths. Also like sound, the speed of light is different in different materials. However, light is different from sound in many ways. For example, light can travel through empty space.

For you to see an object, the object must give off or reflect waves of visible light. The light must then enter your eyes. Different wavelengths of visible light are seen as different colors. When all the colors of visible light are mixed, the result is white light. If you shine white light on an object, some wavelengths bounce off the object and some are absorbed. The wavelengths that bounce off the object can enter your eyes, and they determine the color you see. The other wavelengths are absorbed by the object.

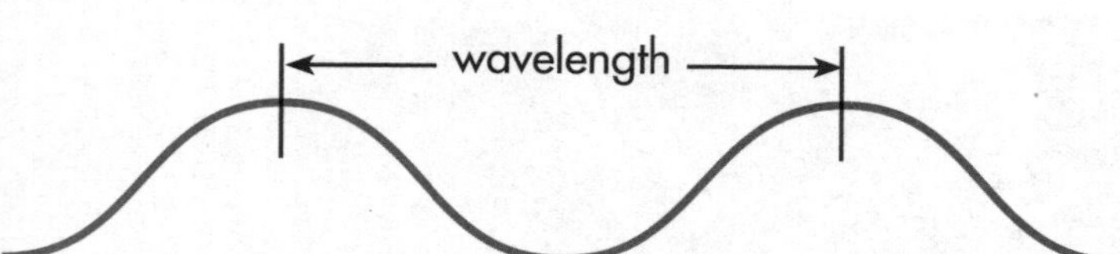

The distance between two crests of a wave is equal to the wavelength.

Visible light has wavelengths between violet and red. Our eyes cannot see wavelengths shorter than violet or longer than red.

5. CHALLENGE Why do you think an ultraviolet bulb is called a "black light"?

An infrared photograph shows that some parts of this house are hotter than others.

When food absorbs microwave radiation, its temperature rises.

Radio waves are used for radio, television, and astronomy.

Electromagnetic Spectrum

Unlike sound, light is not a vibration of particles. Light is an electromagnetic wave—that is, a combination of electrical and magnetic energy. Electromagnetic waves can have very long or very short wavelengths. The full range of electromagnetic wavelengths is called the electromagnetic spectrum. It includes visible light, but also short wavelengths such as those of X rays, and longer wavelengths such as those of radio waves.

Heat

When you feel the warmth of the sun or the heat of a light bulb shining a few centimeters from your hand, you are feeling electromagnetic waves. Infrared waves feel especially warm. Warm objects produce more infrared waves than cold objects.

6. **Compare and Contrast** Name one similarity and one difference between visible light and sound.

Quick Lab

Deflecting Light

Pick out a distant object and observe it. Then collect and analyze information using a prism. Have another student hold a prism in your line of sight. Make sure the triangular base of the prism is facing down. What do you need to do so that the image of the distant object becomes visible to you through the prism? TEKS 4A, 6C

Optical Instruments

We have learned about some of the properties of light. Now let's look at how different optical instruments make use of light for various purposes. Microscopes use lenses to refract light and give you a more detailed and close-up image of your subject. They make really small objects appear larger. Telescopes refract light to make things that are very far away seem closer and visible in more detail. In many cases curved mirrors are used as a substitute for lenses. They can reflect light at different angles and magnify images without using refraction.

7. Identify Explore the uses of light energy by drawing lines to match each optical instrument to its use.

microscope	to view faraway objects like stars
telescope	to reflect a person's image
mirror	to improve a human's vision
optical lens	to magnify very small things

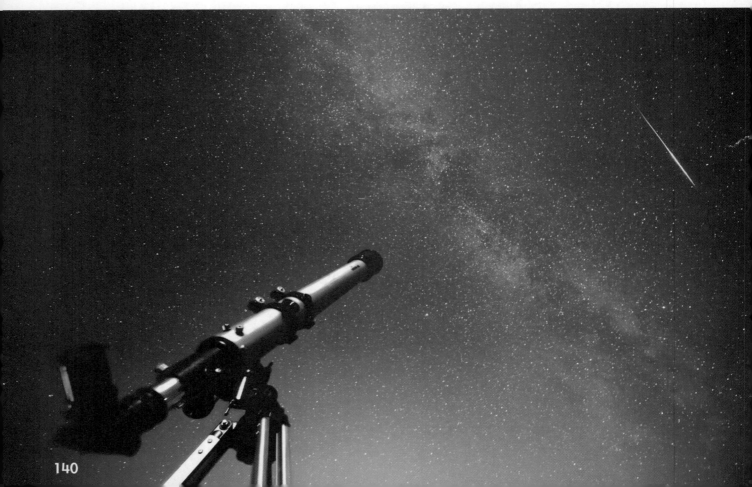

Dispersion

Different colors refract at different angles. Since white light is a mixture of colors, these colors disperse, or separate, when white light is refracted. Rainbows form because water droplets in the air disperse white light into its colors.

A prism can disperse the colors that form white light.

8. **Identify** Look at the picture to the left. What colors refract more than green, and what colors refract less?

got it?

9. **Infer** Things under a microscope often look like they are surrounded by rainbow colors. Why do you think this happens?

10. **Explain** Why do you think most lampshades are made of translucent materials instead of transparent materials?

Stop! I need help with

Wait! I have a question about

Go! Now I know

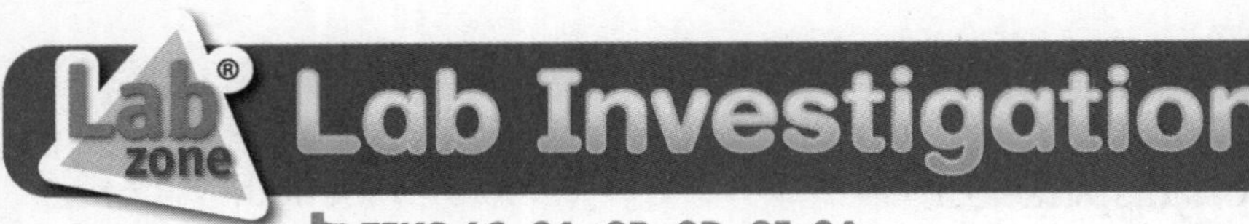

TEKS 6C, 2A, 2B, 2D, 2F, 3A

How can the path of light change?

Light energy travels in a straight line and has a specific speed. It travels too fast to see it move. We can see the path it takes and how that path can be changed by a difference in speed and angle.

Materials

flashlight
clear plastic cup or glass
water
plastic straw

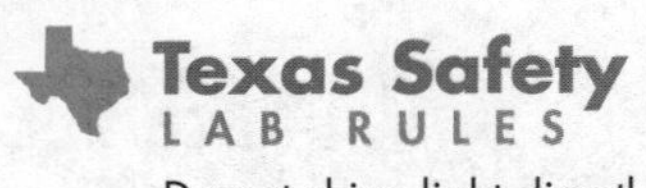

Texas Safety LAB RULES

Do not shine light directly into your eyes.

Follow a Procedure

1. Shine the flashlight at a 90-degree angle onto the front of an empty cup. **Observe** What do you notice about the beam of light?

2. Fill the cup with water. Shine the light through the cup, moving it left and right. **Observe** What do you notice about the beam of light?

3. Now demonstrate that light can be refracted. Place a straw vertically through the water to the center of the cup. **Observe** What do you notice about the straw?

4. Now tilt the straw about an inch or two to the right of the center. **Observe** What do you see?

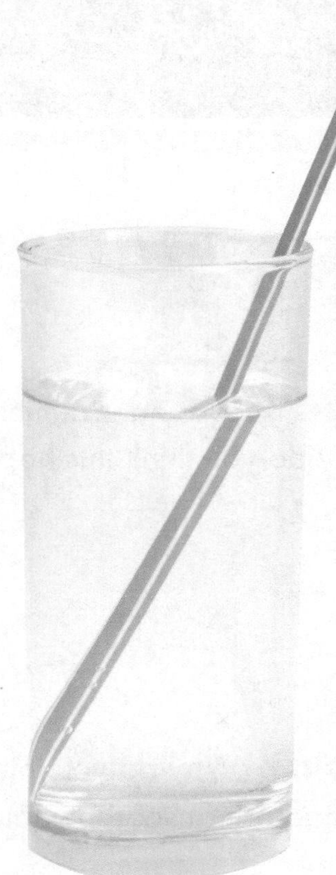

Analyze and Conclude

5. **Compare and Contrast** How was the behavior of the light different when the cup was empty and then filled with water?

6. **Infer** Based on your observations, what can you tell about the path of the light waves when it hits the water and the straw?

7. **Analyze and Evaluate** the scientific explanation of how light travels by using your observational test. How does the explanation support your observations in this investigation?

8. **Form Hypotheses** Food coloring can change the color of the water while still leaving it transparent. Does the color of the water affect how much it can bend light? Write a hypothesis. What experiments might you perform to test this hypothesis?

What is electricity and how is it used?

I will know TEKS 6A, 6B
I will know what electrical energy is. I will know how it can be used. I will know how electricity flows through a circuit. (Also 1A, 2B, 5A)

Vocabulary
transform
electric circuit
conductor
resistor
insulator

Connect to Math

Math TEKS 1A, 3E

Consumers pay electric companies for the use of electricity they supply. Electricity is supplied in kilowatt hours. The electric company bills each building every month for the amount of electricity used.

Suppose that each kilowatt hour costs 6 cents, or $ 0.06. Fill out the following table to figure out the electric bill for each home during one month.

Home	Kilowatt Hours Used	Cost
Home 1	700	
Home 2	1,000	
Home 3	1,200	

Quick Lab

TEKS 6B, 1A, 2B

What can electricity flow through?

1. Make the electric circuit shown.
2. **Predict** which objects electricity will flow through.

3. Test your predictions and demonstrate that the flow of electricity requires a complete path through which an electric current can pass. **Observe.**

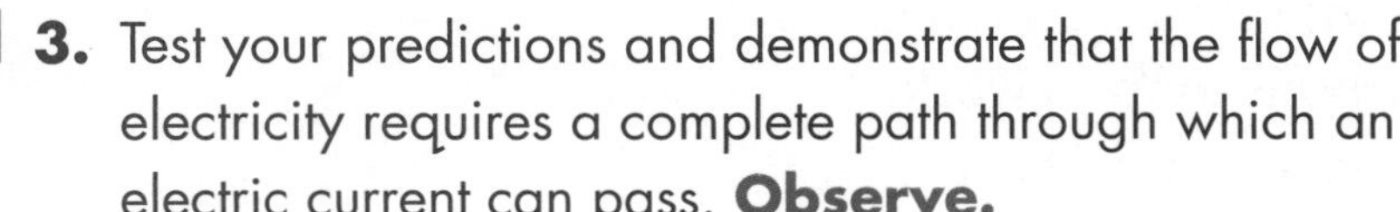

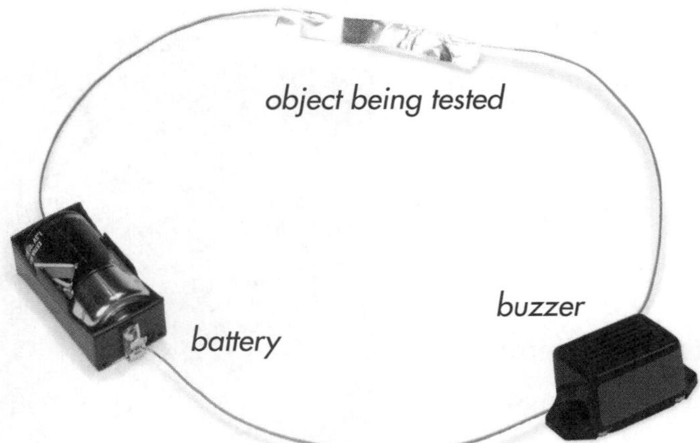

Materials

safety goggles
electric buzzer or bell
3 wires
battery and battery holder
spoon
paper clip
penny
foil
index card

Wear safety goggles.

Explain Your Results

4. **Classify** Name the items that electricity flows through. How many of your predictions were correct?

Uses of Electrical Energy

Energy cannot be made or destroyed. However, it can move from one object to another. Energy can also change from one form into another, or **transform.** Electrical energy can be easily transformed into many other forms. This is why almost everything you use runs on electricity. A lamp changes electrical energy to light energy. A fire alarm changes electrical energy to sound energy.

Many devices contain electric circuits that transform electrical energy. **Electric circuits** are loops that allow electric energy to transform into another energy. When the circuit is open, it no longer forms a loop. It will not work, because the electric energy cannot flow. The circuit needs to be closed and form a continuous loop to work.

Static electricity is another type of electricity. Static electricity is the buildup of static charge on an object. Unlike the electricity in a circuit, it does not need a conductor, such as a copper wire. This electricity is what causes your hair to stand up after it is rubbed with an inflated balloon.

Every time energy changes form, some energy is given off as unusable heat. People can measure the amount of any form of energy that moves or changes. These measurements tell which devices are more energy-efficient or lose less energy as unusable heat.

1. **Predict** If the grinding wheel slows down or speeds up, how do the light, sound, and heat energy change?

2. **Cause and Effect** Write one effect of a device that is energy-efficient.

Most homes run almost entirely on electrical energy.

Electrical energy operates this grinding wheel, which produces motion, heat, light, and sound.

Insulators and Conductors

A material through which an electric charge c
easily is called a **conductor.** Some materials are
conductors than others. Copper, gold, silver, and
are some of the best conductors. Electric wires ar
made from copper and aluminum. Many good
of electrical energy are also good conductors of
energy.

A material through which an electric charge
move easily is called a **resistor.** As current mov
a resistor, some of the electrical energy changes to thermal energy. We can eat toasted bread because of resistors. In toasters, wires of nickel and chromium resist electrical current and turn electrical energy into thermal energy. Under most conditions, all materials, including copper and gold, have at least a little resistance.

Insulators are such strong resistors that they can stop most electrical currents. Rubber, plastic, glass, and dry cotton can be used as insulators. Like conductors, many good insulators of electrical energy are also good insulators of thermal energy.

3. Identify Label the insulator and the conductor in the electric plug below.

4. Explain Someone forgot to turn off the switch before screwing in the light bulb. Why doesn't the hand receive an electric shock when the bulb lights up?

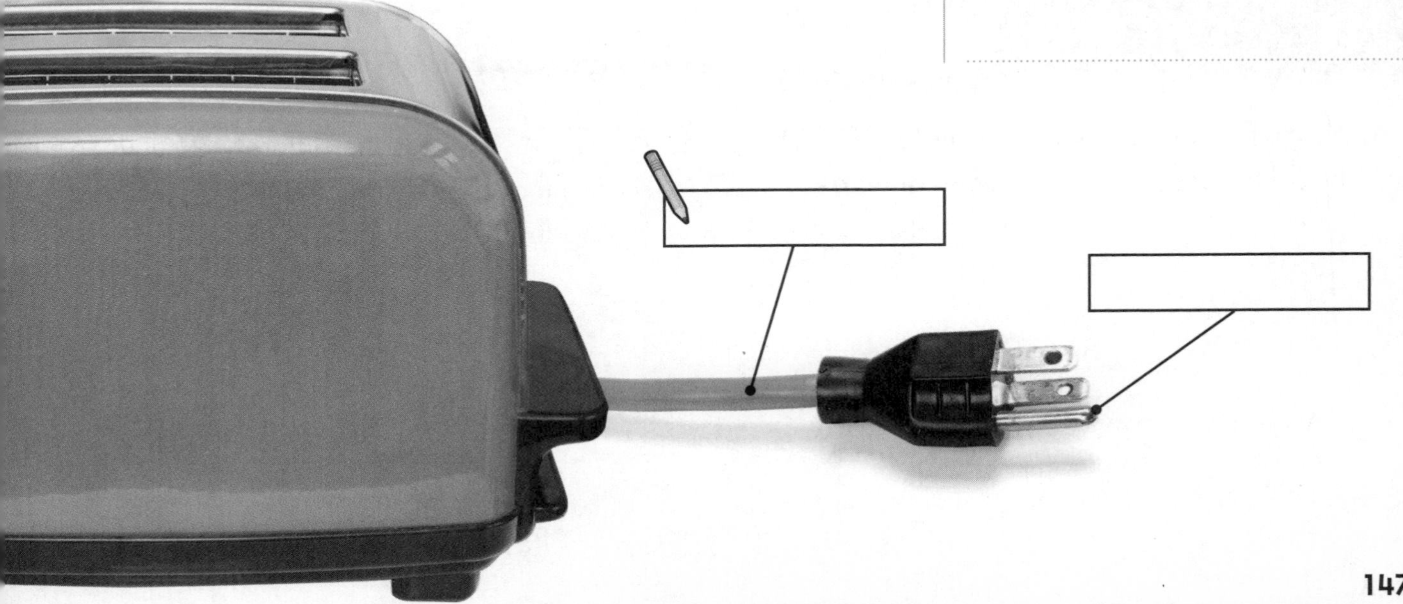

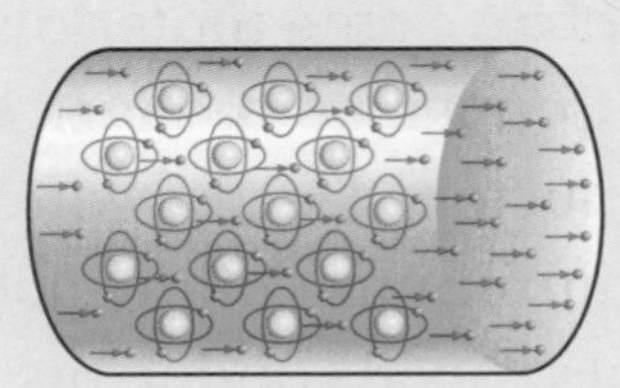

Current *When a power source acts on the charged particles, they flow through the wire in the same direction.*

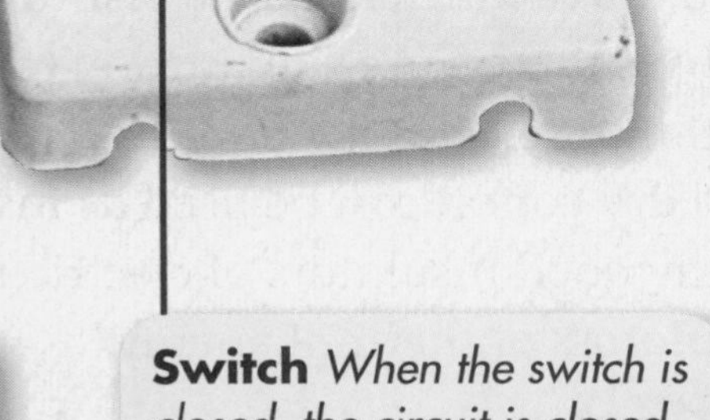

Energy Source
The energy source in this circuit is a battery. Batteries keep the current flowing.

Wires *Electrical wires are usually made of copper, which is an excellent conductor. They are insulated with plastic to ensure that the electricity stays within its path.*

Switch *When the switch is closed, the circuit is closed and electric charges can flow without interruption.*

5. Suggest Name two other materials that could be used to make electrical wires.

6. CHALLENGE What is the difference between saying that an electric circuit is closed and saying that a water pipe is closed?

Electromagnets

Electricity and magnetism are closely related. All electric currents produce a magnetic field. Electromagnets are magnets that use electric current. They consist of a current that flows through a coiled wire connected to a circuit. The strength of an electromagnet can be increased by increasing the number of loops of wire, by increasing the current, or by wrapping the wire around a metal bar.

Ordinary magnets are always magnetic, but electromagnets are only magnetic when an electric current is applied. Their strength can also be varied as needed by changing the current. They are used in many devices, including speakers and electric motors.

12. Compare and Contrast Powerful electromagnets can lift heavy loads of scrap metal. Why can't ordinary magnets be used for this job?

got it? TEKS 6A

13. Support In the space to the right, draw a circuit diagram with two resistors. In the space below, describe what would happen if a gap were created by removing one of the resistors.

14. Explore Explore the uses of electrical energy by naming three things that use electrical energy.

Stop! I need help with

Wait! I have a question about

Go! Now I know

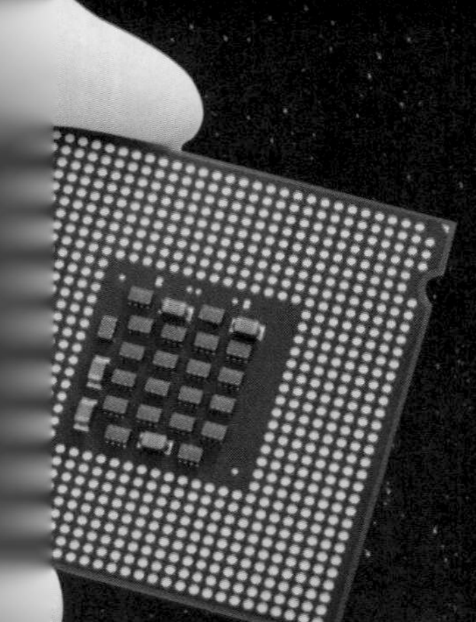

JACK KILBY, INVENTOR OF THE MICROCHIP

TEKS 6A, 6B, 3D

Nobel Prize winner and inventor of the integrated circuit

Who made it possible for your cell phone or calculator to run without plugging it into an outlet, or for a birthday card to play a song when you open it?

An engineer at Texas Instruments made that possible. Jack Kilby, earned a master's degree in electrical engineering and started working at Texas Instruments in 1958. There, he began developing the integrated circuit. An integrated circuit contains all the elements of a large and complex circuit, but it takes up a fraction of the space. It was the first microchip—the small electronic "brain" behind all of our modern electronic devices.

Kilby shares the credit for developing the integrated circuit with Robert Noyce, who was working on a similar project at about the same time. Jack Kilby won the Nobel Prize on December 10, 2000.

Connect Connect science concepts with the contributions of scientists. How did Jack Kilby's breakthrough change the world?

Science Careers

EXECUTIVE CHEF

TEKS 6A, 3D

Science is useful in all kinds of careers. Chefs use thermal energy to cook their meals. Burning wood, natural gas, electricity, or charcoal produces thermal energy. Chefs must know at what temperature and how long to cook every item on the menu. They need to control thermal energy. They need to know how long to roast meat, how to cook each vegetable, and what temperature and length of time to bake. Like scientists, chefs often find their answers through trial and error. They often have to eat the errors!

Infer Connect grade-level appropriate science concepts with science careers. What forms of energy might a biologist observe in penguins while studying their behavior?

FieldTrip

PLANETARIUM

TEKS 6A

The next time you visit a planetarium to learn about the stars, notice how the planetarium transforms energy from one form to another to present information. The planetarium transforms electricity into lights representing the sky, stars, and planets above. The show uses electricity to generate light for movie images and lasers. It transforms electricity into sound for narration, music, and the sound effects to the laser light shows. All this transformation of energy is designed to produce an instructional and entertaining experience.

Lab Investigation

TEKS 6B, 1A, 2D, 2F, 4B

How can electrical energy change forms?

Materials

safety goggles
2 pieces of insulated wire
flashlight bulb and holder
battery and battery holder
thermometer
small electric buzzer

Wear safety goggles.

Inquiry Skill

Scientists make careful observations and record them. They use their observations to help make **inferences.**

Follow a Procedure

☐ **1.** Make a circuit. Use wires to connect each side of a battery holder to each side of a bulb holder.

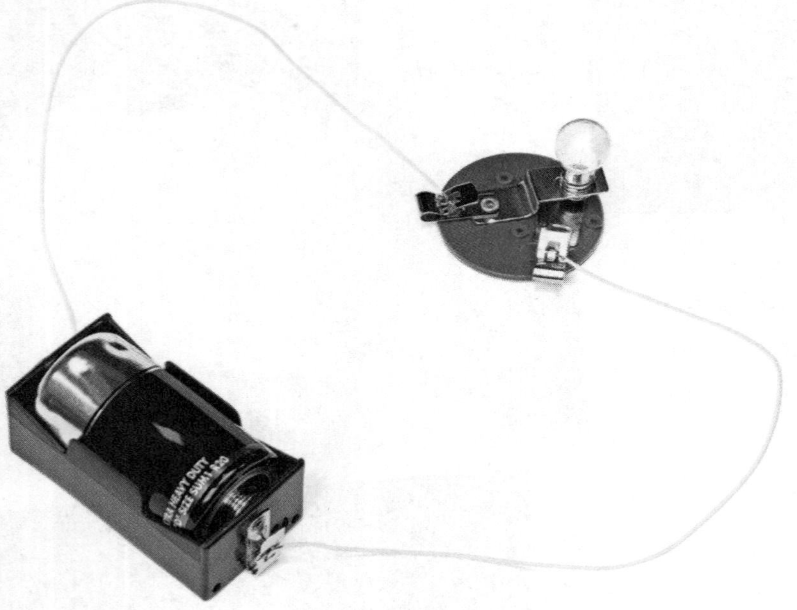

☐ **2. Observe** Demonstrate that the flow of electricity requires a complete path through which an electric current can produce light. In which part of the circuit do you observe light?

☐ **3.** Demonstrate that the flow of electricity requires a complete path through which an electric current can produce heat. Touch the bulb of the thermometer against the flashlight bulb for 1 minute. What do you observe?

4. Demonstrate that the flow of electricity requires a complete path through which an electric current can produce sound. Replace the flashlight bulb and holder with the small electric buzzer. What do you observe?

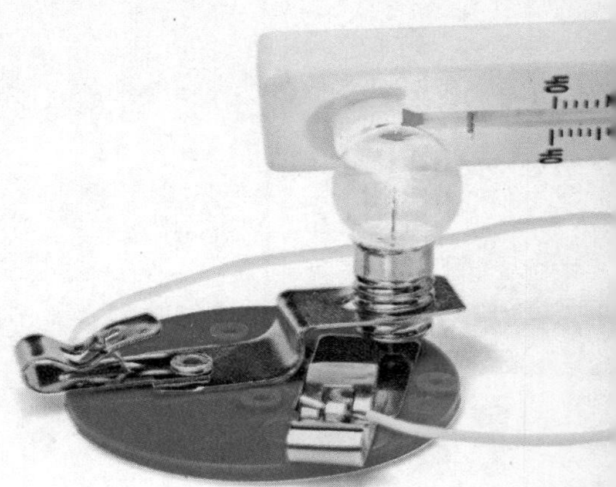

Analyze and Conclude

5. Make a diagram of your circuit. Show where you observed light energy and thermal energy. Identify the source of the electrical energy.

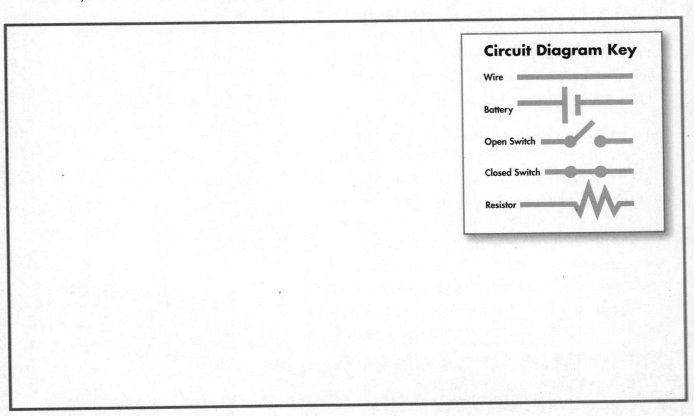

Circuit Diagram Key

- Wire
- Battery
- Open Switch
- Closed Switch
- Resistor

6. **Infer** Tell how energy was transformed in your investigation.

my planet Diary

ENERGY AT A CONSTRUCTION SITE

Think about your town and all the places in it. There are buildings where people live, work, shop, or go for entertainment. People drive cars on streets and highways. You may have bridges that go over rivers, lakes, or other roads. All these places were built using technology and scientific knowledge. Once, they may have looked something like this construction site.

There are many different types of energy in use at a construction site. A wrecking ball is a machine that has a heavy ball tied to it. The ball moves back and forth. The machine uses the energy of the moving ball to crash into buildings and knock them down. Workers use their own energy to move tools and other equipment around the site. Some construction projects include buildings with lights, and the lights in the building use electrical energy to shine brightly so workers can see what they are doing in the dark.

What other things at a construction site use energy?

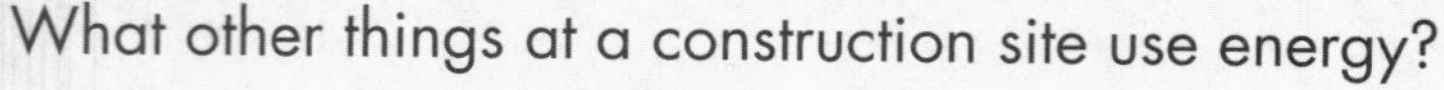

Vocabulary Smart Cards

energy
kinetic energy
potential energy
vibration
transparent
translucent
opaque
reflection
refraction
transform
electric circuit
conductor
resistor
insulator

Play a Game!

Cut out the Vocabulary Smart Cards.

Work with a partner. Choose a Vocabulary Smart Card. Do not let your partner see your card.

Draw a picture to show what the word means. Have your partner guess the word. Take turns drawing and guessing.

ability to do work or cause change

Write three examples.

capacidad de hacer trabajo o causar cambios

the back-and-forth motion of an object

Write three other forms of this word.

movimiento de un objeto hacia adelante y hacia atrás

energy due to motion

Write a sentence using this term.

energía que resulta del movimiento

describes materials that let nearly all light pass through them

Use a dictionary. Find another meaning for this word.

describe materiales que dejan pasar a través de ellos casi toda la luz

energy that is not causing any changes now but could cause changes in the future

Write one example.

energía que no está causando cambios actualmente pero que podría causarlos en el futuro

describes materials that let some light pass through, but not all

Write three examples.

describe materiales que dejan pasar a través de ellos un poco de luz, pero no toda

Interactive Vocabulary

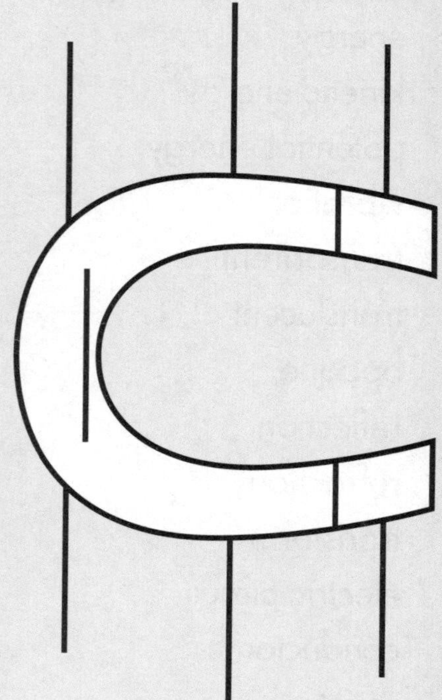

Make a Word Magnet!

Choose a vocabulary word and write it in the Word Magnet. Write words that are related to it on the lines.

resistor

resistencia

transform

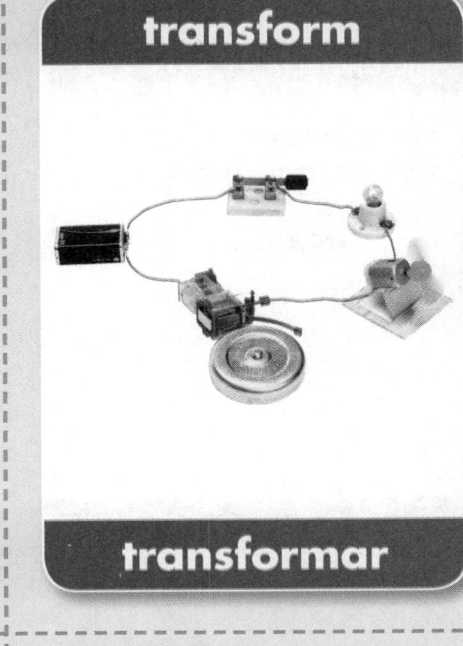

transformar

opaque

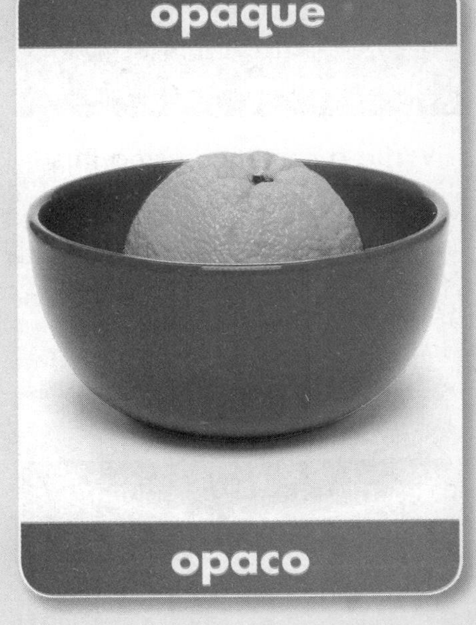

opaco

insulator

aislante

electric circuit

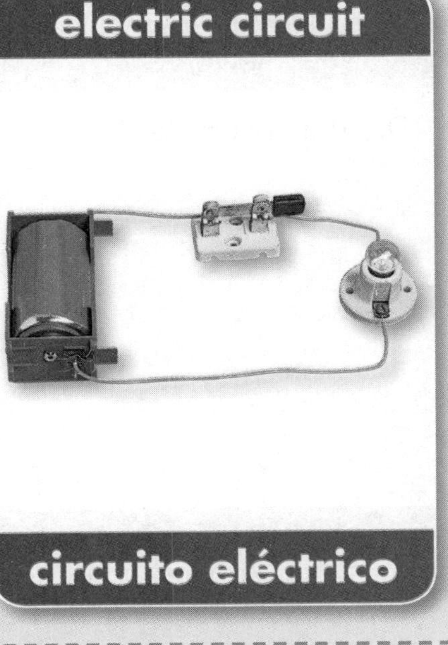

circuito eléctrico

reflection

reflexión

conductor

conductor

refraction

refracción

describes materials that do not let any light pass through them

Write a sentence using this word.

describe materiales que no dejan pasar a través de ellos la luz

to change from one form into another

Write three other words with the same prefix as this word.

cambiar de una forma a otra

a material through which an electric charge cannot move easily

Write a sentence using this word.

material a través del cual una carga eléctrica no puede moverse con facilidad

light bouncing off an object

Use a dictionary. Find as many synonyms for this word as you can.

rebote de la luz contra un objeto

a circular path through which electricity can flow

Draw an example.

camino circular por donde puede fluir electricidad

a strong resistor that can stop most electric currents

Write two examples.

resistencia fuerte que puede impedir el paso de casi cualquier corriente

bending of light

Write a sentence using the verb form of this word.

desviación de la luz

a material through which an electric charge can move easily

What is a different meaning for this word?

material a través del cual fluye fácilmente una carga eléctrica

TEKS Practice

Lesson 1 TEKS 6A

What is energy and how is it used?

1. **Identify** A book sits on a shelf high above the floor. What kind of energy does the book have?

A. thermal
B. kinetic
C. potential

2. **Understand** When someone slides down from the top of a water slide, _________.

A. her kinetic energy becomes potential
B. her potential energy becomes kinetic
C. her total energy doubles

3. **Write About It** If you put your hand on a hot metal pan, what kind of energy causes your hand to get burned and why?

4. **Identify** Which kind of energy travels as waves and moves through empty space?

A. kinetic energy
B. light energy
C. sound energy

Lesson 2 TEKS 6A

What is sound energy and how is it used?

5. Where can sound travel?

A. through solids, liquids, and gases
B. in a vacuum
C. only in air and under water

6. **Cause and Effect** A siren's sound suddenly becomes very loud. What could be the cause of this?

A. The siren is vibrating less.
B. The siren is moving away from you.
C. The siren is moving closer to you.

7. **Write About It** How does sound travel from its source to your ear?

TEKS Practice

Lesson 3 TEKS 6A, 6C

What is light energy and how is it used?

8. Interpret This image shows ________.

A. refraction
B. reflection
C. conduction

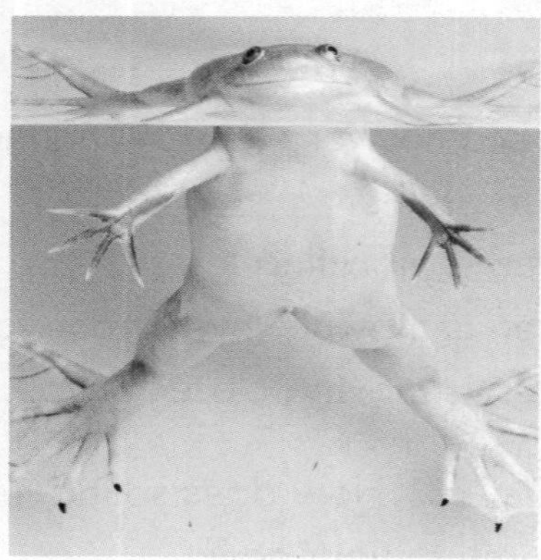

9. Identify Which of the following is opaque?

A. water
B. steel
C. glass

10. Vocabulary When light bounces off Frederick's sunglasses, it is ________.

A. absorbing
B. reflecting
C. refracting

Lesson 4 TEKS 6A, 6B

What is electricity and how is it used?

11. Analyze Why do we use so much electrical energy?

A. It can be transformed into light, sound, and kinetic energy.
B. It is quieter than sound energy or light energy.
C. It will work in a vacuum and underwater.

12. Cause and Effect When a storm knocks down an electric wire, why is the electricity in the neighborhood cut off?

13. List Write two ways you use electrical energy.

TEKS Practice

Lesson 4 TEKS 6A
What is electricity and how is it used?

14. Vocabulary A material that electricity can easily flow through is called a/an ________.

A. insulator
B. resistor
C. conductor

15. Identify Resistors in a circuit ________.

A. oppose electric current
B. conduct electricity
C. insulate from electricity

16. Define What is an electric circuit?

Chapter 3

Lesson 1 What is energy and how is it used?
In Lesson 1, you learned about kinetic and potential energy, sound, light, electrical, and thermal energy and their uses.

Readiness TEKS 6A

Lesson 2 What is sound energy and how is it used?
In Lesson 2, you learned about sound energy and how it is a wave of vibrations sent out from its source. It has many uses, such as in communication and ultrasound.

Readiness TEKS 6A

Lesson 3 What is light energy and how is it used?
In Lesson 3, you learned about light energy and how it travels in a straight line unless it passes from one material to another. You learned that light energy can be reflected or refracted.

Readiness TEKS 6A, 6C

Lesson 4 What is electricity and how is it used?
In Lesson 4, you learned about electrical energy and how it can be easily transformed into many other forms of energy. You learned how electricity flows through a circuit.

Readiness TEKS 6A, 6B

★ TEKS Practice: Chapter Review

Read each question and circle the best answer.

1 When the power goes out during a storm, you might need to use the potential energy stored in a candle to find your way in the dark.

What kind of energy are you using the candle for in this situation?

A Electrical energy

B Light energy

C Sound energy

D Thermal energy

2 The picture below shows a straw in a glass of water.

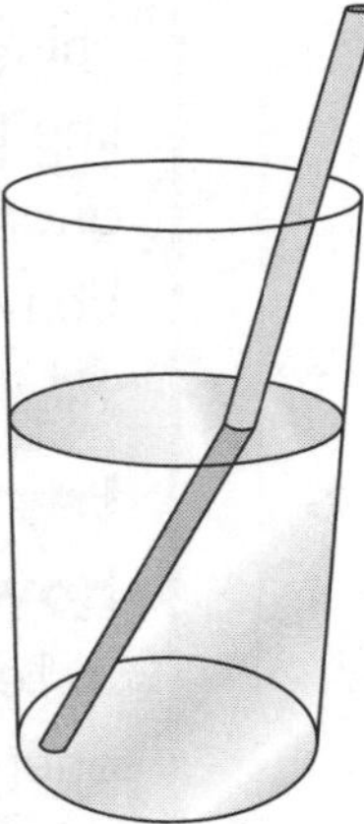

Why does the straw look bent?

F The light transforms into thermal energy.

G The path of the light is blocked by the straw.

H The light bounces off the surface of the water.

J Light can bend when it travels from one material to another.

3 The different parts of a typical computer are labeled in the picture.

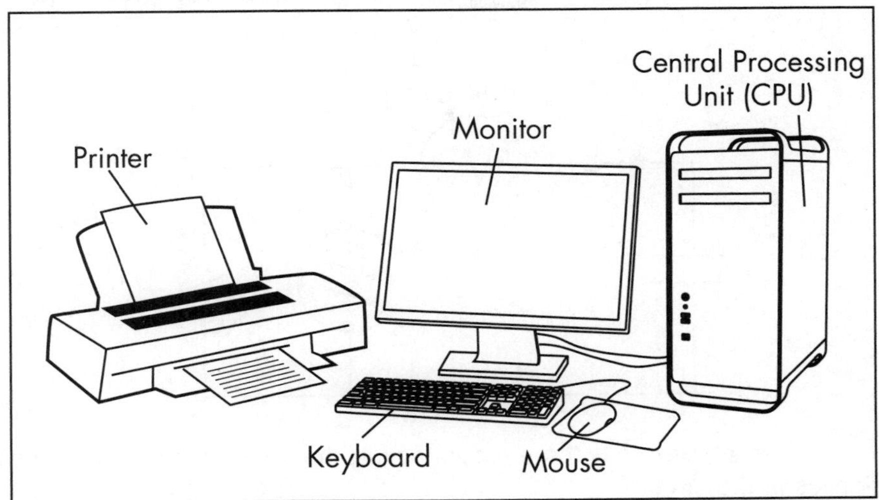

Suppose you want to use the computer to make a graph. Which part of the computer changes electrical energy into light energy so you can see the graph?

A Central processing unit (CPU)

B Keyboard

C Monitor

D Printer

---

4 The sun produces light, which is why it looks so bright in the sky. The moon, however, does not make its own light. The moon looks bright to people on Earth because light from the sun bounces off the moon toward Earth. Which model best represents how light comes from the sun and the moon?

F Two tennis balls

G A flashlight and a mirror

H Two glowing light bulbs

J A burning candle and a lens

5 One way to break the flow of electric charges in an electric circuit is to open a switch. Another way to break the flow of charges is to remove a resistor without reconnecting the wires. Look at the circuit diagram.

Circuit Diagram

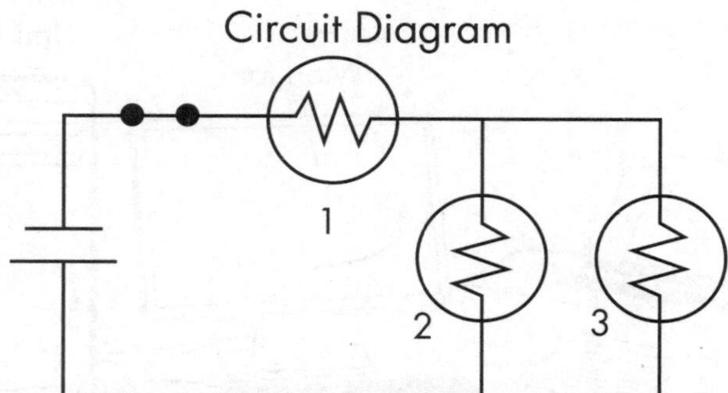

Suppose you removed resistor 2 without reconnecting the wires. How would this affect the flow of electric charges in the circuit?

A Electric charges would stop flowing through all parts of the circuit.

B Electric charges would continue to flow through all parts of the circuit.

C Electric charges would continue to flow only through the open loop that includes resistors 1 and 2.

D Electric charges would continue to flow only through the closed loop that includes resistors 1 and 3.

6 The energy stored in food is a form of potential energy. Plants, like the one in the picture below, make their own food.

How does the plant in the picture transform energy from one type to another?

F It changes the light energy from sunlight into the potential energy of food.

G It changes the thermal energy of sunlight into the potential energy of food.

H It changes the potential energy in food into thermal energy.

J It changes the potential energy in food into light energy.

TEKS Practice: Cumulative Review

7 A student designed an experiment to compare the properties of liquids and gases. She brought two balloons to the top of a very tall building in the elevator.

One balloon was filled with air, and the other balloon was filled with water. When the elevator was on the ground floor of the building, both balloons had the same volume. When the elevator was on the top floor, where the air pressure is lower, the volumes of the balloons were no longer equal. What happened?

A The volume of the liquid in the water balloon increased.

B The volume of the liquid in the water balloon decreased.

C The volume of the gas in the air balloon increased.

D The volume of the gas in the air balloon decreased.

---

8 Which tool measures the amount of matter in an object?

F Graduated cylinder

G Microscope

H Ruler

J None of these

If you have trouble with . . .

Question	1	2	3	4	5	6	7	8
See chapter (lesson)	3 (1)	3 (3)	3 (4)	3 (3)	3 (4)	3 (1)	2 (2)	1 (3)
TEKS	6A	6C	6A	6C	6B	6A	5A	4A

Which way is he MOVING?

Forces and Their Effects

Lesson 1 **What are forces?**

Lesson 2 **What are Newton's laws?**

How do forces and matter interact?

A surfer has to have perfect timing to ride an ocean wave. He has to balance the sideways motion of the water with the upward force of the wave on his board.

Where do you think the surfer will end up after the wave passes? Why?

Texas Essential Knowledge and Skills

Supporting TEKS: 6D Design an experiment that tests the effect of force on an object.

Process TEKS: 1A, 1B, 2A, 2B, 2C, 2D, 2E, 2F, 2G, 3A, 3B, 3C, 3D, 4A

PEARSON Texas.com

Inquiry Warm-Up

TEKS 6D, 1A, 3C

How can you make a paper helicopter drop slowly?

1. Use the Helicopter Pattern to **make a model** of a helicopter. Add a paper clip to the bottom.
2. Drop the helicopter. **Observe** its motion. Describe how it moves.
3. Modify the design to make the helicopter stay in the air longer.

Materials

Helicopter Pattern
scissors
paper clip
additional small or large paper clips (optional)
heavy paper or card stock (optional)

Identify potential hazards and know which precautions to take.

Explain Your Results

4. What force pulls the helicopter down? What force slows its fall?

5. **Interpret Data** How did your change affect the helicopter's motion?

Inquiry Skill

You can **make and use a model** to help explain an object or event.

Focus on Main Idea and Details

You will practice the reading strategy of finding **main idea and details** in this chapter. Learning to find main ideas and details can help you understand and remember what you read.

Connect to Reading

Small but Strong

Small animals can be very strong for their size. For example, tortoise beetles are the size of a ladybug, but it is very difficult to pull them off a leaf or a stem. These beetles have sticky feet and strong legs that allow them to hold on very tight. Leaf-cutting ants use their strength to carry heavy weights. A leaf-cutting ant can carry a leaf that is many times heavier than the ant itself! A flea is able to jump more than 100 times its own height. That would be like a human jumping from street level to the top of a 50-story building!

Practice It!

Use the graphic organizer below to list the main idea and details from the article shown above.

Detail	Detail	Detail

What are forces?

I will know TEKS 6D
I will know that a force can cause motion in an object. I will know that there are different kinds of forces. (Also **2A**, **2D**, **4A**)

Vocabulary
force
contact force
friction
non-contact force
gravity

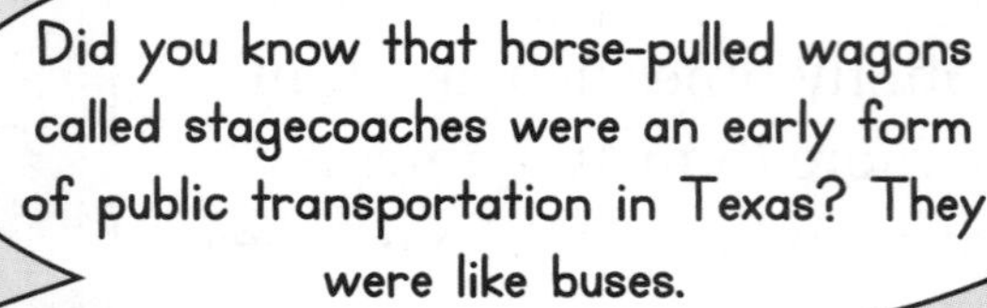

Did you know that horse-pulled wagons called stagecoaches were an early form of public transportation in Texas? They were like buses.

So, horses pulled the wagons, which were loaded with passengers?

Yes. Sometimes six horses pulled a stagecoach that weighed about 11,000 newtons. There might be 12 passengers in the stagecoach too.

That stagecoach weighs a lot. Can you help me find out how much the stagecoach plus 12 passengers weigh? The total weight of the passengers is 8,000 newtons.

Math

Show your work To find the total weight, find the sum of the weight of the stagecoach plus the weight of the passengers. **Math TEKS 1A, 3K**

PEARSON Texas.com

Quick Lab

TEKS 6D, 2D, 4A

Are there different kinds of forces?

Sometimes an object has to touch another object to exert a force on it. In other cases an object can exert a force on another object from a distance.

Materials

string, 1 m long
book, 2 cm thick
spring scale
paper clip, metal
bar magnet

Follow a Procedure

1. Collect information using a spring scale. Tie the string around the book and attach the spring scale as shown in the photo. **Record** the amount of force required to move the book.

Texas Safety LAB RULES
Wear shoes that enclose the feet.

2. Move the bar magnet close to the paper clip. *Do not touch the paper clip with the magnet.* **Observe** and record what happens to the paper clip as you move the magnet closer.

Explain Your Results

3. **Communicate** Explain the difference between how the spring scale and the bar magnet exerted a force on an object.

4. **Analyze** Analyze information using a magnet and a spring scale. Do the spring scale and bar magnet demonstrate two different kinds of forces?

Forces

When one object pushes or pulls another object, each object is exerting a force on the other object. A **force** is a push or pull that acts on an object.

Every force has a strength, or magnitude. This strength is measured in units called newtons (N). A force also has a direction. The direction of a force can be described by telling which way the force is acting.

Forces can change the way objects move. When an object begins to move, it is because a force has acted on it. When an object is already moving, forces can make it speed up, slow down, or change direction.

1. **Main Idea and Details** Use the graphic organizer below to list two details and the main idea found in the last paragraph of the text.

Detail	Detail

Main Idea

When a pitcher throws a baseball, he or she exerts a force on the ball.

When a batter hits a baseball, he or she exerts a force on the ball with the bat

There are a lot of examples of forces in sports such as baseball or softball.

2. **Identify** When you catch a baseball it exerts a force on your glove. What other force is being exerted at the same time?

A. The ground is exerting a force on the ball.
B. The glove is exerting a force on the ball.
C. The ball is exerting a force on the batter.
D. The batter is exerting a force on the ball.

When a player catches a baseball in his or her glove, the ball exerts a force on the glove.

When a player runs from base to base, the player's foot exerts a force on the ground.

Contact Forces

Car mechanics use forces to lift tires and pull tool carts. These forces cannot act unless the mechanic touches the object to be moved. The object may be touched directly with a hand or using a handle or a rope, but there must be contact. A force that requires two pieces of matter to touch is called a **contact force.** You exert a contact force when you push or pull a piece of furniture.

One kind of contact force is friction. **Friction** is the force that results when two materials rub against each other or when their contact prevents sliding. Friction makes it harder for one surface to move past another. The amount of friction between two objects may depend on their texture, shape, speed, and weight. It may also depend on whether or not the surfaces are wet.

Solids are not the only materials that can cause friction. Air and water also resist motion when an object pushes against them. Air resistance is a type of friction that is present when particles of air contact a surface. Water causes a similar type of friction. Submarines and ships are designed with shapes that help them reduce friction and move through water easily.

4. CHALLENGE Why do you think mechanics need to change tires during races?

The smooth, compact shape of race cars reduces air resistance so that the cars can go fast. By contrast, the wide area of an open parachute increases air resistance, slowing the fall.

3. Circle the arrow that shows the direction of air resistance on the parachute.

8
3
5
PIT CREW
PIT CREW
This mechanic is pushing on a lever so she can lift one side of the car.
This member of the pit crew is pulling a worn-out tire off the car.
Many shoes have rough soles that increase friction with the ground and prevent slipping.

The large amount of friction between the tires and the track makes it harder for cars to slide out of control. Friction also causes the brakes on the back of inline skates to slow or stop the skater.

5. **Design** Suppose you are planning an outdoor test to measure the performance of a new design of inline skate brake. Why would rain be an important factor to consider?

Non-Contact Forces

For friction to work, two things need to touch. There has to be contact between two surfaces or contact with a gas or a liquid. But there are forces that can act at a distance. They work even if the object that is pushing or pulling is not touching the object being pushed or pulled! A force that acts at a distance is called a **non-contact force.** Three examples of non-contact forces are gravity, electric forces, and magnetic forces.

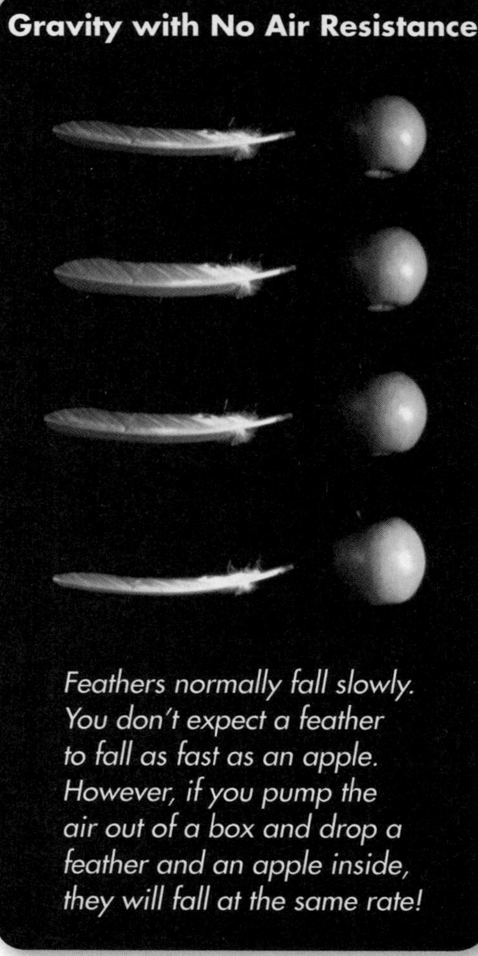

Gravity with No Air Resistance

Feathers normally fall slowly. You don't expect a feather to fall as fast as an apple. However, if you pump the air out of a box and drop a feather and an apple inside, they will fall at the same rate!

Gravity

Every object in the universe exerts a pull on every other object. This force of attraction between any two objects is called **gravity.** Only the gravity of a large object such as Earth is strong enough to cause effects that we can notice easily. Without gravity, things would not fall. Gravity pulls objects toward Earth's center without touching them.

The weight of an object is just the force of Earth's pull on that object. As an object moves away from Earth, the object weighs less and less because the pull of Earth's gravity becomes weaker and weaker with distance.

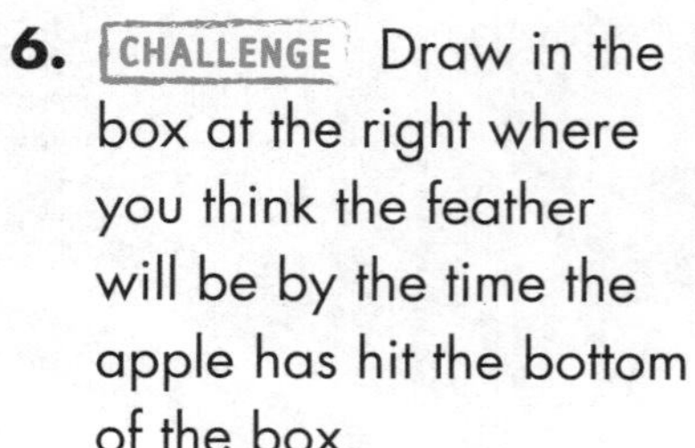

6. CHALLENGE Draw in the box at the right where you think the feather will be by the time the apple has hit the bottom of the box.

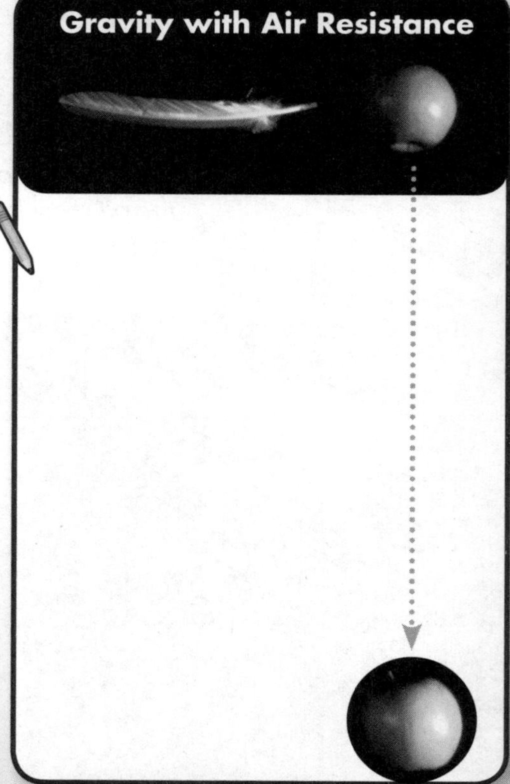

Gravity with Air Resistance

Lab zone Quick Lab

Does Gravity Affect You?

Stand. Stretch your left arm overhead. Leave your right arm at your side. Wait for 1 minute. Then compare the color of the palms of your hands. Share what you notice.

TEKS 2A

Electric and Magnetic Forces

Electric forces act between objects that are electrically charged. Oppositely charged objects are attracted to each other and tend to move toward each other. Objects with the same charge repel each other and tend to move away from each other.

Magnets will pull strongly on objects made of some metals, such as iron, cobalt, and nickel. Every magnet has a north pole and a south pole. Magnetic force is greatest at a magnet's poles. The north pole of one magnet will pull on the south pole of another magnet. The north poles of two magnets will push away from each other. The south poles of two magnets will act in the same way.

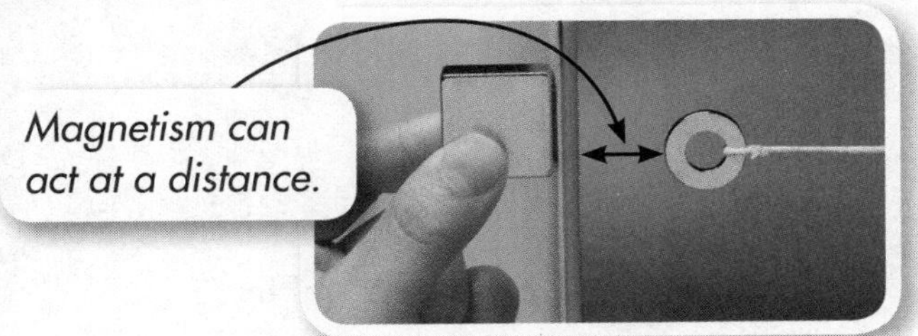

Magnetism can act at a distance.

After this comb was used to straighten dry hair, it became electrically charged.

7. **Analyze** What is happening to the bits of paper?

....

....

....

got it?

8. **Identify** What are some forces that might affect a rock as it tumbles down a hill?

....

....

9. **Conclude** If Earth is pulling down on you, are you pulling up on Earth? Explain.

....

....

Stop! I need help with ....

Wait! I have a question about ....

Go! Now I know ....

What are Newton's Laws?

LESSON 2

I will know TEKS 6D
I will know that forces cause changes in motion. I will know that Newton's three laws of motion describe force and motion.
(Also 1A, 1B, 2D, 2E)

Vocabulary
acceleration

Connect to Math

Math TEKS 7

Jackrabbits are found in most regions of Texas. Jackrabbits are not really rabbits. They are hares. Although hares and rabbits look similar, they do have differences. Jackrabbits are eaten by many other animals, including coyotes, bobcats, owls, and hawks. One way that a jackrabbit defends itself against other animals is running. Jackrabbits are capable of reaching speeds of up to about 40 miles per hour. How many feet are in 40 miles? (Remember that 1 mile = 5,280 ft.)

Quick Lab

TEKS 6D, 1A, 2D, 2E

How can forces affect motion?

Materials

metric ruler with groove
2 metal marbles

Texas Safety
LAB RULES

Do not throw marbles; roll them.
Pick up marbles after each trial.
Avoid stepping on marbles.

- [ ] **1.** Place the ruler on a flat, level surface. Put Marble **A** in the groove of the ruler at the 10 cm mark. Put Marble **B** in the groove at the 20 cm mark.
- [ ] **2.** **Predict** What will happen if you push **A** so that it hits **B**?
- [ ] **3.** Test your prediction. Demonstrate that repeated investigations may increase the reliability of results by repeating your test 4 times. Tell whether your results were the same each time.

Explain Your Results

4. **Analyze and Interpret** Describe the forces that affected each marble.

5. Share your results. Discuss why tests should be repeated. Tell why an **investigation** should be repeatable by others.

6. How would you change the design of this experiment if bowling balls were used instead of marbles?

Marble **A**

Marble **B**

Changes in Motion

Have you ever observed the motion of a car? When the car approaches a red light, the driver steps on the brake pedal. The speed of the car drops to zero. When the light turns green, the driver steps on the gas pedal. The speed climbs from zero. If the car has to turn a corner, the driver turns the steering wheel. The car changes direction.

When an object speeds up, slows down, or changes direction, its motion changes. The rate at which the speed or the direction of motion of an object changes over time is its **acceleration.**

When we speak of acceleration, we usually mean going faster and faster, but in science the word *acceleration* means *any* change in motion. For example, the circular motion of a Ferris wheel is accelerated. Even if the wheel turns with constant speed, the riders change direction all the time. They go up, then forward, then down, and then backward.

An object has no acceleration if it moves in a straight line without changing its speed or direction, or if it is not moving at all. Motion without acceleration is called uniform motion. The word *uniform* tells us that the motion does not change. A train traveling at a steady speed on a straight track has uniform motion. A book sitting on a table also has uniform motion. Its speed is zero.

1. **Explain** Think about a person standing on an escalator as it moves up or down. What kind of motion does that person have? Why?

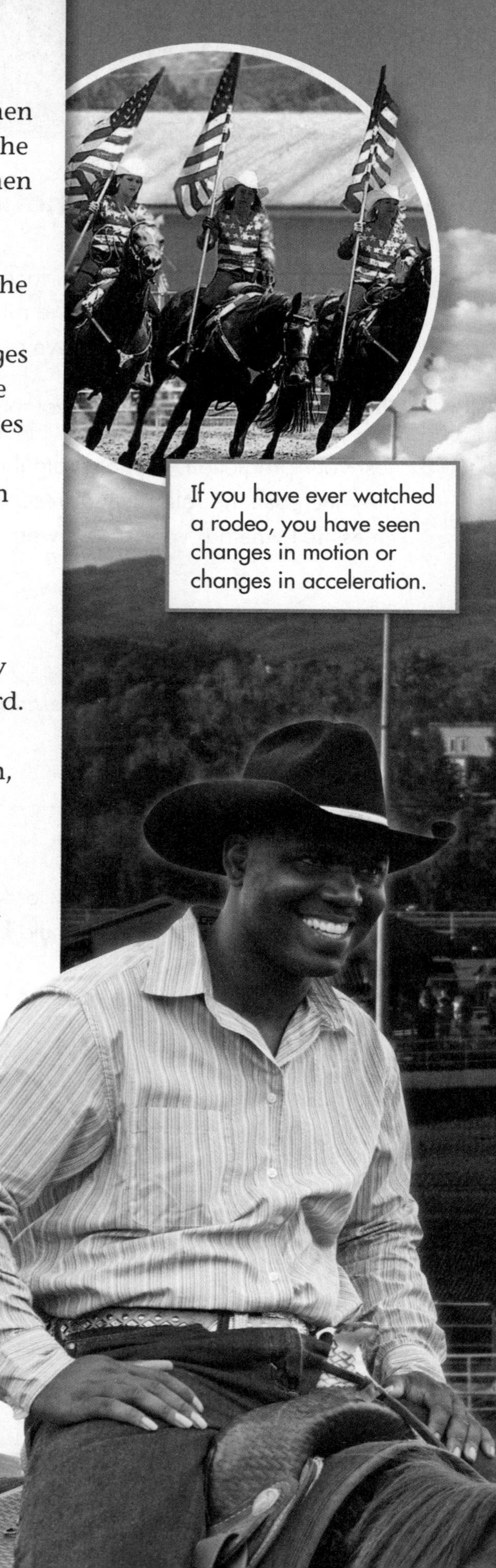

If you have ever watched a rodeo, you have seen changes in motion or changes in acceleration.

When there is no change in motion, such as when an object moves in a straight line without changing speed or if the object is not moving, the object has uniform motion. This horse and rider have no acceleration, and they have uniform motion.

When a horse starts running from a stop, the horse is accelerating because there is a change in speed. The horse's speed is getting faster.

When a horse slows down or stops, the horse also is accelerating because there is a change in speed. The horse is slowing down.

Even though the horse slows down to go around the barrel, the horse is accelerating because it is changing direction.

Newton's First Law

Newton's first law of motion says that an object will stay in uniform motion unless a net force acts on the object. Without that force, an object at rest will stay at rest. An object in motion will keep the same speed and direction. For example, a marble will stay still on the floor unless you push it. If the marble is already moving, it will continue to move at a constant speed in a straight line until a force acts on it.

The tendency of an object to resist any change in motion is known as inertia. Objects with a lot of mass have more inertia than objects with less mass. Your body's inertia is what pushes you against the side of a car when the car turns. Your body tends to keep moving in a straight line when the car changes direction. The car must push you as it turns. Inertia is also what makes your body rise up from your seat when the car goes up and over a steep hill. At the top of the hill, your body tends to continue going forward as the car begins to move down the hill.

Things you push or throw eventually will stop. This is because there are other forces acting on these objects. For example, friction and air resistance will slow down a rolling marble until it stops. However, a space probe will keep moving through space because it has no friction to slow it down. Even without fuel, a space probe can travel a long distance by inertia. It only needs fuel to change direction or to slow down.

2. Main Idea and Details Read the second paragraph again. **Circle** the main idea and **underline** two details.

3. Infer Why do standing passengers fall forward when a bus stops?

4. CHALLENGE Why is fuel needed to change the speed or direction of a probe in space?

A crash-test dummy has inertia. Even if a moving car is stopped in a crash, the inertia of the dummy will keep it moving forward.

The bowling ball has inertia. Inertia will keep it rolling for many meters, even after the player releases it.

5. Use blue to color the part of the arrow where a force is pushing the ball, and red to color the part of the arrow where the ball is moving only by inertia.

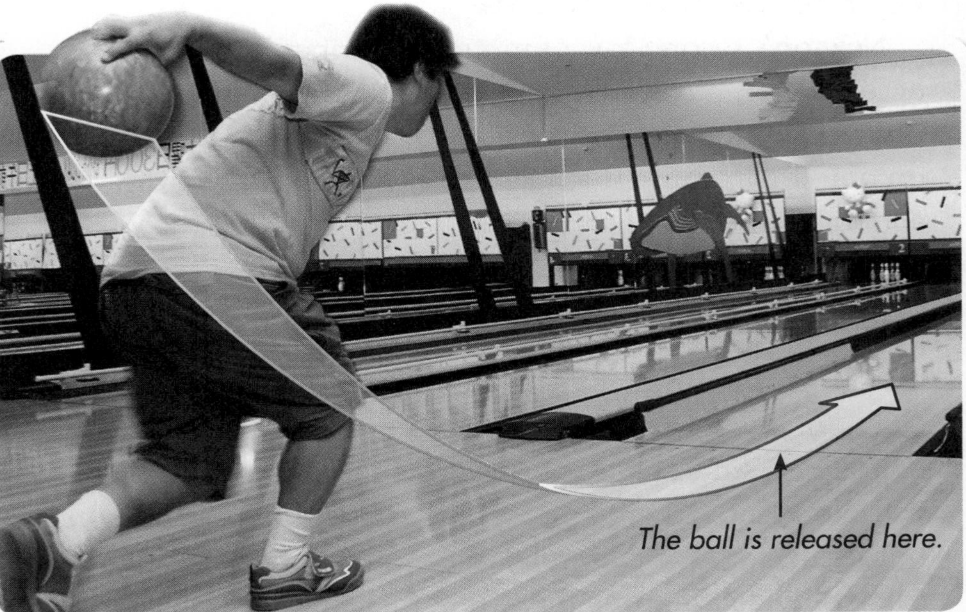

The ball is released here.

6. Suggest What could prevent the test dummy's inertia from carrying the dummy through the windshield?

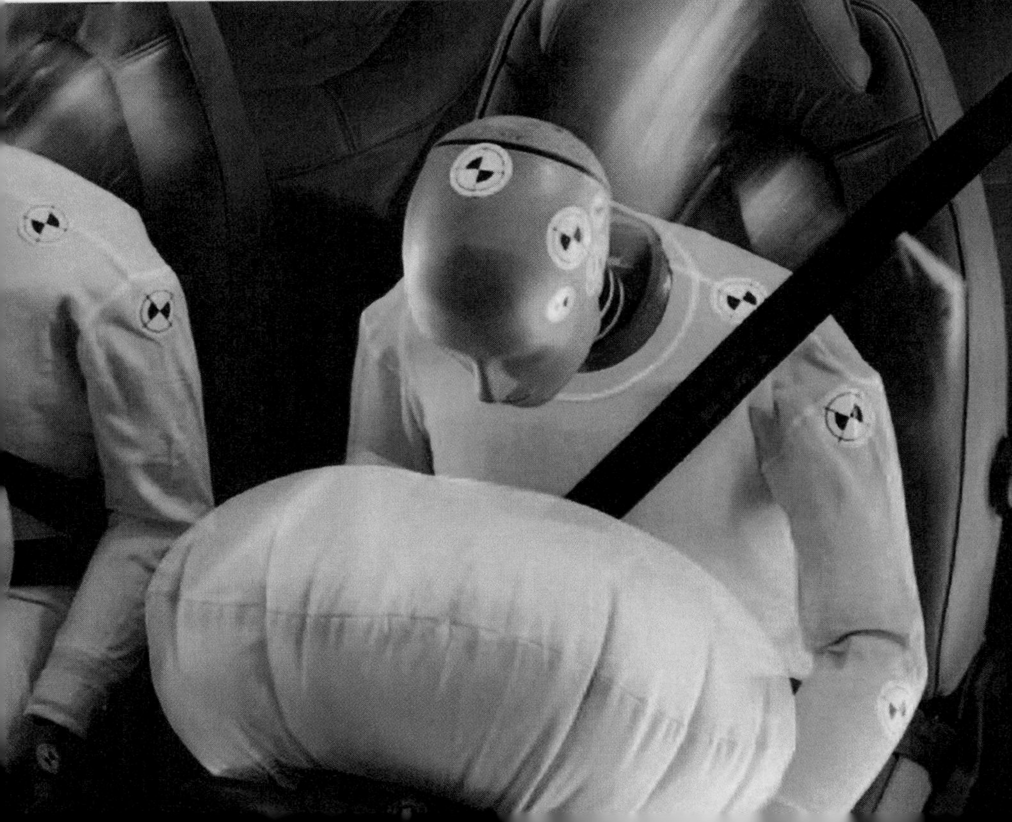

Lab zone Quick Lab

Carry Less, Save Gas
Use your understanding of force and mass to make informed choices in the conservation of materials. More force (and gasoline) is needed to get a heavier car moving. Some people drive with heavy loads they do not need—a bag of fertilizer, sports equipment, and so on. Reducing those loads by 50 kg can reduce fuel use by 2%! Work with an adult to find the mass of unneeded items carried in a car you ride in regularly. Based on your findings, choose a rule that would help the driver conserve gasoline.

TEKS 1B

Newton's Second Law

Newton's second law of motion describes how acceleration, mass, and force are related. Force is the product of mass and acceleration. The force acting on an object can cause the object to speed up, slow down, or change direction.

Same Force, Different Masses

Newton's second law says that the greater the mass of the object, the smaller its change in motion will be for a given force. This means that the same force will cause an object with small mass to accelerate more than an object with large mass. Large masses are harder to accelerate and harder to stop. For example, the engine and brakes of a truck provide the same forces whether the truck is empty or loaded. However, the loaded truck has more mass and will accelerate more slowly. It will also take longer to stop. Truck drivers must be aware of Newton's second law in order to drive safely.

7. Compare The engine shown can push either boat with the same force. **Circle** the boat that is more likely to experience less acceleration with this engine. Tell why.

Same Mass, Different Forces

Newton's second law of motion also says that the greater the force applied, the greater the change in motion for a given mass. In other words, a large force will produce more acceleration than a small force acting on the same object.

You can see this law at work in the Olympic sport of archery. Archers shoot arrows at targets. The archer must be sure that the arrow starts moving with just the right speed and direction in order to reach the target. The arrow starts at rest. The archer bends the bow by pulling on the bow string. The amount of bending controls the force that will accelerate the arrow. This force changes the motion of the arrow. When the arrow leaves the bow, it is traveling very fast. The same arrow can experience different accelerations depending on the amount of stretching of the bow.

8. Predict If the archer pulls the string to B instead of to A, there will be less force on the arrow. How will this affect the acceleration of the arrow?

A

B

9. Infer Look at the shape of the bow and string to the right. How can you tell that a force will act on the arrow when the string is released?

Connect to

Math

Math TEKS 4B, 7

Using Formulas

The formula that describes the relationship between force, mass, and acceleration is:

Force = Mass × Acceleration

This means that the stronger the force acting on an object, the more that object will accelerate. The formula is often written as follows:

$$F = m \times a$$

The unit of force in the metric system is called a newton (N). The unit of mass in the metric system is the kilogram (kg).
The unit of acceleration is the meter per second squared $\left(\frac{m}{s^2}\right)$.

$$1\ N = 1\ kg \times \frac{m}{s^2}$$

Example

A block with a mass of 12 kg is being pushed. Its acceleration is $5\ \frac{m}{s^2}$. What force is acting on the block?

Solve for the force, F. Use $m = 12$ kg, $a = 5\ \frac{m}{s^2}$

$F = m \times a$

$F = 12\ kg \times 5\ \frac{m}{s^2}$

$F = 60\ kg \times \frac{m}{s^2}$

$F = 60\ N$

Think: I know that $1\ kg \times \frac{m}{s^2} = 1\ N$, so $60\ kg \times \frac{m}{s^2} = 60\ N$

The force being applied to the block is 60 N.

1. A 25 kg block is being pushed and is accelerated at a rate of $6\ \frac{m}{s^2}$. What force is being applied to the block? Show your work.

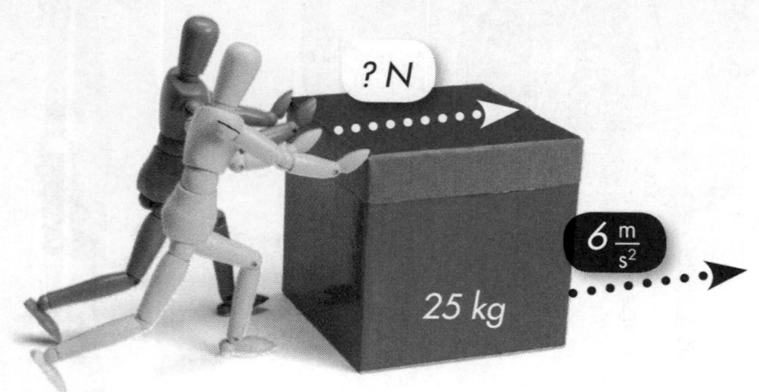

Work Area

Newton's Third Law

Newton's third law of motion states that when one object exerts a force on a second object, the second object exerts a force on the first. These forces are equal in strength and opposite in direction.

It is impossible to have one force without an equal and opposite force. For example, if you have ever ridden bumper cars, you know that when a moving car collides with a stationary car, both drivers feel the force of the collision. The driver of the stationary car feels a force and starts to move. The driver of the moving car feels an opposite force that slows the moving car.

10. Choose Suppose the girl on the left bumps the car on the right. Which girl feels a bigger bump? Explain.

....

....

got it?

11. Explain What is needed to give a large boulder a large acceleration?

....

....

12. Suppose a train engine is pulling ten cars. The last car becomes separated from the train. What happens to the motion of the rest of the train?

....

....

Stop! I need help with ....

Wait! I have a question about ....

Go! Now I know ....

TEXAS

Forces and Their Effects

Evaluating Promotional Materials

TEKS 3B Promotional materials are used to get you to purchase a product or service. Often, advertisers use scientific information in their promotional materials. However, the information may or may not be factual. You must think carefully and draw inferences about the accuracy of the information. Ask yourself questions such as: Is there something that seems too good to be true? Are there data that don't match what I already know? What information am I not seeing?

Read the following promotional materials. Can you spot the inaccurate information?

Evaluate Evaluate the accuracy of the information related to promotional materials for services. Circle two statements in the advertisement that you believe to be inaccurate.

Lightning-Fast Tutoring Service

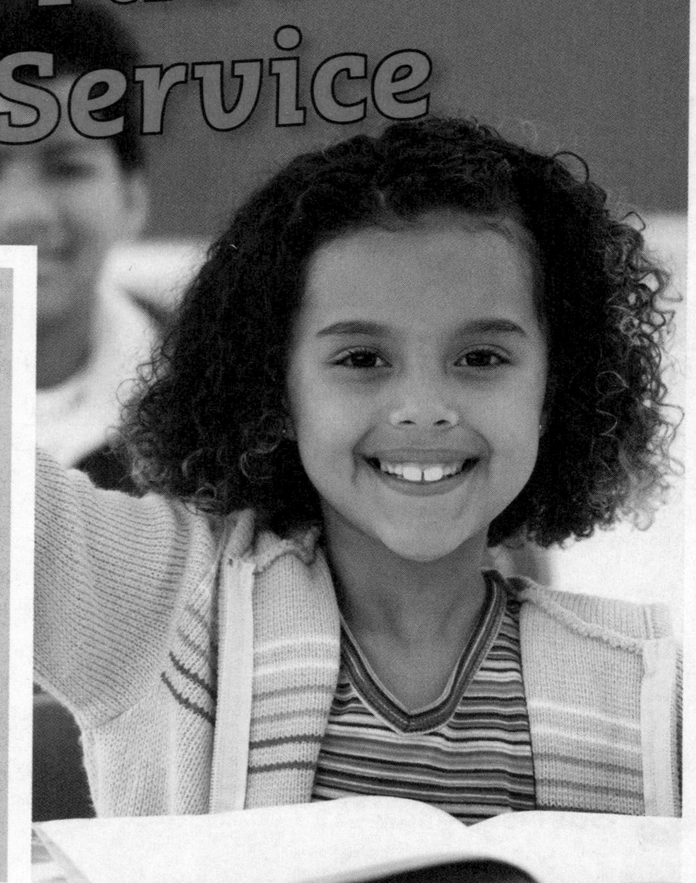

Learn everything about forces and their effects in just 5 minutes!

Are you struggling to understand forces and their effects? If so, struggle no more! Scientists have discovered an amazing new tutoring process.

In just 5 minutes, our specially trained tutors can teach you everything there is to know about forces and their effects. Over 150 percent of the students who use our tutoring services pass the Texas standardized tests with outstanding scores!

What are you waiting for? Change your life!

Our scientifically engineered bicycles are perfect for you! Ride them to work, school, or the gym. Our bikes:

Have frames made of 100% aluminum, the lightest metal. This makes our bikes light and very easy to steer and to transport. And you can brake on a dime!

Keep you healthy! Aluminum has magnetic properties that protect your joints.

Save the environment! We use only recycled aluminum, which does not use up energy resources.

Have no-slip hyper-friction tires that never slip, no matter how hard you apply the brakes.

Evaluate Evaluate the accuracy of the information related to promotional materials for products. Which statements in the advertisement sound too good to be true? Don't forget to use what you have learned about forces and their effects!

Lab zone® Lab Investigation

TEKS 6D, 1A, 2C, 2D, 2E, 2F, 4A

What forces affect the motion of a rocket?

Materials

safety goggles
string
straw
tape
paper bag
balloon
meterstick

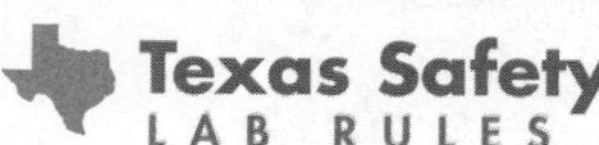

Wear safety goggles.
Do not blow up the balloon too much.

Follow a Procedure

- [ ] **1.** Tie one end of a 10-meter piece of string to a chair. Slide a straw onto the string. Tape a paper bag to the straw. Tie the other end of the string to another chair. Make the string tight by pulling the chairs apart. Slide the bag to the middle of the string.
- [ ] **2.** Blow up a long balloon. Hold the neck end closed. Put the other end in the bag. This will be your rocket.
- [ ] **3.** **Observe** Let go of the balloon. What happened?

....

Inquiry Skill

Before you **predict,** think about what you have already observed.

- [ ] **4.** Slide the bag to one end of the string. Blow up the balloon again. Place the balloon in the bag.
- [ ] **5.** **Predict** how far the rocket will move.

....

....

- [ ] **6.** Let go of the balloon. Collect information by accurate measuring by using a meterstick to measure how far the rocket moved. Repeat 2 more times.

7. **Record** your data below. Find the average distance for the 3 trials. Add the 3 distances and divide by 3.

Rocket Data	
	Distance (m)
Trial 1	
Trial 2	
Trial 3	
Average	

Scientists often make observations again and again. Repeating trials helps them be sure what they have observed is accurate.

Analyze and Conclude

8. **Observe** Analyze information using a meterstick. Compare how far the rocket moved in each trial.

9. **Infer** What caused the rocket to move in the direction that it moved?

10. What made the rocket move? How do you know?

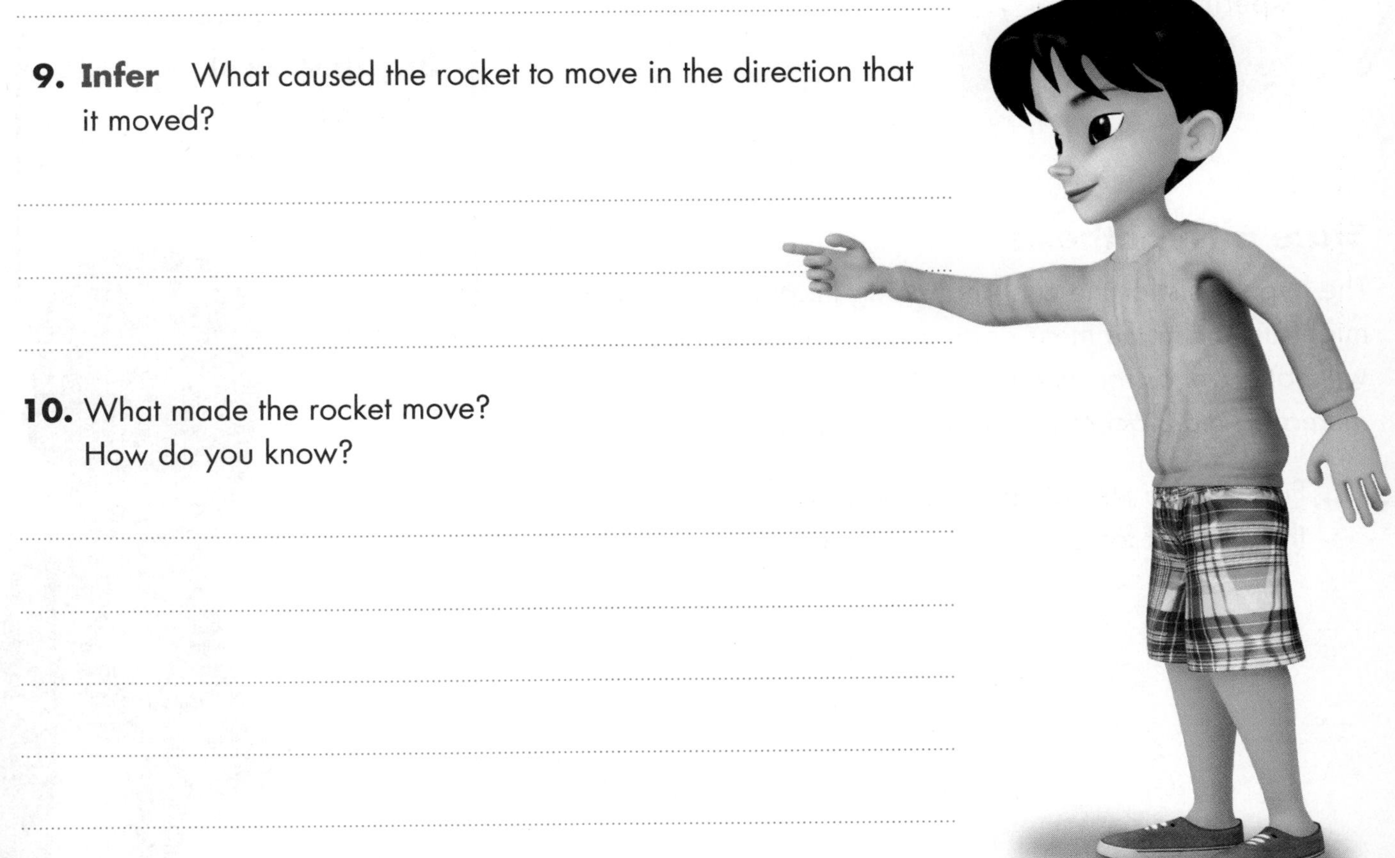

Lab Investigation

TEKS 6D, 1A, 2A, 2B, 2C, 2D, 2F, 2G, 3A, 4A

How does force affect the motion of different masses?

A force can cause an object to move. You will design an experiment that tests the effect of force on objects with different masses.

Materials

2 metric rulers

$\frac{1}{2}$ of a plastic cup and metal marble

2 books

tape and 4 pennies

pan balance and gram cubes

graphing calculator or computer

Note: These materials would be used to test the effect of a rolling marble on the motion of a cup. Other materials may be needed depending on your design.

Ask a Question

If you were designing an experiment to test the effect of a rolling marble when it hits a plastic cup, you might wonder how far the cup will travel when the marble pushes it. In that case, you could ask a question like, *What effect does the mass of a cup have on the distance a rolling marble will move the cup?*

1. With the help of your teacher, think of a question you would like to investigate about the effect of forces on objects. Write a well-defined question for your experiment.

Texas Safety LAB RULES

Identify potential safety hazards and know which precautions to take.

State a Hypothesis

The hypothesis for the cup and rolling marble experiment might be this: *If the mass of a cup is increased, then the cup will not travel as far when it is hit by the rolling marble. The increased mass decreases the distance traveled by the cup.*

2. Formulate a testable hypothesis for your experiment on the effect of force on objects with different masses.

Inquiry Skill

A **hypothesis** is a statement that explains an observation. It can be tested by an experiment.

Identify and Control Variables

In the cup and marble experiment, the distance the cup moves is measured. You can change only one variable. Everything else must remain the same. Possible variables that can change include ramp height, ramp length, mass of marbles, mass of cups or toy cars, roughness of rolling surface, etc.

☐ **3.** Plan a simple experimental investigation testing one variable. What is the one variable that you will change in your experiment?

Design Your Test

☐ **4.** Describe a simple experimental investigation testing one variable. Draw how you will set up your test.

☐ **5.** Select appropriate equipment. What equipment or materials will you need to perform your experiment?

☐ **6.** List your steps in the order in which they will be performed.

Do Your Test

7. Follow the steps you wrote.

If you are testing the effect of a force on objects of different masses, you might use a balance and gram cubes to find the masses of objects.

8. Make sure to **measure** accurately. **Record** your results in a table.

9. Scientists repeat their tests to improve their accuracy. Repeat your test if time allows.

Collect and Record

10. Collect information by detailed observation and measuring. Fill in the chart.

Work like a Scientist

Clear and active communication is an essential part of performing scientific investigations. Talk with your classmates. Compare your methods and results.

Interpret Your Data

☐ **11.** Use your data construct a simple graph, using a computer, to organize and evaluate your information.

☐ **12.** Look at your graph closely. Describe the effect of force on the object or objects you chose for your test. Identify the (observable or inferred) evidence you used to answer the question.

Technology Tools
Select and use appropriate technology to collect, organize, examine, evaluate, and present data. Use a computer (with the right software) or a graphing calculator. These tools can help you construct appropriate tables, charts, and simple graphs.

State your conclusion.

13. Communicate valid conclusions in written form. Compare your hypothesis with your results. Compare your results with those of others.

MY PLANET DIARY

Free Fall

You may have seen video clips of astronauts floating around in a spacecraft. People often think astronauts have no weight at all in space, but they do. Most astronauts work just 300 km above ground. This is relatively close to Earth. At that height, they are only a few pounds lighter. They seem to float because their spacecraft is moving along with them. However, the spacecraft and the astronauts are both falling, just like a skydiver. The spacecraft and the astronauts don't crash because they are also moving forward fast enough to follow the curvature of Earth.

Which everyday activities do you think would be easier in orbit?

....

....

....

Earth exerts a force on the astronauts even when they are 300 km from the surface of Earth.

The skydiver falls to the surface of Earth because Earth exerts a force on him.

Vocabulary Smart Cards

force
contact force
friction
non-contact force
gravity
acceleration

Play a Game!

Cut out the Vocabulary Smart Cards.

Work with a partner.

Choose a Vocabulary Smart Card.

Say as many words as you can think of that describe that vocabulary word.

Have your partner try to guess the word.

a push or pull that acts on an object

Use this word in a sentence.

empujón o jalón que se le da a un objeto

a force that acts at a distance

Use this word in a sentence.

fuerza que actúa a distancia

a force that requires two pieces of matter to touch

Draw an example of this word.

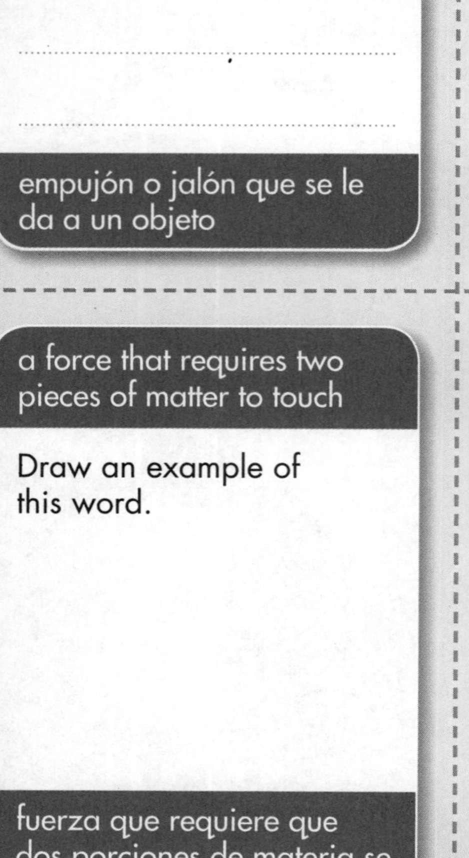

fuerza que requiere que dos porciones de materia se toquen

the force of attraction between any two objects

Use this word in a sentence.

fuerza de atracción entre dos cuerpos cualesquiera

the force that results when two materials rub against each other or when their contact prevents sliding

Write an example of this word.

fuerza que resulta al frotar un material contra otro o cuando el contacto entre ambos impide el deslizamiento

the rate at which the speed or direction of motion of an object changes over time

Write three other forms of this word.

ritmo al cual cambia la rapidez o la dirección del movimiento de un objeto con el tiempo

Interactive Vocabulary

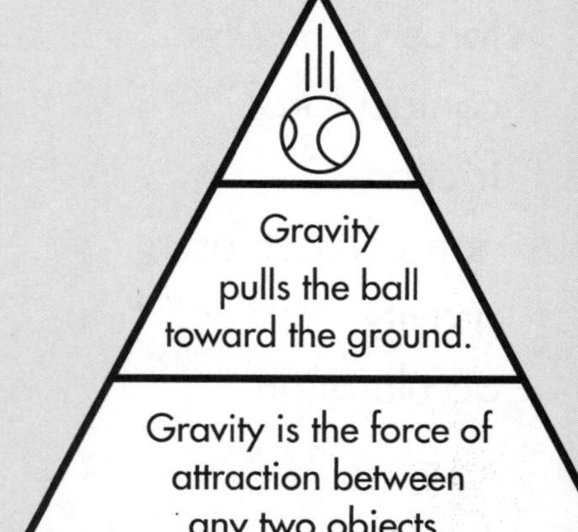

Gravity pulls the ball toward the ground.
Gravity is the force of attraction between any two objects.

Make a Word Pyramid!

Choose a vocabulary word and write the definition in the base of the pyramid. Write a sentence in the middle of the pyramid. Draw a picture of an example, or of something related, at the top.

TEKS Practice

Lesson 1 TEKS 6D

What are forces?

1. **Main Idea and Details** Underline the main idea and circle the details in the following paragraph.

When you ride a roller coaster, the roller coaster exerts forces on you in many ways. You could test this statement by riding a roller coaster. When the roller coaster starts, it might feel like something is pushing you back against the seat. What really happens is the roller coaster is pushing your body forward. When you go downhill, your body falls forward. The safety bar exerts a force on you to keep you in your seat.

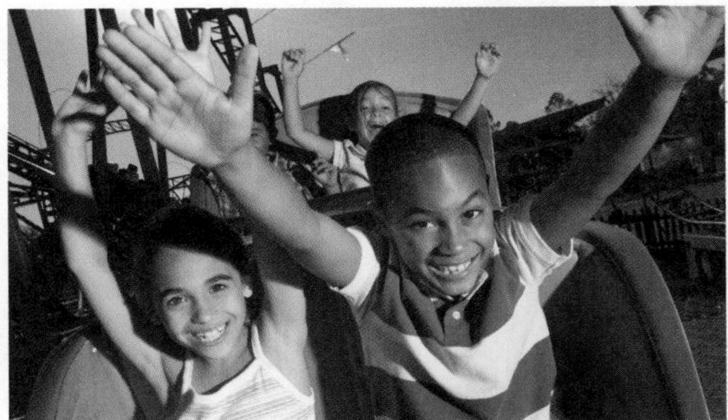

2. **Interpret** Write a *T* for true or an *F* for false.

_________ Magnets exert forces on objects from a distance.

_________ Friction exerts forces on objects from a distance.

_________ Gravity exerts a force on objects by contact.

3. **Explain** How can the shapes of a boat and an airplane affect how water and wind forces act on the objects?

4. **Identify** Which of the following is a contact force?
   A. electric
   B. friction
   C. gravity
   D. magnetic

5. **Analyze** What type of force is acting on the object?

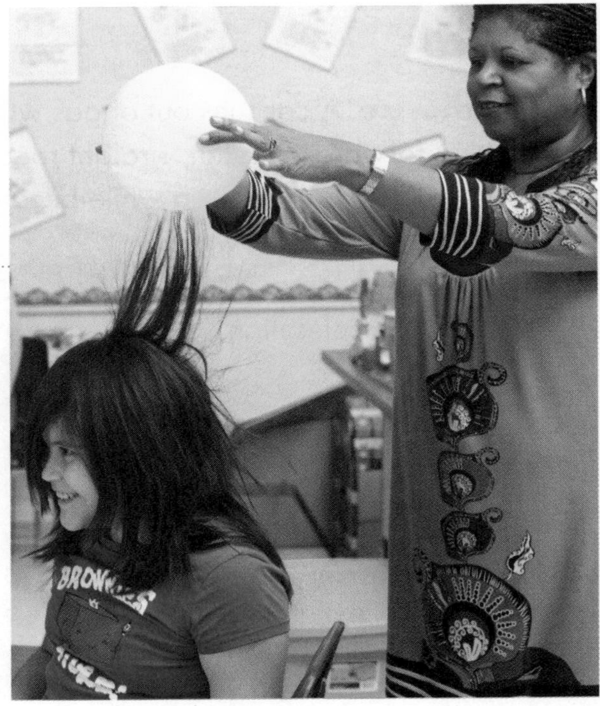

TEKS Practice

Lesson 2 TEKS 6D

6. Synthesize Which laws of motion are demonstrated when a hammer exerts a force on a nail?

7. Explain A batter hits a baseball with a bat. The bat exerts a force on the ball. Does the ball exert a force on the bat? Explain.

8. Synthesize A car runs out of gas while moving forward on a flat, straight road. The car keeps rolling for a while because

A. gravity pulls it forward.
B. it still has force.
C. it has acceleration.
D. it has inertia.

9. Think About It In space, where there is no air and gravity is weak, space probes can travel millions of miles without using any fuel. How do forces affect the motion of a space probe?

10. A force of 20 N accelerates a 2-kg object. How much force is needed to give the same acceleration to a 20-kg object?

A. 10 N
B. 10 kg
C. 200 N
D. 400 kg

11 Identify Which of the following is NOT an example of accelerated motion?

A. an elevator going up at a constant speed
B. an elevator slowing down
C. an elevator speeding up
D. a car taking a curve at constant speed

TEKS Practice

12. Conclude A drummer hits a drum with a drumstick. The drumstick exerts a force on the drum. The reaction

A. is stronger than the action.
B. changes the motion of the drumstick.
C. drives the drum forward.
D. creates inertia.

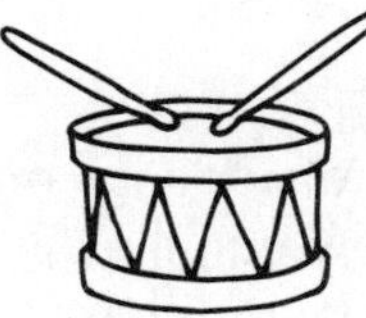

13. Plan If you are trying to design an experiment that tests the effect of a force on an object, which should you do first?

A. draw conclusions
B. make observations
C. write a well-defined question
D. formulate a testable hypothesis

14. Write About It A student kicks a soccer ball by applying a force. Describe what happens to the soccer ball.

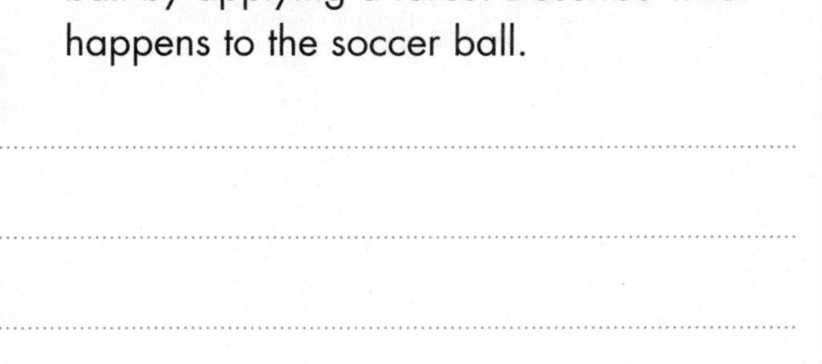

Chapter 4

Lesson 1 What are forces?

In Lesson 1, you learned that a force can cause motion in an object. You learned that there are different kinds of forces. Contact forces and non-contact forces are two different kinds of forces.

Supporting TEKS 6D

Lesson 2 What are Newton's Laws?

In Lesson 2, you learned Newton's three laws of motion that describe force and motion. You designed an experiment that tests the effect of force on an object.

Supporting TEKS 6D

★ TEKS Practice: Chapter Review

Read each question and circle the best answer.

1 A spring scale is a tool that measures the strength of a force. It has a scale marked with units of force, such as newtons. When you pull on the scale's hook, a pointer lines up with the marking that describes the strength of your pull in newtons. A student attaches a spring scale to a block, as shown below.

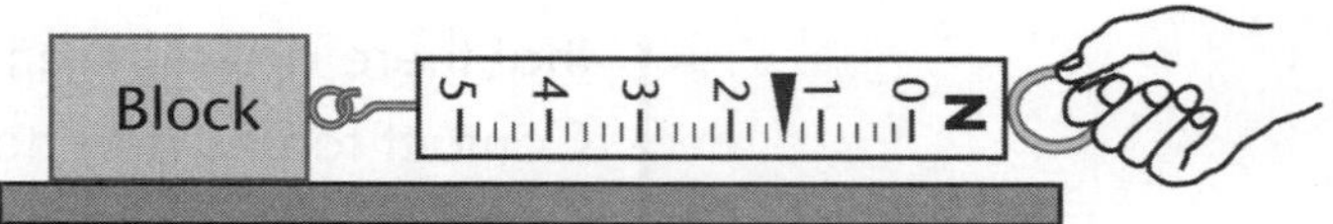

The student drags the block across a surface by pulling on the spring scale. The markings on the scale tell her the number of newtons of force needed to drag the block. How can the student use the spring scale to compare the force of friction between the block and different types of surfaces?

A She can pull harder on the spring scale.

B She can pull a bigger block across the surface.

C She can pull the block a greater distance across the surface.

D She can pull the same block across two different surfaces.

2 A skydiver's parachute is closed as he falls. Suddenly, he opens the parachute and his speed decreases. What caused this change in motion?

F Air resistance increased.

G Air resistance decreased.

H Gravity increased.

J Gravity decreased.

3 An object's motion will not change unless an outside force acts on it. Which graph shows the motion of an object that is moving with no outside force acting on it?

A

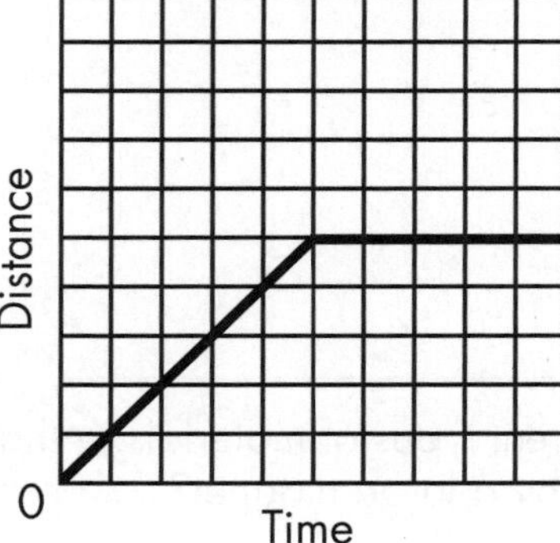

B

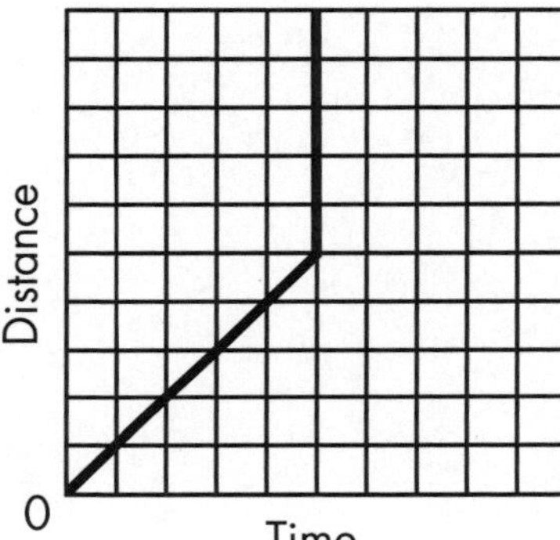

C

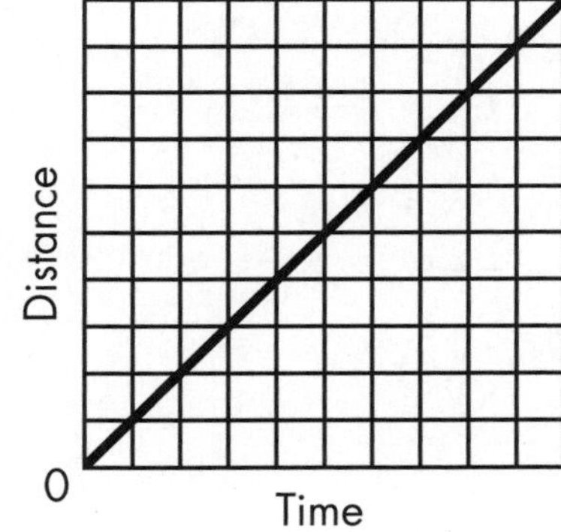

D

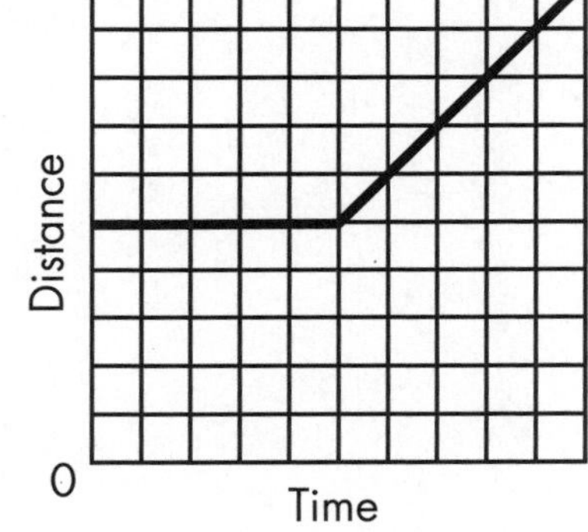

4 A 30-newton force can —

F give a 2 kg mass an acceleration of 15 m/s^2

G give a 3 kg mass an acceleration of 10 m/s^2

H give a 5 kg mass an acceleration of 6 m/s^2

J All of the above

5 Many recycling plants use a large magnet to separate different types of materials. What is one type of material that can be pulled from a pile of trash by a large magnet?

A Scrap iron

B Newspaper

C Glass bottles

D Aluminum cans

TEKS Practice: Cumulative Review

6 Sonar uses sound energy to find and map objects on the ocean floor. The picture below shows how sonar works.

Sonar

A boat's sonar device sends sound waves down to the ocean floor. A device on the boat records how long the sound waves take to travel back to the boat. Sound waves that return to the boat in a short time have struck nearby objects. Sound waves that take a long time to return to the boat have struck faraway objects. Which behavior of light waves is most like sonar?

F Light shining on your hand and warming it

G Light reflecting off a mirror

H Light refracting as it passes from air into water

J Light being separated into its different colors by a prism

---

7 The electric circuit shown in the diagram contains two batteries and two light bulbs connected by wires. Both light bulbs are lit.

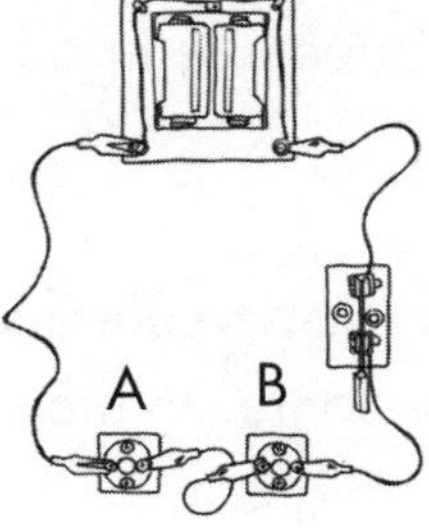

How would cutting the wire between light bulb A and the battery affect the circuit?

A Both light bulbs would stay lit.

B Both light bulbs would go out.

C Only light bulb A would go out.

D Only light bulb B would go out.

If you have trouble with . . .

Question	1	2	3	4	5	6	7
See chapter (lesson)	4 (1)	4 (1)	4 (2)	4 (2)	4 (1)	3 (3)	3 (4)
TEKS	6D	6D	6D	6D	6D	6A	6B

Lab zone® Open-Ended Inquiry

TEKS 5A, 1A, 1B, 2A, 2B, 2C, 2F, 3A, 4A

Materials

cup, clear plastic 9 oz
triple-beam balance
graduated cylinder
dark corn syrup
vegetable oil
water
calculator

If water or any other liquid spills, notify your teacher immediately.

Inquiry Skill

You **control variables** when you make sure the amounts you test for each item are the same. Controlling variables helps you make sure your experiment is a fair test.

How can you use density to classify matter?

You can compare relative density of matter by observing whether it floats or sinks. Matter will sink in a liquid if its density is greater and it will float if its density is lower.

Ask a question.

Can you use density to classify matter?

State a hypothesis.

☐ **1.** Write a **hypothesis** by finishing the sentence.

If different kinds of liquids are poured into a cup, then

....

Identify and control variables.

☐ **2.** When you conduct an **experiment,** you must change only one variable. The **variable** you change is the **independent variable.** What will you change?

....

☐ **3.** The **dependent variable** is the variable you observe or measure in an experiment. What will you observe?

....

☐ **4.** **Controlled variables** are the factors you must keep the same. Which factor are you keeping the same?

....

Design your test.

☑ **5.** Draw how you will set up your test.

☑ **6.** List your steps in the order in which you will do them.

Do your test.

☑ **7.** Follow the steps you wrote.

☑ **8.** Make sure to **record** your results in the table.

☑ **9.** Dispose of your materials. It is not good for the building's pipes or the environment to pour oil down the drain. Discuss other ways of dealing with oil waste, such as reusing, recycling, or throwing it away. Then make an informed choice in the disposal of your materials based on what you think is best.

Collect and record your data.

☑ **10.** Collect and analyze information using tools, including a triple-beam balance, graduated cylinder, and calculator, by filling in the chart.

To find the mass of the liquid, subtract the mass of the empty graduated cylinder from the mass of the graduated cylinder with liquid.

$$\text{mass of liquid} = \text{mass of graduated cylinder (with liquid)} - \text{mass of graduated cylinder (empty)}$$

To find the density, divide the mass of the liquid by the volume of the liquid.

$$\text{density} = \frac{\text{mass of liquid}}{\text{volume of liquid}}$$

Data Table

	Water	**Corn Syrup**	**Vegetable Oil**
Mass of graduated cylinder (empty)			
Mass of graduated cylinder (with liquid)			
Mass of liquid			
Volume of liquid			
Density of liquid			

Interpret your data.

11. Observe the items in the cup.

Which item floated on top? ....

Which item was in the middle? ....

Which item sank to the bottom? ....

12. How do your density calculations compare to the order of the layers in your cup?

....

....

....

State your conclusion.

13. Review the information on relative densities at the beginning of the inquiry. Critique this scientific explanation by using observational testing and empirical evidence from your investigation. Do you think density can be used to classify matter? What evidence supports your conclusion?

....

....

14. Evaluate and Critique Critique scientific explanations by examining all sides of scientific evidence of those scientific explanations. Compare your results with those of other groups. Does their evidence support the explanation of relative densities? Why or why not? Does their evidence make sense, based on what you observed? Why or why not?

....

....

....

....

15. Analyze Use a triple-beam balance to analyze information. Find three objects that have the same volume. Measure their masses using a triple-beam balance. Analyze this information to determine which object has the highest density.

....

....

Earth Science

Texas Essential Knowledge and Skills

Content TEKS

Earth and Space: 7A, 7B, 7C, 7D, 8A, 8B, 8C, 8D
Matter and Energy: 5A

Process TEKS

1A, 1B, 2A, 2B, 2C, 2D, 2E, 2F, 2G, 3A, 3C, 3D, 4A, 4B

What makes this ROCK look like a WAVE?

Earth's Surface

What kinds of processes cause Earth's surface and its resources to constantly change?

Wave Rock is a formation in Australia. It is about ten meters high and 100 meters long and is made of solid granite. Wave Rock's curved shape has taken millions of years to form.

What forces might have shaped this formation?

Texas Essential Knowledge and Skills

Readiness TEKS: 5A Classify matter based on physical properties, including mass, magnetism, physical state (solid, liquid, and gas), relative density (sinking and floating), solubility in water, and the ability to conduct or insulate thermal energy or electric energy. **7A** Explore the processes that led to the formation of sedimentary rocks and fossil fuels. **7B** Recognize how landforms such as deltas, canyons, and sand dunes are the result of changes to Earth's surface by wind, water, and ice. **7C** Identify alternative energy resources such as wind, solar, hydroelectric, geothermal, and biofuels.

Supporting TEKS: 7D Identify fossils as evidence of past living organisms and the nature of the environments at the time using models.

Process TEKS: 1A, 1B, 2A, 2B, 2C, 2D, 2F, 3A, 3C, 4A, 4B

Lab zone® Inquiry Warm-Up

TEKS 7A, 7D, 2D, 2F, 3A, 3C

How can you make a model of the fossil record?

Sedimentary rock forms when bits of rock and materials settle on top of one another and harden into layers over time. Dead plants and animals leave their marks or remains in the layers, forming fossils. Scientists study the fossils found in layers of sedimentary rock to understand past environments.

Materials

paper
colored markers
metric ruler
scissors
glue or tape

Be careful with sharp objects.

Inquiry Skill

Making a model can help you understand a process.

1. **Make a model** of sedimentary rock layers. Use a ruler and colored markers to draw 4 layers on a piece of paper. Make each layer at least 4 cm thick.
2. Research how horses, elephants, sharks, or horseshoe crabs and their environments have changed over time. Take notes and gather pictures of fossils from four different times in Earth's past. Print the pictures or draw them on paper.
3. Cut out the pictures and glue or tape them on the layers, in order of age. The oldest fossil should be in the bottom layer.

Explain Your Results

4. **Communicate** Identify the nature of the environment at the time when your organism lived. Using your model and your notes, describe how your organism and its environment changed over time.

5. **Infer** Explain why you placed the oldest fossil in the bottom layer.

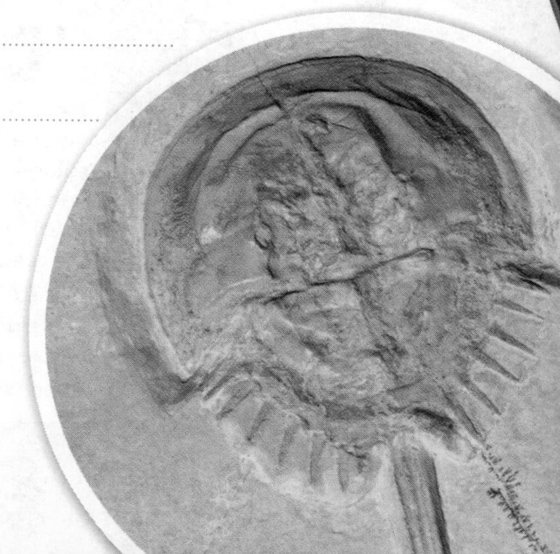

Focus on Sequence

You will practice the reading strategy of finding the **sequence** of events. The order in which events happen is the sequence. Signal words such as *first, next, then,* and *last* tell the order of events.

Fossils

A fossil is the preserved remains or traces of living things. Fossils such as this fish took many years to form. Millions of years ago this fish died and sank into shallow water. Next, mud and sand, or sediment, covered the fish. Last, the sediment became rock, preserving parts of the fish. Weather and the wearing away of land eventually exposed a fossil at the surface. Fossils are clues to how Earth's surface has changed.

Practice It!

Use the graphic organizer below to list a sequence of events found in the example paragraph.

First

....

Next

....

Last

....

Texas

LESSON 1

How do rocks form?

I will know TEKS 7A
I will know how sedimentary rocks and fossil fuels are formed. (Also 1A, 2A, 2B, 2C, 2D, 2F, 4A, 5A)

Vocabulary
mineral
igneous
sedimentary
metamorphic
rock cycle
nonrenewable resources

Connect to Social Studies

Social Studies TEKS 9A

Spanish explorers in what is today Texas noticed oil seeping from the ground in the 1500s. However, the quest for Texas oil did not begin until after the Civil War. Spurred by the demand for kerosene and other products made from oil, Texans drilled for the precious resource. The first Texas oil boom was launched when oil was discovered at Spindletop, south of Beaumont, in 1901. The find marked the beginning of the modern oil industry in Texas.

Explain Why were people eager to drill for oil after the Civil War?

Lab zone Quick Lab

TEKS 5A, 1A, 2A, 2B, 2C, 2D, 2F, 4A

What causes some rocks to float?

Materials

3 rocks
hand lens
plastic cup of water

Texas Safety LAB RULES

Wash your hands thoroughly upon completing the activity.

1. Hold and feel 3 rocks with your hands. Think of ways to describe them.
2. Analyze information about the rocks using a hand lens. List differences and similarities between the rocks.

....

....

....

3. Drop each rock into the cup of water. **Observe.**

Explain Your Results

4. **Communicate** Within your group and with other groups, communicate your valid conclusions in verbal form. Which of the rock samples floated? Explain why you think it floated.

....

....

....

Kinds of Rocks

There are three kinds of rocks. Each kind of rock is formed in a different way, but all rocks are made of minerals. A **mineral** is a nonliving, naturally occurring solid that has its own regular arrangement of particles in it. Some rocks are made up of just one mineral. Other rocks are made up of combinations of minerals. By looking at how the minerals in the rock are arranged, you can often determine how the rock was formed.

Igneous Rocks

Rocks that form when melted rock cools and hardens are called **igneous** rocks. Igneous rocks can form deep inside Earth or from lava that hardens on Earth's surface. As hot, liquid rock cools, crystals of minerals form. Melted rock that cools slowly results in igneous rocks with large crystals of minerals. Melted rock that cools quickly results in igneous rocks with small crystals.

Granite and basalt are examples of igneous rock. Granite forms when magma slowly cools far underground. Because it cools slowly, granite has large crystals of minerals you can see without a microscope. The texture of granite is rough. Basalt forms when lava cools quickly near Earth's surface. It has small crystals of minerals that can only be seen with a microscope. Basalt has a smoother texture than granite.

Pumice is a rock formed when lava is quickly cooled by air at the surface. It often has many tiny holes where gases were trapped in the lava as it cooled.

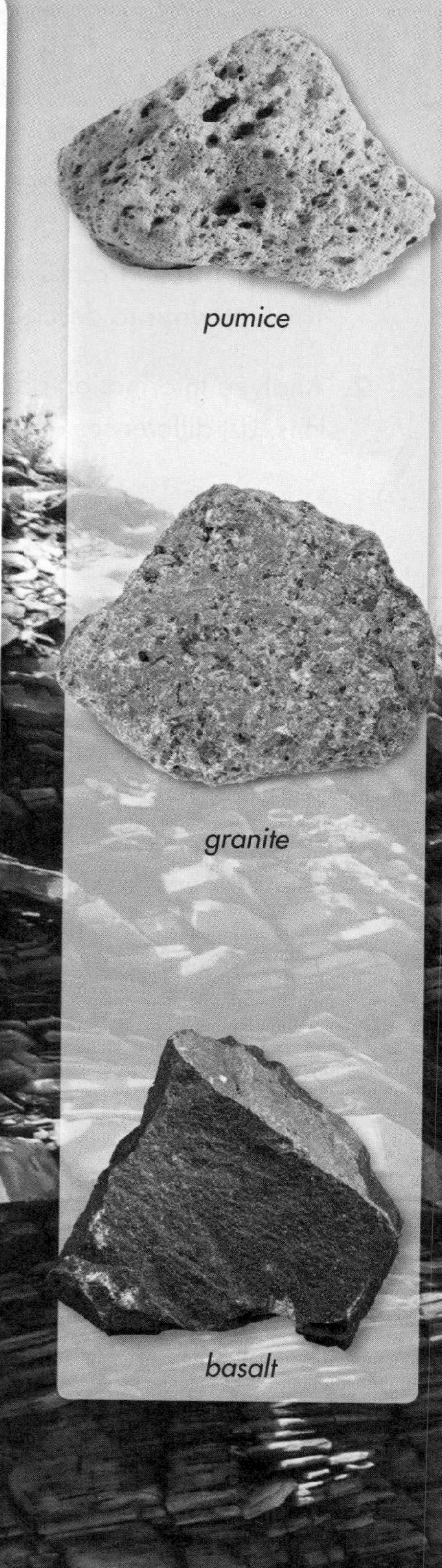
pumice

granite

basalt

1. **Apply** Does basalt have large or small crystals? What does this tell you about how and where basalt forms?

Sedimentary Rocks

Most **sedimentary** rocks form when layers of materials and rock particles settle on top of one another and then harden. This process takes thousands of years.

The process begins when water, ice, and wind cause existing rocks to break down to form pebbles, sand, or mud. Sometimes these small pieces mix with other materials such as plants or animal shells and bones. This loose material is called sediment.

Wind, water, and gravity carry the sediment away. It settles in low areas and along the shores of rivers, lakes, and oceans. Some sediment settles in the bottom of lakes or oceans.

Over time, layers of sediment build up. The weight of new layers presses down on older layers. Minerals from water may act like cement, holding the particles together. Eventually, the squeezed layers become rock.

Sandstone and conglomerate are examples of sedimentary rock. Sandstone can form when layers of sand are buried and put under pressure. Large, rounded particles that have been pressed together form conglomerate.

2. Sequence Explore the processes that led to the formation of sedimentary rocks by completing the graphic organizer below.

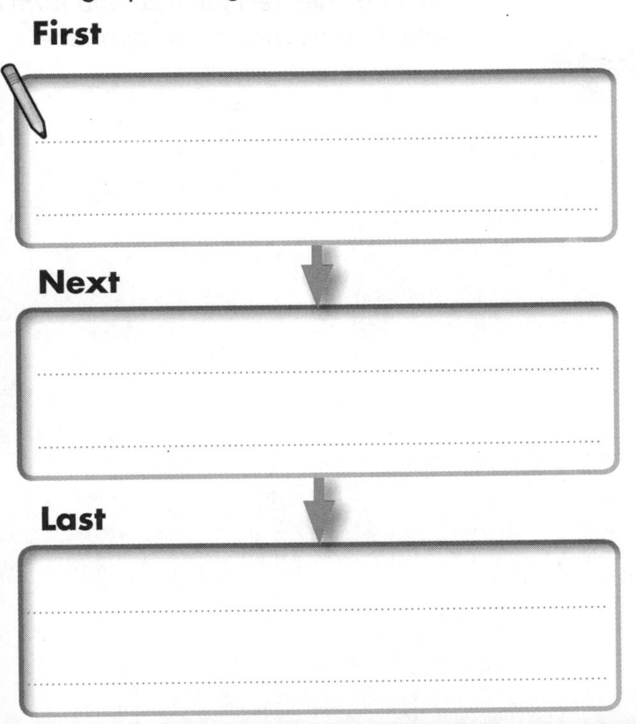

3. Identify Name each sedimentary rock below. Complete the captions.

________ is formed from large, rounded particles.

________ is formed from sand.

Rock It

Write a "rock" song that describes how igneous, sedimentary, and metamorphic rocks are formed. Give examples of each kind of rock.

TEKS 7A

gneiss

slate

marble

Metamorphic Rocks

When solid rock is squeezed and heated to very high temperatures, the particles inside the rock can take on different arrangements. New minerals may also be formed. These rocks are metamorphic rocks. **Metamorphic** rock is rock formed inside Earth from other rocks under heat and pressure. Under very high temperature and pressure, solid rock particles form rough layers, as seen in gneiss. At lower pressure, fine, thin layers are formed, as seen in slate.

Heat and squeezing can change igneous and sedimentary rocks into metamorphic rocks. Gneiss is formed when granite—an igneous rock—is heated and squeezed. Slate is formed when shale—a sedimentary rock—and other materials are squeezed and heated. Quartzite and marble are also formed from sedimentary rocks. Quartzite is formed from sandstone, and marble from limestone.

4. Sequence What can happen to rock particles after they are squeezed and heated to high temperatures?

When quartz crystals, like these, are exposed to increased temperature and pressure, they recrystallize and form a metamorphic rock called quartzite.

The Rock Cycle

Rocks are constantly being formed and destroyed in a process called the **rock cycle.** Rocks may be changed from one kind to another in any order or stay the same for millions of years. The remains of organisms can be part of the rock cycle. The diagram shows the different ways that one type of rock can become another type of rock.

5. **Interpret** Use the rock-cycle diagram to determine the type of rock that igneous rock can become.

....

....

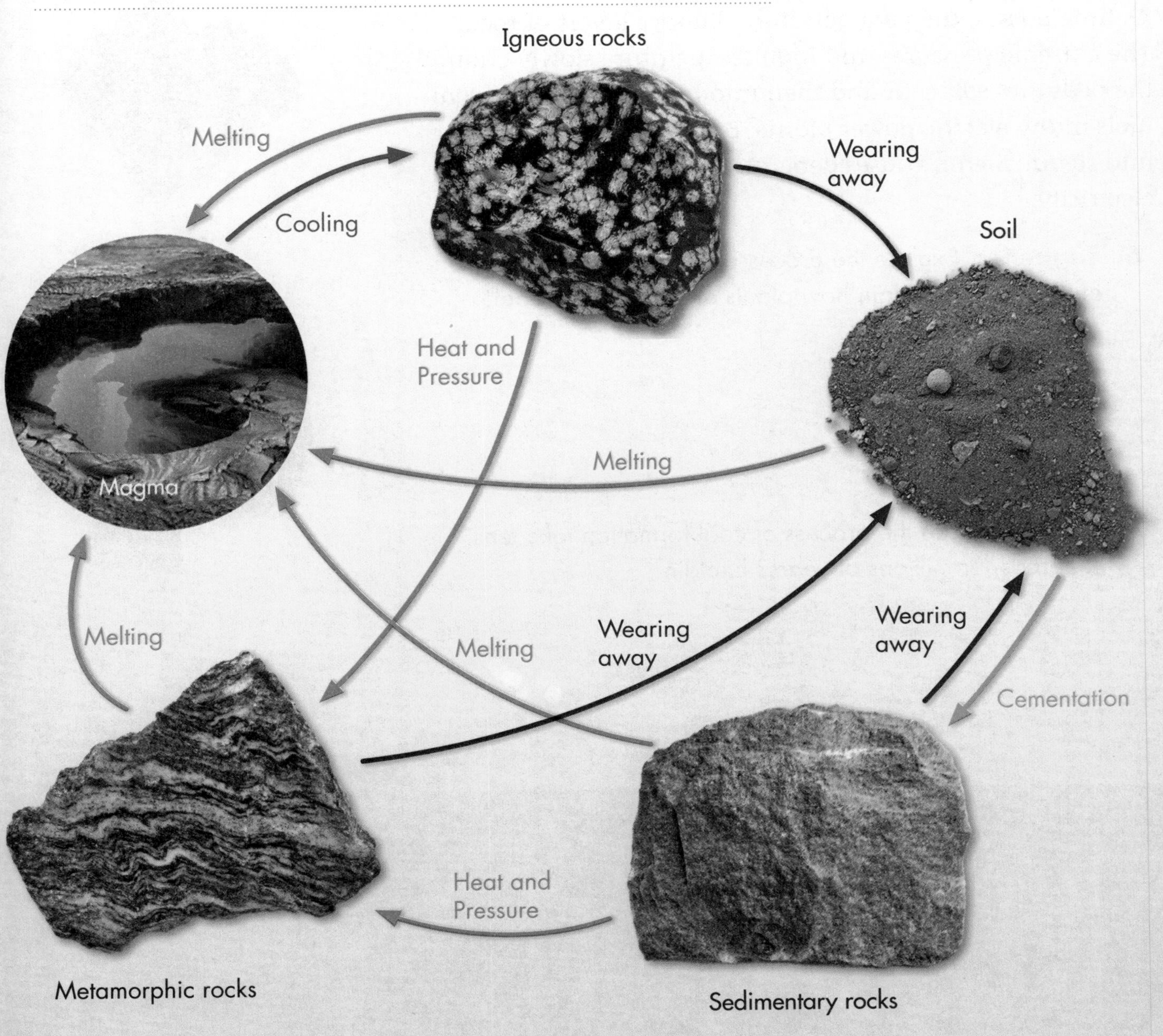

Fossil Fuels

Coal, oil, and natural gas are fossil fuels. They are important energy resources. Like rocks, fossil fuels form over long periods of time. The coal, oil, and natural gas we use today formed millions of years ago from the fossil remains of organisms. This is why they are called fossil fuels. Fossil fuels are nonrenewable resources. **Nonrenewable resources** either cannot be replaced at all or cannot be replaced as fast as people use them.

Coal

Coal forms from plants. Under certain conditions, layers of dead plants build up and form a material called peat. As time passes, the peat gets buried under layers of rock. The extreme pressures and high temperature slowly change the peat into soft coal and then into hard coal. Today, coal fuels many electric power plants. Burning coal turns water into steam. Steam causes generators to spin and make electricity.

6. **Sequence** Explore the processes that led to the formation of fossil fuels. Explain how plants are turned into coal.

7. **Estimate** Does the process of coal formation take tens, hundreds, or millions of years? Explain.

Coal Formation

plant life

peat

coal

Oil and Gas

Most scientists think that oil and natural gas form in basically the same way that coal forms, except that oil and natural gas form from the remains of tiny sea organisms, not dead plants. The remains are buried under layers of sediment. The heat and high pressure help turn the organic material into oil. If the temperature is high enough, natural gas is formed. Oil may be found beneath land or beneath the ocean floor. Drills make deep holes in Earth's surface to reach the oil. Millions of cars, trucks, trains, and ships use the fuels made from oil. Oil is also used to heat homes.

Natural gas is often found where oil is found. The gas is usually pumped into pipelines. Pipelines carry the gas to storage tanks until it is needed. Natural gas is a common fuel used for heating homes and household appliances such as grills, stoves, and water heaters.

Oil is pumped out of the ground and then heated and separated to make different products. In addition to fuel, oil is made into products such as asphalt, plastic, grease, and wax.

8. Differentiate What is one way that the formation of oil and natural gas differs from the way coal is formed?

....

....

got it? TEKS 7A

9. Analyze What role might igneous rocks play in forming sedimentary rocks?

....

....

10. Compare How is the formation of all fossil fuels similar?

....

....

Stop! I need help with ....

Wait! I have a question about ....

Go! Now I know ....

What are erosion and deposition?

I will know TEKS 7B
I will recognize that landforms such as deltas, canyons, and sand dunes are the result of changes to Earth's surface by wind, water, and ice. (Also **1A**, **2C**, **2D**, **2F**, **3C**, **4B**)

Vocabulary
erosion
deposition

Connect to Math

Math TEKS 7

The Palo Duro Canyon is sometimes called the "Grand Canyon of Texas." Carved by the Red River, the canyon is about 800 feet or 243.84 meters deep at its deepest point. How deep is the canyon in inches and centimeters? Convert feet to inches and meters to centimeters using these formulas:

feet x 12 = inches
meters x 100 = centimeters

Use paper to convert feet to inches.

800 feet = ... inches

Use a calculator to convert meters to centimeters.

243.84 = ... centimeters

PEARSON Texas.com

Quick Lab

TEKS 7B, 1A, 2C, 2D, 2F, 3C, 4B

How does melting ice cause erosion?

- [x] **1.** Put 1 cup of sand on each container. **Make a model** of 2 landforms. Make a hill on one container. Make a flat plain on the other container.
- [x] **2.** Place 1 ice cube in the middle of each pile of sand. **Observe.**

Materials

safety goggles
2 plastic cups with sand
2 containers
2 ice cubes

Texas Safety LAB RULES

Use safety equipment, including safety goggles. Wear protective equipment until your work area is clean.

Explain Your Results

3. Which landform **model** eroded more?

....

....

4. Analyze and Interpret How does the shape of the land affect erosion?

....

....

....

Erosion and Deposition

Landforms—the natural land features on Earth's surface—are constantly changing shape. This is because materials such as rock particles move. Water, wind, ice, and gravity transport tiny particles of rocks, soil, and other sediments from one place to another place. Often the changes are so gradual that you might not even notice them. Over time, though, this process reshapes the land. The movement of materials away from a place is called **erosion.**

Erosion

Water, wind, temperature, and other forces wear away rock and soil. Once materials break into small enough pieces, flowing water, wind, and gravity can carry them away.

Gravity is one of the main forces causing erosion. In a landslide, gravity quickly pulls rocks and soil downhill. Landslides often occur during earthquakes and after heavy rains. Landslides are more likely to happen on steep slopes with no trees.

1. **Infer** How might trees on steep slopes help prevent landslides?

Deposition

Sooner or later, the materials carried away by erosion will be unable to keep moving. The wind will die down. A river's water will slow or empty into the ocean. A mountain or a canyon floor will block movement. The material will be dropped in a new place. **Deposition** is the process of laying down materials, such as rocks and soil.

As deposition causes more and more materials to build up, new landforms take shape. This process may happen quickly, or it may take a long time. The materials that make up the new landforms are sediments. Some may eventually harden into sedimentary rock.

2. **Infer** How does deposition help explain the layers that are often found in sedimentary rock?

3. **Identify** Look at the photos of the Rio Grande and the Padre Island National Seashore. What evidence of deposition do you see?

4. **Conclude** Recognize how landforms are the result of changes to Earth's surface by water. How does water create canyons?

5. **Cause and Effect** Reread the paragraph on rivers. **Underline** how deltas are formed.

As the brownish water of the Mississippi River flows along, it can carry sediment thousands of miles to the Gulf of Mexico.

Water Erosion and Deposition

Moving water causes much of the erosion that shapes Earth's surface. Water can also deposit materials in other places to create new landforms. Rivers, rain, waves, ocean currents, and glaciers are all forms of moving water.

Rivers

Gravity causes rivers to flow. As rivers flow downhill, they pick up and carry sediments. The sediments can erode the riverbeds by grinding against the riverbeds again and again. The faster a river flows, the more sediments it can carry and the heavier those sediments can be. Rivers also erode the land around them. A fast-flowing river can form V-shaped valleys and cut deep canyons from rock. Slow rivers form looping bends, which erode the sides of the valley and make it wider. The deposited material from rivers forms areas called deltas. Deltas form where river waters slow and drop their sediments when they enter an ocean or lake.

Rain

Rain can loosen sediments from the soil and carry them away. Rain can cause flooding in low, flat areas. Flooding damages soil, roads, and buildings. Rainwater flowing over bare farm fields on slopes can erode tons of soil and deposit it downhill. To prevent soil erosion, farmers plow furrows perpendicular to the field's slope. The furrows catch rainwater, keeping the rain from carrying soil away.

Waves

Waves cause erosion along coastlines. As waves hit against rocks, the rocks can break. Sand and gravel in the waves act like sandpaper, weathering the rocks over time. Waves that erode one shoreline may drop sand somewhere else to form other beaches. Storms, tides, and currents can erode beaches. Grasses and plants can help hold soil in place to prevent beach erosion.

Glaciers

Glaciers are large masses of ice. This ice can cause erosion. Gravity pulls glaciers down along a valley. As this movement happens, glaciers grind rocks beneath them into sediments. The glaciers deposit sediments downhill. Over a long time, the action of glaciers wears away the bottom of a valley, which becomes U-shaped.

6. **Analyze** Recognize how landforms are the result of changes to Earth's surface by ice by explaining how glacier ice helps form valleys.

Connect to Math

Math TEKS 1A, 1B, 1G

Calculate Rates

Because of water erosion, a sandy coast can erode about 5 meters every 5 years.

1. Suppose that the coast continues to erode at the same rate. How much will the coast erode in 50 years? Show your work.

2. Suppose that during each severe storm the coast erodes an additional 4 meters. If there were 15 severe storms in one year, how much did the coast erode because of the storms?

Blown Over

Put on your safety goggles. Cover the bottom of a pan with a flat layer of sand 1–2 cm deep. Use a straw to gently blow over the sand. What can you place in the pan to prevent the sand from blowing all over? How might your idea help prevent wind erosion?

TEKS 1A, 4B, 7B

Wind Erosion and Deposition

Wind erosion is caused by wind blowing dust, soil, or sand from one place to another. When sand and dust blow against a rock, tiny bits of the rock might break off. These bits are immediately blown away. Wind erosion also changes sand dunes and fields.

Sand Dunes

Sand dunes are large, loose deposits of sand. The size and shape of a sand dune depend on the speed and direction that the winds are blowing, the amount of sand available, and the number of plants that live in the area. The stronger the wind, the farther sand particles can move. Winds that move in a steady direction can move a dune. This kind of wind will consistently pick up sand from one side and deposit it on the other side. This process causes the entire dune to move slowly in the same direction the wind moves.

7. CHALLENGE Why is wind erosion more likely to happen in dry areas than moist areas?

8. **Hypothesize** How could sand dunes be held in place to keep them from drifting onto a road?

Fields

Wind erosion can be a serious problem on farms. Bare, plowed fields can become very dry. Winds can blow topsoil off the fields. This topsoil is the best kind of soil for growing crops. It cannot be quickly replaced. Farmers often plant rows of tall trees along the edges of fields to prevent wind erosion of topsoil. The trees prevent some of the wind from blowing on the field. Some farmers are able to grow their crops with less plowing. In this way, the soil stays in larger clumps that do not get blown away.

9. **Explain** How is wind erosion being prevented in the photo?

....

....

....

got it? TEKS 7B

10. **Identify** What is one cause of erosion? How can it be prevented?

....

....

11. Give an example of how deposition changes Earth's surface.

....

....

Stop! I need help with ....

Wait! I have a question about ....

Go! Now I know ....

TEXAS

Earth's Surface

TEKS 7B

Dust Storm!

On October 17, 2011, wind gusts of more than 70 miles an hour pushed an 8,000-foot-high cloud of rust-colored dust across the West Texas plains toward Lubbock. The huge dust storm roared through the city around 6:00 in the evening, blotting out the sun and everything in its path.

The state was in the grip of a massive drought. Dry conditions had robbed the soil of moisture and killed the plants needed to hold the soil in place. High winds picked up the fine, loose soil and sent it rolling toward the city.

Lubbock is located on the windy Southern High Plains. Over millions of years, high winds have shifted the soil during periods of drought. The result is the flat, open land and sand dunes we see in the region today.

Although the dust storm that struck Lubbock on October 17 2011 was much larger than usual, people in the region are used to dust storms.

Summarize Recognize how landforms are the result of changes to Earth's surface by wind. Explain how wind and drought helped shape the Southern High Plains.

....

....

....

FieldTrip

The Canyons of Big Bend

The Rio Grande is proof that a flowing river is a powerful force for shaping the land. The Rio Grande flows through the Big Bend National Park in West Texas. Over millions of years, the river has carved deep canyons in the mountains of the area.

The steep walls of the canyons tell the story of how the rocks and mountains were made. They show that the mountains were lifted up, buried by rocks or ancient seas, and then lifted up again. Pressure, heat, and the cementing effects of lime created sedimentary rock. Volcanic eruptions left igneous rock trapped inside the mountains and twisted and tilted the sedimentary rock. Scientists study the patterns in the canyon walls to understand the effects of erosion, deposition, and twisting at different times in Earth's history.

Big Bend National Park is a popular vacation destination. Visitors can hike through the park or take guided tours to observe how erosion has carved the landscape.

Identify How did water help create the canyons of Big Bend National Park?

Explain How were the sedimentary rocks in the mountains formed?

The Rio Grande flows for 107 miles through Big Bend National Park.

What are some alternative energy resources?

I will know TEKS 7C
I will know how to identify alternative energy resources such as wind, solar, hydroelectric, geothermal, and biofuels. (Also **1A**, **1B**, **2A**, **2B**, **2C**, **2D**, **2F**, **4A**)

Vocabulary
renewable resource
inexhaustible resource

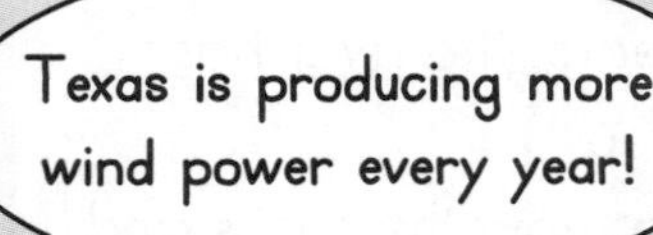

Texas is producing more wind power every year!

In 2010, Texas produced 26,828,660 megawatt-hours of wind power.

In 2011, the megawatt-hours jumped to 30,769,674.

Can you help us figure out how much of an increase that was?

Show your work To find the increase, subtract the 2010 rate from the 2011 rate. **Math TEKS 1A, 3K**

PEARSON Texas.com

Quick Lab

TEKS 7C, 1A, 2A, 2B, 2C, 2D, 2F, 4A

Can you capture energy from the sun?

Materials

graduated cylinder
500 mL water
2 resealable clear plastic bags
2 Celsius thermometers

1. Use the graduated cylinder to pour 250 milliliters of water into each of the sealable clear plastic bags.
2. **Record** the water temperature in each bag in degrees Celsius. Seal the bags. Put one bag in a dark or shady place. Put the other bag in a place where it will receive direct sunlight.
3. **Formulate a testable hypothesis** based on the question this investigation will answer.
4. **Predict** what the temperature of the water in each bag will be in degrees Celsius after 30 minutes. Record the temperatures after 30 minutes.

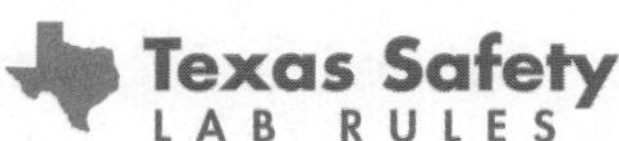

If any water spills, notify your teacher immediately.

Explain Your Results

5. **Compare and Contrast** How did the water temperature in each bag change compared with your hypothesis and prediction?

6. **Identify** What alternative energy resource accounts for these results? How did the alternative energy source affect the water temperature?

Energy Resources

A resource is something that will meet a need. An energy resource is something that will meet energy needs. The sun is an energy resource. It gives off energy in the forms of light and heat. People can use this light to make electricity. Trees are also an energy resource. Trees provide wood. Wood produces heat when it burns, so people can use it to heat their homes. There are different kinds of energy resources. Renewable, nonrenewable, and inexhaustible resources are three major types of natural resources. Oil, coal, and natural gas are nonrenewable resources.

Hydroelectric power is an example of a resource that cannot be used up. People use the force of flowing water to generate hydroelectric energy. Most hydroelectric stations use a dam to block the flow of a river. The water flows through pipes in the dam, which causes the blades of the turbine to spin. The blades are similar to fan blades. The spinning motion in the turbine causes the parts of the generator to turn, making electricity.

1. Sequence Complete the graphic organizer below. Explain how hydroelectric energy is generated.

First

....

Next

....

Last

....

2. Classify Identify the energy resource in this photo.

....

....

Renewable and Inexhaustible Resources

Resources that can be replaced are **renewable resources.** Renewable energy resources include the wood from trees, leaves, food wastes, and even manure. These resources belong to a group of fuels called biomass fuels, or biofuels, which are made by living things or from recently living things. Some biomass, such as corn, is turned into fuels that can run cars and trucks. People will never run out of biomass because garbage is always being made. By using biomass as a resource, less garbage will be taken to landfills. One disadvantage is that burning biomass causes air pollution.

Sun, wind, moving water, and energy from inside Earth are inexhaustible resources. **Inexhaustible resources** will not run out.

3. Cause and Effect **Underline** two effects of using biomass for energy.

Compost It!

Make informed choices in the recycling of materials by making your own compost pile. Ask an adult to cut off the top of a plastic gallon jug. Fill it with leaves, grass clippings, and fruit and vegetable wastes. Cover your jug with plastic wrap. Then wait for your biomass to become soil!

TEKS 1B

Connect to **Math**

Math TEKS 3A, 9

Read a Circle Graph

The circle graph shows the percentage of energy from inexhaustible and renewable resources used in 2007 in the United States.

5% Wind

6% Other

36% Water

Biomass

Use the graph to answer these questions.

1. What percentage of energy use from these resources came from biomass fuels?

2. The energy from these resources is measured in energy units. In 2007, energy use from these resources was 6.8 energy units. Estimate how many energy units came from biomass fuels. Explain how you got your answer.

Biomass

Trees provide wood. Wood is probably the first fuel that people ever used for both heat and light. Although wood is a renewable fuel, it takes time for new trees to grow that will replace those that have been cut down. Also, burning wood increases the amount of carbon dioxide in the air, which may contribute to global warming.

Wind

Wind is the motion of air. People have used the wind for energy for thousands of years. For example, the blades of windmills were connected to machines that ground grain and pumped water. Today, a wind turbine uses the wind's energy to spin a generator that makes electricity. Wind is an inexhaustible resource.

Solar Energy

Solar energy is energy from sunlight. A device called a solar cell changes solar energy into electrical energy. When light hits the cell, an electric current is produced. Groups of solar cells form solar panels. Some homes, buildings, and cars have solar panels to provide energy. Solar energy is also used to heat things, such as the air in greenhouses.

Geothermal Energy

The rock material deep inside Earth is very hot. Energy from the high temperature inside Earth is called geothermal energy. One way to get geothermal energy is to pump water down deep holes into hot rock. The hot rock heats the water or turns the water into steam. The steam rushes back to Earth's surface and can be used to make electricity.

4. CHALLENGE Tell where the energy in wood originally comes from.

Conserving Resources

The use of alternative energy resources helps conserve nonrenewable energy resources like oil, coal, and natural gas. It is good practice to conserve all resources. One way to conserve is to make informed choices about how you use, dispose of, and recycle materials. The three R's—*reduce, reuse, and recycle*—can help you do that. Reduce the amount of resources you use throughout the day. When you wash your hands or the dishes, turn off the water between soaping up and rinsing off. When possible, reuse products rather than throw them out. Carefully wash and refill a plastic water bottle or rinse out a plastic sandwich bag. Find out your community's policies on recycling. Take the time to recycle what you can.

5. **Conclude** Why is it important to find out about your community's policies on recycling?

got it? TEKS 7C

6. **Identify** Identify an alternative energy resource that is renewable.

7. **Analyze** Is wind a renewable or an inexhaustible resource? Explain.

Stop! I need help with

Wait! I have a question about

Go! Now I know

What can fossils tell us?

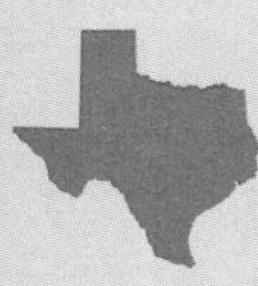

I will know TEKS 7A, 7D
I will explore the processes that led to the formation of fossils. I will identify fossils as evidence of past living organisms and use models to identify the nature of the environments in which the fossils lived. (Also **1A, 1B, 2F, 3C**)

Vocabulary
fossil
extinct
paleontologist

I went fossil hunting over the weekend. You should see all the fossils I found!

What did you find?

I found 6 snail shells, 15 pieces of rock that had plant impressions on them, and 3 pieces of something I think might be bone.

Can you help us find what fraction of the whole were snail shells?

Connect to Math

Show your work How many fossils were found all together? How many were snail shells? What fraction of the whole is that? **Math TEKS 1A, 1F**

PEARSON Texas.com

Quick Lab

TEKS 7D, 1A, 2F, 3C

What can a fossil tell you?

1. **Make a model** of a fossil. Press a shell into clay.
2. Make a fossil model with an object.
3. Guess what your partner's fossil model shows.

Materials

shell
modeling clay
objects

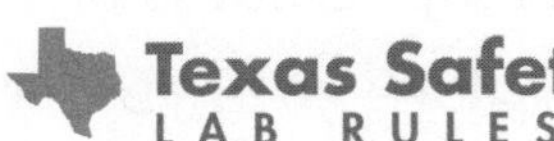

Texas Safety LAB RULES

Wash your hands thoroughly upon completing the activity. Be sure to return lab materials to their proper location.

Explain Your Results

4. How did you **infer** what your partner's fossil model showed?

5. How do fossils give clues about living things?

Fossil Clues

Some plants and animals that lived millions of years ago have left clues about their lives. A line of footprints preserved in rock can show how an animal walked. The skeleton of a small animal can help scientists understand what the animal looked like.

Skeletons and footprints are examples of fossils. A **fossil** is the remains or mark of an animal or plant that lived long ago. Scientists can study fossils to learn about species that are extinct. An **extinct** species no longer exists. More than one million species currently live on Earth, but many more have become extinct. In fact, most types of organisms that have lived on Earth no longer exist.

Scientists can also use fossils to understand how plants, animals, and environments have changed over time. By studying fossils, scientists can create models of environments that existed long before written records. These models help scientists compare plants, animals, and environments at different times in Earth's history.

1. **Main Idea and Details** Read the first paragraph again. **Underline** the main idea.

2. **Explain** Read the caption below. What is one thing scientists might learn by examining a trilobite fossil?

Trilobites are now extinct. These animals had hard shells and lived in the sea hundreds of millions of years ago.

Windows to the Past

A scientist who studies fossils is called a **paleontologist.** By studying fossils, a paleontologist can learn what extinct organisms looked like and how they lived. For example, paleontologists have found skulls from dinosaurs called sauropods. Sauropods were a group of dinosaurs that had small heads, long necks, and enormous bodies. They ate plants and may have used their long necks to reach tall trees.

Because of their size, these dinosaurs needed huge amounts of food. However, their small heads meant that they could only take small bites. How did they get enough to eat? Paleontologists studied the dinosaurs' skulls and the shape of their teeth. They concluded that some sauropods may have swallowed their food without chewing it. Doing this allowed the dinosaurs to get food to their stomachs more quickly and take more bites.

3. Recall What did paleontologists conclude about sauropods by studying their skulls and teeth?

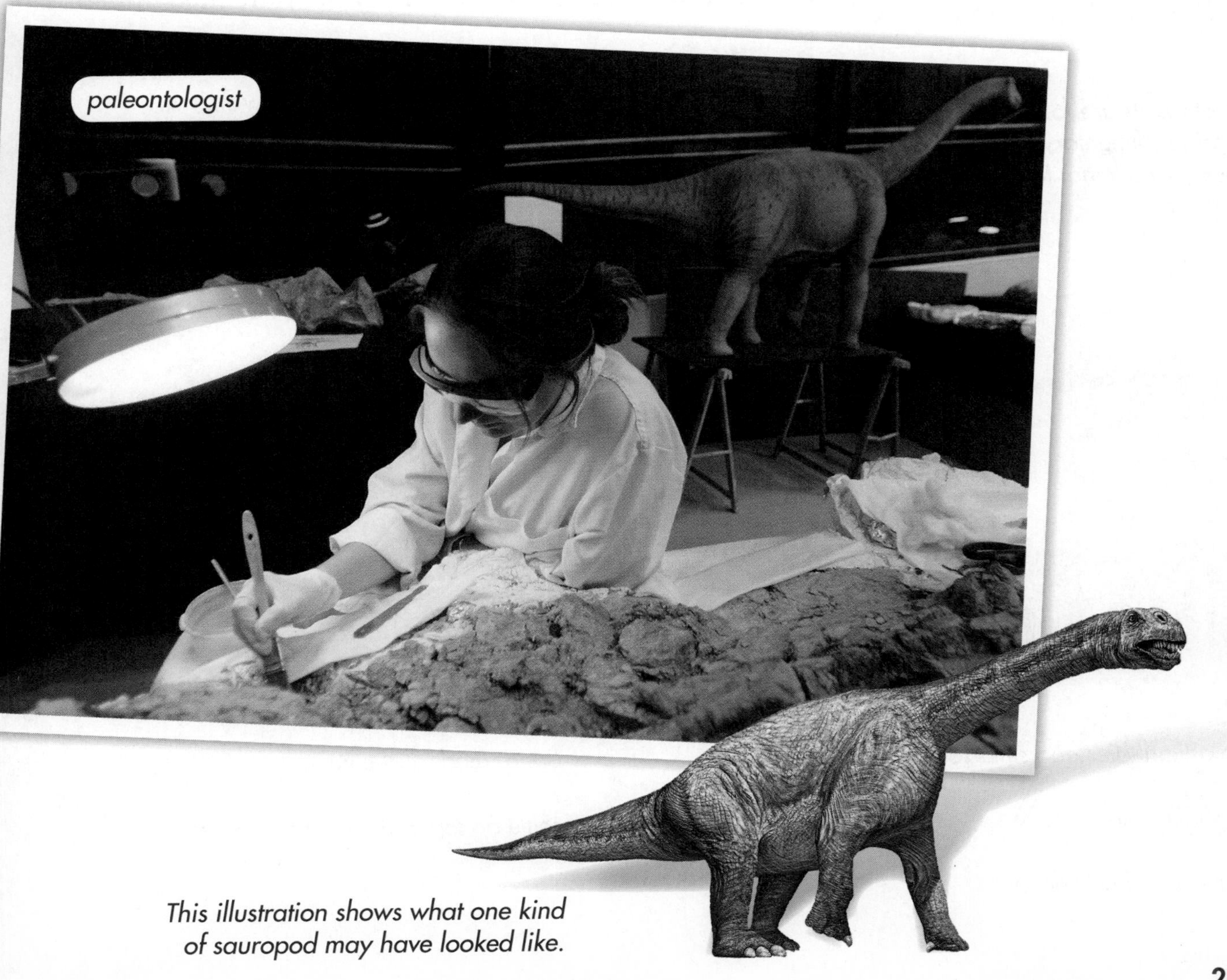

This illustration shows what one kind of sauropod may have looked like.

How Fossils Form

Fossils form in different ways. Most fossils form when a plant or animal dies and becomes buried under layers of sediments. Sediments are bits of rock, sand, shell, and other material. Over time, the sediments harden into rock and preserve the shape of the buried plant or animal. The diagram below shows this process.

Usually only the hard parts of animals, such as bones and shells, become fossils. The soft parts decay or may be eaten by other animals. Once the remains of an animal are buried, different things can happen. Sometimes the buried remains break down and disappear, leaving an empty space in the sedimentary rock. A space in rock in the shape of a living thing is called a *mold fossil.* Later, minerals from the surrounding rock might fill the mold fossil. Over time, these minerals harden into the shape of the mold. This type of fossil is called a *cast fossil.* Dinosaur "bones" that come from cast fossils are not bones at all! They are hardened minerals.

Most fossils are found within sedimentary rock, or rock that forms in layers.

4. Fill in the Blanks Complete the captions in the diagram below. Fill in each blank with the correct word.

An animal dies and sinks to the bottom of a lake or shallow sea. The .... parts of its body decay.

Sand, mud, and other .... settle on top of the animal's remains.

5. **Identify** **Draw** an X on the mold fossils. **Circle** the cast fossil.

6. **Infer** Many dinosaurs once roamed Earth, but fossils do not exist for all of them. Look at the diagram. What might be some reasons why not all dinosaurs left fossils?

....

....

....

These are ammonite fossils.

More layers of sediments form. The sediments harden into .... , preserving the shape of the animal's parts.

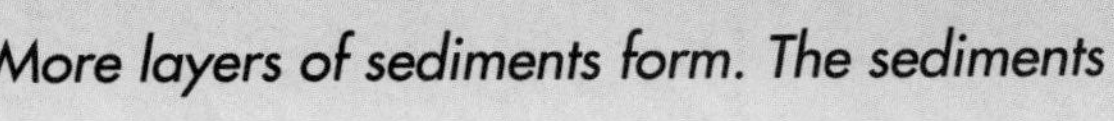

Over time the rock layers above the fossil wear away. The fossil appears at or near Earth's surface.

Fossils and Living Organisms

One way paleontologists learn about extinct plants and animals is by comparing them with plants and animals that exist today. For example, fossils show that some dinosaurs called hadrosaurs had large, hollow crests on their heads. Paleontologists have different ideas about the purposes of these crests. One idea came from comparing hadrosaurs to birds called peacocks. Male peacocks have large, brightly colored tails. They use their tails to attract mates. Paleontologists hypothesize that hadrosaurs may have used their crests in the same way.

Fossils can also show how plants and animals have changed over time. Many living things today are related to plants and animals of the past. Fossils show that some extinct plant species looked a lot like modern plants. For example, compare the pictures of the horsetail fossil and the modern horsetail plant. Some horsetail plants of the past grew to the size of trees. Modern horsetail plants are much smaller. This suggests that the plants changed slowly over time.

8. **Analyze** Tell what we may infer from a horsetail fossil about the nature of the environment in the past.

This illustration shows what one kind of hadrosaur might have looked like.

7. **Hypothesize** What is another possible use of the hadrosaur's hollow crest?

Fossils and the Environment

Fossils also show that Earth's environment has changed. For example, scientists in Kansas have found the remains of sea animals called ammonites. Ammonites are related to modern squids, but they died out 65 million years ago. In South Dakota, scientists have discovered fossils of giant sea turtles. These turtles lived about 70 million years ago but are now extinct. What do these discoveries tell us? They show that areas of present-day states such as Kansas and South Dakota were once covered with water!

9. **Describe** How has the environment of Kansas changed?

10. **Main Idea and Details** What details support the idea that Earth's environment has changed?

Now

Then

ammonite

Geologic Time Scale

Present
Cenozoic Era
In the last 65 million years, dogs, cats, and humans appeared.
65 million years ago
Mesozoic Era
The Mesozoic Era, also called the Age of the Dinosaurs, was the time of hadrosaurs and Tyrannosaurus rex. Most dinosaurs became extinct at the end of this period.
248 million years ago
Paleozoic Era
Fish, simple plants, insects, and early land animals lived during this time.
544 million years ago
Precambrian
Some rocks from the late Precambrian time have fossils of jellyfish.

Scientists divide Earth's history into time spans of millions of years. These time spans are labeled on the geologic time scale.

Fossil Age

Scientists determine the age of fossils in two ways. Many fossils are located within layers of rock. Older layers of rock are under newer layers of rock. Scientists can conclude that fossils found in deeper or lower layers are older than those found in layers above.

Scientists can also determine the age of fossils by examining how quickly certain materials in the fossils change. These materials change at steady rates after a plant or animal dies. Scientists can measure these materials in a fossil to determine how long ago the organism died.

Geologic Time Scale

Scientists have used information about the ages of fossils and rocks to make a timeline of the history of Earth. This timeline is called the geologic time scale. When they draw the scale, scientists place the earliest time span at the bottom. They put the most recent time span at the top. This matches the way rock layers of different ages are arranged. The time scale helps scientists show when different animals, including the dinosaurs, existed.

11. Infer What era are the sea turtle fossils of South Dakota from?

12. Draw Conclusions Suppose that you found two different fossils in two different layers of rock. How could you tell which fossil was older?

Fossil Fuels

You have already learned that fuels such as coal and oil are a kind of fossil. Most of these fossil fuels come from the remains of organisms that lived millions of years ago. Scientists sometimes use fossils as clues to where to explore for fossil fuels. If they find fossils of plants or animals from a certain geologic time, there is a chance that they might also find fossil fuels nearby. It took millions of years for the remains to become coal or oil. At power plants, fossil fuels are used to produce electricity.

Fossil Fuel Use

With a partner, list three things you and your classmates can do to reduce electricity use and conserve fossil fuels. Share your list with the class.

TEKS 1B

13. CHALLENGE What might happen if people use up all the fossil fuels currently available? Explain your answer.

....

....

....

....

....

got it? TEKS 7D

14. Draw Conclusions A scientist finds the fossil of a sea creature on top of a mountain range. What can the scientist conclude about the land around the fossil?

....

15. Summarize Identify fossils as evidence of past living organisms. Summarize what paleontologists can learn from studying fossils.

....

....

....

Stop! I need help with ....

Wait! I have a question about ....

Go! Now I know ....

Lab Investigation

TEKS 7B, 1A, 2A, 2B, 2C, 3C, 4A

How does the steepness of a stream affect how fast it flows?

Materials

clear plastic tubing
protractor
plastic cup
water
graduated cylinder
funnel
masking tape
stopwatch

Follow a Procedure

☐ 1. **Make a model** of a stream. Have one student hold a piece of tubing up. Set the stream angle to 10°. Place a cup at the low end of the stream.

☐ 2. **Measure** 50 mL of water into a graduated cylinder.

☐ 3. Attach a funnel to the top of the tubing. Then, collect information using a stopwatch. Start the stopwatch as you pour the water into the tubing. Stop the stopwatch when all the water has flowed into the cup. **Record** the time.

☐ 4. Change the stream angle to 25°, 40°, and 55° and repeat Steps 2 and 3.

Report spilled water or other unsafe conditions to your teacher immediately.

Inquiry Skill

Recording data on a chart can help you make **inferences** based on the data.

☐ **5. Record** Record information using the stopwatch. Use the table below.

Observations of Model Stream	
Stream Angle (°)	**Flow Time** (seconds)
10	
25	
40	
55	

Analyze and Conclude

6. Communicate Analyze information using a stopwatch. Summarize your results.

....

....

....

....

7. Infer Where might you find a stream that flows at a 55° angle? Where might you find a stream that flows at a 15° angle?

....

....

....

TEXAS

my planet Diary

TEKS 7B, 7D

Fun Fact

Look closely at the photo on this page. It shows the Guadalupe Mountains, which run through West Texas. Can you guess how these mountains formed?

The Guadalupe Mountains are actually an ancient fossil reef! Hundreds of millions of years ago, this area was part of a vast inland sea called the Permian Basin. There was a large ridge-like reef in the Permian Basin. The reef was formed from the skeletons and cemented remains of tiny animals and plants that lived in the ocean.

Eventually, changes in Earth's surface caused the Permian Basin to fill in and the mountains we see today to rise up. Over millions of years, erosion from wind and water uncovered the ancient fossil reef!

Infer How can the fossil reef help paleontologists understand the ancient past?

Vocabulary Smart Cards

- mineral
- igneous
- sedimentary
- metamorphic
- rock cycle
- nonrenewable resource
- erosion
- deposition
- renewable resource
- inexhaustible resource
- fossil
- extinct
- paleontologist

Play a Game!

Cut out the Vocabulary Smart Cards. Work with a partner. One person puts the cards picture-side up. The other puts the cards picture-side down. Take turns matching each word with its definition.

metamorphic

metamórfica

mineral

mineral

rock cycle

ciclo de las rocas

igneous

ígnea

nonrenewable resource

recurso no renovable

sedimentary

sedimentaria

a nonliving, naturally occurring solid that has its own regular arrangement of particles in it

Write three examples of this word.

sólido natural, sin vida, cuyas partículas están regularmente organizadas

rocks formed inside Earth from other rocks under heat and pressure

Write an example of this word.

rocas que se forman dentro de la Tierra a partir de otras rocas, bajo calor y presión

Interactive Vocabulary

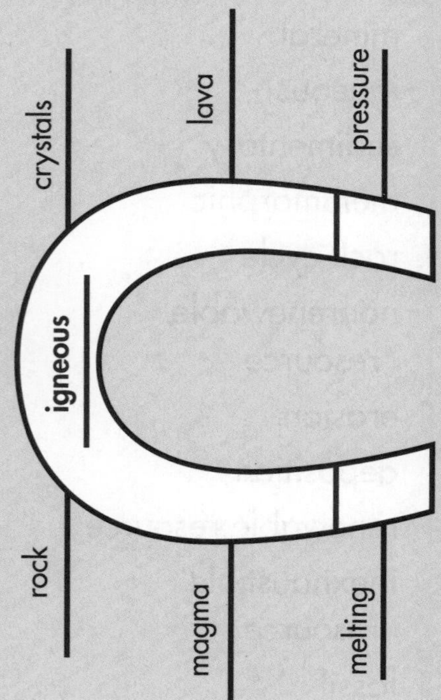

rocks that form when melted rock cools and hardens

Write an example of this word.

rocas que se forman cuando la roca derretida se enfría y se endurece

a process in which rocks are constantly being formed and destroyed

Draw an example.

proceso en el cual las rocas se forman y se destruyen constantemente

Make a Word Magnet!

Choose a vocabulary word and write it in the Word Magnet. Write words that are related to it on the lines.

rocks that form when layers of materials and rock particles settle on top of each other and then harden

Write an example of this word.

rocas que se forman cuando materiales y partículas de roca se asientan unos sobre los otros y se endurecen

a type of energy resource that cannot be replaced at all or cannot be replaced as fast as people use it

What is the prefix of resource?

tipo de recurso energético que no se puede reemplazar o que no se puede reemplazar con la misma rapidez con que se lo usa

paleontologist

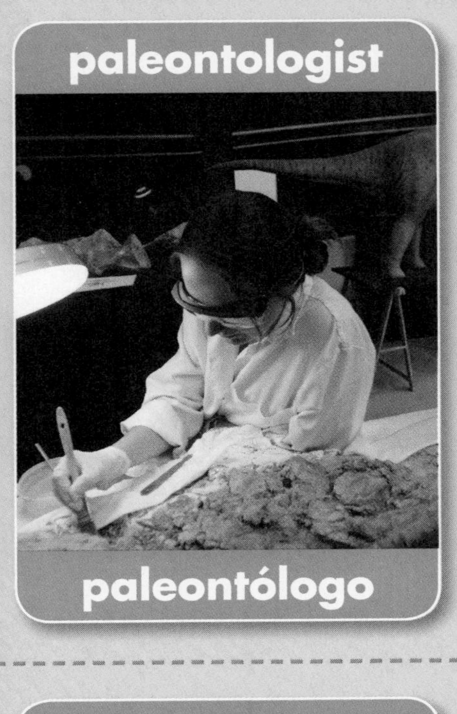

paleontólogo

inexhaustible resource

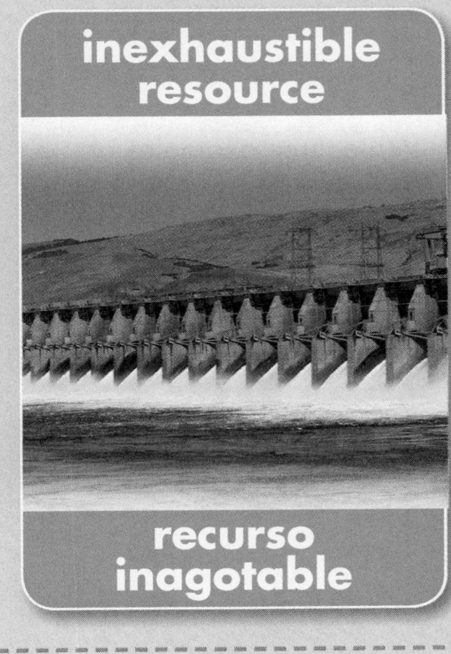

recurso inagotable

erosion

erosión

fossil

fósil

deposition

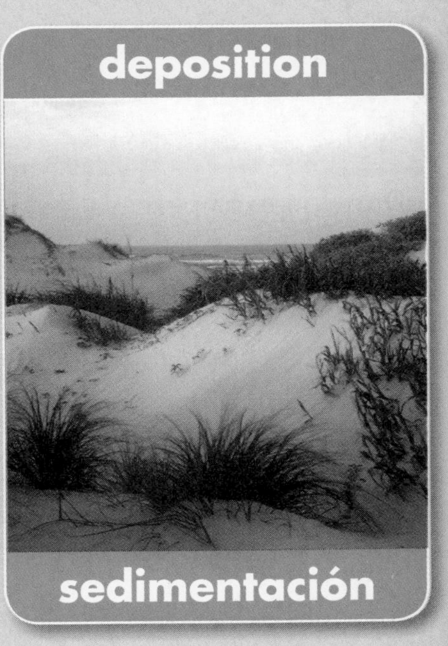

sedimentación

extinct

extinto

renewable resource

recurso renovable

the movement of materials away from a place

Write a sentence using the verb form of this word.

movimiento de materiales que se alejan de un lugar

a type of energy resource that will not run out

Write three examples of this word.

tipo de recurso energético que nunca se agota

a scientist who studies fossils

What is the suffix of this word and what does it mean?

científico que estudia los fósiles

process of laying down materials, such as rocks and soil

Draw an example.

proceso por el cual materiales como rocas y partículas de suelo se asientan

remains or mark of an animal or plant that lived long ago

Draw an example.

restos o marca de un ser vivo que existió hace mucho tiempo

a type of energy resource that can be replaced

Write a sentence using this word.

tipo de recurso energético que puede reemplazarse

no longer existing as a species

Write a sentence using the word.

ya no existe más como especie

TEKS Practice

Lesson 1 TEKS 7A

How do rocks form?

1. **Write About It** Explain how sedimentary rock forms.

2. **Identify** Is the rock shown an igneous, sedimentary, or metamorphic rock? Explain.

3. **Communicate** How do fossil fuels form?

Lesson 2 TEKS 7B

What are erosion and deposition?

4. **Explain** How do water, erosion, and deposition form deltas?

5. **Explain** Are U-shaped valleys most likely formed by river water, ice, or wind? Explain.

6. **Identify** What kind of landform is pictured below? How did it form?

TEKS Practice

Lesson 3 TEKS 7C

What are some alternative energy resources?

7. Communicate What form of alternative energy is made by using hot rocks deep inside Earth? How is it produced?

8. Identify What form of alternative energy is shown in the photo? How is it produced?

9. Name Which alternative energy source is made by capturing the power of running water?

10. Summarize How can wind be used as an alternative source of energy?

11. In 2010, Texas produced 97,535 megawatts of biofuel from biomass. In 2011, the amount of biofuel produced from biomass was 137,004 megawatts. By how many megawatts did fuel produced from this alternative energy source increase in 2011?

Lesson 4 TEKS 7D
What can fossils tell us?

12. Sequence Explain how a once-living organism turns into a cast fossil.

First

Next

Last

13. Infer How might a paleontologist use a model to explain how Texas looked 70 million years ago?

Chapter 5

Lesson 1 How do rocks form?
In this lesson, you learned how sedimentary rocks form. You also learned how fossil fuels form.
Readiness TEKS 7A

Lesson 2 What are erosion and deposition?
In this lesson, you learned that water, wind, and ice help create landforms such as deltas, canyons, and sand dunes.
Readiness TEKS 7B

Lesson 3 What are some alternative energy resources?
In this lesson, you learned that wind energy, solar energy, hydroelectric energy, geothermal energy, and biomass are alternative energy resources.
Readiness TEKS 7C

Lesson 4 What can fossils tell us?
In this lesson, you learned that fossils are evidence of past living organisms. You also learned that paleontologists use models to represent past environments.
Supporting TEKS 7D

★ TEKS Practice: Chapter Review

Read each question and circle the best answer.

1 Lamar looked at the rock shown below with a hand lens.

He decided that it is a sedimentary rock. What clue would support this conclusion?

A The rock has many small, shiny crystals.

B The rock looks like it formed under heat and pressure.

C The rock looks like layers of sand that have been pressed together.

D The rock has many tiny holes where gases were trapped as the rock formed.

2 The fossil in the picture is a trilobite. Trilobites were animals that lived in Earth's oceans long ago. They are now extinct.

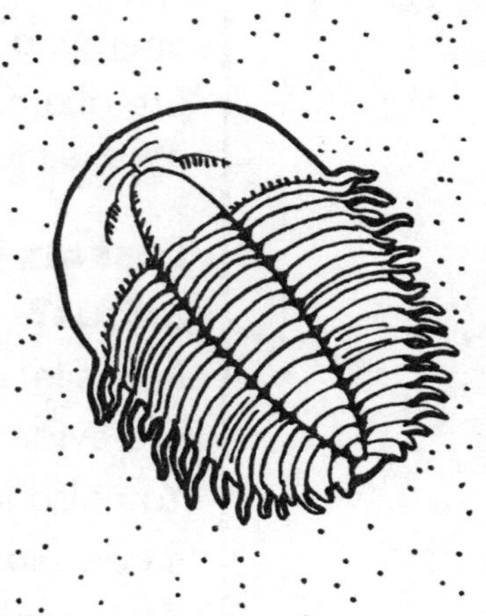

What can finding this fossil in a rock near your home tell you?

F There are trilobites living in the area near your home.

G The rock containing this trilobite formed under the ocean.

H The trilobite's shell was as hard as rock when it was alive.

J The trilobite died because the water where it lived dried up.

3 Elena took a trip with her family to see a beautiful canyon. The canyon contained many interesting and colorful shapes. She sketched the picture below in her notebook.

What most likely formed this canyon?

A River water deposited sediment as it emptied into the ocean.

B River water eroded rock as it flowed through the area.

C Lava from a volcano hardened and cooled to form rock.

D An earthquake caused parts of the land to fall to a lower level.

---

4 Michael models a renewable energy source using a pinwheel. When he blows on the pinwheel, it spins.

What energy source is he modeling?

F Wind

G Water

H Biomass

J Sunlight

5 The graph shows the types of energy sources used by a city.

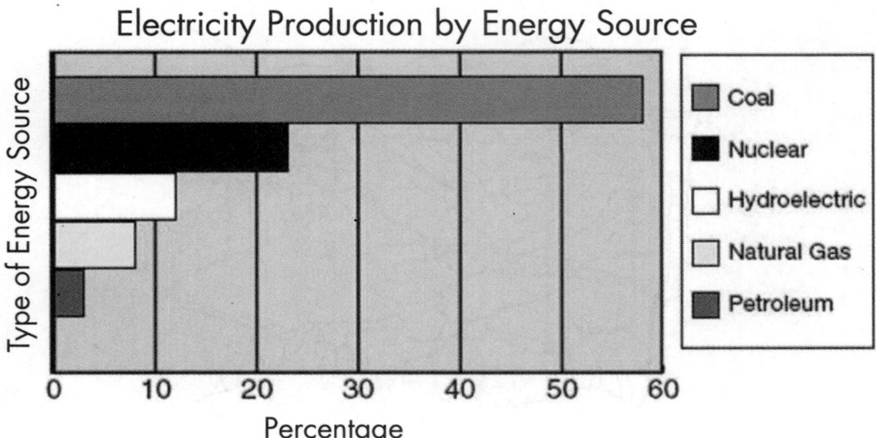

What percentage of these energy sources is renewable?

A 43%

B 35%

C 23%

D 12%

6 Many power plants burn oil or coal to produce electricity. What is another way oil and coal are alike?

F They both formed from the remains of ancient organisms.

G They are both nonrenewable sources of energy.

H They both formed underground through high temperatures and extreme pressure.

J All of the above

 TEKS Practice: Cumulative Review

7 A worker at a factory pushes boxes across the floor of a warehouse and loads them into a truck. A scientist wants to calculate the force that the worker uses to push the boxes. The scientist measures the mass of several boxes. Then he measures the acceleration of the boxes as the worker pushes them. The chart shows his findings.

Force Needed to Push 10 Kg Boxes

Box Mass (kg)	Acceleration (m/s^2)
10.0	2.0
10.0	2.0
9.9	2.0
10.0	2.1

What force does the worker use to push a box?

A 2 N

B 10 N

C 20 N

D 40 N

---

8 The picture shows how a flashlight works.

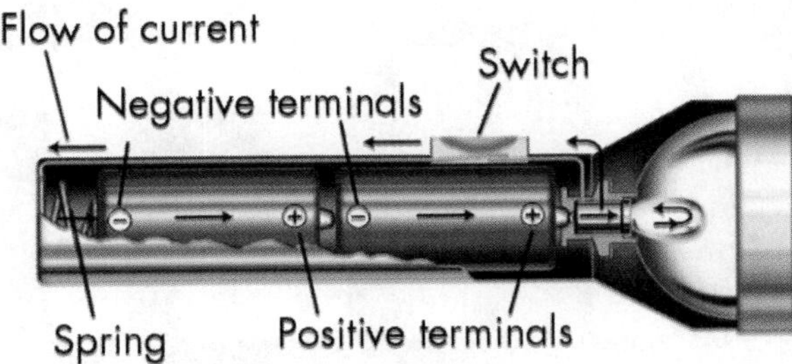

The flashlight's electric circuit has two batteries, a light bulb (a resistor), and a switch. How does turning the switch off affect the electricity in the circuit of the flashlight?

F Turning the switch off opens the circuit and stops the flow of electric charges.

G Turning the switch off closes the circuit and stops the flow of electric charges.

H Turning the switch off opens the circuit and allows the electric charges to flow.

J Turning the switch off closes the circuit and allows the electric charges to flow.

If you have trouble with . . .

Question	1	2	3	4	5	6	7	8
See chapter (lesson)	5 (1)	5 (4)	5 (2)	5 (3)	5 (3)	5 (1)	4 (2)	3 (4)
TEKS	7A	7D	7B	7C	7C	7A	6D	6B

WHERE did these drops come from?

The Water Cycle, Weather, and Climate

How does water move through the environment?

It has not rained, but after spending the night resting, this fly was covered with droplets in the morning.

Where do you think this water came from?

Texas Essential Knowledge and Skills

Supporting TEKS: 8A Differentiate between weather and climate. **8B** Explain how the Sun and the ocean interact in the water cycle.
Process TEKS: 1A, 2A, 2C, 2D, 2F, 2G, 3C, 3D

PEARSON Texas.com

Lab zone® Inquiry Warm-Up

TEKS 8B, 1A, 2C, 3C

How can groundwater move in the water cycle?

1. Make the model shown below.
2. Slowly add water until the lake is 1.5 cm deep.
3. Make it rain. Move the cup with holes over the land as your partner pours a cup of water into your cup. **Observe** the water level. Record your observations.

4. Cover the bottom end of a spray nozzle with nylon. Tape on the nylon. Put the end deep into the gravel. Pump the nozzle. Spray water into a resealable plastic bag held by your partner. **Observe** and record.

Materials

safety goggles
plastic container
gravel
paper cups
pitcher of water
metric ruler
pencil
tape
spray nozzle
piece of nylon
resealable plastic bag

Wear safety goggles.
If any water spills, notify your teacher immediately.

Inquiry Skill

You can **communicate** by using drawings and labels.

Explain Your Results

5. **Communicate** Explain how adding or removing water from the ground can affect the water level in lakes and rivers.

6. **Predict** how changing the water level in the lake or river might affect the level of the groundwater.

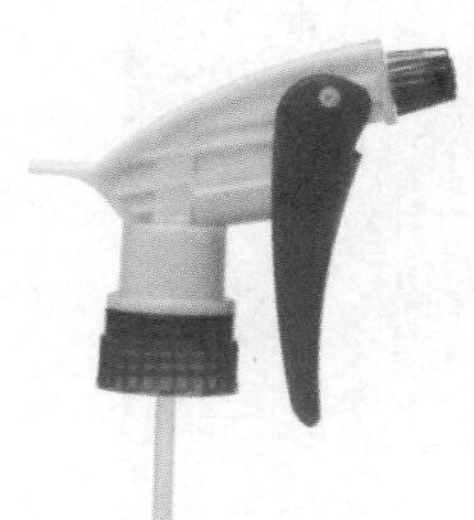

Focus on Cause and Effect

You will practice the reading strategy of identifying **cause and effect.** A cause is the reason something happens. The effect is the result of the action. Learning to understand cause and effect relationships can help you understand what you read and observe.

Coastal Climates

Communities located near oceans or other large bodies of water usually have a moderate climate. Water is the reason for this moderating effect. Water can absorb and store more thermal energy than air. When there is a change in temperature, air cools or warms quickly. However, water cools and warms slowly when the temperature changes. Since water temperatures influence air temperatures, land masses located near large bodies of water, such as oceans, usually have moderate climates.

Practice It!

Use the graphic organizer. List one cause and one effect from the example paragraph above.

Cause and Effect

Cause	Effect

Corpus Christi has a moderate climate because it is located on the Gulf of Mexico.

What is the water cycle?

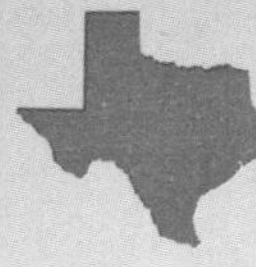

I will know TEKS 8B
I will know how to explain how the sun and the ocean interact in the water cycle. (Also **1A**, **2A**, **2C**, **2D**, **2F**)

Vocabulary
water vapor
water cycle
evaporation
condensation
precipitation

Connect to Social Studies

Social Studies TEKS 7D

When it rains, sleets, or snows, water falls to the ground. The soil, plants, and other things absorb some of the water. When no more water can be absorbed, the water flows into area streams, rivers, and lakes. A river basin is the area in which excess water flows. Streams and rivers carry the excess water to the oceans. The Rio Grande is one of the river basins in Texas.

Use a map to find where the Rio Grande starts and what body of water it flows into.

The Rio Grande starts San juans Mountain

The Rio Grande flows into Golf of mexico

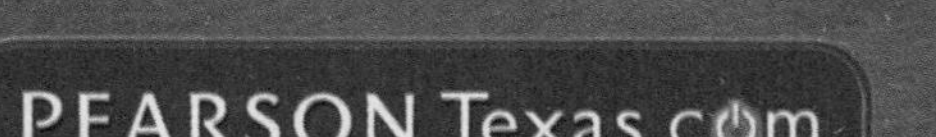

Quick Lab

TEKS 8B, 1A, 2A, 2C, 2F

Does a cloud form?

☑ **1.** Fill one bowl about $\frac{1}{3}$ full with warm water. Put nothing in the other bowl. Close both lids. Put the same number of ice cubes on each lid.

☑ **2. Observe** Collect information by detailed observations after 1 minute, 5 minutes, and 10 minutes.

Materials

2 plastic bowls with lids
warm water
ice cubes

Texas Safety
LAB RULES
If any water or ice spills, notify your teacher immediately.

Cloud or No Cloud?

	Observations	
Time	**Bowl With Warm Water**	**Bowl Without Water**
After 1 min	Cloudy	No clouds
After 5 min	Cloudy	No clouds
After 10 min	Cloudy	No clouds

Explain Your Results

3. Communicate Where did water condense? Did a cloud form? Discuss with a partner and record your conclusions.

Water in the Air

Look around you. Can you see any water? Even if you do not see it, water surrounds you all the time. This water is not in a liquid form as in rivers or a solid form as in glaciers. This water is an invisible gas called **water vapor.** Air always has some water vapor in it, even in the driest deserts. This water vapor was liquid water at some time in the past. A water particle from a plant, a tropical river, or the Arctic Ocean could become water vapor, and eventually it could return to Earth's surface in the form of rain.

Water vapor makes up a small percentage of the gases in the air. Particles of water vapor, like particles of other gases, are constantly moving.

1. **Sequence** Use the graphic organizer to sequence the events described above.

First

Water vaper surrounds us

Next

Water vaper is in the form of a gas

Finally

Its a small percentige of air

2. **Synthesize** Moisture has frozen on this man's beard. Where might the moisture have come from?

Water waper and snow

You can see water vapor forming tiny water droplets as it escapes the tea kettle into the cool room.
Water vapor forms tiny water droplets in the cool air as the warm air escapes from the tower.
The air in contact with the warm lake water is warmer than the surrounding air. It can hold more water vapor. As the warmer air cools, water vapor forms tiny droplets of water called fog.
Warm air can hold more water vapor than cold air. When it is cold outside and warm inside, tiny droplets of water form on the window that separates the two areas.

The Water Cycle

Water is always moving on, through, and above Earth as it changes from one form to another in the water cycle. The **water cycle** is the repeated movement of water through the environment in different forms. The water cycle is continuous, but we can talk about the different processes as steps. The steps of the water cycle include evaporation, condensation, precipitation, and runoff. These steps can be affected by temperature, pressure, wind, and the elevation of the land. A diagram of the water cycle is shown here.

Evaporation is the changing of a liquid, such as water, to a gas. When oceans or other bodies of water absorb energy from the sun, the temperature of the water increases. As a result, water evaporates into the atmosphere. Water vapor is water in the form of a gas in the air. In **condensation,** a gas, such as water vapor, turns into liquid. Clouds form when water vapor condenses into water droplets and ice crystals. In **precipitation,** the water falls from clouds as rain, snow, sleet, or hail. The water cycle can follow different paths. For example, condensation forms clouds, but it can also form dew.

Sublimation and deposition are other possible paths in the water cycle. Sublimation occurs when ice changes into water vapor without first melting. Deposition occurs when water vapor turns into ice without first becoming liquid water. The ice crystals that form on surfaces from deposition are called frost.

3. Fill in the Blank In the diagram to the right, complete the sentences to finish the labels.

4. CHALLENGE Look at the diagram below. Where do you think the water cycle begins?

....

....

....

....

Some water vapor rises and .... to form clouds. Some water vapor turns into frost or dew. Frost and dew often form in the morning and evaporate soon after sunrise.

Water .... from the ocean, lakes, and puddles.

5. **Apply** How might pesticides and fertilizers on land become a problem in an ocean ecosystem?

....

....

Very slowly, snow and ice turn into water vapor by sublimation.
Raindrops and snowflakes fall to Earth. Most .... falls on the ocean.
Some rain or melted snow soaks into the ground and becomes groundwater.
Runoff is water that flows off the land into streams, rivers, lakes, and the ocean.
Groundwater slowly moves into rivers, lakes, and the ocean.

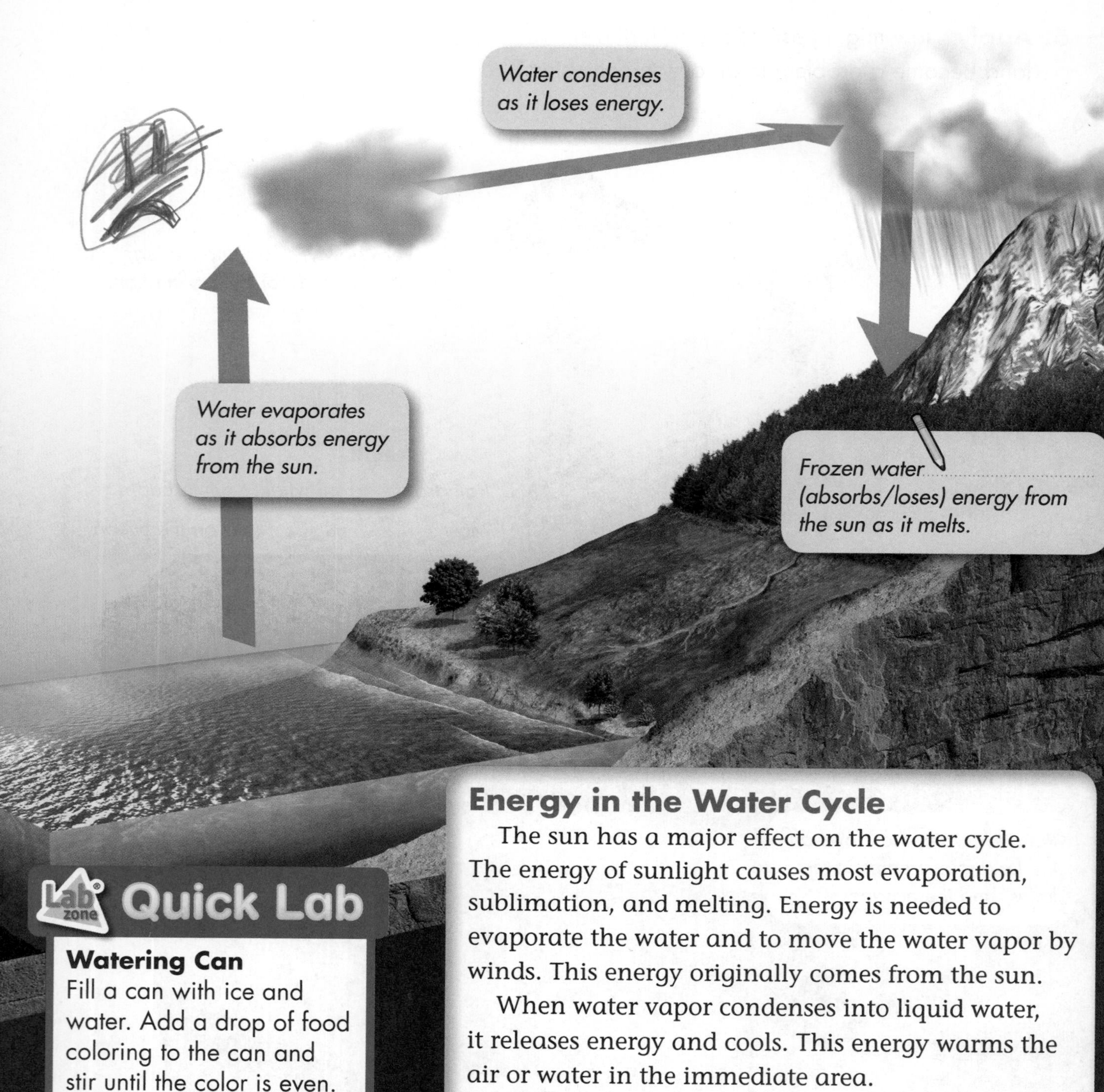
Water condenses
as it loses energy.
Water evaporates
as it absorbs energy
from the sun.
Frozen water
(absorbs/loses) energy from
the sun as it melts.

Quick Lab

Watering Can

Fill a can with ice and water. Add a drop of food coloring to the can and stir until the color is even. Observe. When droplets form on the outside of the can, wipe them with a white paper towel. What are the droplets and where did they come from? How do you know?

TEKS 2C, 2D

Energy in the Water Cycle

The sun has a major effect on the water cycle. The energy of sunlight causes most evaporation, sublimation, and melting. Energy is needed to evaporate the water and to move the water vapor by winds. This energy originally comes from the sun.

When water vapor condenses into liquid water, it releases energy and cools. This energy warms the air or water in the immediate area.

6. **Main Idea and Details** **Circle** the main idea and **underline** two details in the first paragraph above.

7. **Determine** Read and complete the captions in the diagram above. **Circle** the part of the diagram that shows water vapor turning into liquid water.

Connect to **Math**

Math TEKS 1C

Estimating Area

One way to estimate the area of a shape is to use a grid that divides the shape into square units. On the map below, each square unit represents 1 square kilometer. The lake completely covers 6 squares. Also, 8 squares are about half covered, making 4 more whole squares. A good estimate for the area of the lake is 10 square kilometers.

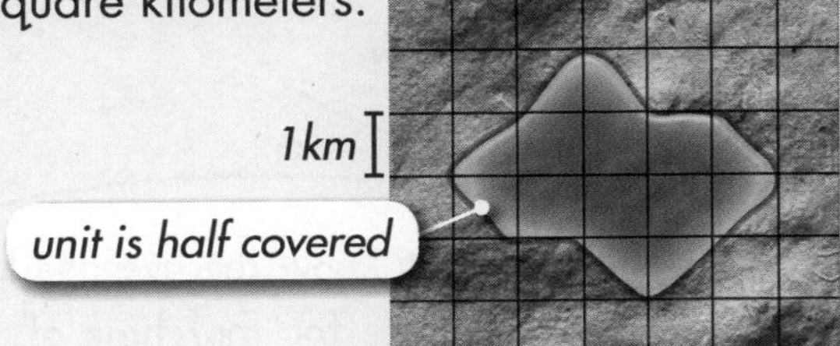

On the map below, each square unit represents 1 square kilometer. Estimate the area of the lake below.

....

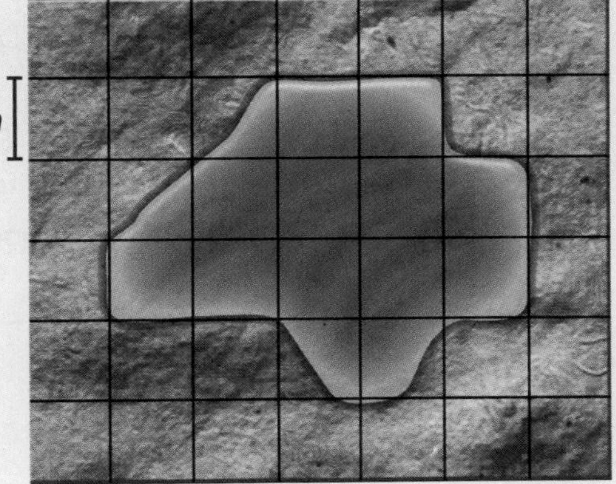

got it? TEKS 8B

8. Explain Explain how the sun and the ocean interact in the water cycle.

....

....

....

9. Think about what you learned in this lesson. How does water move through the environment?

....

....

Stop! I need help with ....

Wait! I have a question about ....

Go! Now I know ....

What is weather?

I will know TEKS 8A
I will know what weather is. I will know some tools that are used to study weather. (Also 2C, 2F, 2G)

Vocabulary
weather
meteorologist
barometric pressure
wind

We are going tubing down the Guadalupe River in New Braunfels in September. I wonder if it will be cold that time of year?

Do you know the average low temperature for that time of year?

The average low temperatures in September for New Braunfels for the last five years were 13°C, 11°C, 14°C, 14°C, and 17°C.

Can you help me find the average low temperature in New Braunfels for the last five years?

Show your work To find an average, you add all of the temperatures in your list and divide by the number of temperatures in your list. Math TEKS 1A, 1B, 3K

Quick Lab

TEKS 8A, 2F, 2G

How accurate are weather forecasts?

Materials

local 5-day weather forecast

1. Look at the current 5-day weather forecast. **Record** the forecasted high temperatures.
2. Construct an appropriate table, using technology including computers, to examine and evaluate forecasted highs, actual highs, and the difference between the two.
3. Check the weather report each day for the next 5 days. Record the actual high for the previous day.
4. Compare the forecast data with the actual data.

Weather Report Predictions

Day	Forecast High (°C)	Actual High (°C)	Difference Between Forecast and Actual (°C)
1			
2			
3			
4			
5			

Explain Your Results

5. What was the largest difference between the forecast and actual temperatures?

6. **Draw a Conclusion** Do you see a pattern in the accuracy of the forecasts? Explain.

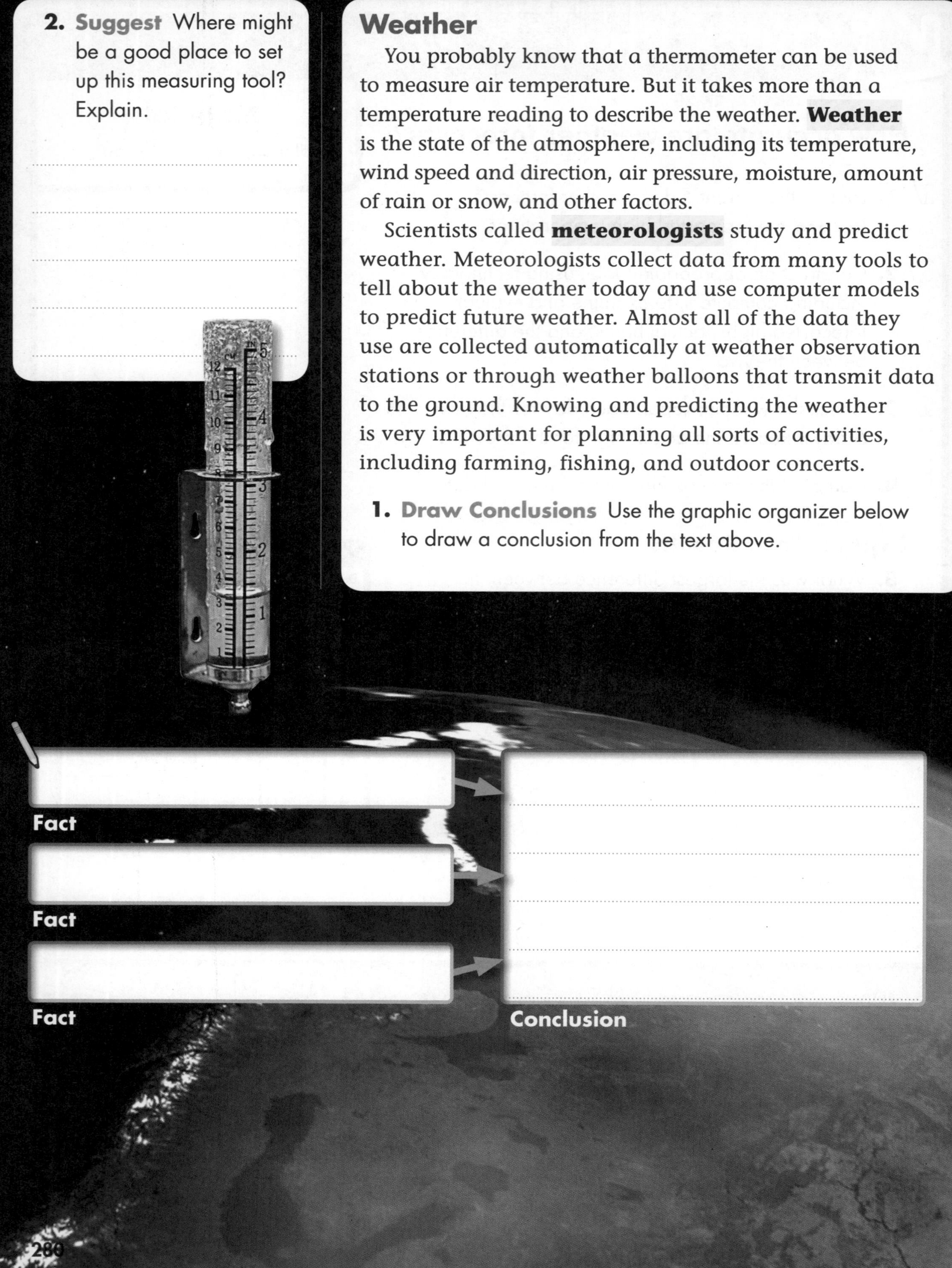

2. Suggest Where might be a good place to set up this measuring tool? Explain.

Weather

You probably know that a thermometer can be used to measure air temperature. But it takes more than a temperature reading to describe the weather. **Weather** is the state of the atmosphere, including its temperature, wind speed and direction, air pressure, moisture, amount of rain or snow, and other factors.

Scientists called **meteorologists** study and predict weather. Meteorologists collect data from many tools to tell about the weather today and use computer models to predict future weather. Almost all of the data they use are collected automatically at weather observation stations or through weather balloons that transmit data to the ground. Knowing and predicting the weather is very important for planning all sorts of activities, including farming, fishing, and outdoor concerts.

1. Draw Conclusions Use the graphic organizer below to draw a conclusion from the text above.

Fact

Fact

Fact

Conclusion

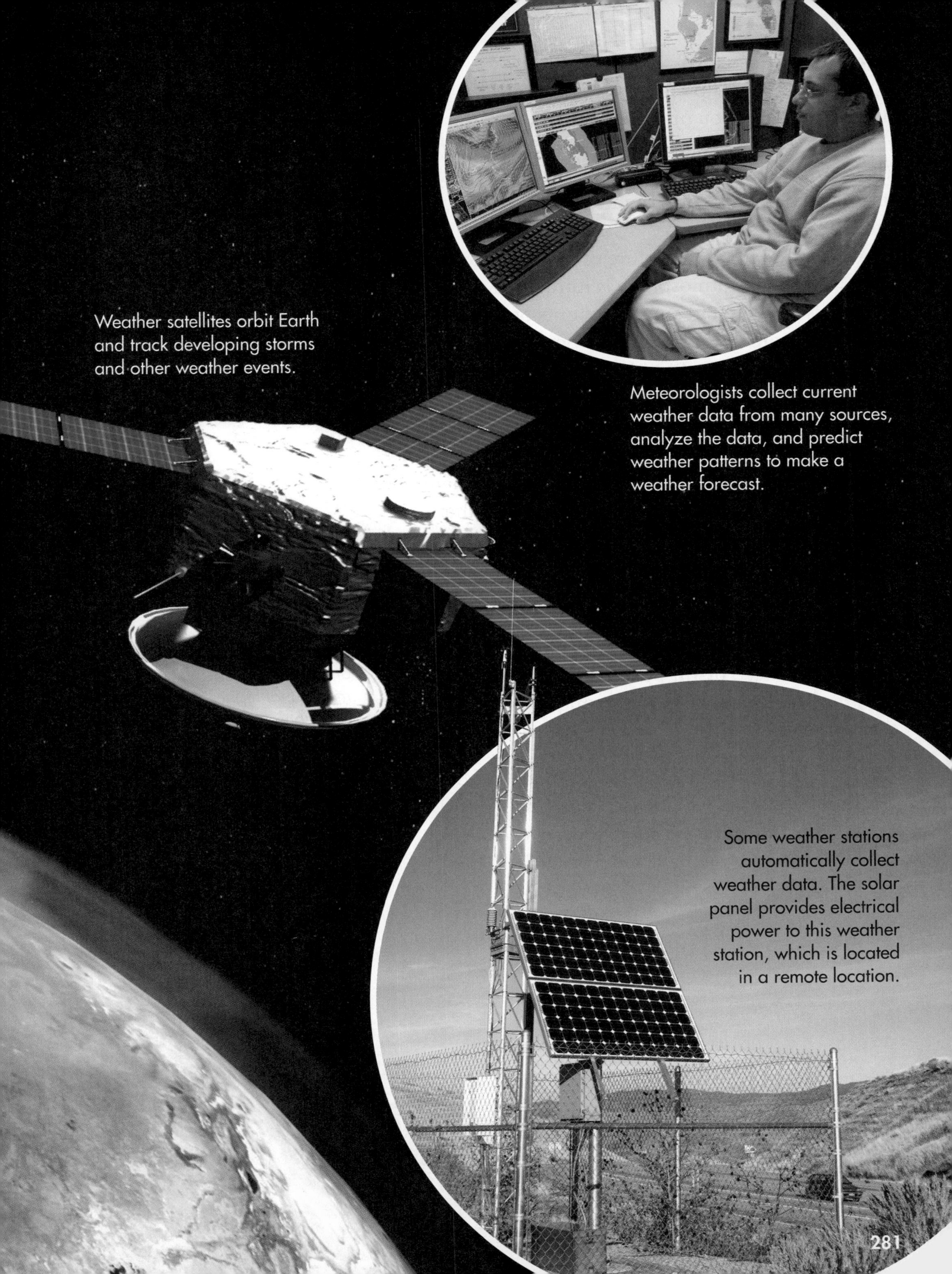

Weather satellites orbit Earth and track developing storms and other weather events.

Meteorologists collect current weather data from many sources, analyze the data, and predict weather patterns to make a weather forecast.

Some weather stations automatically collect weather data. The solar panel provides electrical power to this weather station, which is located in a remote location.

Barometric Pressure

When you look up on a clear day, you see a high, blue sky. You are really looking through 9,600 km (about 6,000 mi) of air. The blanket of air that surrounds Earth is its atmosphere. Like other matter, air has mass and takes up space.

Air is made up of a mixture of invisible gases. Over $\frac{3}{4}$ of Earth's atmosphere is nitrogen. Most of the rest is oxygen, but small amounts of carbon dioxide gas are also present. The part of the atmosphere closest to Earth's surface contains water vapor. The amount of water vapor depends on time and place. For example, air over the ocean or a forest has more water vapor than air over a desert.

Gravity pulls the mass of air in the atmosphere toward Earth's surface. The pushing force of the atmosphere is called **barometric pressure.** Air pushes with equal force in all directions. Many kilograms of gas are pressing down on your school building. They do not crush it because the air inside the building exerts pressure too. Air pushing down is balanced by air pushing up and sideways. Air pressure decreases as you go higher in the atmosphere.

A barometer is an instrument that shows air pressure.

Air particles are represented here by small, blue spheres. As you move upward through the atmosphere, air particles are farther apart. This means that higher in the atmosphere, the pressure is lower.

12 km
11 km
10 km
9 km
8 km
7 km
6 km
5 km
4 km
3 km
2 km
1 km
0 km

3. CHALLENGE Suppose you take two readings from a barometer. One reading is taken at the top of a tall building and the other at ground level. Which reading is likely to be higher? Why?

Temperature

Air temperature also affects weather. As the sun warms Earth's surface, air that is in contact with the surface becomes warmer. As the air particles move farther apart, the air becomes lighter. The warm air rises, causing an area of low pressure to form, and air from areas with higher pressure rushes in. If the air near Earth's surface cools, the particles in the air become more closely packed. This denser, cooler air pushes down with more pressure. An area of high pressure forms. Air from this area flows into lower-pressure areas. The temperature of the air also affects the type of precipitation—rain, snow, or sleet.

4. **Predict** What would happen if the air outside the hot air balloon were as hot as the air inside?

Connect to **Math**

Line Graphs

Math TEKS 1A, 1D, 9

Look at the graph of average monthly high temperatures for Port Isabel, Texas.

Average High Temperatures in Port Isabel, Texas

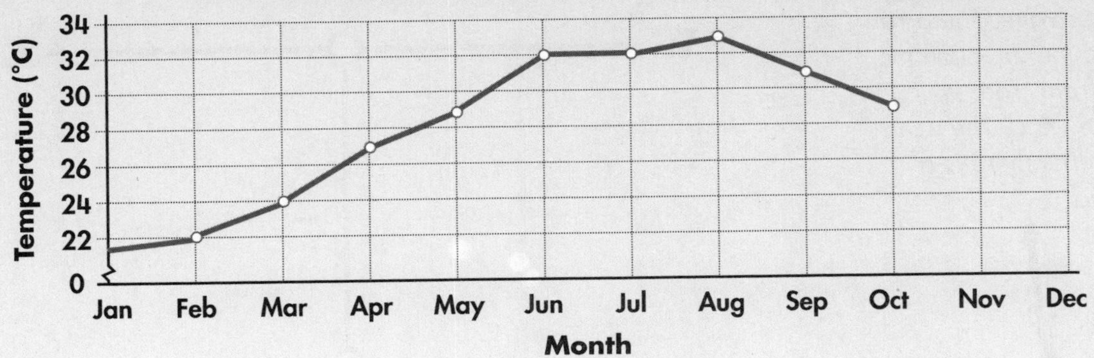

1. In November, the average high temperature was about 26°C. In December, it was about 22°C. Use a computer to copy the graph. Plot the missing data points and complete the graph.

2. Between which two months did Port Isabel have the greatest decrease in average temperature? About how many degrees did the temperature decrease?

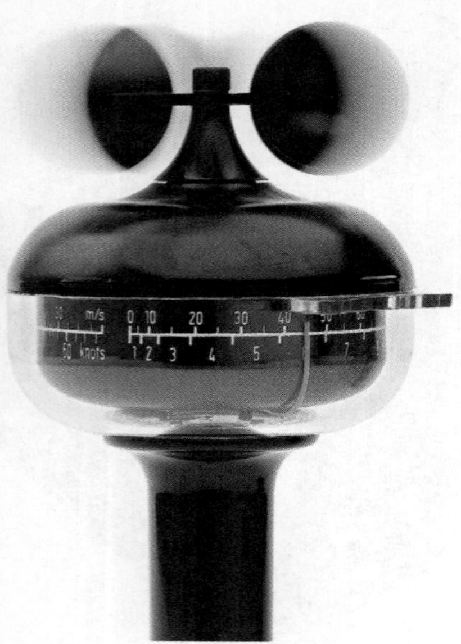

Meteorologists measure wind speed using an instrument called an anemometer.

Winds

Wind is air movement caused by differences in pressure. In general, air moves from areas of high pressure to areas of low pressure. Think about a balloon. When you let air out of a balloon, air rushes from inside the balloon where pressure is higher to where pressure is lower outside the balloon. You can feel wind.

Wind speed and direction affect weather. Local weather can be affected by special winds called jet streams. A jet stream is a narrow band of high-speed wind. A polar jet stream blows from west to east high in the atmosphere over North America. The jet stream affects day-to-day weather and seasons. In the winter, the jet stream can bring cold air from the north to states as far south as Kentucky. In the summer, the jet stream brings warmer air north into Canada.

The name of a wind is the direction from which it blows. A north wind comes from the north and moves toward the south. Winds near the ocean are sometimes named differently.

Wind direction can be observed with a weather vane. The arrow points toward the direction the wind comes from. That is, it points into the wind. The vane below shows that there is a northerly wind.

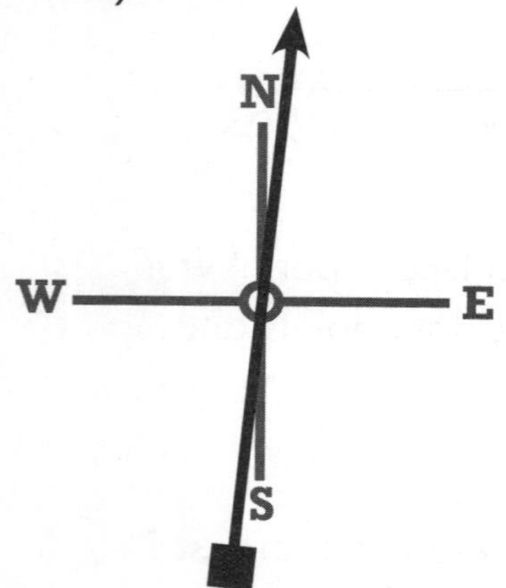

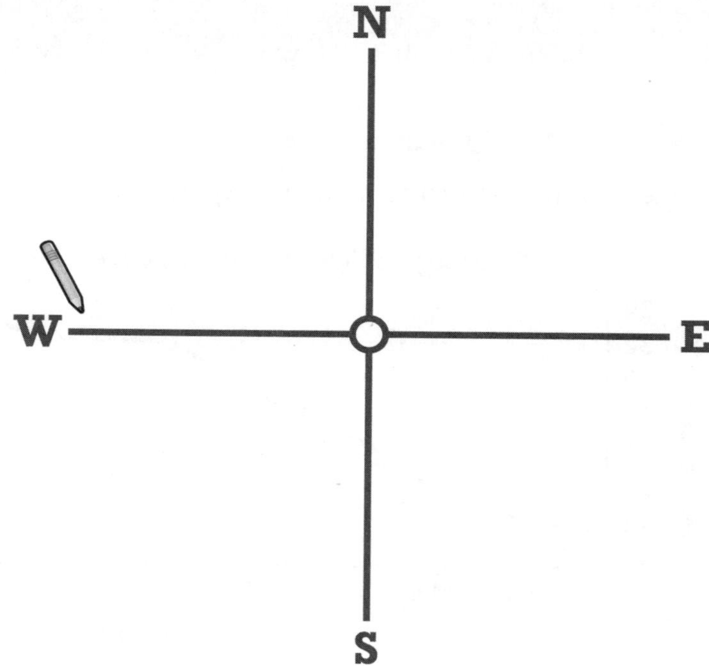

5. Draw On the blank weather vane diagram above, draw an arrow to represent a southeasterly wind.

Water in the Atmosphere

Three other factors for determining weather are humidity, clouds, and precipitation. Humidity is the amount of water vapor in the air. The particles of water vapor are too small to be visible, but when conditions are right, they can come together to form small water droplets and ice crystals. These droplets and crystals are bigger than water vapor particles and can reflect light from the sun. At this point, we can see the water as a cloud. If the droplets or crystals get large enough, they can fall to the ground as precipitation, such as rain or snow.

Running Hot and Cold
Work with an adult. Fill a bottle with hot water and then wait a minute or so. Gently pour the water out and immediately cap the bottle. Now run cold water over the bottle. What happens? Can you reverse this process?
TEKS 2C

6. **Summarize** What do the factors humidity, clouds, and precipitation have in common? List two things.

TEKS 8A

7. **Describe** What is weather?

8. List four factors that are commonly used to describe the weather.

Stop! I need help with

Wait! I have a question about

Go! Now I know

What is climate?

I will know TEKS 8A
I will know what climate is. I will know how to differentiate between weather and climate. (Also 1A, 2C, 2D, 2F, 3C)

Vocabulary
climate
latitude
elevation

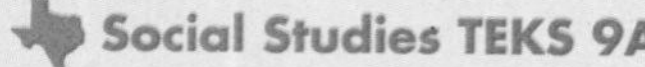

Social Studies

Social Studies TEKS 9A

Many parts of the Southwestern United States can get very hot during the day and very cold at night. Houses there are often designed to protect the people inside from uncomfortable temperature swings and reduce heating and cooling expenses.

Adobe is a building material that has been used for thousands of years. It is made of clay, water, sand, and organic matter. Adobe walls warm up and cool down relatively slowly. After sunrise, as outdoor temperatures quickly rise, the walls of an adobe house help keep the indoors cool. After sunset, the walls slowly release some of the heat they absorbed during the day, keeping the house warm.

Describe how and why people in the Southwest have adapted to their environment in the United States with adobe.

PEARSON Texas.com

Quick Lab

TEKS 6A, 8A, 1A, 2C, 2D, 2F, 3C

How does a thermometer work?

Materials

Make a Thermometer worksheet
plastic jar
room-temperature water
metric ruler
red food coloring
modeling clay
plastic bowl with very warm water
plastic bowl with very cold water
plastic straw

1. Use the Make a Thermometer sheet. Make a thermometer. Will it work like a regular thermometer? Discuss.

2. Place your thermometer in warm water. What do you **observe?**

3. **Predict** what will happen if you place your thermometer in cold water. Tell how you made your prediction. Test your prediction.

Texas Safety
LAB RULES
Do not use dangerously warm water.

Explain Your Results

4. **Analyze and Interpret** Analyze information to construct a reasonable explanation about how the thermometer might work. Use indirect, or inferred, evidence from the lab to construct your explanation.

Average Weather

The words *weather* and *climate* do not have the same definitions. The difference between climate and weather is the time interval. Weather describes the conditions of the atmosphere for short periods of time, such as days, weeks, months, and years. **Climate** describes the conditions of the atmosphere (weather) for longer periods of time, such as decades or centuries. Climate includes information such as the average amount of precipitation, the average temperature, and how much the temperature changes over time.

Texas is a large state with a range of climates. Climate and plants are related. Plants grow best in certain types of climates. It is unwise to plant tropical plants in north Texas because they will freeze and die during the winter. Plants that thrive in north Texas might die in the coastal areas of Houston or Corpus Christi. Plants that live for many years, such as trees, are dependent on the climate. Plants that live only for a season are less dependent on the climate.

1. **Explain** the difference between weather and climate.

Texas Hill Country is one example of a climate in which peaches thrive. Fredericksburg, Texas is located in the Hill Country, and several peach orchards are located near there. Peach trees can withstand freezing temperatures in the winter, but a late freeze can destroy the peach crop for the year.

Parts of western Texas near El Paso and Presidio are located in the Chihuahuan Desert. Shrubs grow in this region, but trees do not grow well there. Water is scarce, and only plants that can survive on little water can grow there, unless the plants are irrigated.

These bald cypress trees (or swamp cypress as they are sometimes called) thrive in the swamp-like Caddo Lake. These trees need lots of water to grow well.

Citrus fruits, such as grapefruits, grow in the lower Rio Grande valley. Citrus crops often are damaged if the temperatures drop below freezing. The Rio Grande valley is the best place to grow citrus trees in Texas.

Factors That Affect Climate

Different areas of the world have different climates. Some factors that affect climate include latitude, elevation, and closeness to large bodies of water.

Latitude

One factor that affects the climate of a place is its latitude. **Latitude** is a measure of how far a place is from the equator. Latitude is measured in degrees, starting at 0° at the equator. Energy from the sun hits Earth's surface more directly at the equator. An area nearer to the equator is usually hotter than places farther away.

There are three major zones of climate according to latitude. The tropical zone extends from 23.5° south to 23.5° north latitude and contains the equator itself. Here, the sun's energy hits most directly all year. The tropical zone is usually warm.

You may know that places like the North and South Poles are generally quite cold. The polar zones receive energy from the sun less directly than the tropical zone. The polar zone extends from 66.5° to 90° north and from 66.5° to 90° south.

In between the polar and tropical zones are the temperate zones. Most of the United States is in a temperate zone. Here, energy from the sun is more direct during the summer, causing the temperature to be higher. The sun's energy is less direct in the winter, which causes winters to be colder.

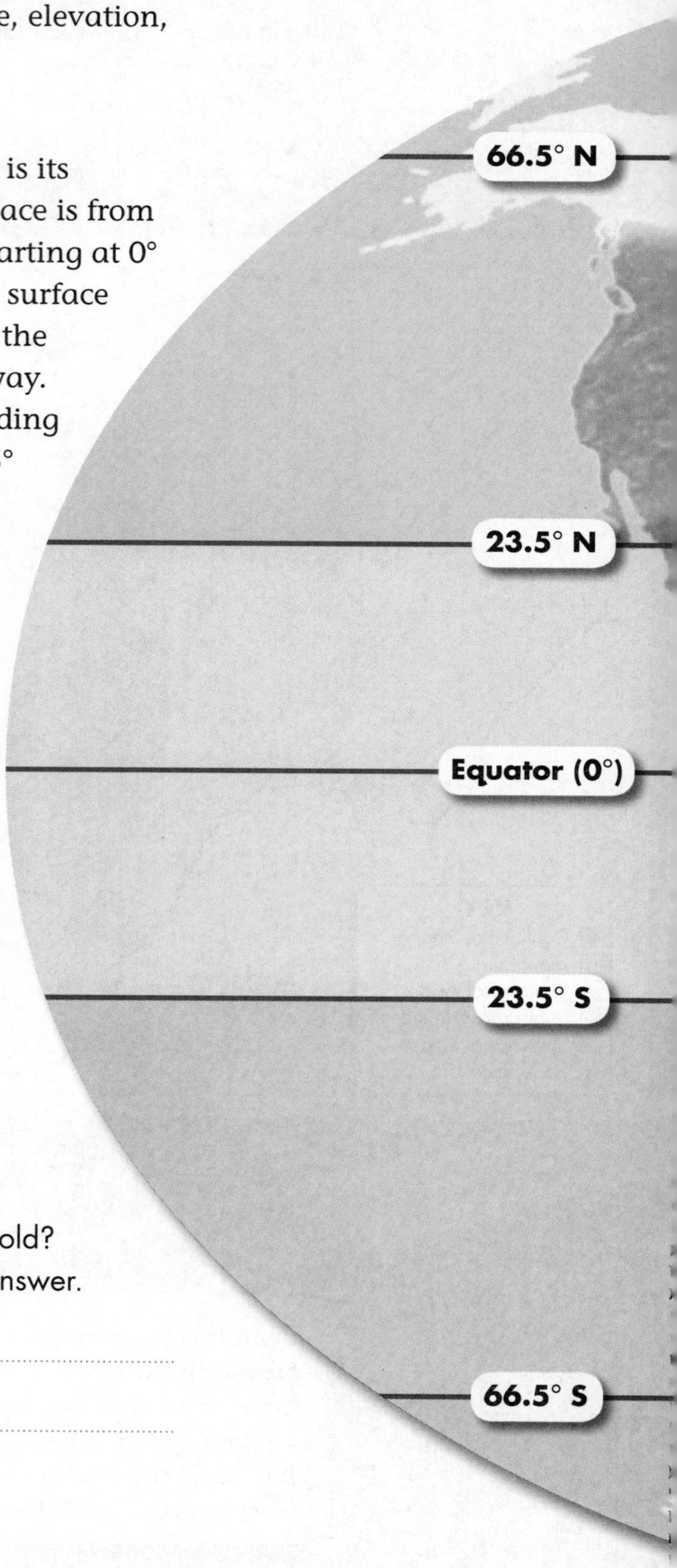

66.5° N

23.5° N

Equator (0°)

23.5° S

66.5° S

2. Support Why are the polar regions usually cold? **Underline** one statement that supports your answer.

3. Describe Write two words to describe each climate zone.

polar zone

temperate zone

tropical zone

temperate zone

polar zone

4. Justify Deciduous trees have leaves that fall off during some seasons. Might you find deciduous trees in the tropical zone? Why?

Quick Lab

Climate Zones

Find your city or town on a relief map. Note its latitude. Note nearby features such as lakes or mountains. Look for another city on the map that is at about the same latitude. Would you expect this city to have a similar climate to yours? Explain.

Bodies of Water

The ocean can affect a climate by slowing the rise and fall of air temperature. Remember that bodies of water become warm and cool more slowly than land. Because of this, the temperature of the air near water does not change as quickly as air inland. In the winter, large beaches often do not get as cold as areas just a few miles inland. In the summer, the air over beaches is often cooler than air over areas inland.

Ocean currents can make a climate warmer or cooler. The Gulf Stream and the North Atlantic Drift are large currents that carry warm water northward. The water warms the winds above it. These winds make northern Europe's climate much warmer than it would be otherwise. A change in these currents could change the climate of Europe. On the other hand, cold currents that flow from Alaska to California make that coastal climate cooler.

5. Infer Think of the effect of the ocean. Would Dallas, Texas be warmer or colder than Charleston, South Carolina in the winter? Explain.

Charleston, South Carolina

Dallas, Texas

Elevation

Mountain ranges may have different climates than areas around them. Higher land is cooler because in the lower part of the atmosphere temperature decreases with increased elevation. **Elevation** is the height above sea level.

Areas on opposite sides of a mountain range can have very different climates. This happens because the air does not have much moisture in it by the time it reaches the other side.

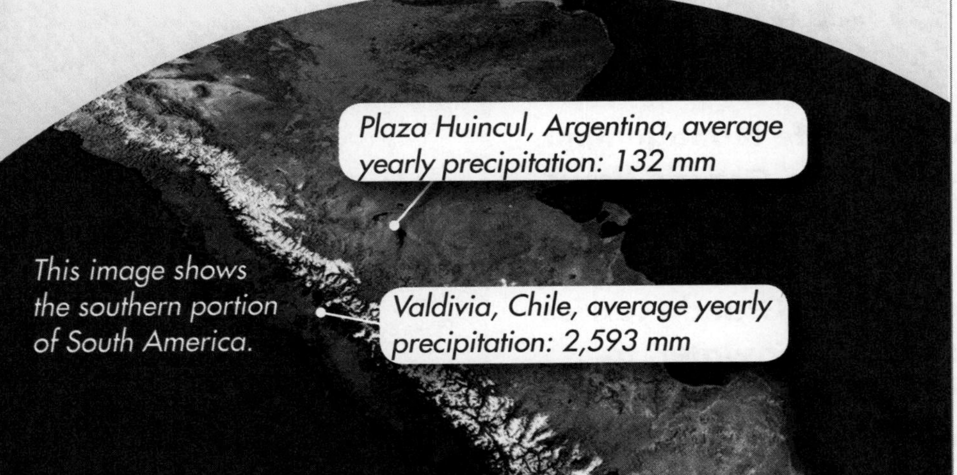

This image shows the southern portion of South America.

6. Show Draw an arrow to show how wind flows between the cities shown on the map. Explain your answer.

got it?

7. Cause and Effect It is December. You take a bus trip from San Antonio, Texas—which is in the southern part of the state—north to Amarillo, Texas, in the panhandle. What temperature change would you expect? Explain.

8. Name three factors that can influence climate.

Stop! I need help with

Wait! I have a question about

Go! Now I know

The Water Cycle and Weather

South of the Las Palomas Wildlife Management Unit near Port Isabel, Texas, the Rio Grande flows into the Gulf of Mexico. Precipitation from areas in Colorado, New Mexico, Texas, and Mexico drains into the Rio Grande. The Rio Grande carries this precipitation, in the form of river water, to the Gulf of Mexico. All along the route, the water evaporates, condenses, and forms clouds. At some point, the water falls in the form of precipitation again. The water that falls onto land that is drained by the Rio Grande flows once again to the Gulf of Mexico, and the cycle repeats.

The water cycle and weather are closely related. All forms of precipitation—rain, sleet, snow, and ice—are part of the water cycle. Humid weather is caused by water vapor from the water cycle. The sun provides energy for the water in the oceans, rivers, and other waterways to evaporate. Coastal cities like Houston and Port Isabel can be very humid because of the evaporated water in the air.

Explain how water in the water cycle affects weather in your city.

Precipitation that falls in the Rio Grande river basin flows to the Gulf of Mexico. Water that evaporates from the flowing river, as well as the water in the river, are both part of the water cycle.

STEM

Go Green!

Straw Bale Homes

TEKS 3D

Texas is hot during the summer. It can be expensive to cool the inside of a house. Early pioneers on the prairie discovered that homes made of straw bales were sturdy. These homes also were cooler on the inside during the summer and warmer during the winter. The straw insulated the inside of the home from the weather outdoors. Straw bale construction is used today to build homes that are energy efficient. Straw is harvested from fields and used to construct the walls of the home. The home might be made of straw, but it doesn't have to be rustic. Some homes have the modern touches that you see in more conventional homes. Straw is a "green" building material because you can grow a new crop of straw every year. Trees, on the other hand, take several years before they are mature enough to use for lumber.

Analyze What are some advantages of homes built from straw bales?

TEKS 8A, 2F

Where is the hurricane going?

Weather forecasters record where a hurricane was and where it is. They find the direction it was going. They consider other factors, too. Then they predict its path. They warn people in the path that a hurricane might be coming.

Materials

Storm Map worksheet

Inquiry Skill

To help **predict** where a hurricane might go, you make inferences based on what you already know (where the hurricane has been and where it is currently).

Follow a Procedure

1. Look at the Storm Map.
Find where the hurricane was on Day 1 and Day 2. Think about its direction. **Predict** where it will go. What places would you warn that a hurricane might come? Record your first prediction in the Prediction Chart.

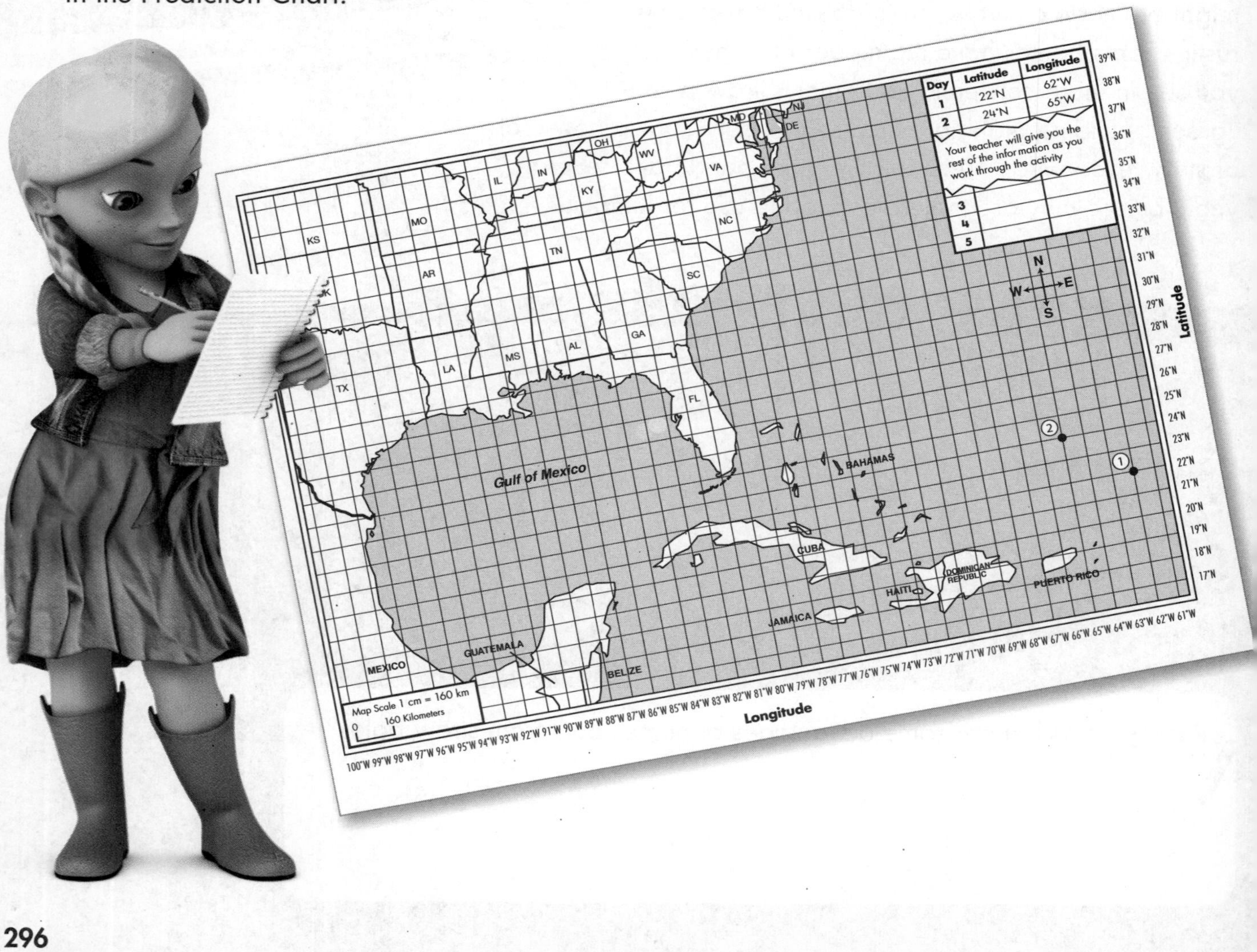

Day	Latitude	Longitude
1	22°N	62°W
2	24°N	65°W
Your teacher will give you the rest of the information as you work through the activity		
3		
4		
5		

Prediction Chart		
	Prediction What places would you warn that a hurricane might be approaching?	**Accuracy** How accurate was your prediction?
1st prediction (from Step 1)		
2nd prediction (from Step 2)		

☐ **2.** Your teacher will tell you the hurricane's location on Day 3.
Mark this position on the Storm Map.
Predict where the hurricane will go next.
What places would you warn? Record your second prediction.

☐ **3.** Your teacher will tell you the hurricane's locations on Day 4 and Day 5.
Mark these locations on the Storm Map.
Complete the Prediction Chart.

Analyze and Conclude

4. Communicate Share with a partner how you **predicted** where the hurricane might go. Use the lines below to write some notes on what your partner said.

5. How might people be affected by an accurate prediction? How might they be affected by one that is not accurate?

Lab Investigation

TEKS 8A, 2F, 2G

How do you construct a weather map?

Forecasters use weather charts and maps to organize, examine, and evaluate current weather conditions. Most weather maps display air temperature, air pressure, and precipitation.

The weather map on the next page shows red and blue lines called fronts. A front is a boundary between two large masses of air with different temperatures, amounts of water vapor, and pressures. Cold fronts, represented by blue lines, bring colder weather. Warm fronts, represented by red lines, bring warmer weather. The triangles or half-circles on the lines point in the direction the front is moving. Fronts are boundaries between air masses. They often bring cloudy weather. Areas of high pressure that are away from fronts have clear skies.

Materials

computer
Internet access
blank map of the United States
colored pencils

Inquiry Skill

You can construct a map to **evaluate** information.

Follow a Procedure

☐ **1.** Look at the weather map. What is the weather like in north Texas?

....

☐ **2.** Look at the weather map. What feature on the map indicates why it is raining in north Texas?

....

☐ **3.** Use the Internet to find a weather map for the current day. Examine and evaluate the map to determine in which direction the weather is moving.

☐ **4.** Find an area 100 km away in the direction of the weather movement. Observe the weather for that area for the next four days. Organize the weather information in a table.

5. Get a copy of a blank map of the United States from your teacher. With your table, construct a weather map, using technology including computers, to organize, examine, and evaluate information you collected about weather. Use the Common Weather Symbols key on this page to find the symbols that you might need.

Analyze and Conclude

6. **Communicate** How can fronts affect weather?

7. Prepare a weather forecast for the location on your weather map and tell it to a partner. Be sure to include high and low temperatures for the day in your forecast. Use the Internet to find any additional information that you might need for your forecast.

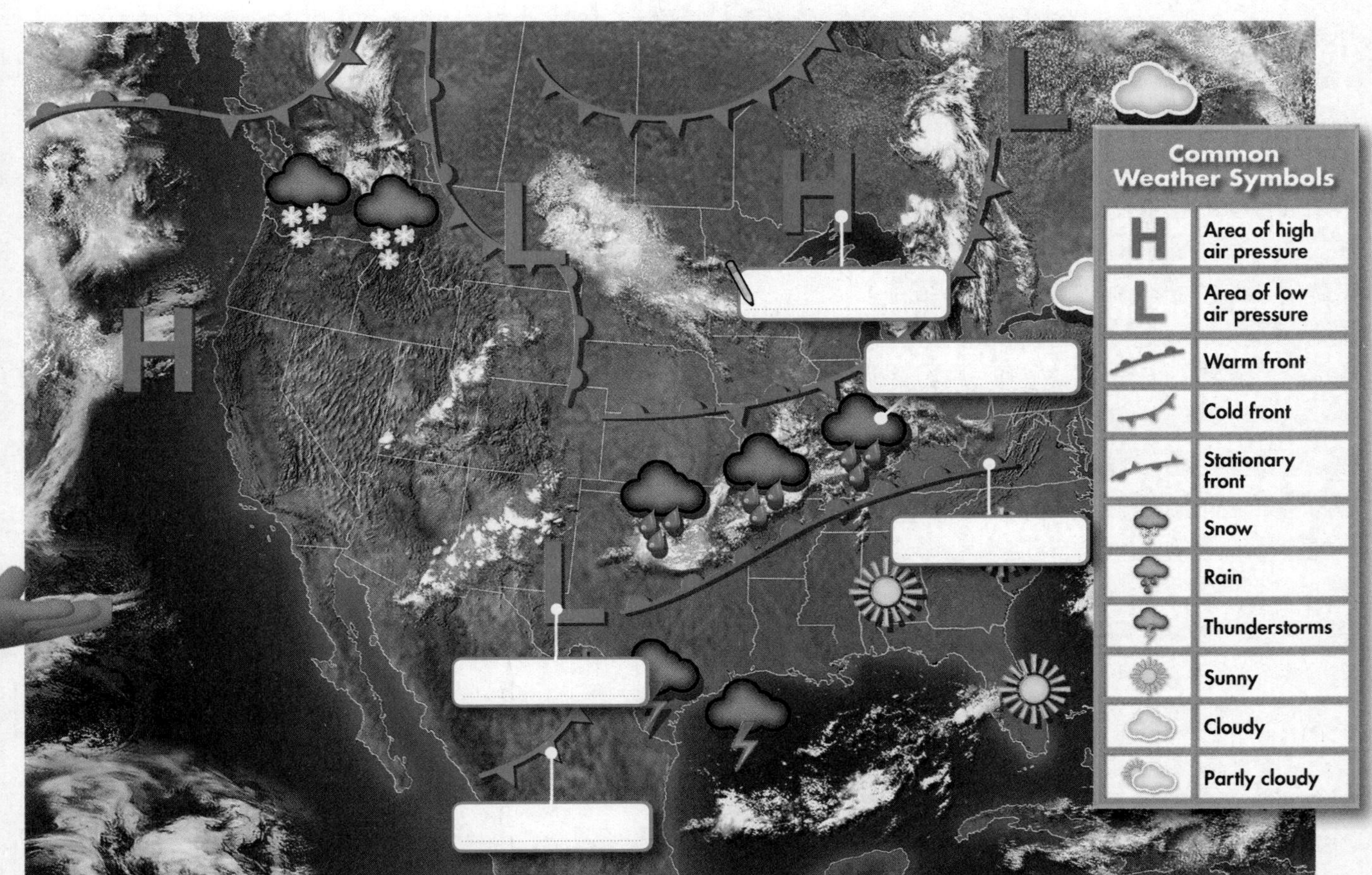

TEXAS

my planet Diary

TEKS 2F

One liter of sea water contains around 35 g of salt.

There's nothing like a tall glass of cool water on a hot day. People in all parts of the world need fresh water to drink and to grow crops. While much of our planet is covered in water, the water in the ocean is salt water.

There are places around the world that do not have much fresh water. However, people can use water from the sea after the salt has been removed from it. Desalination removes salt from seawater to get fresh water. Seawater can be distilled. This involves boiling seawater to make water vapor, which condenses into fresh water and leaves the salt behind. Desalination takes a lot of energy and is expensive, but costs are decreasing as technology improves. In Texas, a desalination pilot study at Laguana Madre Water District in Port Isabel was conducted to determine the cost of a desalination plant. Desalination plants could increase the amount of fresh water available in Texas.

What do you think might happen to the salt that comes out of seawater during desalination?

Vocabulary Smart Cards

water vapor
water cycle
evaporation
condensation
precipitation
weather
meteorologist
barometric pressure
wind
climate
latitude
elevation

Play a Game!

Cut out the Vocabulary Smart Cards.

Work with a partner. One person puts the cards picture-side up. The other person puts the cards picture-side down.

Take turns matching each word with its definition.

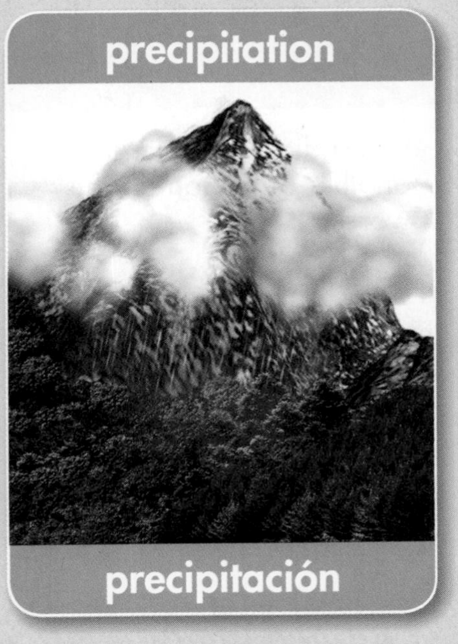

water in the form of an invisible gas

Write an example of where you might find water vapor.

agua en forma de gas invisible

the process in which a gas turns into a liquid

Write a sentence using this word.

proceso en el que un gas se convierte en líquido

Interactive Vocabulary

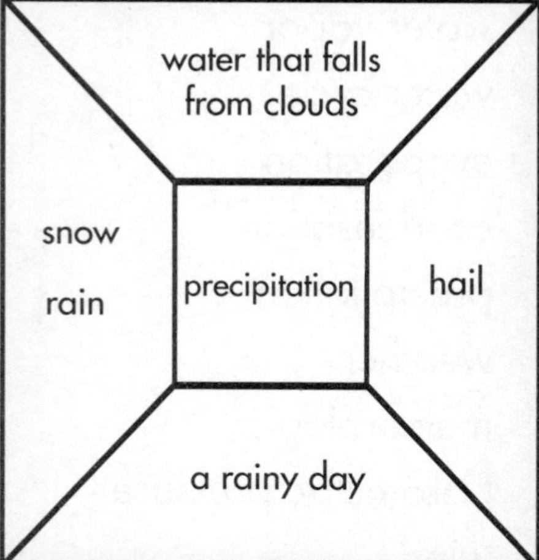

Make a Word Frame!

Choose a vocabulary term and write it in the center of the frame. Write details about the vocabulary term.

repeated movement of water through the environment in different forms

Draw a picture that represents the term.

movimiento repetido del agua en formas distintas a través del medio ambiente

water that falls from clouds as rain, snow, sleet, or hail

Use a dictionary. Find another definition for this word.

agua que cae de las nubes en forma de lluvia, nieve, aguanieve o granizo

the changing of a liquid to a gas

Write a sentence using the verb form of this word.

cambio de líquido a gas

the state of the atmosphere

Write three examples.

condición de la atmósfera

climate

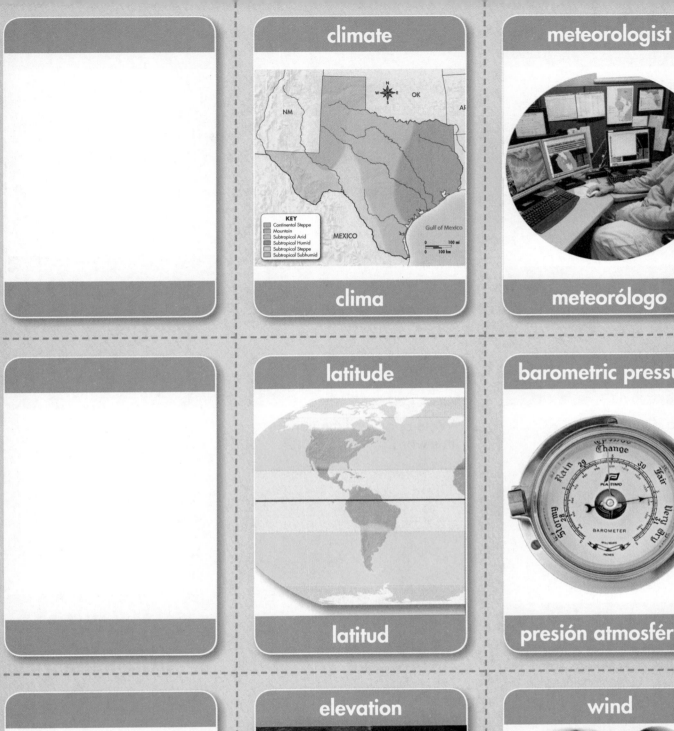

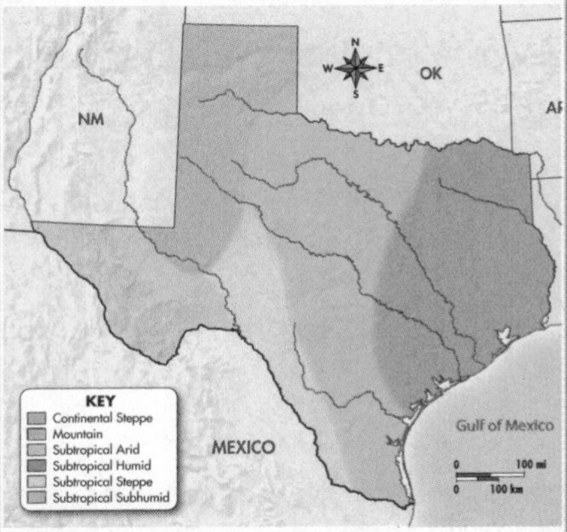

clima

meteorologist

meteorólogo

latitude

latitud

barometric pressure

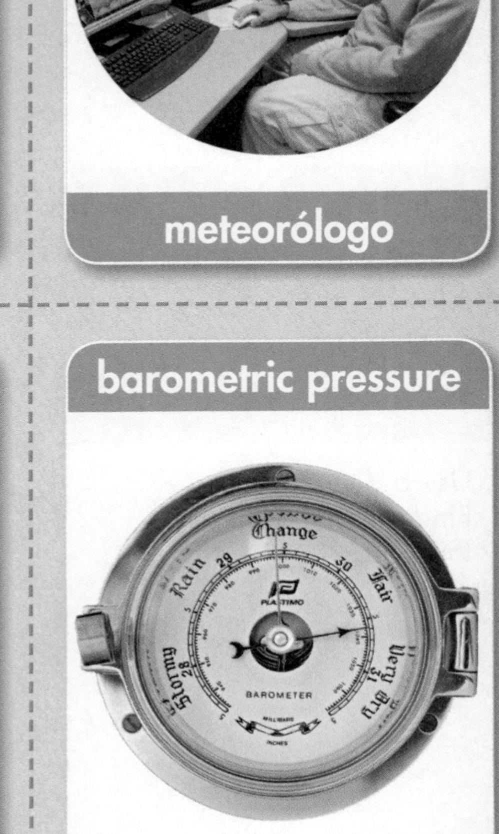

presión atmosférica

elevation

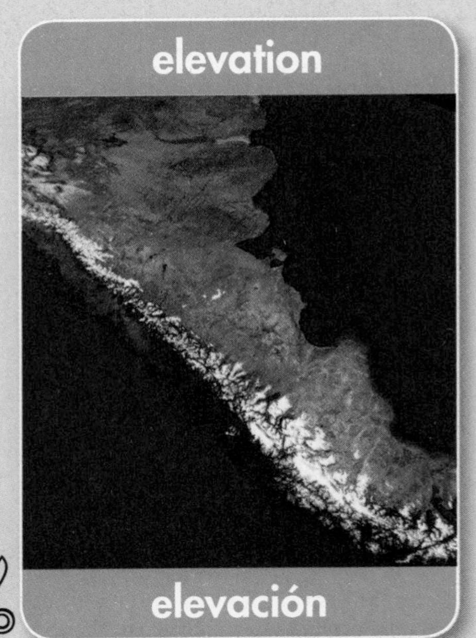

elevación

wind

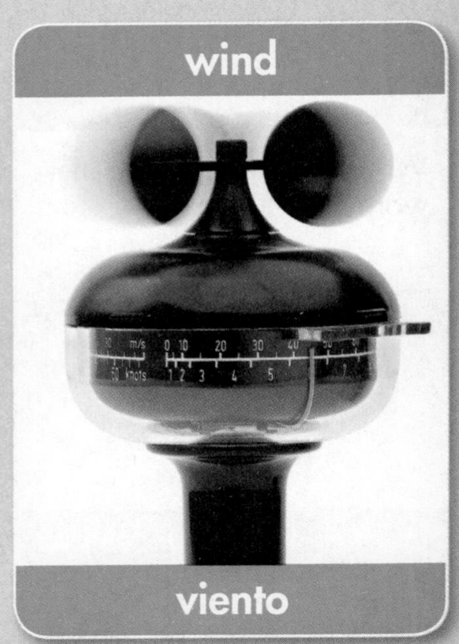

viento

scientist who studies and predicts weather

What is the suffix of this word?

científico que estudia y predice el estado del tiempo

the average of weather conditions over a long time

Write another definition for this word.

promedio de las condiciones del tiempo durante un período largo

the pushing force of the atmosphere

Use a dictionary.
Find another term for this phrase.

fuerza que ejerce la atmósfera

a measure of how far a place is from the equator

Write another definition for this word.

medida de la distancia entre un objeto y el ecuador

air movement caused by differences in air pressure

Write a sentence using this word.

movimiento del aire debido a diferencias en la presión del aire

height above sea level

What is the suffix of this word?

altura sobre el nivel del mar

TEKS Practice

Lesson 1 TEKS 8B

What is the water cycle?

1. Recognize The particles of water vapor

A. are always moving.
B. are as small as a drop.
C. form a liquid.

2. A certain cloud contains 220 water droplets per cubic centimeter. If 1 cubic meter = 1,000,000 cubic centimeters, how many drops are in one cubic meter of the cloud?

....

3. Vocabulary The change of a gas, such as water vapor, into a liquid is called ________.

A. condensation
B. evaporation
C. precipitation

4. Describe In the water cycle on Earth, water is in which form?

A. solid
B. liquid
C. gas
D. all of the above

5. Identify Precipitation includes

A. rain, snow, and air.
B. rain, wind, and snow.
C. snow, sleet, and hail.
D. all of the above

6. Write About It How does the water cycle affect the salinity of the ocean?

....

....

....

....

....

....

TEKS Practice

Lesson 1 TEKS 8B

What is the water cycle?

7. Explain How does water move through the environment where you live?

8. Explain How do the sun and the ocean interact in the water cycle?

Lesson 2 TEKS 8A

What is weather?

9. Identify Which of the following land features affects weather?

A. mountains
B. swamps
C. deserts
D. all of the above

10. Vocabulary The state of the atmosphere at a given time and place is called

A. climate.
B. weather.
C. circulation.
D. altitude.

11. Write About It How does a difference in barometric pressure cause wind?

12. List Write three factors that determine the weather shown below.

TEKS Practice

Lesson 3 TEKS 8A
What is climate?

13. Predict St. Louis, Missouri, experiences large differences in temperature between summer and winter. Predict how the temperature difference might change if St. Louis were next to the ocean.

14. Identify *Tropical, temperate,* and *polar* describe climate zones due to
A. latitude.
B. rainfall amount.
C. temperature.

15. Recognize An area's latitude helps determine its
A. climate zones.
B. elevation.
C. precipitation.
D. time zone.

16. Contrast Differentiate between weather and climate.

Chapter 6

Lesson 1 What is the water cycle?
In Lesson 1, you learned that water can be a solid, liquid, or gas and can change state. Evaporation, condensation, precipitation, and runoff are parts of the water cycle.
Supporting TEKS 8B

Lesson 2 What is weather?
In Lesson 2, you learned that air temperature, pressure, humidity, wind speed and direction, and precipitation determine the weather in a given place and time. Air circulates throughout the planet in predictable patterns.
Supporting TEKS 8A

Lesson 3 What is climate?
In Lesson 3, you learned that climate is affected by latitude, elevation, and distance from water. The climate in a region may change over time.
Supporting TEKS 8A

★ TEKS Practice: Chapter Review

Read each question and circle the best answer or fill in the grid.

1 A scientist is conducting a study in a region with latitude 72° S.

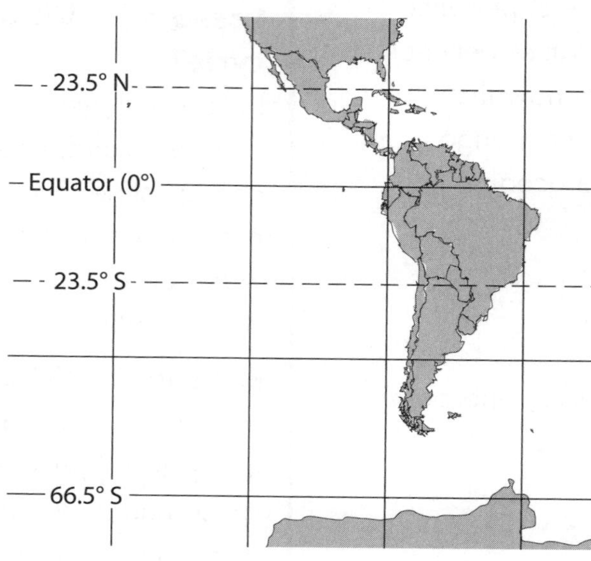

What kind of conditions should the scientist expect?

A Mild temperatures

B Extreme cold

C High heat

D Heavy rain

2 Mrs. Sanchez models a step in the water cycle by placing a pot of water onto a hot stove.

As the water heats, it gradually becomes water vapor. In this model of part of the water cycle, what does the stove represent?

F The atmosphere

G A cloud

H Sunlight

J None of these

3 David kept track of the weather conditions in Littleville over five days. He recorded the daily precipitation in the table below.

Day	Precipitation (cm)
1	4
2	2
3	1
4	0
5	2

Which bar graph represents his data for precipitation?

A

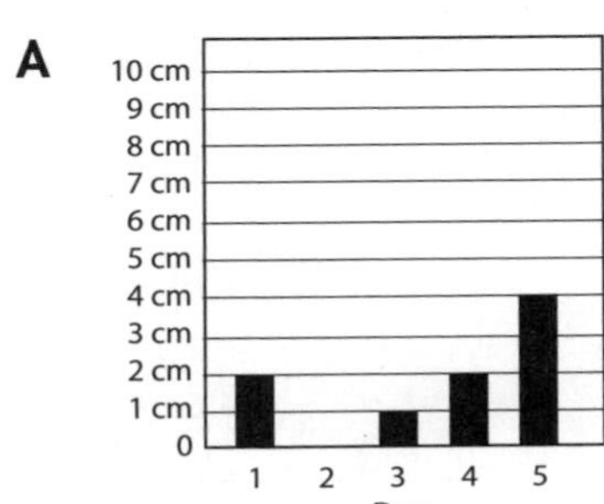

B

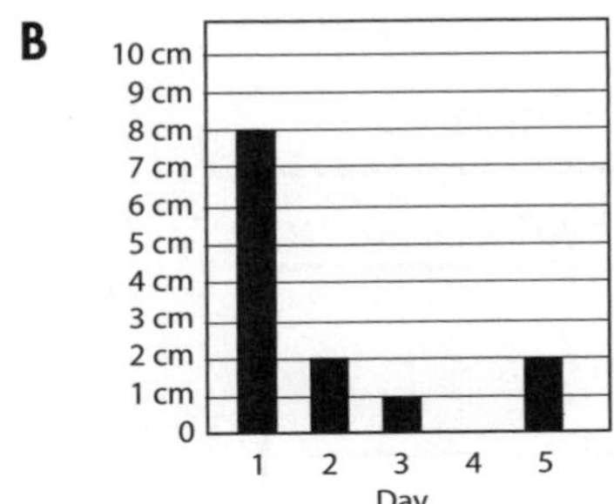

C

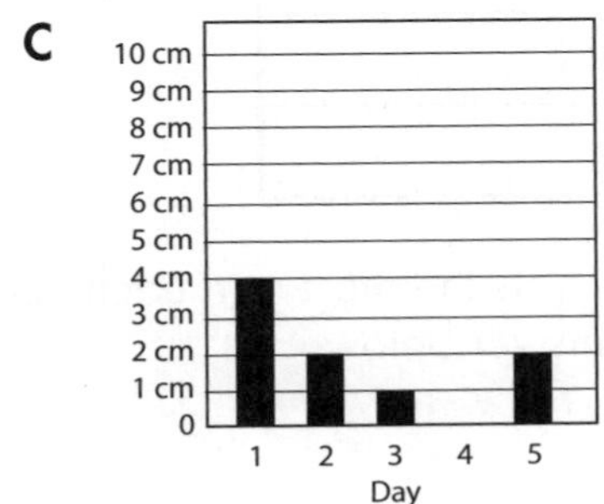

D

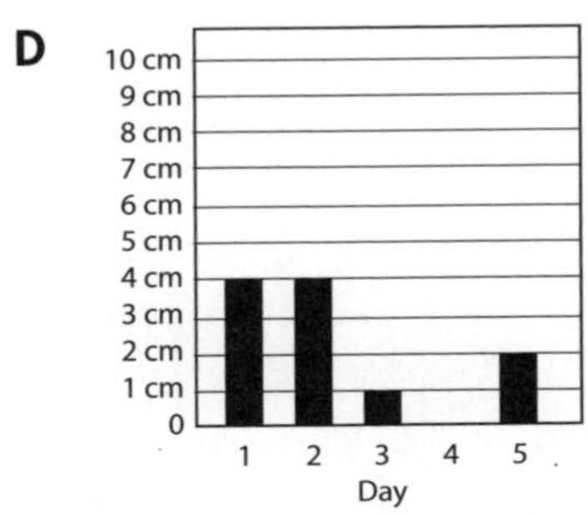

4 The picture shows a natural place.

Which statement best describes the climate in this place?

F Yesterday it did not rain.

G It is generally hot and dry.

H This month has had high temperatures.

J Last year, it rained only 10 centimeters.

---

5 The table gives the average yearly rainfall in five U.S. cities.

Average Yearly Rainfall in Five U.S. Cities

City	Average Yearly Rainfall (cm)
Chicago	88
New York City	102
San Francisco	50
Seattle	92
Washington, D.C.	99

What is the difference in centimeters of rain between the city that gets the most rain each year and the city that gets the least rain? Record and bubble in your answer below.

			.
⓪	⓪	⓪	
①	①	①	
②	②	②	
③	③	③	
④	④	④	
⑤	⑤	⑤	
⑥	⑥	⑥	
⑦	⑦	⑦	
⑧	⑧	⑧	
⑨	⑨	⑨	

TEKS Practice: Cumulative Review

6 The diagram shows a river that empties into the ocean.

River System

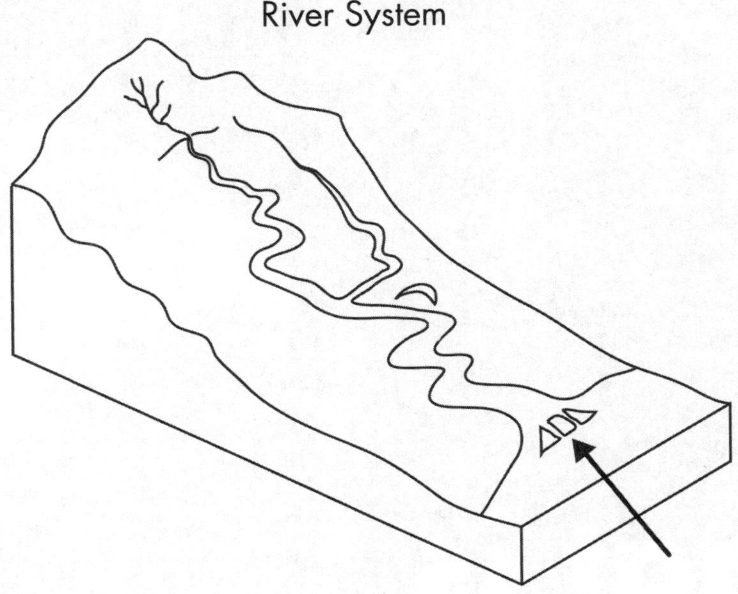

What most likely formed the triangular areas of land marked by the arrow?

F Lava from a volcano hardened and cooled to form rock.

G River water eroded all the rock surrounding these bits of land.

H Wind eroded dust, soil, and sand along the shore at the base of the river.

J River water deposited sediment as it slowed down and entered the ocean.

---

7 British fossil hunter Mary Anning was born in 1799. She and her brother learned how to hunt for fossils from their father. After their father died, they continued to hunt for fossils and sell them to collectors. Mary dug up her first important fossil in 1811. It was an *ichthyosaur*, a reptile that lived in the ocean. She found many other important fossils before she died in 1847, including other swimming reptiles called *plesiosaurs* and a flying reptile called a *pterodactyl*. Which of the following is an example of a fossil?

A Ancient animal footprints preserved in rock

B A plant or animal that has become extinct

C The skeleton of a small animal

D An animal that eats other animals

If you have trouble with . . .

Question	1	2	3	4	5	6	7
See chapter (lesson)	6 (3)	6 (1)	6 (2)	6 (3)	6 (2)	5 (2)	5 (4)
TEKS	8A	8B	8A	8A	8A	7B	7D

What is happening in the SKY?

Earth and Space

How can you compare the physical characteristics and motion of the sun, Earth, and moon?

You may have seen the moon when it looks like a crescent, a shape that looks like a circle with a bite taken out of it. This happens when we can see only part of the moon's sunlit side. The sun usually looks like a full circle, but sometimes the sun can look like a crescent too.

When do you think the sun might look like a crescent?

Texas Essential Knowledge and Skills

Readiness TEKS: 8C Demonstrate that Earth rotates on its axis once approximately every 24 hours causing the day/night cycle and the apparent movement of the Sun across the sky.

Supporting TEKS: 8D Identify and compare the physical characteristics of the Sun, Earth, and Moon.

Process TEKS: 1A, 2B, 2C, 2D, 2F, 2G, 3C, 3D, 4A

Lab zone® Inquiry Warm-Up

TEKS 8C, 1A, 2C, 2D, 2F, 2G, 4A

Does the formation of shadows relate to the position of the sun?

1. Insert a meterstick into the ground outside. Make sure the stick is perpendicular to the ground.
2. Write N on a craft stick. Place the craft stick one meter to the north of the meterstick in the ground. Repeat this for E (east), S (south), and W (west).
3. **Observe** the shadow of the meterstick. Create a table like the one below to **record** your data. Repeat your observations at regular intervals all day and at the same times the next day. Record the sun's position as its height above the horizon (low, medium, or high).

Materials

craft sticks
compass (directional)
marker
metersticks
clock

Texas Safety LAB RULES

Do not look directly at the sun.
Stay in the area directed by your teacher.

Inquiry Skill

You can **interpret data** by using a data table.

Sun and Shadow Observations Over Time

Day and Time	Shadow Direction	Shadow Length	Sun Position	Sun Direction

Explain Your Results

4. **Analyze and Interpret** Information in the table using the tools from the lab, including the clock. How is the length of a shadow related to the height of the sun in the sky?

5. **Draw Conclusions** How many hours does it take Earth to rotate on its axis once? Explain.

Connect to Reading

Focus on Draw Conclusions

You will practice the reading strategy of **draw conclusions.** A good reader can put together facts and observations to build a new idea, or a conclusion. Learning to draw conclusions or make inferences can help you evaluate what you read and observe.

A Trip to the Moon

The moon has basically no atmosphere. It also has no liquid water on its surface. As a result, the moon does not have weather as we do on Earth. There is no wind. There is no rain or snow. Astronauts could confirm this when they walked on the moon many years ago. As they walked, they made footprints on the moon's surface.

Practice It!

Use the graphic organizer to draw a conclusion about what happened to the footprints Apollo astronauts left on the moon.

The moon has no liquid water on its surface.

Fact

The moon has no wind.

Fact

The moon has no rain or snow.

Fact

Conclusion

Texas

LESSON 1

What are the sun, Earth, and moon like?

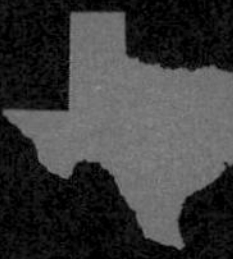

I will know TEKS 8D
I will know how to identify and compare the physical characteristics of the sun, Earth, and moon.
(Also 2B, 2C, 2D, 2F, 3C, 4A)

Vocabulary
galaxy
photosphere
corona
sunspot
solar flare
hydrosphere
atmosphere
moon

Connect to Math

STEM

Math TEKS 1B, 3E

You are part of a group of students in charge of building a scale model of the solar system to decorate your classroom. You already have a globe, so you decide that it would be practical to use it as a model of Earth. The list below has facts about Earth, your classroom globe, and the sun. From the list, find the facts that you need to calculate the required diameter for your model of the sun. Describe your procedure and state your result. What problem could be caused by using the globe as a model of Earth?

- Sun's diameter: about 1,392,684 km
- Diameter of your classroom globe: about 0.30 m
- Earth's diameter: about 12,742 km
- Sun's general size: about 109 times that of Earth

Quick Lab

TEKS 2B, 2F, 3C, 4A, 8D

How can you compare the size of Earth with the size of the moon?

Materials

calculator
drawing compass
paper
pencil

Be careful of sharp objects.

1. **Make a Model** Use the data in the table to create a scale for your model. To determine your scale, first compare the radius of Earth with the radius of the moon.

2. **Calculate** Record information using tools, including calculators. Divide Earth's radius by the moon's radius to see how much bigger Earth's radius is. Round off to the nearest whole number. Then fill in this statement:

   Earth is about .... times larger than the moon. In my model, Earth will be .... times larger than the moon.

Data for Earth and the Moon	
Earth's Radius	6,371 km
Moon's Radius	1,738 km

3. **Determine** Choose a size for the radius of the moon in your model. Multiply that number by the number you calculated in Step 2. This is the radius of Earth in your model.

4. **Draw** the moon and Earth side-by-side on a sheet of paper using your compass.

Explain Your Results

5. **Communicate** Explain how a model such as this helps you understand the Earth-moon system.

....

....

6. **Analyze and Interpret** For this to be a true model of Earth and the moon in space, what else would you add?

....

....

Stars

What would you say if someone asked you what a star looks like? You might say it looks like a bright dot in the night sky. Stars are only dots in the sky when stars are far away. Up close, they look like our sun. They are gigantic balls of very hot, bright gases.

The sun is part of a galaxy. A **galaxy** is a large group of stars. The sun's galaxy is called the Milky Way. The Milky Way has a spiral shape. It contains billions of stars.

Within the Milky Way, the sun is just an average, medium-sized star. Many stars are much larger. Stars known as giants may be eight to 100 times as large as the sun. Supergiants are even larger. They may be up to 300 times as large as the sun. There are also stars much smaller than the sun. A star at the end of its life can collapse and become very small—only about the size of Earth.

1. **Draw Conclusions** How does the size of the sun compare to the size of Earth?

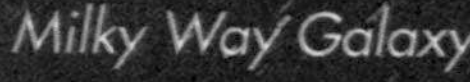
Milky Way Galaxy

Earth, pictured to scale with the sun

Even though the sun is only a medium-sized star, it is the largest object in our solar system. Scientists have been able to calculate the sun's mass from the speeds of the planets and the shapes of their orbits around the sun. The sun's mass is nearly two million trillion trillion kilograms—you can write that as a two followed by 30 zeros! The sun has almost 100 percent of the mass in the solar system. The sun is huge when compared to Earth. In fact, the sun has more than one million times the volume of Earth.

The temperature at the center of a star such as the sun can reach millions of degrees. There is also great pressure. The intense heat and pressure in a star's core cause reactions that release abundant energy—which we sense as heat and light.

2. **Recognize** How can scientists determine the mass of the sun?

3. **Identify** From which part of a star does the star's energy come?

Quick Lab

Put a magnet on a table and place a sheet of white paper over it. Put some iron filings on a folded sheet of notebook paper. Hold it in one hand as you gently shake the filings down onto the white paper. Observe the pattern the filings make on the paper. Why do they form this pattern?

TEKS 2C, 2D, 2F, 4A

Characteristics of the Sun

The sun is a fiery ball of hot gases with no hard surface. It gives off enormous amounts of light and heat—the energy that makes life on Earth possible.

The Visible Sun

Like Earth, the sun has several layers. The sun produces great amounts of energy at its core, where temperatures can reach 15 million degrees Celsius (C°). Energy from the core moves out toward the photosphere. The **photosphere** is the surface of the sun that we see from Earth. The photosphere is much cooler than the core, but is still a scorching 5,500°C.

The sun also has a layered atmosphere. The lower layer of the atmosphere is called the chromosphere. It blends with the upper photosphere. The outermost layer of the sun's atmosphere is called the **corona.** During a total solar eclipse, you see the corona as a halo around the sun's disk.

The sun has a very strong magnetic field. Lines of magnetic force twist and turn inside the sun. In places where they break through, the surface is cooler. These cooler areas, called **sunspots,** look darker. Scientists can look at the sun with special equipment. They see sunspots moving on the face of the sun. Sunspots are part of the photosphere. They may be the size of Earth or larger. The number of sunspots increases and decreases in cycles of about eleven years.

4. **Identify** the physical characteristics of the sun.

Gravity and Movement of the Sun

Because the sun has a very large mass, it has very strong gravity. The sun's gravity is so strong that it can hold Earth and the other planets in the solar system in orbit around it—even some that are billions of kilometers away. Earth is small compared to the sun. It has only a fraction of the sun's gravity. Because the moon is even smaller, its gravity is even less than that of Earth.

The sun spins, just like Earth. Because the sun is not solid, bands of the sun's gases turn at different rates. The sun's equator turns once every 27 days. Its poles move slower. They take 31 days for one complete turn.

Solar Eruptions

Two types of eruptions that take place on the sun are prominences and solar flares. A prominence looks like a ribbon of glowing gases that leaps out of the chromosphere into the corona. Prominences may appear and then disappear in a few days or months.

A **solar flare** is an explosive eruption of waves and particles into space. A solar flare is similar to a volcano here on Earth. It causes a bright spot in the chromosphere that may last for minutes or hours. Along with extra-bright light, a solar flare also gives off other forms of energy. This energy can be powerful enough to interrupt radio and satellite communication on Earth.

5. **Identify** What is a solar flare similar to on Earth?

6. **Apply** Why might an astronaut in space want to monitor solar flares?

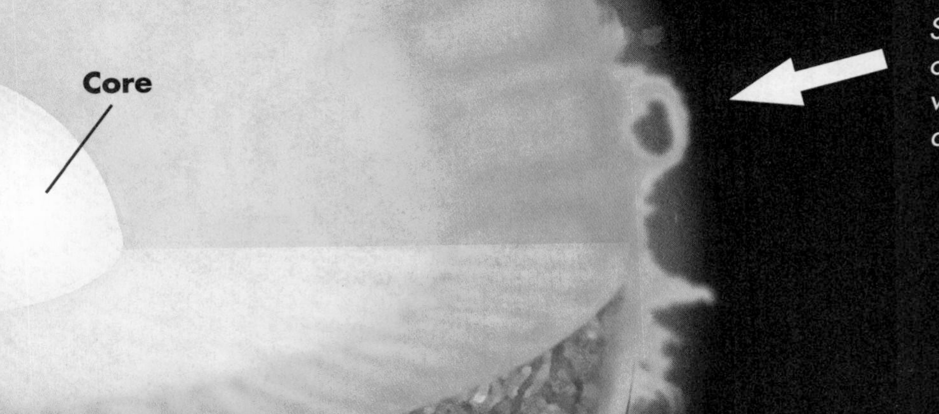

Solar flares give off more light than other parts of the sun. They emit radio waves, visible light, X rays, plasma, and other radiation.

Characteristics of Earth

Earth is just one of the solar system's eight planets. It is not remarkable in size. Four planets are larger than Earth. It doesn't have rings or dozens of moons. Still, Earth is unusual. It is the only planet known to have life. Earth is also the only planet covered mostly by water.

If you could look at Earth from space, you would see why it is sometimes called a water planet. Huge oceans cover about 3/4 of Earth's surface. Earth's waters form the **hydrosphere**, which helps regulate the planet's temperature. Oceans absorb and release heat energy more slowly than land. Without oceans, Earth's temperatures would be more extreme. Earth would be less suitable for life as we know it.

Layers of Rock

If you could slice Earth open like an apple, you would see layers. At the center is the core. The inner core is a solid sphere of mostly iron. The outer core is a layer of hot, liquid iron and nickel that surrounds the inner core. Above the core is the rock mantle. Its upper zone is solid, but soft like taffy. Earth's hard, rocky crust sits on the upper mantle. The crust is broken into huge pieces called plates. The plates hold Earth's continents and ocean basins.

7. Sequence Imagine a machine that could drill all the way through Earth in a straight line, passing through the center of the planet. From first to last, list the layers that the machine would have to pass through.

Earth's Atmosphere

Earth is wrapped in a layer of gases that is about 100 kilometers thick. This layer of gases, or **atmosphere,** makes life on Earth possible. It filters out some of the sun's harmful rays. Earth's atmosphere is also the only one in the solar system that is mostly nitrogen and oxygen. Plants and animals use nitrogen, oxygen, carbon dioxide, and water vapor from the atmosphere. Life on Earth would not be possible without these gases. The atmosphere also holds in Earth's heat, making Earth warm enough to support life as we know it.

Earth's Magnetic Field

A strong magnetic field surrounds Earth. Like a magnet, Earth has a north magnetic pole and a south magnetic pole. Earth's magnetic field causes compass needles to point north. It also creates the glowing lights in polar skies called auroras. When charged particles from the sun hit Earth's magnetic field, auroras glow as bands of bright light in the sky.

Earth has one moon, which is about ¼ its size. Like both the sun and the moon, Earth spins. Unlike the sun and the moon, it makes one complete spin every 24 hours. This is one Earth day.

8. CHALLENGE The circles below represent Earth and the moon. Measure the diameter of the large circle, and multiply it by 30. That would be the correct distance from Earth to the moon at this scale. Draw the two circles in the space provided. Use the correct distance you found.

● = *Earth* • = *moon*

9. **Illustrate** Identify the physical characteristics of the Earth. Name three characteristics that make it a better place than the moon for life as we know it.

Characteristics of the Moon

Earth has one large moon, which is about 1/4 as wide as Earth. A **moon** is a natural object that revolves around a planet. Although the moon can look quite bright at night, it produces no light of its own. It reflects light from the sun.

Like Earth, the moon is a rocky body with several layers. It has a solid inner core and a mostly liquid outer core. There is a partly molten layer between the core and mantle. The moon has a thick mantle and a thin outer crust.

It takes the moon 27 days to revolve around Earth.

Surface and Temperature

The moon's surface is dry and barren. There are rocky highlands, and large flat areas that ancient astronomers named "seas." The surface also has thousands of depressions called craters. On Earth, falling meteoroids are slowed down or burned by the atmosphere before they hit the surface. However, the moon has almost no atmosphere. Meteoroids slam into the moon at full speed, leaving craters.

Heat and cold are extreme on the moon because of its lack of an atmosphere. Temperatures rise as high as 123°C in sunlight and can drop as low as –233°C in darkness.

Gravity and Mass

Gravity keeps the moon circling around Earth, just as it keeps Earth circling around the sun. Because the moon's mass is much less than that of Earth, gravity on the moon is only about $\frac{1}{6}$ as strong as gravity on Earth.

10. Draw Conclusions Why are there so many more craters on the moon than on Earth's land?

Large craters on the moon are often named after famous scientists, scholars, and artists.

Magnetic Field, Rotation, and Orbit

Unlike Earth, the moon does not have a magnetic field. Yet it does have magnetic rocks. Some scientists think the rocks formed billions of years ago, when the moon might have had a magnetic field of its own.

The moon spins once every 28 days. It takes about the same amount of time to circle once around Earth. As a result, the moon always keeps the same side turned toward Earth. The first pictures of the far side of the moon were taken by a space probe. Apollo 8 astronauts flew behind the moon for the first time in 1968. They were the first humans to observe the far side of the moon directly.

11. Explain Why did people on Earth see the far side of the moon for only the first time in 1968?

got it? TEKS 8D

12. Draw Conclusions Identify the physical characteristics of the moon and explain how these characteristics make the moon easier for scientists to study than the sun.

13. Analyze Earth makes one spin every 24 hours. The moon makes one spin about every 28 days. Do Earth and the moon both have day/night cycles? If so, how are they different on the moon and on Earth?

Stop! I need help with

Wait! I have a question about

Go! Now I know

How does Earth move?

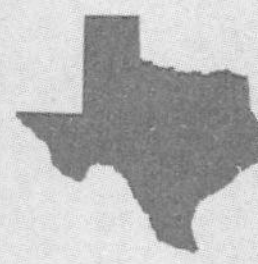

I will know **TEKS 8C, 8D**
I will know how to demonstrate that Earth rotates on its axis causing the day/night cycle and the apparent movement of the sun across the sky. (Also **1A**, **2B**, **2C**, **2D**, **2F**, **3C**)

Vocabulary
axis
rotation
orbit
revolution

Each day is 24 hours long. That is how long it takes Earth to spin around once.

That's why there are 24 time zones. On a time zone map, you can see a one-hour difference between zones that are next to each other.

I need a time zone map. I want to call my cousin in San Diego. But it's not the same time there as it is here in Dallas.

Check the map. It's 8:00 A.M. here. Find out what time it is in San Diego.

Social Studies

Compare the time in Dallas and San Diego to find the answer. Is it too early to call?

Social Studies TEKS 6A

PEARSON Texas.com

Quick Lab

TEKS 8C, 1A, 2B, 2C, 2D, 2F, 3C

What causes day and night?

Materials

globe
lamp without a shade
light bulb, 40-watt (or smaller)
marker
meterstick
table
small piece of tape

1. **Make a Model** Place a lamp on the table, and place the globe on the table about 1 meter from it. Place a piece of tape on the globe to represent where you live. Turn on the lamp and darken the room.

2. **Observe** which parts of the globe have light shining on them and which parts are unlit.

3. **Demonstrate** Slowly turn the globe all the way around. Note when your location is lit and dark.

Never touch a hot light bulb.

Explain Your Results

4. **Make Models** What do the lamp and globe represent in this model?

5. **Explain** what happened as you turned the globe. How did this demonstrate that Earth rotates on its axis once approximately every 24 hours, causing the day/night cycle?

6. **Draw Conclusions** How did your turning of the globe demonstrate that Earth rotates on its axis once approximately every 24 hours, causing the apparent movement of the sun across the sky?

Earth and the Sun

Think about a time thousands of years ago, before telescopes had been invented and before astronauts had ever traveled into space. Just as we do today, people looked up at the sky. They saw the sun travel across it each day. The sun appeared to rise in the east and set in the west. People naturally thought the sun was moving around Earth. In fact, people thought Earth was the center of the solar system. They believed the sun and all of the planets moved around it.

1. Compare and Contrast Use the graphic organizer below to list what is alike about and different between the way people used to think about Earth and the sun and what we know now.

Time-lapse photography shows how the sun appears to move through the sky as it sets.

Then **Now**

Earth Moves Around the Sun

Before the 1600s, careful observations had led some astronomers to propose that it was in fact Earth and the planets that moved around the sun. Beginning in the 1600s, astronomers began to use a new tool to look at the night sky: the telescope. This helped them prove that Earth is not the center of the solar system. Now we know that the center of the solar system is a star we call the sun. Earth and the other planets move around the sun. The sun appears to circle Earth because Earth spins. As our planet spins, the sun and other objects, such as other stars, appear to move across the sky.

2. Identify Connect appropriate science concepts with the history of science. What discovery showed that the sun does not really travel across the sky each day?

Before telescopes and space exploration, some people thought Earth was the center of the universe.

Earth's Rotation

Earth and the other planets of the solar system rotate, or spin, much like a top spins. They each rotate around an imaginary line called an **axis.** The northern end of Earth's axis is the North Pole. The southern end of Earth's axis is the South Pole. One whole spin of an object on its axis is called a **rotation.** One full rotation is what we call a *day*.

Earth rotates around its imaginary axis from west to east. As Earth spins, the sun, moon, stars, and planets only seem to rise in the east and set in the west. When you watch the sun set, remember that it is you who are moving. You are riding on the rotating Earth.

3. Explain Why does the sun appear to move from east to west across the sky?

....

....

4. Fill in the Blank In the illustration below, fill in the missing words in the labels.

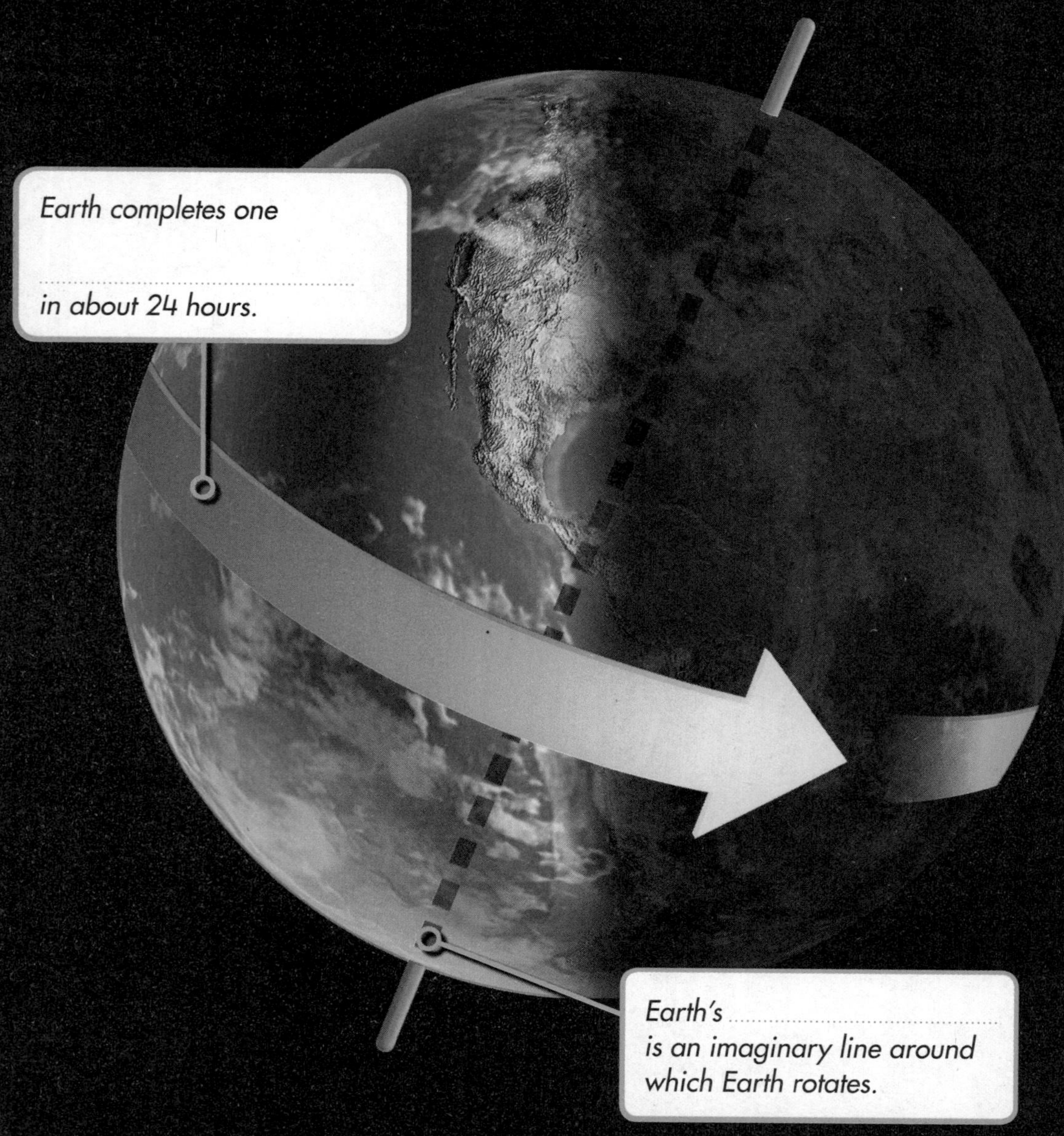
Earth completes one
....
in about 24 hours.
Earth's ....
is an imaginary line around which Earth rotates.

Earth's Revolution

Earth also moves in an orbit. An **orbit** is the path an object takes as it revolves around a star, planet, or moon. Earth's orbit is elliptical—it has an oval shape. The moon's orbit around Earth is also elliptical. One full orbit of an object around another object is called a **revolution.** Earth's revolution around the sun lasts for just a few hours longer than 365 days. This period may sound familiar to you. It is one year. The moon's revolution around Earth takes 27.3 days, or about a month.

Just as gravity keeps you on Earth, gravity keeps Earth in its orbit around the sun. Because the sun is so massive, its gravity pulls all the planets toward it. This pull keeps the planets from moving in straight lines into space.

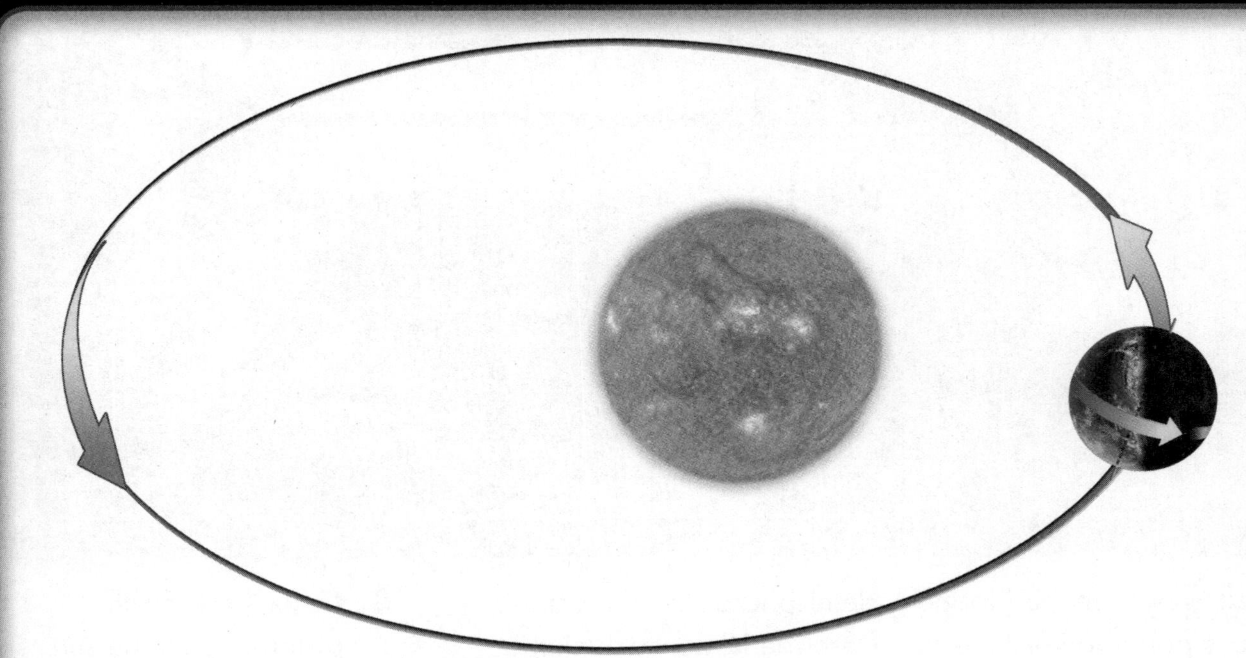

5. **Infer** Draw a representation of the moon's orbit in the diagram above.

6. **Compare and Contrast** How are the orbits of Earth and the moon alike? How are they different?

Seasons

Earth always tilts the same way during its revolution around the sun. Earth's tilt affects how much sunlight parts of Earth receive. The amount of sunlight an area receives affects its climate and seasons. Seasons change as Earth's axis tilts either toward or away from the sun at different times during its revolution. When the North Pole is tilted away from the sun, sunlight is less concentrated in the Northern Hemisphere. Temperatures drop, and winter sets in. At the same time, the South Pole is tilted toward the sun. The Southern Hemisphere receives concentrated sunlight and has the warm temperatures of summer.

Quick Lab

Earth's Tilt
Hold a globe so that its axis is tilted toward the front of the room. Slowly move around the outer edge of the room. Keep the globe's axis tilted toward the front of the room. Explain how this is a model of Earth in its orbit around the sun.
TEKS 3C

In this diagram, look at how the sun's rays strike Earth. During the Southern Hemisphere summer, the sun's rays strike Earth more directly south of the equator. The rays are concentrated, not spread out. Concentrated energy gives this region warm summer weather.

7. CHALLENGE In the Northern Hemisphere summer, Earth's axis points toward the sun. Describe how you think the axis looks in the spring.

8. Calculate Earth's distance from the sun in January is about 147,000,000 km. In July its distance from the sun is about 152,100,000 km. About how much closer is Earth to the sun in January than in July?

The number of daylight hours also changes as the seasons change. On the first day of its summer, a hemisphere has more hours of daylight than at any other time of the year. The least number of daylight hours occurs on the first day of winter. Twice a year the hours of day and night are equal. At this time, Earth's axis points neither toward nor away from the sun.

9. Identify In the diagram, label each part of Earth's orbit with the Northern Hemisphere season that it represents.

got it?

10. Describe What is a rotation? What is a revolution?

11. Explain In what direction do stars, the moon, and the sun seem to move across the sky? Why?

Stop! I need help with

Wait! I have a question about

Go! Now I know

TEKS 3D

JOHNSON SPACE CENTER

When people think of space exploration, they usually think of Florida's Kennedy Space Center. Still, Texas has a NASA center that is just as important: Houston's Johnson Space Center (JSC). JSC is the main mission control center for NASA's crewed space flights. It is a research center and a place where astronauts train. Houston is also the place astronauts call home.

JSC has guided NASA missions since the 1960s. Mission controllers at Houston oversaw the Apollo missions that placed the first person on the moon. The first space shuttle was designed and tested here. JSC directed more than 100 space shuttle missions. It now manages the International Space Station.

Almost 14,000 engineers, scientists, and other specialists work at JSC. When NASA begins the newest crewed missions to the moon and beyond, JSC will keep Texas at the center of space flight.

Summarize NASA's launch facilities are at the Kennedy Space Center in Florida. Why is Texas's Johnson Space Center just as important to NASA?

HIGH NOON IN TEXAS

Earth's axis is tilted 23-1/2°. So the sun is never directly overhead north of the Tropic of Cancer or south of the Tropic of Capricorn.

"up"

to sun

Equator

Tropic of Cancer

Tropic of Capricorn

Noon is the time of day when the sun is highest in the sky. Does that mean it's right overhead? In some places, the answer could be yes. That is never the case in Texas. Because of Earth's tilt, the sun can be directly overhead only in a wide band around the equator. The regions within that band are known as the tropics. The boundaries of the tropics are the Tropic of Cancer in the north and the Tropic of Capricorn in the south. In the tropics, it is possible to see the sun shining directly overhead at different times of the year. Texas is north of the Tropic of Cancer. So, even on the hot first day of summer, when the sun is highest, the sun's most direct

USE A MAP

The sun is never directly overhead in Texas. Using the Internet or other resources, determine whether the sun can be directly overhead in other parts of the United States. Explain your answer.

Lab Investigation

TEKS 8D, 1A, 2F, 3C

How can spinning affect the shape of a planet or the moon?

Materials

construction paper
hole punch
pencil
ruler
scissors
stapler

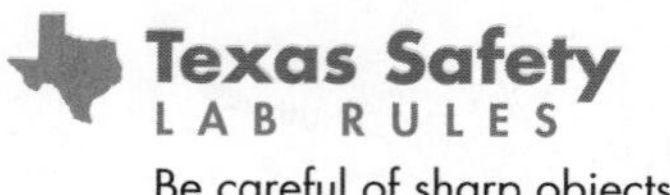

Be careful of sharp objects.

Inquiry Skill

Scientists **use a model** when the real object is hard to study.

Follow a Procedure

☐ **1.** Cut 2 strips of construction paper, each 2 cm × 45 cm. Cross them at the center and staple them to make an X.

☐ **2.** Bring the 4 ends together and overlap them. Staple them to form a sphere.

☐ **3.** Punch a hole through the center of the overlapped ends.

☐ **4.** Push a dull pencil through the hole. Only about 5 cm of the pencil should go in.

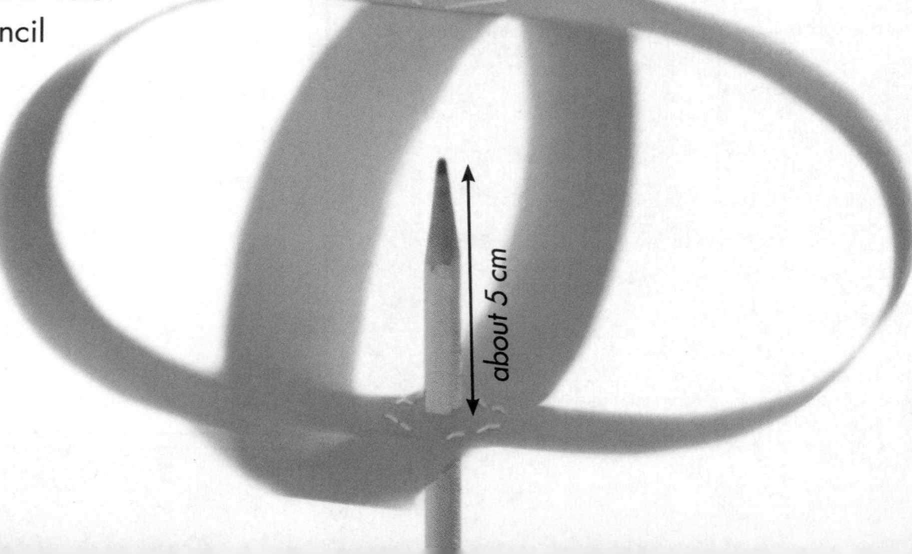

☐ **5.** Hold the pencil between your palms. Move your hands back and forth to make your **model** spin.

☐ **6.** What shape do you **observe** when it spins?

☐ **7.** **Record** your observations.

Effect of Spinning on a Planet's Shape	
Shape When Not Spinning	**Shape When Spinning**
○	

Analyze and Conclude

8. How did the sphere change shape when you spun it? Make an **inference** about what happened.

9. How is your **model** similar to a spinning planet, such as Earth, or a spinning moon? How is it different?

A solar eclipse occurs when the moon's orbit causes it to pass in front of the sun. The moon blocks sunlight and casts a shadow on Earth. That's pretty amazing, since the moon's diameter is only about 1/400 the diameter of the sun.

The sun, Earth, and moon need to be in just the right positions for an eclipse to occur. At least 2 solar eclipses occur somewhere on Earth every year. The maximum number of eclipses possible is 5 eclipses in one year. A total solar eclipse only occurs once every 1.5 years.

During a total solar eclipse, the sun is completely covered by the moon. The shadow of the moon travels across the globe as Earth rotates. At any one spot on Earth, the maximum time of a total solar eclipse is 7.5 minutes. The path where you can see the total eclipse is a maximum of about 269 kilometers wide. Within that path, the sun is completely blocked, the sky gets dark, and the stars become visible. It is an extraordinary event.

For this reason, some people travel all over the globe. These eclipse chasers, or "umbraphiles," often travel long distances to places such as Bolivia, Bulgaria, Zambia, or China. Sometimes the eclipse is visible in the United States. The next total solar eclipse visible from Texas will take place in 2024.

Special precautions need to be taken to view a solar eclipse. Looking directly at the sun can damage your eyes.

Infer The moon is much smaller than the sun, but the moon covers the sun completely during a total solar eclipse. What can you infer about the relative distances of the sun and the moon from Earth?

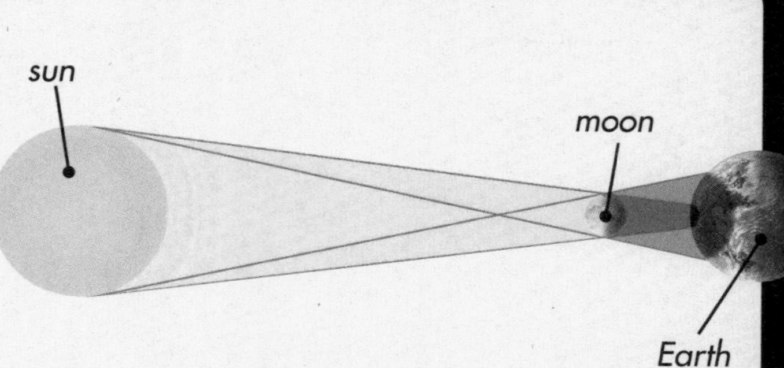

Vocabulary Smart Cards

galaxy
photosphere
corona
sunspot
solar flare
hydrosphere
atmosphere
moon
axis
rotation
orbit
revolution

Play a Game!

Work with a partner. Choose a Vocabulary Smart Card. Do not let your partner see your card.

Play Password. Try to get your partner to say the word or phrase by giving only one-word clues, one at a time. Take turns giving clues and guessing.

sunspot

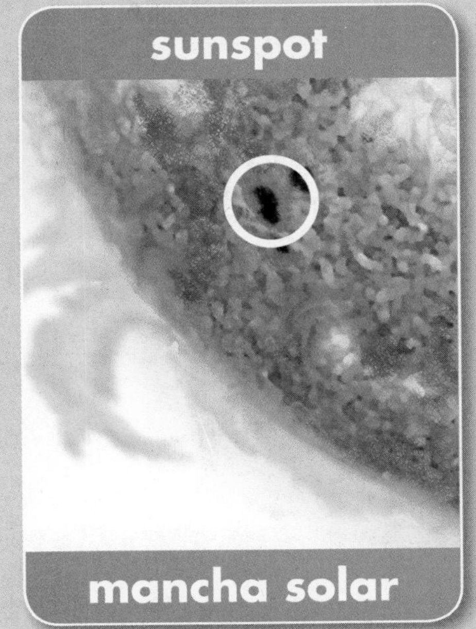

mancha solar

galaxy

galaxia

solar flare

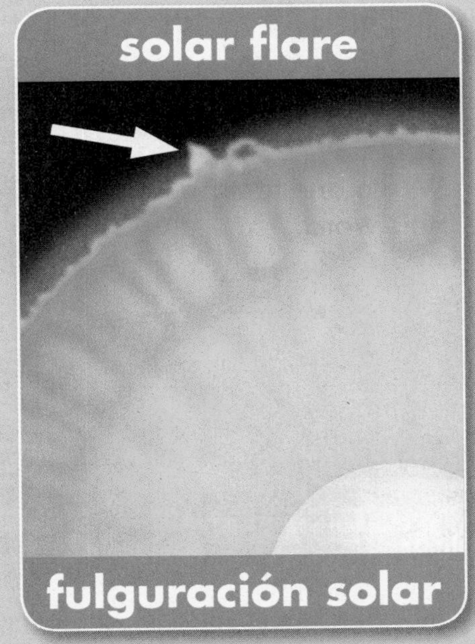

fulguración solar

photosphere

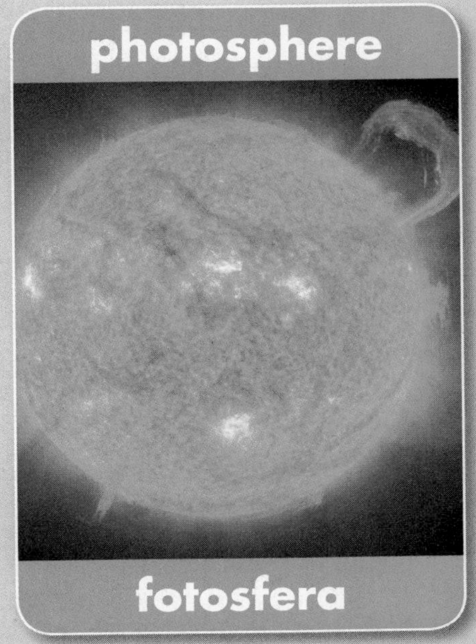

fotosfera

hydrosphere

hidrosfera

corona

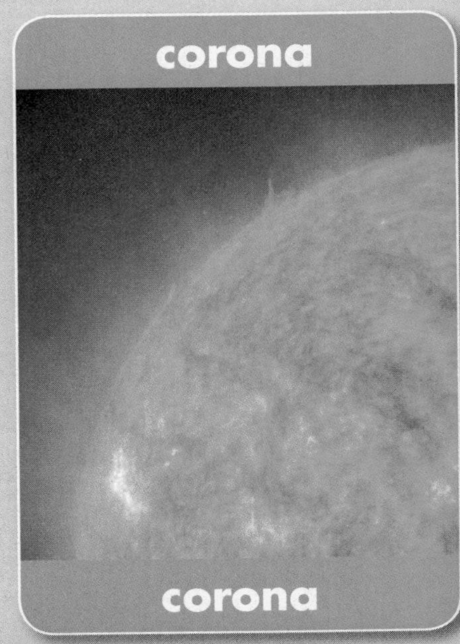

corona

a large group of stars

Write a sentence using this word.

enorme grupo de estrellas

dark spot on the surface of the sun

Divide this compound word into the two smaller words that make it up.

mancha oscura en la superficie del Sol

the surface of the sun visible from Earth

Write a sentence using this term.

superficie del Sol visible desde la Tierra

an explosive eruption of waves and particles into space

Write one fact about this word.

erupción explosiva de ondas y partículas emitidas hacia el espacio

the outer layer of the sun's atmosphere

Write a fact about this word.

capa más externa de la atmósfera del Sol

Earth's waters

Give an example of a part of it.

toda el agua de la Tierra

Interactive Vocabulary

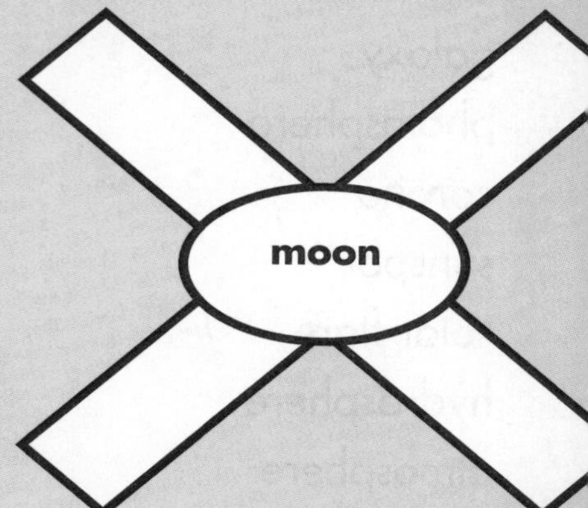

Make a Word Wheel!

Choose a vocabulary word and write it in the center of the Word Wheel graphic organizer. Write examples or related words on the wheel spokes.

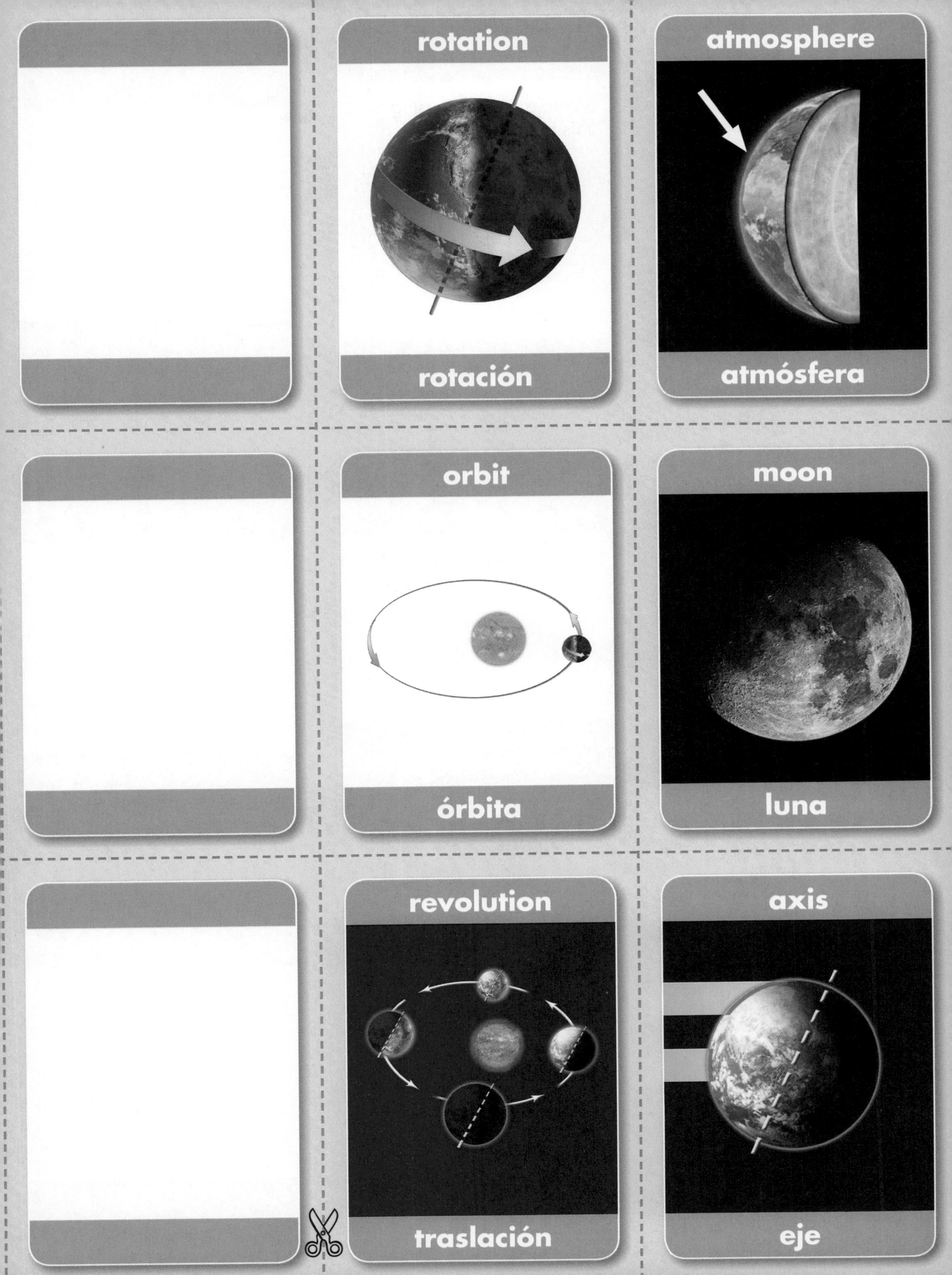
rotation
rotación
atmosphere
atmósfera
orbit
órbita
moon
luna
revolution
traslación
axis
eje

layer of gases wrapped around Earth that makes life possible

What does the word root *sphere* mean?

capa de gases que envuelve la Tierra y hace posible la vida

one whole spin of an object on its axis

Write a sentence using this term.

una vuelta completa de un objeto en torno a su eje

a natural object that revolves around a planet

Draw an example.

satélite natural que orbita un planeta

the path an object takes as it revolves around a star, planet, or moon

Write a sentence using the verb form of this word.

el camino que sigue un objeto al girar alrededor de una estrella, un planeta o una luna

an imaginary line around which an object spins

Draw an example.

línea imaginaria en torno a la cual gira un objeto

one full orbit around the sun

Write a sentence using this word.

una órbita completa alrededor del Sol

TEKS Practice

Lesson 1 TEKS 8D

What are the sun, Earth, and moon like?

1. **Identify** Which layer of the sun gives off the light energy we see?

2. **Write About It** Explain the difference between the surface of the moon and the surface of Earth.

3. **Infer** How would sunspots appear if they were the same temperature as the rest of the sun's surface?

4. **Explain** Compare the physical characteristics of the sun, Earth, and the moon by explaining how they differ in size.

5. **Analyze** Would it be easier for a rocket to blast off from the moon or Earth? Think about the difference in gravity between Earth and the moon when you write your answer.

6. **Predict** At certain times of the month, sunlight does not shine on the side of the moon facing Earth. Predict how the moon would look from Earth at this time. Explain your answer.

TEKS Practice

Lesson 2 TEKS 8C, 8D

How does Earth move?

7. Explain The picture below shows how the sun moves in the sky. Why does the sun appear to move from east to west?

....

....

....

8. Vocabulary Earth's .... on its axis once every 24 hours causes day and night.

A. rotation
B. revolution
C. orbit
D. tilt

9. Predict What would happen to the seasons of the world if Earth's axis tilted in the opposite direction?

....

....

....

....

....

10. Show Use the space below to make two drawings of Earth that show the difference between rotation and revolution.

TEKS Practice

Lesson 2 TEKS 8C, 8D

How does Earth move?

11. Identify What is the force that keeps Earth in orbit around the sun, and the moon in orbit around Earth?

12. Determine Which season starts on the day with the fewest number of daylight hours? Which season starts on the day with the greatest number of daylight hours?

13. Describe How have ideas about the structure of the solar system changed since hundreds of years ago?

Chapter 7

Lesson 1 What are the sun, Earth, and moon like?

In Lesson 1, you learned to identify and compare the physical characteristics of the sun, Earth, and moon.

Supporting TEKS 8D

Lesson 2 How does Earth move?

In Lesson 2, you learned that Earth rotates on its axis once approximately every 24 hours, causing the day/night cycle and the apparent movement of the Sun across the sky. You learned more about identifying and comparing the physical characteristics of the sun, Earth, and moon.

Readiness TEKS 8C, Supporting TEKS 8D

★ TEKS Practice: Chapter Review

Read each question and circle the best answer or fill in the grid.

1 The table shows some physical characteristics of the sun, Earth, and moon.

Physical Characteristics of the Sun, Earth, and Moon

Name	Shape	Composition	Atmosphere	Light Properties
Sun	Sphere	Hot gases	Yes	Radiates light
Earth	Sphere	Rocky surface, with water	Yes	Reflects light
Moon	Sphere	Rocky surface	No	Reflects light

According to the data, which of these bodies from our solar system have the greatest number of characteristics in common?

A The sun and the moon have the greatest number of characteristics in common.

B Earth and the moon have the greatest number of characteristics in common.

C Earth and the sun have the greatest number of characteristics in common.

D None of the above

2 Earth rotates from west to east once every 24 hours. As the planet rotates, some areas experience day, while other areas experience night.

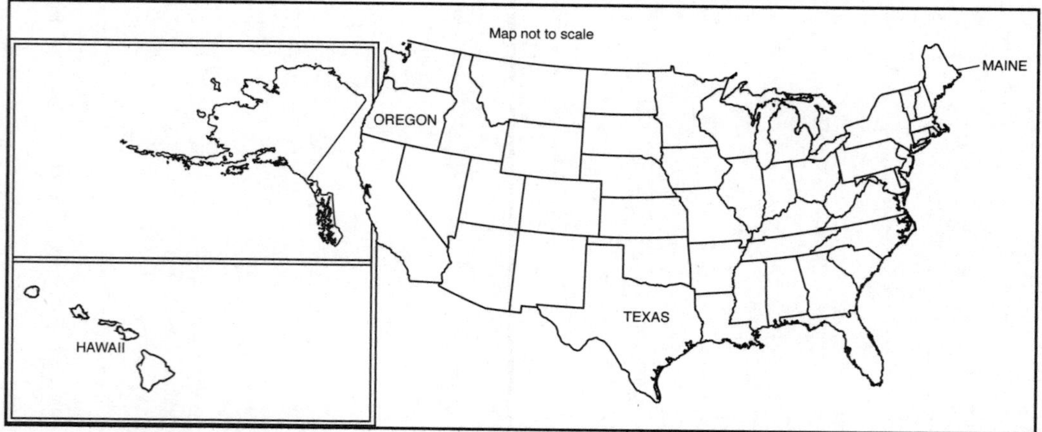

If Earth rotated from east to west, which area of the United States would experience sunrise first?

F Texas

G Oregon

H Hawaii

J Maine

3 The table shows some characteristics of Earth and the moon, including the range of temperatures found on each body.

Some Characteristics of Earth and the Moon

Characteristic	Earth	Moon
Distance from sun	149,700,000 km	149,200,000 km
Length of day	About 24 hours	27.3 Earth days
Orbit	Orbits the sun once every 365 days	Orbits Earth once every 27.3 days
Makeup of mantle and core	Rocks and minerals—mainly iron, magnesium, and nickel	Rocks and minerals—mainly iron, magnesium, and nickel
Atmosphere: depth and components	About 100 km deep; composed mainly of nitrogen (78%) and oxygen (21%)	Almost no atmosphere, but small amounts of CO_2, CO, and methane are present
Surface temperature	–89°C to 57°C	–173°C to 127°C

What is the main cause of the difference between temperatures found on Earth and temperatures found on the moon?

A The moon's very long days

B The moon's lack of atmosphere

C Earth's rotation on its axis

D Earth's distance from the sun

4 If you stayed up all night and watched the moon, what would you expect to see the moon do?

F The moon would rise in the east and set in the west.

G The moon would rise in the west and set in the east.

H The moon would change from a crescent to a full moon.

J The moon would change from a full moon to a crescent.

5 Mia wants her class to build a scale model of the sun-Earth-moon system on the playground. She knows that the sun is about 109 times larger in diameter than Earth. She also knows that the moon is about $\frac{1}{4}$ the size of Earth.

For the scale model, Mia wants the class to use a weather balloon to represent the sun, a tennis ball to represent Earth, and a marble to represent the moon. Mia's data are shown in the table.

Scale Model of Sun-Earth-Moon System

Name	Physical Model	Diameter of Model (cm)
Sun	Weather balloon	?
Earth	Tennis ball	6.66
Moon	Marble	1.8

Based on the data in the table, what is the diameter in centimeters of the weather balloon representing the sun? Round to the nearest whole number. Then record and bubble in your answer below.

			.
0	0	0	
1	1	1	
2	2	2	
3	3	3	
4	4	4	
5	5	5	
6	6	6	
7	7	7	
8	8	8	
9	9	9	

6 In the 1600s the scientist Galileo made improvements to the telescope and used it to study objects in space in a scientific way. His studies convinced him that the theories of his day about the sun and planets were wrong. What can you infer is one way that Galileo changed our knowledge of the solar system?

F Galileo helped prove that Earth is the center of the solar system.

G Galileo helped prove that Venus is the center of the solar system.

H Galileo helped prove that the sun is the center of the solar system.

J Galileo helped prove that the moon is the center of the solar system.

★ TEKS Practice: Cumulative Review

7 Which diagram best shows how the sun and ocean interact in the water cycle?

A Sunlight + Clouds ⟶ Ocean water

B Water vapor + Ocean water ⟶ Sunlight

C Sunlight + Water vapor ⟶ Ocean water

D Sunlight + Ocean water ⟶ Water vapor

---

8 A scientist found several fossils in some layers of rock. She made the diagram below of rock layers A–D to show her findings.

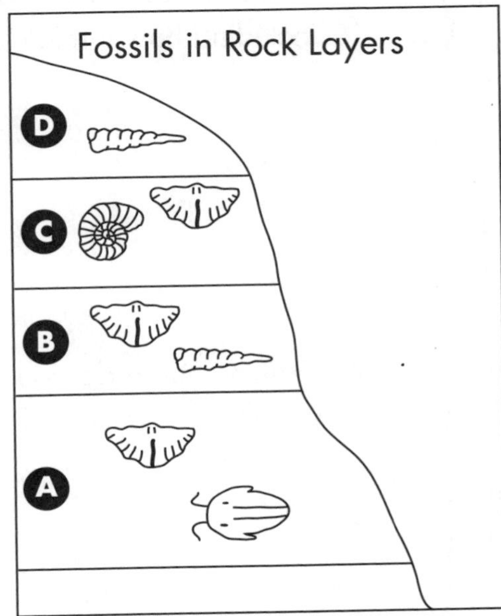

Two of the fossils had the same long, pointed shape. She found one in layer D. She found the other in layer B. Her student concluded that these fossils were the same age because they came from the same kind of animal. Which evidence shows this conclusion is wrong?

F Layer B is older than layer D because it is below layer D.

G Layer B is newer than layer D because it is below layer D.

H Layer B is older than layer D because it has more than one type of fossil.

J Layer B is newer than layer D because it has more than one type of fossil.

If you have trouble with . . .								
Question	1	2	3	4	5	6	7	8
See chapter (lesson)	7 (1)	7 (2)	7 (1)	7 (2)	7 (1)	7 (2)	6 (1)	5 (4)
TEKS	8D	8C	8D	8C	8D	8C	8B	7D

Lab zone® Open-Ended Inquiry

TEKS 8D, 1A, 2A, 2B, 2C, 2D, 2E, 2F, 2G, 3A, 3C, 4A, 4B

Materials

safety goggles
copy paper box lid
metal marble
meterstick
metric ruler
plastic cup of flour
plastic spoon
calculator or computer (optional)

Wear safety goggles.

Inquiry Skill
Controlled variables are things you must keep the same in an experiment if you want a fair test. The **independent variable** is the variable that you change in an experiment. The **dependent variable** is the variable you measure in an experiment.

How does the speed of a meteorite affect the crater it makes?

Will meteorites that move faster make a smaller or larger crater than meteorites that move more slowly?

Form a hypothesis.

1. Find sources that discuss the formation of impact craters. Analyze and evaluate the scientific explanations. Which do you think best explains the process of crater formation, including how it relates to the speed of a meteorite?

2. Which source do you think was least helpful? What do you think it's missing?

3. Based on what you've learned, formulate a testable **hypothesis** about speed of a meteorite and size of the crater it creates.

Identify and control variables.

4. Controlled variable:
   Independent variable:
   Dependent variable:

Design your test.

☐ **5.** Draw how you will set up your **model.**

☐ **6.** Plan and describe a simple experimental investigation testing one variable. List your steps in the order in which you will do them. Select appropriate equipment to use and list it here.

Do your test.

☑ **8.** Implement your simple experimental investigations testing one variable by following the steps you wrote.

☑ **9.** Collect and analyze information using a metric ruler to **measure** the width of the crater in millimeters.

☑ **10.** Scientists repeat their tests to improve their accuracy.

Collect and record your data.

☑ **11.** Collect information using a computer to record your information in a chart like the one below.

Interpret your data.

☑ **12.** Use appropriate technology, such as a computer or graphing calculator, to make a bar graph with your data.

Work Like a Scientist

Scientists work with other scientists. They compare their methods and results. Talk with your classmates. Compare your methods and results.

☐ **13.** Study your chart and graph. What patterns do you see?

☐ **14. Analyze and Interpret** Analyze your information using tools, including computers. What can you infer from your results?

Technology Tools
Your teacher may want you to use a computer (with the right software) or a graphing calculator to help collect, organize, analyze, and present your data. These tools can help you make tables, charts, and graphs.

State your conclusions.

15. Communicate your conclusion. Compare your **hypothesis** with your results. Share your results with others.

Life Science

Texas Essential Knowledge and Skills

Content TEKS

Organisms and Environments: 9A, 9B, 9C, 9D, 10A, 10B, 10C

Process TEKS

1A, 1B, 2A, 2B, 2C, 2D, 2F, 2G, 3A, 3C, 3D, 4A, 4B

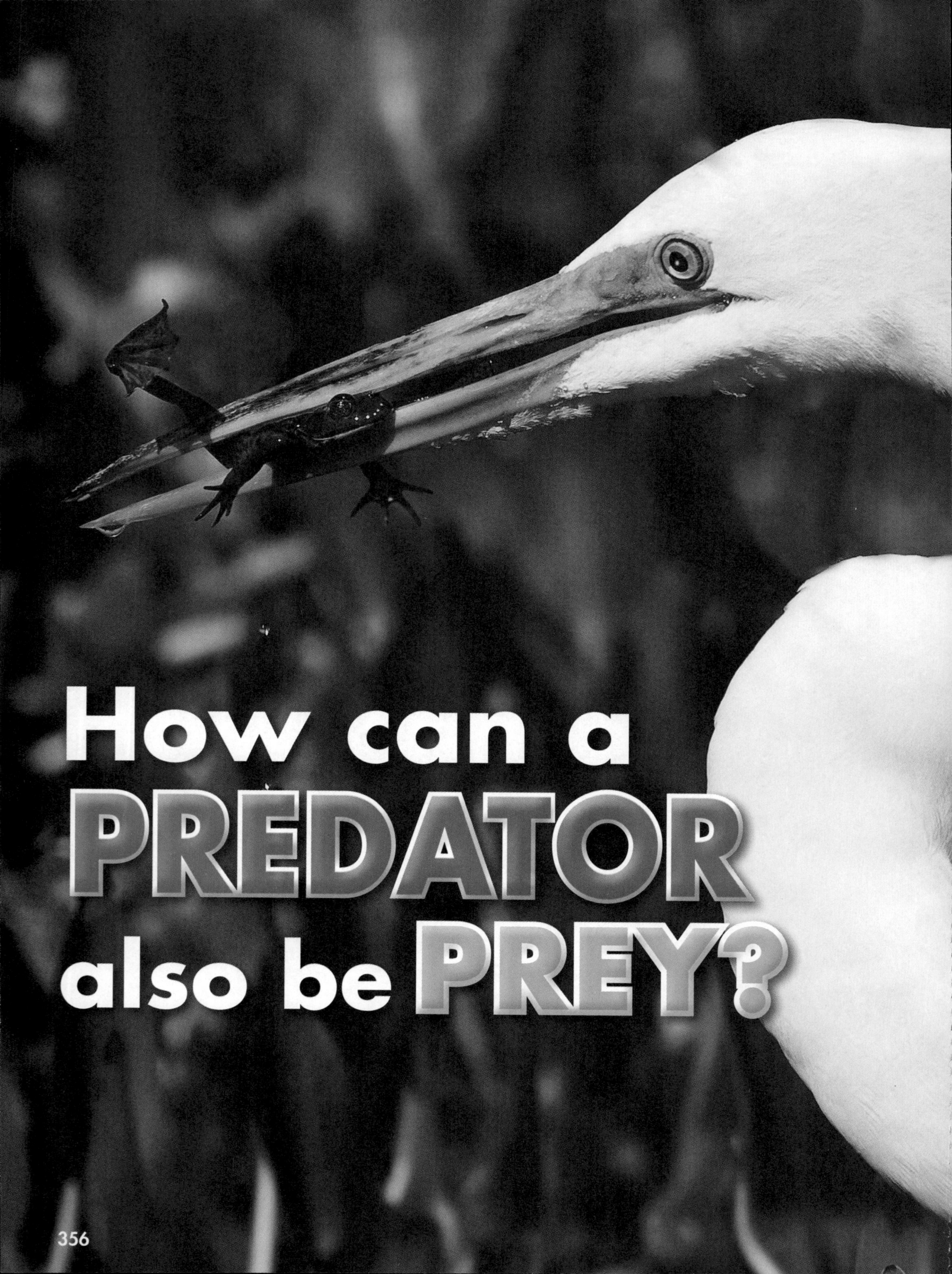

How can a PREDATOR also be PREY?

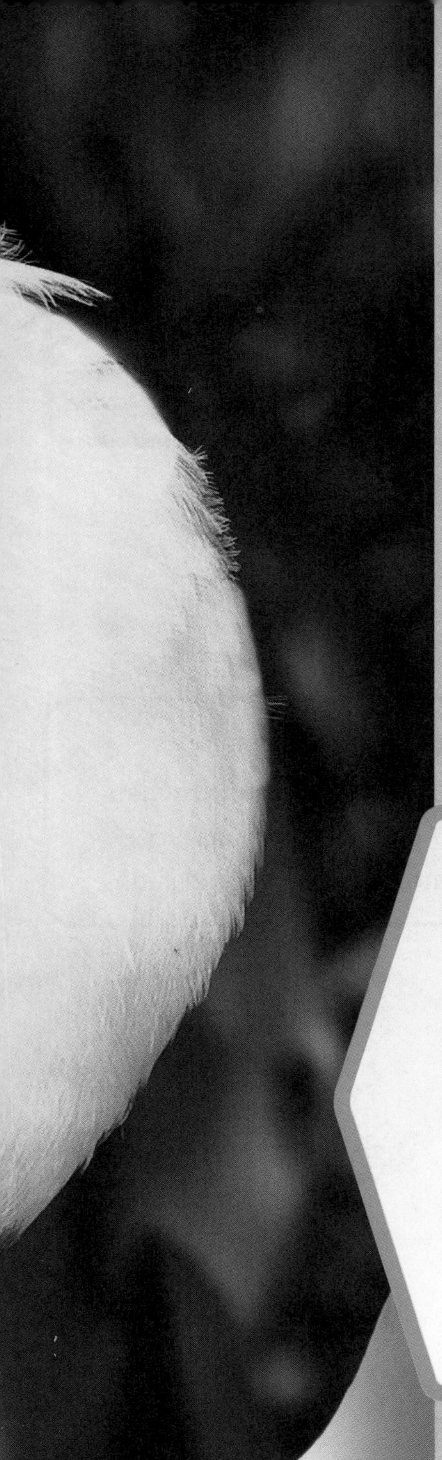

Ecosystems

How do living things interact with their environments?

The great white egret, the frog, and the plants all live in the same swamp. Many different living things interact with one another in this ecosystem.

If the great white egret left this swamp, what would happen to the frogs there?

Texas Essential Knowledge and Skills

Readiness TEKS: 9A Observe the way organisms live and survive in their ecosystem by interacting with the living and non-living elements. **9B** Describe how the flow of energy derived from the Sun, used by producers to create their own food, is transferred through a food chain and food web to consumers and decomposers. **Supporting TEKS: 9C** Predict the effects of changes in ecosystems caused by living organisms, including humans, such as the overpopulation of grazers or the building of highways. **9D** Identify the significance of the carbon dioxide-oxygen cycle to the survival of plants and animals.

Process TEKS: 1A, 1B, 2A, 2B, 2C, 2D, 2F, 3C, 3D, 4A, 4B

Inquiry Warm-Up

TEKS 9A, 1A, 2C, 2D, 2F, 3C, 4A

What can happen if an environment changes?

1. Place a water plant in the bowl with soil and water. Put the bowl in a warm place with bright light.
2. Every other day, add 4 seeds into the bowl.
3. Collect and analyze information using the materials that support the observation of habitats and organisms. **Observe** and **record** how the **model** of an environment changes.

Changes in a Model of an Environment

Day	Daily Observations
1	
2	
3	
4	
5	
6	
7	
8	
9	
10	
11	

Materials

bowl with soil and water
water plant
birdseed

Texas Safety LAB RULES

Always wash your hands with soap and warm water for at least 20 seconds before leaving the laboratory.

Inquiry Skill

You **interpret data** when you use information in a chart to draw a conclusion.

Explain Your Results

4. **Interpret Data** How did the changes in the **model** of an environment affect the plants that grew?

Focus on Main Idea and Details

Connect to Reading

You will practice the reading strategy of identifying **main idea and details.** The **main idea** is the most important idea in a reading selection. Supporting **details** tell more about the main idea.

Wetlands

A wetland is partly covered with water or is flooded at least part of the year. There are many kinds of wetlands, including swamps, marshes, and bogs. A swamp has many trees and bushes. Plants such as water lilies, vines, and cypress trees grow in some swamps. Animals such as alligators, turtles, frogs, and insects may live there too.

Another kind of wetland is a marsh, which is grassy with no trees. Muskrats and wading birds often live in this kind of wetland. Bogs are another kind of wetland. Bogs contain peat, a material that floats on the water and is formed by decomposing plants. Evergreen trees, shrubs, and moss are some plants that grow in bogs. Moose, deer, and lynx are some animals that live near bogs.

muskrat in wetlands

Practice It!

Complete the graphic organizer below to show the main idea and details in the example paragraph.

Main Idea

Detail

Detail

Detail

What are the parts of an ecosystem?

I will know **TEKS 9A**
I will know how organisms live and survive by interacting with living parts of their ecosystem. I will know how organisms live and survive by interacting with nonliving parts of their ecosystem. (Also **1A**, **2A**, **2B**, **2C**, **2D**, **4A**, **4B**)

Vocabulary
ecosystem
habitat
population
community

Did you know that the Panhandle of Texas is part of the Great Plains?

What are the Panhandle of Texas and the Great Plains?

The Panhandle is the part of Texas that borders Oklahoma and New Mexico. On a map, the area looks like the handle of a pan. The Great Plains is a vast area with a grasslands ecosystem. It is located in the middle of the United States.

Can you help me find the Panhandle of Texas on the map?

Connect to Social Studies

Identify a large Texas city that is located in the Texas Panhandle. **Social Studies TEKS 7B**

....

Quick Lab

TEKS 9A, 1A, 2A, 2B, 2C, 2D, 4A, 4B

What do some molds need to grow?

Materials

protective gloves
moldy strawberry
bread slice (without preservatives)
foil square
2 resealable plastic bags
plastic cup with water
dropper
hand lens

1. Put on the gloves. Rub some mold from a strawberry onto a piece of bread and onto a piece of foil.

2. Put the bread in a bag. Put the foil in the other bag. Place 10 drops of water onto the areas where you rubbed the mold.

3. Place the sealed bags in a warm, dark place for 4 days. Use a hand lens to **observe** the way the mold organism lives and survives in the ecosystem by interacting with nonliving elements.

4. **Communicate** What did you observe in each bag?

Texas Safety LAB RULES

Tell your teacher if you have allergies, such as to certain foods or to latex gloves.

Use safety equipment by wearing protective gloves. Wash your hands thoroughly upon completing the activity.

Explain Your Results

5. **Draw a Conclusion** Why did the mold grow only in one bag?

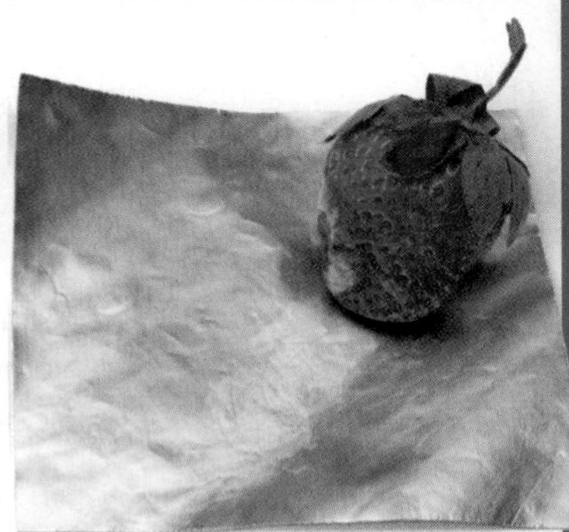

Ecosystems

An **ecosystem** is all the living and nonliving things in an area and their interactions. Ecosystems can be large, like a desert, or small, like a puddle. Even your classroom can be considered an ecosystem. The organisms in an ecosystem live in a habitat. A **habitat** is a place that provides all the things an organism needs to live. These things include food, water, and shelter.

There are many parts to an ecosystem. For example, ecosystems contain biotic and abiotic factors. Biotic factors are all the living organisms in an ecosystem, such as plants, animals, bacteria, and fungi. Abiotic factors are the nonliving parts in an ecosystem. Air, water, soil, temperature, and sunlight are some abiotic factors.

1. **Main Idea and Details** Complete the graphic organizer below. Write two details about ecosystems.

An aquarium ecosystem has similar elements to a pond ecosystem. Organisms live and survive in their ecosystem by interacting with living and nonliving elements.

Main Idea

There are many parts to an ecosystem.

Detail	Detail	Detail
	Ecosystems can be large or small.	

Algae interact with the nonliving elements (abiotic factors) in an aquarium ecosystem when it uses sunlight that comes through the glass to make its food.

Freshwater snails interact with other living organisms when they eat algae that grow on the glass and other items inside the tank of an aquarium.

Plants and animals in the aquarium interact with nonliving elements: carbon dioxide and oxygen. Plants use carbon dioxide exhaled by fish and other animals to make their food. The animals use the oxygen the plants give off to live.

Living elements in the aquarium ecosystem interact when they mate and when they eat other organisms. When fish mate, they produce young that can be food for other species.

2. Identify Read the description of the ecosystems on these pages. **Underline** the details in each description that tell how some organisms survive in their environment.

3. Classify What is an example of a population in the picture below of the coral reef?

Types of Ecosystems

There are many different types of ecosystems. The abiotic factors in an ecosystem often determine what kinds of organisms live in it. For example, only organisms that can withstand the extreme heat and dryness of a desert can live there.

Organisms in an ecosystem often have similar traits, or characteristics. These traits help them survive in their ecosystem. Frogs, turtles, and alligators have webbed feet that help them swim in a water ecosystem, such as a swamp.

All types of ecosystems contain populations and communities. A **population** is a group of organisms of one species that live in an area at the same time. A population may be all the oak trees in an area. Different populations in an area make up a **community.** A community may have populations of oak trees, maple trees, and pine trees. Members of a community depend on one another to fill their needs, such as food and shelter.

Coral Reef

Organisms that live in a coral reef have traits that help them live in warm, clear, shallow water. For example, some algae carry on photosynthesis. As a result, they grow only in shallow water where sunlight can reach them. The coral reef can support the algae, which produce food for other organisms, including the coral. A coral reef may have many colorful animals, such as clown fish, anemones, and sponges. A reef is made up mostly of the skeletons of dead coral animals. The coral animals on the top part of the reef are alive.

panda butterflyfish

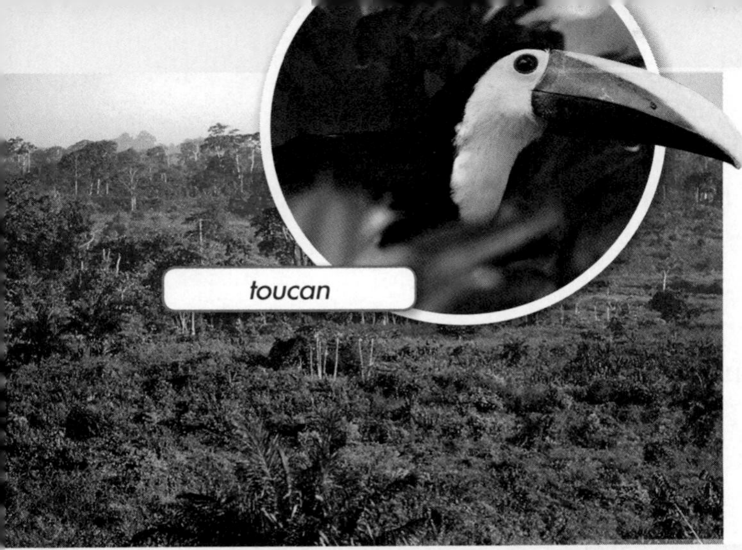
toucan

Tropical Rain Forest

The traits of organisms that live in a tropical rain forest help them survive in a warm, rainy climate all year long. The shape of the leaves of some plants cause rain drops to fall off the plants quickly. The high amount of moisture in the air allows other plants, such as orchids, to grow on trees, not in soil. Butterflies, tree frogs, monkeys, and parrots are some animals that live in this ecosystem.

Desert

Deserts have little rain. Most have hot days and cool nights. Some deserts have sand dunes. Some are rocky. Others are covered by a layer of salt. Organisms living in the desert have traits that help them survive the hot, dry conditions. Plants, such as cactuses, can store water in their stems when it rains. To deal with high temperatures, many animals rest during the day. Animals such as coyotes, desert tortoises, lizards, and rattlesnakes live in deserts in the United States.

desert tortoise

arctic fox

Tundra

The traits of organisms that live in a tundra help them survive cold weather with little rain. Thick fur coats cover many of the animals that live there. Most tundras are found in the most northern areas of Earth or high up in mountains. Rodents, rabbits, and caribou feed on small plants and grasses. Weasels, polar bears, and foxes also live on the tundra.

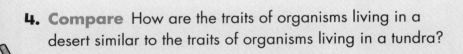

4. **Compare** How are the traits of organisms living in a desert similar to the traits of organisms living in a tundra?

Balance in Ecosystems

Every organism in an ecosystem has a niche and a habitat. A *niche* is the role that an organism has in an ecosystem. The niche of a northern pygmy owl in the mixed forest is that of a hunter. It eats small animals, such as mice and chipmunks. A habitat is the place where an organism lives. A habitat is made up of the soil, air, and water, as well as the plants of the area. The habitat of northern pygmy owls is the trees and the land on which they live. The trees' habitat is the land.

All the relationships among the parts of an ecosystem keep it balanced. For example, in a forest owls eat small animals, such as mice. If the number of mice in the forest decreases, the owls have less food. So, the number of owls will decrease. But with fewer owls hunting, fewer mice will be eaten. As a result, the population of mice will grow. Then, with more mice to hunt, the number of owls will increase again. In this way, the populations of owls and mice balance.

northern pygmy owl hunting a mouse

5. **Main Idea and Details** Read the first paragraph again. **Underline** the main idea. **Circle** the details.

6. CHALLENGE Think of a local ecosystem. Draw an organism you might find there. Label your organism and describe its niche.

Limiting Factors

The number of organisms that can live in a habitat is called the carrying capacity. Factors that limit the carrying capacity of a habitat are the amount of food, water, space, and shelter. With the right conditions, such as plenty of food, few diseases, and few predators, a population in a habitat will grow larger. But a population may grow only to a certain size and still have all its needs met. Overcrowding may happen if a population grows larger than the carrying capacity. When overcrowding occurs, food supplies can run out. Organisms must move to another area or they will not survive.

Quick Lab

Eco-Walk
With an adult, take a walk outside. Observe and record the living and nonliving things you see. Then read about ecosystems in your region and compare what you learn with what you observed outside.
TEKS 9A

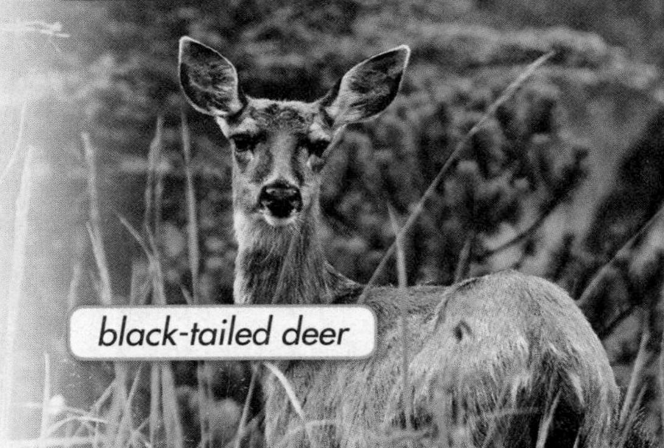

black-tailed deer

7. **Predict** What may happen to the population of deer if it increases too much?

got it?

8. **Describe** Identify an ecosystem near where you live. Describe the living and nonliving things in that ecosystem.

9. **Compare** How are the traits of some plants living in a tropical rain forest similar?

Stop! I need help with

Wait! I have a question about

Go! Now I know

How do organisms interact in ecosystems?

I will know TEKS 9A, 9B
I will know how organisms interact with living and nonliving elements in their ecosystem. I will describe how energy flows and is transferred through an ecosystem. (Also 1A, 2B, 2C, 2D, 2F, 4A)

Vocabulary
predator
prey
producer
consumer
decomposer
food chain
food web

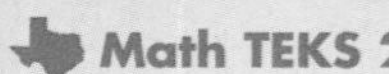

Connect to Math

Math TEKS 2B

Zebra mussels are not a native species in North America. They were first discovered in the mid-1980s in Lake St. Clair, Michigan. It is believed that the zebra mussels were brought in on ships from eastern Europe. Zebra mussels multiply quickly, and they have no natural predators in North America.

Zebra mussels are now found in many lakes in North America, including some in Texas. They are a threat to native species because they out-compete these species. Zebra mussels consume food, shelter, and other resources quickly.

Very young zebra mussels are extremely small and are able to swim. If the shells of two young zebra mussels measure 0.099 mm and 0.110 mm, use the symbol > or < to indicate which shell is larger.

0.099 mm ____ 0.110 mm

PEARSON Texas.com

Quick Lab

 TEKS 9A, 1A, 2B, 2C, 2D, 2F, 4A

How do organisms survive in their ecosystems?

Materials

hand lens

science notebook

Texas Safety LAB RULES

Demonstrate the use of safety equipment during outdoor investigations.

Wear shoes that enclose the feet.

In hot weather, you may want to wear lightweight, loose-fitting, and light-colored clothing.

Stay in the area directed by your teacher.

Tell your teacher if you have allergies, such as to certain plants or foods.

Wash your hands thoroughly upon completing the activity.

☐ **1.** Your teacher will take you to the area where you will observe interactions in an ecosystem. Demonstrate safe practices during an outdoor investigation by observing the boundaries of the area you are studying and by staying within those boundaries. Demonstrate the use of safety equipment during an outdoor investigation by wearing the kinds of shoes and clothing described on the right.

☐ **2. Observe** the way organisms in the area live and survive in their ecosystem by interacting with the living and nonliving elements. Using your hand lens, collect and analyze information by observing plants or other tiny living organisms.

☐ **3. Record and analyze** information, including your detailed observations, using your science notebook. Make sketches of any interactions that you want to illustrate.

Explain Your Results

4. Draw a Conclusion Analyze and interpret your information to construct reasonable explanations from direct (observable) evidence. Explain how an organism survives in its ecosystem by interacting with other living organisms.

....

....

....

Interactions in Ecosystems

Ecosystems are made up of living and nonliving things. The living things in ecosystems interact with each other in a variety of ways. Some organisms help one another meet their needs. Some organisms may eat other organisms and get energy or nutrients from them. Some organisms compete with one another for space or food.

In some ecosystems, birds may flock near larger animals. The animals may disturb insects in high grasses. As the insects fly or jump away, the birds are able to catch them for food. The birds are helped by this relationship, but the larger animal is not affected.

Some animals in an ecosystem must hunt other organisms to fill their energy needs. In this type of interaction, only one organism is helped. An animal that hunts and eats another animal is called a **predator.** Any animal that is hunted by others for food is called **prey.** The predator gets energy from the prey when the predator eats the prey.

Ticks are parasites. They often feed on the blood of deer, birds, and other organisms. If too many ticks feed on an animal or if the tick infects the animal with a disease, the animal can become weak and die.

Each environment or ecosystem has its own relationships among organisms. These white-tailed deer eat the grass in the field. The grass is a living organism that makes its own food by photosynthesis.

Cottontail rabbits often are found in the same environments as white-tailed deer. Rabbits also eat plants. So white-tailed deer and cottontail rabbits could compete for the same plants as food.

1. **Classify** Classify each animal in these pictures as predator or prey. Explain their roles.

Great horned owls also might share the ecosystem with the other organisms.

Snakes also are found in this type of ecosystem. This rat snake eats mice, rats, and other small animals, as well as eggs. The snake is the predator, and a mouse or a rat is the prey in this relationship.

Energy Roles in Ecosystems

These plants make their own food. They are producers.

The moose eats the plants. Moose are herbivores.

Bears are omnivores. They eat plants and animals.

Perhaps the most common interaction in an ecosystem occurs when organisms get energy. All organisms need energy to live. How an organism gets its energy determines its energy role. An organism's energy role makes up part of its niche in an ecosystem. Each organism in an ecosystem fills the energy role of producer, consumer, or decomposer.

Producers

Plants and some other organisms are producers. **Producers** make their own food for energy. Most producers use energy from the sun to make food. Some producers use chemicals from their environment for energy. Producers either use the energy to grow or store it for later. The food they make is often a source of energy for other organisms.

Consumers

Many organisms depend on producers to get energy. **Consumers** are organisms that cannot make their own food. They get energy from producers or other consumers. All animals and some microorganisms are consumers.

There are several kinds of consumers. They are classified by what they eat. Herbivores, such as moose, eat only plants. Carnivores eat only other animals. One example of a carnivore is a lion. Omnivores eat both plants and animals. Black bears are omnivores.

Some carnivores feed on dead animals. These consumers are called *scavengers*. Vultures and hyenas are two examples of scavengers.

2. **Give an Example** Write two examples of consumers. Tell whether they are herbivores, omnivores, carnivores, or scavengers.

Decomposers

Producers and consumers take in nutrients from the environment as they use energy and grow. **Decomposers** are organisms that get their energy by breaking down wastes and dead organisms. During this process, decomposers return materials to an ecosystem. In turn, other organisms reuse these materials for their own needs. Most decomposers are too small to see without a microscope.

3. **Classify** Read the caption to the right about the organisms shown. Use the key to label the organisms.

Key		
C = consumer	**P** = producer	**D** = decomposer

The plant gets its energy from sunlight. The hummingbird sips nectar from the plant's flower for food. The mushrooms get energy from the dead tree.

These decomposers are too small to be seen without a microscope. They are breaking down a dead leaf.

You in the Food Chain
Think about a fresh food you ate or drank yesterday, such as an apple or a glass of milk. Describe how the flow of energy derived from the sun, used by producers to create their own food, is transferred through a food chain to you. TEKS 9B

Food Chains

Energy passes through an ecosystem when food is eaten. This energy often begins as the sunlight that producers, like plants, use to make food. Energy can take many different paths in an ecosystem. This movement of energy through an ecosystem can be shown in food chains. A **food chain** is a series of steps by which energy, derived from the sun, moves from one type of living thing to another. The shortest food chains involve only a producer, which uses the energy from the sun to create its own food, and a decomposer. Other food chains involve a carnivore or an omnivore too. Arrows on a food chain show the path in which energy moves.

4. **Fill in the Blanks** Write a word that best describes each part of the Prairie Food Chain diagram below.

Prairie Food Chain

Grass is an example of a ....

Deer eat grass. They are ....

Coyotes eat deer. They are ....

5. **Sequence** Water oak trees are a source of food for termites. Black bears often look in rotting logs for insects such as termites to eat. Make a food chain for these organisms.

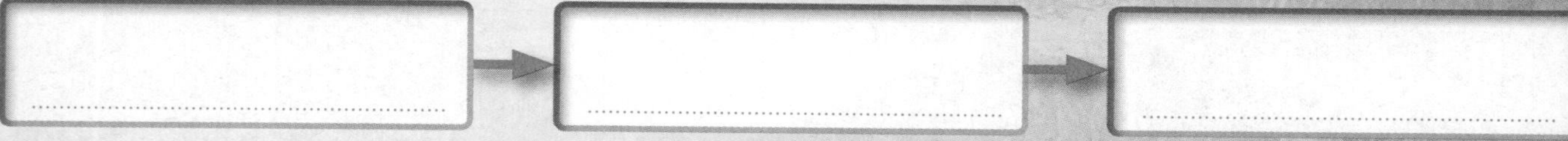

Food Webs

Relationships among organisms in an ecosystem can be complicated. There are many food chains in an ecosystem, but a food chain can describe only one way energy flows in an ecosystem. To see how these food chains are all connected in an ecosystem, you can use a food web. A **food web** is a diagram that combines many food chains into one picture. Like a food chain, a food web uses arrows to show the energy relationships among organisms as the energy flows from the sun to producers that use it to make their own food, and then to consumers.

At any point in the food web, a consumer or a producer may die. The energy from the Sun that has been stored in its body can then be used by decomposers, such as fungi and bacteria.

6. Main Idea and Details **Underline** the main idea in the paragraph about food chains. **Circle** the supporting details.

7. Look at the food web below. Describe how the energy derived from the sun, used by producers to create their own food, is transferred through the web to consumers and decomposers.

This food web shows the complex flow of energy in a salt marsh ecosystem.

kudzu

Roles in Ecosystems

Every organism in an ecosystem has a niche, or role in that ecosystem. A niche includes the type of food the organism takes in, how it gets its food, and which other species use the organism as food. An organism may compete for the things it needs. Plants may compete for sunlight, soil, or water. Animals may compete for territory, water, light, food, or mates. For example, male black bears will compete with each other for territory and mates. Rabbits, mice, and other animals of a desert community compete with one another for plants to eat. An animal that cannot compete may die or be forced to move away.

8. Infer Kudzu is a vine that quickly grows and covers other plants. What is one resource for which kudzu competes with other plants?

Connect to Math

Math TEKS 1A, 1B, 9C

Read a Graph

The graph shows how the population sizes of a hunter, such as an owl, and the animal it hunts might change over time. Use the graph to answer these questions.

1 Which is a reasonable estimate for the difference between the greatest and the least number of hunters?

A. 5 **B.** 12 **C.** 22 **D.** 40

2 What happens after the hunter's population becomes greater than the hunted animal's population?

A. This never happens.

B. The hunter's population decreases to zero.

C. The hunter's population decreases.

D. The hunted animal's population increases.

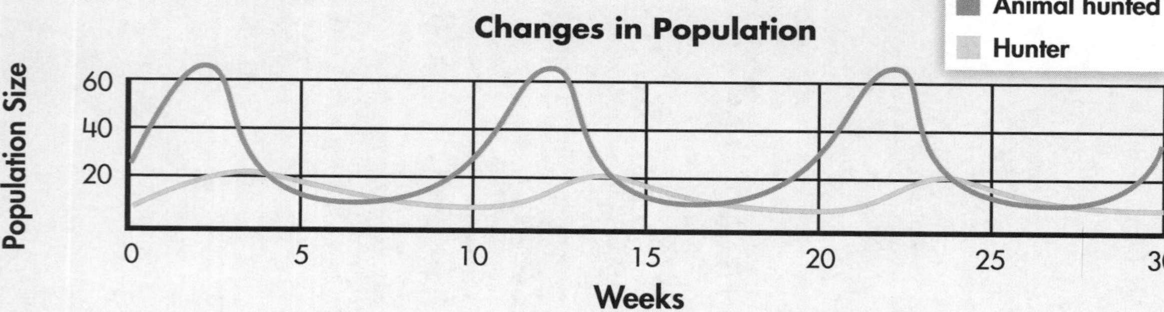

Symbiosis

A long-term relationship between two different organisms is called symbiosis. One organism is always helped. The other organism might be harmed, helped, or not affected. A *parasite* is an organism that lives on or inside of another organism. Parasites take nutrients away from the organisms where they live, which harms organisms.

In other relationships, both organisms are helped. For example, the cleaner shrimp eats parasites from the eel's mouth. The shrimp gets food and the eel keeps its teeth clean and free of parasites.

moray eel with cleaner shrimp

9. CHALLENGE Think about the interaction between bees and apple trees. How is this an example of symbiosis?

....

....

got it?

10. Compare and Contrast How are food chains and food webs alike and different?

....

....

11. Describe What are the roles of producers, consumers, and decomposers in a food chain?

....

....

....

Stop! I need help with ....

Wait! I have a question about ....

Go! Now I know ....

Fungal Gardens

APPLY THE TEKS 9B

***Atta texana*, a species of leaf-cutter ant in Texas, grows its own food in underground gardens. These leaf-cutter ants cut green leaves from plants. Then, they carry the leaves through underground tunnels to garden chambers. Inside these chambers, specific kinds of fungi decompose the leaves. The fungi grow and reproduce using the leaves as their food source. The fungi are the ants' primary food source. The ants and fungi have a symbiotic relationship in which both species benefit from the relationship. The fungi get food and shelter, and the ants get a food source.**

These ants are carrying ant larvae in the fungal garden. The green pieces in the photo are fragments of green leaves.

This colony of Texas leaf-cutting ants has collected leaves from several species of plants. They use the chewed-up leaves to grow a fungus in their nest. Describe how the flow of energy derived from the sun, used by producers to create their own food, is transferred through a food chain to a decomposer.

Entomologist

Science Careers

TEKS 3D

If you find insects interesting, you might want to become an entomologist. An entomologist studies insects, which are a large group of organisms on Earth. Some insects, like mosquitoes, are considered pests. Mosquitoes can carry diseases, such as malaria and West Nile virus, that infect humans. Other insects, like honeybees, are considered beneficial. Honeybees pollinate crops and help ensure that farmers get a good crop yield. Entomologists might study how to control mosquitoes to keep people from getting sick, or they might study factors that reduce bee populations.

Symbiotic Relationships in Texas

TEKS 9A

Symbiotic relationships are common in Texas. Cattle egrets are birds that follow grazing animals and eat the insects that the cattle scare with their movements. When the insects fly, the egrets catch them and eat them. Brown-headed cowbirds lay their eggs in the nests of other birds. When the cowbirds hatch, they compete for food against the baby birds from the nest. The offspring of the nest builders die, and the nest builders raise the cowbirds.

Infer What might happen if the population of brown-headed cowbirds increases in an ecosystem?

Texas

LESSON

3

How do ecosystems change?

I will know TEKS 9C
I will know that living things, including humans, can change ecosystems. I will know how to predict the changes in ecosystems caused by living organisms, including humans. (Also **1A**, **1B**, **2B**, **2C**, **2D**, **2F**, **4A**)

Vocabulary
environment
competition

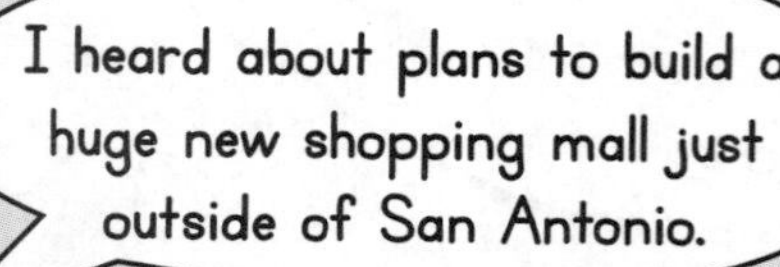

I heard about plans to build a huge new shopping mall just outside of San Antonio.
What is going to happen to the ecosystem where they want to build the mall?
I am not sure. They didn't say anything about that on the news.

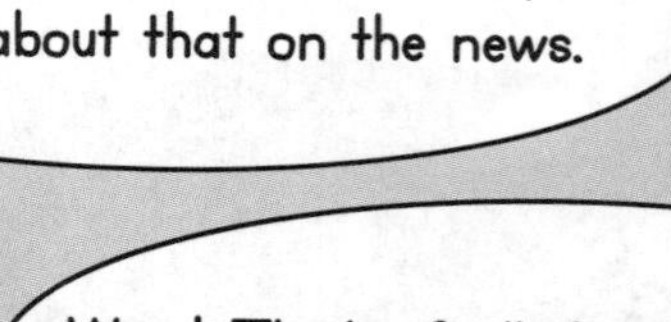

Wow! Think of all the organisms that the mall will affect.

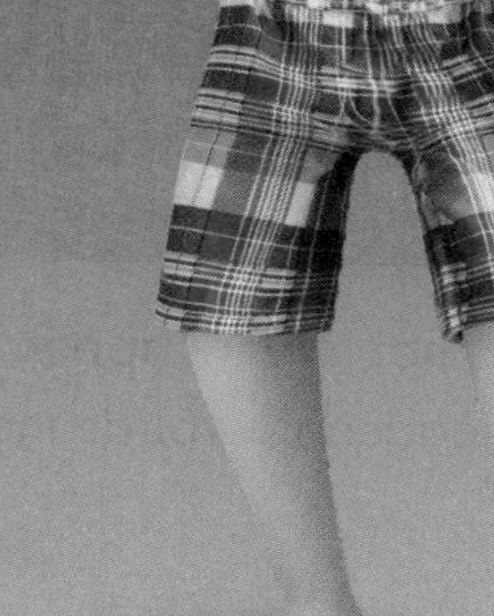

Connect to Social Studies

Write two well-organized paragraphs that describe how you think the ecosystem might be affected if a new shopping mall is built. **Social Studies TEKS 26A**

Quick Lab

TEKS 9C, 1A, 2B, 2C, 2D, 2F, 4A

What does a microscopic ecosystem look like?

1. Use a marker and masking tape to label your plastic jar or bottle. If possible, your teacher will take you to collect a sample of pond water from an outdoor pond.
2. Demonstrate the use of safety equipment by wearing protective gloves. Use your jar or bottle to transport your pond water sample.
3. Follow your teacher's instructions and prepare a microscope slide with cover using the pond water.
4. **Observe** Collect information by using a microscope to observe the pond water. **Draw** a picture of what you see under the microscope in your science notebook.
5. Use the lid to *loosely* cover the jar or bottle. Place the jar in a sunny window for a week.
6. Repeat Steps 3 and 4. Note: Pond water often contains water fleas, insect larvae, and other organisms that are small but not microscopic. These are easy to observe. Collect and analyze information about these organisms using a collecting net to catch and observe them separately.

Materials

marker
masking tape
clear plastic jar or bottle with lid
protective gloves
pond water sample
dropper
microscope slide
microscope slide cover
microscope
collecting net (optional)

Texas Safety LAB RULES

In hot weather, you may want to wear lightweight, loose-fitting, and light-colored clothing.

Wear shoes that enclose the feet.

Wear protective gloves when collecting pond water.

Stay in the area directed by your teacher.

Tell your teacher if you have allergies, such as to certain plants or foods.

Wash your hands thoroughly upon completing the activity.

Explain Your Results

7. **Communicate** Analyze information using a microscope. Explain what happened in the jar or bottle during the week.

8. **Analyze and Interpret** Did the ecosystem change over time?

Environmental Changes

All organisms live in particular environments where their needs are met. An **environment** is all of the conditions surrounding an organism. Environments may be hot or cold and on land or in water.

Environments change naturally as resources change. For example, a population of millipedes lives in an environment with dead plant matter. As the population grows, it needs more food, water, and living space. As these resources decrease, each millipede will have less food, water, and space. Some millipedes will die or move away. More resources will be available for the remaining millipedes. The population will grow, and the cycle will start again. Species must change to take advantage of new opportunities and protect themselves from new dangers in a changed environment.

1. **Explain** Puddles like this may be home to frogs, fish, worms, or fairy shrimp. Which of these animals might be able to survive after the puddle is dry? Why?

2. **Cause and Effect** Use the graphic organizer to list one cause and one effect from the text.

Cause

Effect

This puddle has been drying up for some time, and the mud around it is cracking as it dries.

Life in a modern American city requires a lot of resources and generates a lot of waste. Getting those resources and disposing of wastes causes environmental changes. Making informed choices in the disposal of materials helps conserve ecosystems.

Forests are being cut to plant crops and to make wood products, such as lumber and paper. When the forests are removed, the forest ecosystem is destroyed.

Huge landfills are built to bury trash or waste. Many kinds of waste, such as batteries, have to be disposed of carefully so that they do not cause environmental damage.

Sometimes toxic materials are accidently released into the environment. This happens in oil spills. Fish, birds, and other organisms are affected by such spills.

Mining for copper, sulfur, and other natural resources causes environmental changes. Many of these resources can be recycled to reduce environmental damage.

Slow Changes

Sometimes environments change very slowly. For example, the climate in a region may become drier and drier over thousands of years. This has happened in the Sahara, which has had both wet and dry periods in the past.

Seasons change slowly every year. This gives animals time to grow winter fur. Plants have time to grow new leaves for the summer.

The continents also change their position over millions of years. For example, Antarctica used to be much closer to the equator, and much warmer.

Rocks are slowly broken down by the weather and by plants and animals. They become part of the soil.

Very slowly, the orange lichens growing on this rock are helping break down the rock to form new soil.

Fast Changes

Hurricanes, floods, and fires, along with volcanic eruptions and earthquakes, are natural events that can quickly change the environment. A hurricane's strong winds can rip up trees and flatten plants. Heavy rains and huge waves can flood a coastal community. When lightning strikes a tree, it can start a forest fire that burns almost everything in its path.

These rapid changes may force species to leave the area because the resources they need are no longer available.

3. **Underline** two examples of slow environmental changes. **Circle** two examples of fast changes.

4. **Give an Example** What is another type of fast environmental change?

Quick Lab

Long Ago
Work with an adult. Find out what your region was like 10 years ago. What was it like 100 years ago? What was it like 1,000 years ago? Discuss how your region has changed.

A volcano can quickly destroy or bury many organisms, but it can also cover the soil with nutrients that other organisms can use.

Changes Caused by Organisms

Organisms themselves may alter their environment as they feed, grow, and build their homes. For example, locusts are insects that travel in large groups called swarms. The members of these large swarms can quickly eat all the plants in large fields and destroy farm crops. After locusts pass through, an area that was green and full of plants will look dead and bare.

Plants also cause changes. In fact, plants affect the quality of the air for the entire planet. They absorb carbon dioxide from the air and release oxygen back into the atmosphere.

A swarm of locusts can be many kilometers long and eat tons of plant matter.

5. Suggest What kind of animal might benefit from a locust swarm?

A water mold is using this potato for food. The water mold starts consuming the potato in the field. An entire crop can be destroyed before it can be harvested.

A healthy potato has cream-colored flesh.

This microscopic organism is a water mold. It uses the leaves, stems, and potatoes as food. This water mold destroyed potato crops in Ireland during the 1800s and caused widespread famine.

When a single type of plant is grown close together, it is easy for organisms to go from plant to plant. An entire crop can be destroyed in a short period of time.

Changes Caused by Humans

Humans are one of the most important causes of environmental change. We change the land to plant crops, build dams to get energy, fish to get food, and clear forests to get construction materials. We change the environment when we build buildings and highways, and when we burn fuel.

There are many ways in which we can reduce the impact of human activity on the environment. For example, tunnels have been built in some places with busy traffic so that animals can cross from one side of the road to the other without getting hit by cars. We can recycle things like paper or construction materials to reduce the number of trees we cut down.

6. **Classify** Look at the picture of a farm on this page. What parts of this environment probably were not there before people arrived?

7. Predict the effects of changes in ecosystems caused by living organisms, including humans, in the case of a forest being removed to plant crops.

Farming often requires flat land with no trees or rocks.

Adapting to Changes

Changes that are harmful for some organisms may be beneficial for others. A forest fire destroys trees and bushes that help protect the soil from being washed away by rainwater. In addition, a forest fire adds smoke and carbon dioxide to the atmosphere and destroys the habitats of many animals. However, a forest fire may also help organisms in a forest. A forest fire clears away dead and dying plant matter, making room for new plants to grow. It also returns nutrients to the soil in the form of ashes.

In any environment, resources are limited. The struggle of organisms for the same limited resources is called **competition.** Organisms must succeed in this struggle in order to survive.

8. Explain How can competition affect a group of organisms in an environment?

The thick bark of the sequoia tree protects it from the fire. This bark helps the sequoia tree survive in its environment.

Some trees, such as the Table Mountain pine, have sealed cones that open only with the heat of a fire.

Some seeds only start to grow when there is smoke.

The growing parts of grasses are underground. They can quickly grow back after a fire. This helps them in the competition for nutrients.

Resurrection plants can survive very dry seasons because they can dry up without dying. The plant below is the same plant as above, only one day after being watered.

Survival

In any species of plant or animal there are differences among individuals. A plant that has deeper roots than other plants may be able to reach deeper into the soil to get water. An animal that runs a little faster than others of its kind has a better chance of escaping from a predator. Even a small advantage can help a plant or animal survive. Only the individuals that survive will be able to reproduce and pass along their beneficial characteristics to their offspring.

9. Infer How do you think the environment of a resurrection plant might change over time?

Connect to **Math**

Math TEKS 3H

Subtracting Fractions

When subtracting fractions from a whole, use equivalent fractions.

Example

A forest fire destroys $\frac{1}{3}$ of a forest. If another $\frac{1}{4}$ of the forest area burns, what fraction of the forest is left unburned?

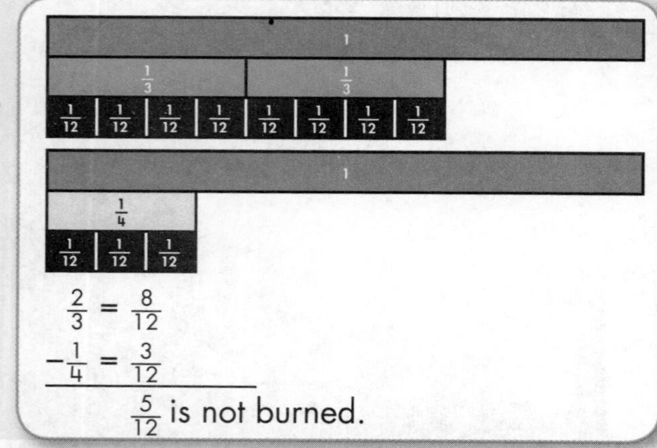

$$\frac{2}{3} = \frac{8}{12}$$
$$-\frac{1}{4} = \frac{3}{12}$$
$\frac{5}{12}$ is not burned.

1 One year, $\frac{1}{2}$ of a sea turtle population could not find nest space on a beach. The next year, another $\frac{1}{3}$ of the population relocated. What fraction of the turtle population is left?

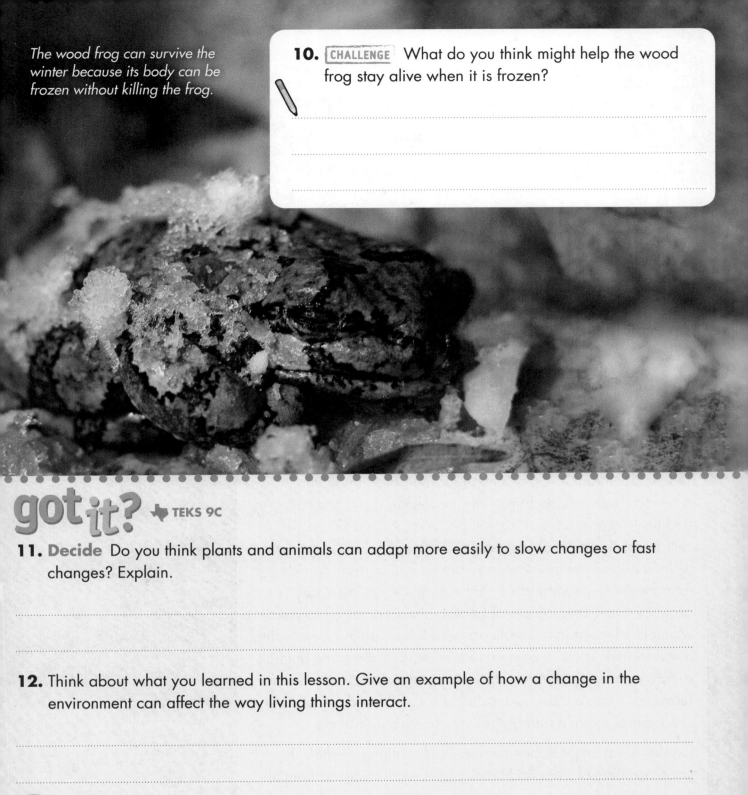

The wood frog can survive the winter because its body can be frozen without killing the frog.

10. CHALLENGE What do you think might help the wood frog stay alive when it is frozen?

got it? TEKS 9C

11. Decide Do you think plants and animals can adapt more easily to slow changes or fast changes? Explain.

12. Think about what you learned in this lesson. Give an example of how a change in the environment can affect the way living things interact.

Stop! I need help with

Wait! I have a question about

Go! Now I know

Texas LESSON 4

What are some natural cycles?

I will know TEKS 9C, 9D
I will know how to predict the effects of changes in an ecosystem caused by living organisms, including humans. I will know how to identify the significance of the carbon dioxide–oxygen cycle to the survival of plants and animals.(Also 1A, 2C, 2D, 2F, 4B)

Vocabulary
nitrogen cycle
carbon cycle

Connect to Social Studies

 **TEKS Social Studies 25B, 25E**

The Amazon rain forest is a huge forested area in South America. Tropical rain forests are located in warm climates, and they receive a lot of rainfall per year. As a result, tropical rain forests have an abundance of different kinds of organisms, including green plants. Green plants take in carbon dioxide from the atmosphere and use it during photosynthesis to produce food. The process of photosynthesis gives off oxygen, which is released into the atmosphere. Many animals, including humans, must breathe oxygen to survive, and the same animals exhale carbon dioxide into the atmosphere. The Amazon rain forest contains so many plants that it is considered a global producer of oxygen and global user of carbon dioxide.

Explain what might happen to oxygen-breathing animals if large numbers of trees and other plants were removed from the Amazon rain forest.

PEARSON Texas.com

Quick Lab

TEKS 9D, 1A, 2C, 2D, 2F, 4B

How do plants use carbon dioxide?

BTB water turns greenish yellow when there are high levels of CO_2. It turns blue when there are low levels.

1. Push a straw through the covering of a cup of BTB water. Breathe out through the straw into the water. Stop when the color starts to change.
2. Put elodea into the cup. Put it in a bright place. **Observe** every 10 minutes. **Record** any changes.

Observations

Conditions	Color of BTB Water
Before breathing out into the water	
After breathing out into the water	
After adding elodea to the water	

Materials

safety goggles
straw
cup $\frac{1}{3}$ full of BTB water, covered with plastic wrap
elodea

Texas Safety LAB RULES

Wear safety goggles.
Do not drink the BTB water.
Use the straw to breathe OUT only!

Explain Your Results

3. **Infer** Discuss why the BTB water changed color.
4. **Communicate** Describe the movement of carbon dioxide in this activity.

Earth's Natural Cycles

One reason that life on Earth is possible is because of the gases that make up its atmosphere. Most of Earth's atmosphere is nitrogen gas. Most of the rest is oxygen, but small amounts of carbon dioxide gas are also present. Nitrogen, oxygen, and carbon dioxide are renewable resources because they cycle, or go through a complete series, in the environment.

If resources that living things need, such as water, nitrogen, carbon, and oxygen, were not cycled, they would soon run out. Earth's natural cycles allow living things to use the same materials over and over. Two important cycles are the nitrogen cycle and the carbon cycle.

1. **Draw Conclusions** What might happen to living things if important resources ran out?

2. **Predict** How do you think nutrients will continue to flow in this ecosystem from the banana slug?

A fungus is a decomposer that breaks down materials from a log into nutrients.

This banana slug eats material on the forest floor.

Earth supports life because it has the resources available for life to survive. Many of these resources cycle through the environment and are used over and over again. The recycling of these resources makes it possible for life to continue on Earth. If nitrogen, carbon, and oxygen did not cycle, they would eventually become unavailable and plants and animals would not survive.

All living things on Earth, including you, are made up of carbon compounds. Often, oxygen atoms and carbon atoms cycle together. When you breathe in and breathe out, you are participating in the carbon dioxide–oxygen cycle. Plants and animals could not survive for long without the carbon dioxide–oxygen cycle.

Water and the cycling of water are important for the survival of plants and animals, including humans, to survive.

Nitrogen Cycle

Nitrogen is all around us. Almost $\frac{4}{5}$ of Earth's atmosphere is nitrogen gas. Nitrogen cycles through ecosystems. It moves through the food chain and other processes. The **nitrogen cycle** is the repeated movement of nitrogen through the environment in different forms.

Cells in plants and animals need nitrogen to do their work, but most organisms cannot use nitrogen gas from the air. They must use nitrogen compounds, which are chemicals that contain nitrogen. Nitrogen compounds form in many ways. For example, they can form in the atmosphere. Lightning can cause nitrogen to combine with other gases in air and make nitrogen compounds. These compounds reach Earth's soil and water in rainfall.

Some kinds of bacteria are able to take nitrogen gas directly from the air to make nitrogen compounds. Plants can then absorb and use these compounds. Some of these bacteria live in the soil or in the special roots of some kinds of plants. Some live in plants that grow in the upper branches of tropical rain forests.

Herbivores, or animals that eat plants, get the nitrogen they need from the plants they eat. Animals that are carnivores get nitrogen when they eat the herbivores.

Nitrogen returns to the soil or air when animals and plants die. It also returns in animals' waste products. Decomposers break down the remains of dead organisms and waste products. They change the animals' nitrogen compounds into kinds that plants can use. The compounds return to the soil or air and the cycle repeats.

A bromeliad is a plant that contains certain bacteria. These bacteria can make nitrogen compounds from nitrogen in the air.

3. **Sequence** What happens after lightning causes nitrogen compounds to form?

4. **Identify** Where is the nitrogen cycle found?

5. **Describe** Tell the process of the nitrogen cycle.

6. **Explain** If carnivores do not eat plants, how do they get nitrogen?

Herbivores get nitrogen compounds when they eat plants.

Lightning produces nitrogen compounds from gases in the air.

Microorganisms make nitrogen compounds and put them in soil.

carnivore

Plants absorb nitrogen compounds from the soil.

7. **Produce** Write a caption that describes how decomposers help nitrogen return to the soil or air.

Carbon and Oxygen Cycles

Oxygen is the second most abundant gas in the atmosphere. It makes up about 20% of the air. Carbon dioxide is much less abundant. It makes up 0.04% of the air. Even so, there is enough carbon dioxide to meet the needs of all the world's plants.

Volcanoes spew lava, ash, and carbon dioxide.

How Carbon Dioxide and Oxygen Flow

Carbon dioxide and oxygen gases are always being made and used in the world's ecosystems. Plants take in carbon dioxide and give off oxygen. Animals take in oxygen and give off carbon dioxide. The repeated movement of carbon through the environment in different forms is called the **carbon cycle.** Oxygen is often involved in the processes in which carbon dioxide moves. As this diagram shows, the give-and-take of oxygen and carbon dioxide has many paths through an ecosystem.

8. **Identify** **Circle** in the text how plants are involved in the carbon dioxide and oxygen cycles. **Underline** how animals are involved.

9. **Represent** In each box in the diagram, draw arrows to show how plants, fire, and organisms in the water give off or take in oxygen and carbon dioxide. Use blue for oxygen and green for carbon dioxide.

10. **Identify** the significance of the carbon dioxide–oxygen cycle to the survival of plants and animals.

Carbon dioxide is released when materials are decomposed.

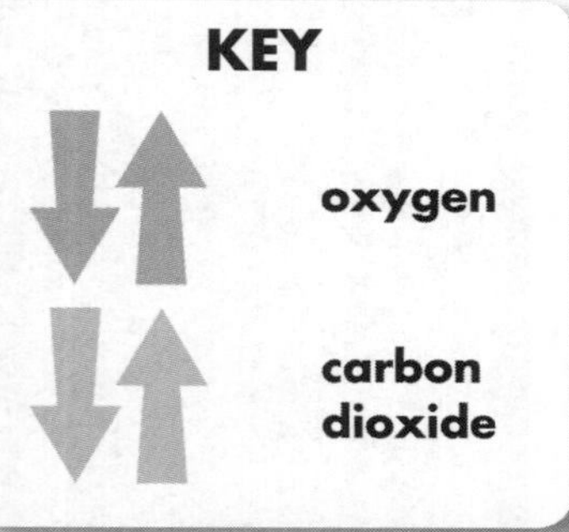

In most cells, the process of cellular respiration combines oxygen with sugar and releases carbon dioxide.

Burning trees and other plants takes oxygen from the air and gives off carbon dioxide.

In photosynthesis, plants use carbon dioxide with water and release oxygen.

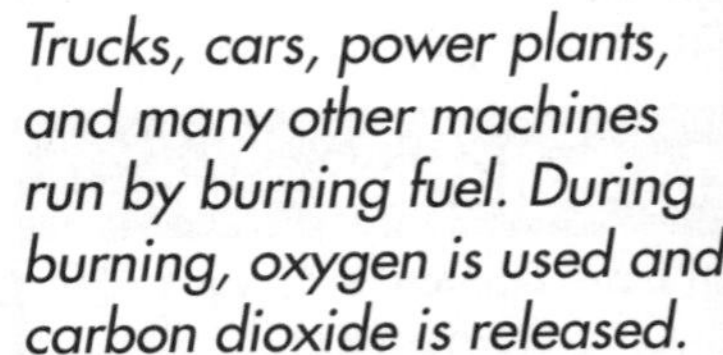

Trucks, cars, power plants, and many other machines run by burning fuel. During burning, oxygen is used and carbon dioxide is released.

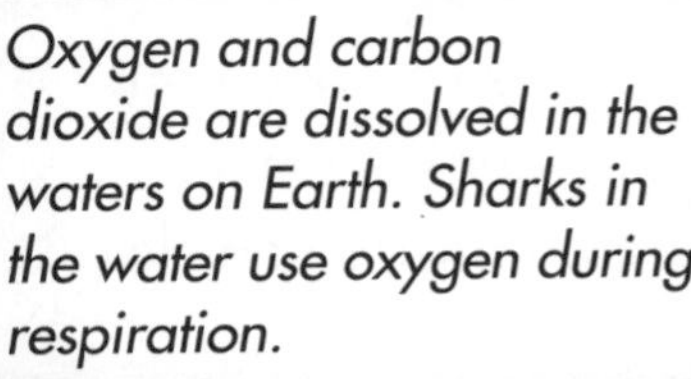

Oxygen and carbon dioxide are dissolved in the waters on Earth. Sharks in the water use oxygen during respiration.

Much of the oxygen in the atmosphere comes from photosynthesis by microscopic ocean organisms called plankton.

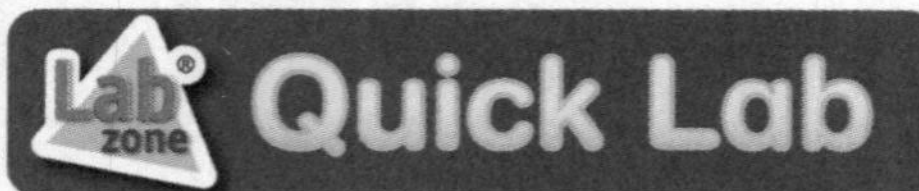

Carbon Dioxide and the Environment

With an adult, research the ways that people can help to reduce the amount of carbon dioxide that is released into the atmosphere. Make an informative brochure to share your research.

Human Effect on Carbon and Oxygen Cycles

People's activities can have an impact on the carbon and oxygen cycles. These impacts can change Earth's ecosystems.

Combustion is the burning of materials. Carbon dioxide forms as a result of combustion. Combustion occurs in machines such as cars, power plants, and home furnaces. When people use these machines, they put carbon dioxide into the atmosphere.

11. CHALLENGE Why do you think it is important for people to limit the amount of carbon dioxide released into the atmosphere?

Connect to Math

Math TEKS 3K

Use a Data Table

The data in the table show how much carbon dioxide a car and a light truck give off on average each year.

Vehicle Pollution

Vehicle	Carbon Dioxide Given Off (pounds)
Car	11,450
Light truck	16,035

1 **Compute** About how much more carbon dioxide does a light truck give off than a car each year?

2 **Solve** Suppose a family has one light truck and two cars. About how much carbon dioxide do the family's vehicles give off in one year?

People clear forests for lumber, fuel, and farmland. Trees and other plants use carbon dioxide in photosynthesis. With fewer plants, there is less photosynthesis. This leaves more carbon dioxide in the atmosphere. If people burn trees to clear the forests, even more carbon dioxide is released into the atmosphere.

12. Infer How does the clearing of this forest affect the amount of oxygen in the atmosphere?

got it? TEKS 9D

13. Describe Describe the carbon cycle and identify some places where carbon is found.

14. How do plants and animals interact with the carbon and oxygen cycles?

15. Identify Where is one place the carbon, oxygen, and nitrogen cycles are found?

Stop! I need help with

Wait! I have a question about

Go! Now I know

Lab Investigation

TEKS 9A, 1A, 2B, 2C, 2D, 2F, 4A, 4B

What is inside an owl pellet?

Follow a Procedure

- [x] **1.** Place an owl pellet on a sheet of paper. **Measure** its length.
- [x] **2.** **Observe** the pellet. Separate the contents of the pellet. Use the hand lens to observe and analyze the pellet's contents.

Materials

safety goggles
owl pellet
forceps
wooden probe
hand lens
sheet of paper
metric ruler

Texas Safety
LAB RULES

Wear safety goggles.
Wash your hands thoroughly upon completing the activity.

Inquiry Skill

You **infer** when you explain your observations.

3. Fill in the chart to **classify** the contents of the pellet.

4. **Record** your observations below.

Owl Pellet Observations					
	Pellet Length	**Skulls**	**Other Bones**	**Teeth**	**Fur or Feathers?** (describe)
Pellet contents					

Analyze and Conclude

5. **Draw a Conclusion** Communicate valid conclusions in written form by explaining what you can **infer** about the diet of the owl.

6. How does examining an owl pellet help you learn how the owl interacted with other living elements in its environment?

Fun Fact

The first sign the fisherman saw was smoke rising from the ocean along the southern coast of Iceland. Was it a ship on fire? No, it was Surtsey, a volcanic island, being born on November 15, 1963.

At first, Surtsey was bare. But soon, life began to colonize the new land. Insects arrived early. Mosses, lichens, and then more complex plants established themselves. Birds nested on the island, and migrating birds stopped there. Seals basked on its shores. The island is now a nature reserve and has been named a World Heritage site.

Surtsey covers an area of about 3 square kilometers.

Infer How might plants have arrived on Surtsey?

Vocabulary Smart Cards

ecosystem
habitat
population
community
predator
prey
producer
consumer
decomposer
food chain
food web
environment
competition
nitrogen cycle
carbon cycle

Play a Game!

Cut out the Vocabulary Smart Cards.

Work with a partner. Choose a Vocabulary Smart Card. Do not show the word to your partner.

Say clues to help your partner guess what your word is.

Have your partner repeat with another Vocabulary Smart Card.

all the living and nonliving things in an area and their interactions

Write a sentence using this word.

todos los seres vivos y los objetos inertes que hay en un área y sus interacciones

the group of all populations in an area

Write a word that is not an example.

grupo de todas las poblaciones de un área

a place that provides all the things an organism needs to live

Draw an example.

lugar que proporciona todas las cosas que necesita un organismo para vivir

a consumer that hunts and eats another animal

Write a sentence using the plural form of this word.

consumidor que atrapa a otro animal y se lo come

a group of organisms of one species that live in an area at the same time

What is another meaning of this word?

grupo de organismos de la misma especie que viven en un área al mismo tiempo

any animal that is hunted by others for food

Write an example of this word.

cualquier animal que es cazado por otros para alimentación

Interactive Vocabulary

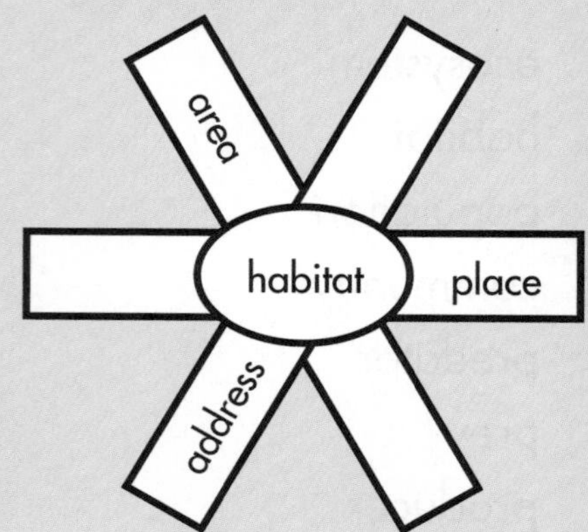

Make a Word Wheel!

Choose a vocabulary word and write it in the center of the Word Wheel graphic organizer. Write synonyms or related words on the wheel spokes.

competition
competencia

food chain
cadena alimenticia

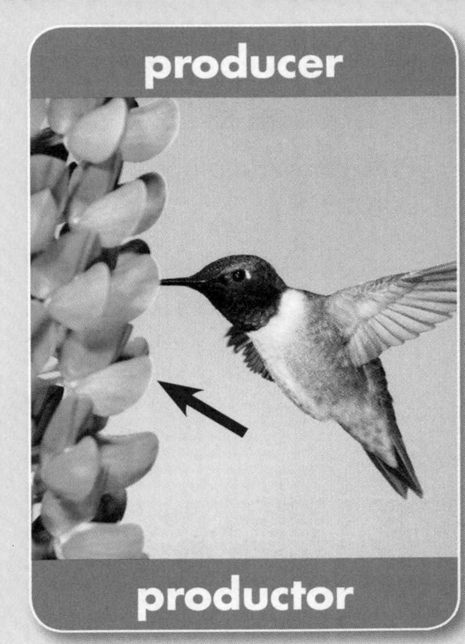
producer
productor

nitrogen cycle
ciclo del nitrógeno

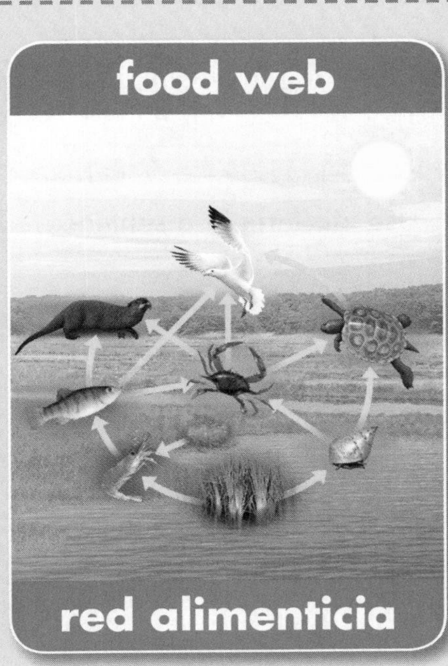
food web
red alimenticia

consumer
consumidor

carbon cycle
ciclo del carbono

environment
medio ambiente

decomposer
descomponedor

organism that makes its own food for energy

Draw an example.

organismo que hace su propio alimento para obtener energía

a series of steps by which energy moves from one type of living thing to another

Draw an example.

serie de pasos mediante los cuales la energía pasa de un ser vivo a otro

the struggle among organisms for the same limited resources

Use a dictionary. Find another definition for this word.

lucha entre organismos por los mismos recursos limitados

organism that cannot make its own food

Use this term in a sentence.

organismo que no puede hacer su propio alimento

a diagram that combines many food chains into one picture

Use this term in a sentence.

diagrama que combina varias cadenas alimenticias en una sola imagen

repeated movement of nitrogen through the environment in different forms

Draw a picture that represents the term.

movimiento repetido del nitrógeno en formas diferentes a través del medio ambiente

organism that gets its energy by breaking down wastes and dead organisms

Draw an example.

organismo que obtiene su energía descomponiendo desechos y organismos muertos

all of the conditions surrounding an organism

Write a sentence using this word.

todas las condiciones que rodean a un ser vivo

repeated movement of carbon through the environment in different forms

Draw a picture that represents the term.

movimiento repetido del carbono en formas diferentes a través del medio ambiente

TEKS Practice

Lesson 1 TEKS 9A

What are the parts of an ecosystem?

1. **Identify** Which of the following is an example of a community?
   A. squirrels, blue jays, and oak trees
   B. a group of twenty sandhill cranes
   C. a school of tuna
   D. rocks, soil, and air

2. **Write About It** How are an organism's niche and habitat related?

3. **Main Idea and Details** **Underline** the main idea and **circle** the details in the following paragraph.

> An organism may compete for the things it needs. Plants may compete for sunlight, soil, or water. Animals may compete for territory, water, light, food, or mates.

4. **Identify** With which nonliving elements does an arctic fox interact?
   A. rodents
   B. rabbits
   C. plants
   D. rocks

Lesson 2 TEKS 9A, 9B

How do organisms interact in ecosystems?

5. **Vocabulary** When organisms need the same limited resources, there is
   A. an extra resource.
   B. competition.
   C. extinction.
   D. mutation.

6. **Write About It** Give an example of how an organism might interact with a nonliving element of its ecosystem.

7. **Determine** A nonnative plant in an ecosystem spreads quickly. This will **most directly** affect the native plants by
   A. leaving them less space.
   B. giving them more food.
   C. helping them grow.
   D. leaving them more sun.

8. **Identify** In one ecosystem, snakes eat birds, plants make fruit, and birds eat fruit. Which is the correct food chain?
   A. snake → plant → bird
   B. bird → plant → snake
   C. plant → bird → snake
   D. snake → bird → plant

TEKS Practice

Lesson 2 TEKS 9A, 9B

How do organisms interact in ecosystems?

9. **Describe** What is the role of this organism in a food chain?

A. It breaks down wastes and dead organisms.
B. It uses the sun's energy to make food.
C. It eats other organisms.
D. It cannot make its own food.

10. **Summarize** Choose a food web with a decomposer in it. Describe how the flow of energy derived from the sun, used by producers to create their own food, is transferred through a food web to decomposers.

Lesson 3 TEKS 9C

How do ecosystems change?

11. **Analyze** How can a forest fire have both beneficial and harmful changes?

12. In a forest, high winds blow away $\frac{1}{4}$ of the birds' nests and a flood destroys $\frac{2}{5}$ of the nests. What fraction of the birds' nests is left?

13. **Identify** Which of the following is an environmental change caused by humans?
A. farming crops
B. lichen on rocks
C. heavy rain
D. beaver dam

14. **Predict** Predict the changes in an ecosystem when a river is dammed to make a large lake.

Lesson 4 TEKS 9D

What are some natural cycles?

15. Vocabulary The repeated movement of carbon through the environment in different forms is called the

A. carbon cycle
B. nitrogen cycle
C. oxygen cycle
D. water cycle

16. Identify Describe the significance of the carbon dioxide–oxygen cycle to the survival of plants and animals.

Chapter 8

Lesson 1 What are the parts of an ecosystem?

In Lesson 1, you learned that organisms interact with living and nonliving elements in their ecosystem. You also learned that these interactions are important for organisms to survive in their ecosystems.

Supporting TEKS 9A

Lesson 2 How do organisms interact in ecosystems?

In Lesson 2, you learned about interactions between organisms in an ecosystem, and how these interactions involve the transfer of energy from the sun to organisms.

Supporting TEKS 9A, 9B

Lesson 3 How do ecosystems change?

In Lesson 3, you learned how organisms, including humans, can cause environmental changes. You also learned how to predict the effect of these changes.

Supporting TEKS 9C, Readiness TEKS 9A

Lesson 4 What are some natural cycles?

In Lesson 4, you learned that some resources cycle through the environment. You also learned that the carbon dioxide–oxygen cycle is important to the survival of plants and animals.

Supporting TEKS 9D, Readiness TEKS 9B

TEKS Practice: Chapter Review

Read each question and circle the best answer or fill in the grid.

1 What is one way that living organisms use abiotic factors of an ecosystem?

A By eating plants

B By drinking water

C By taking shelter in trees

D By preying on animals

2 This drawing shows a forest ecosystem.

Which of the animals eats only plants?

F Fox

G Frog

H Deer

J Ducks

3 All organisms need energy to survive. How do scavengers and decomposers get the energy they need?

A Scavengers break their food down into chemical nutrients, and decomposers take their energy from those chemicals.

B Scavengers make their own food. Decomposers eat some nutrients that scavengers produce. Decomposers then return chemicals to the soil.

C When scavengers kill and eat animals, decomposers eat some of the food they leave behind. The decomposers then return chemical nutrients to the soil.

D Scavengers feed on dead animals or plants. The food that scavengers leave behind is broken down by decomposers into chemical nutrients and returned to the soil.

4 Which two living things interact in a way that helps each one?

F Fleas and a dog

G Flowers and bees

H A hawk and a mouse

J None of the above

5 Tyler investigates temperatures around his school. He believes that different types of land cover affect temperature. On a hot day Tyler places thermometers in direct sunlight on the concrete sidewalk, the asphalt parking lot, and the sunny front lawn. He also places a thermometer in a shady place on the lawn. The table shows the temperatures Tyler records from hottest to coolest.

Location	Temperature (°C)
	44
	38
	27
	21

Tyler has not yet entered the location next to each temperature in the table. Predict which location goes with each temperature, from hottest to coolest.

A Concrete sidewalk, asphalt parking lot, shaded lawn, sunlit lawn

B Asphalt parking lot, concrete sidewalk, sunlit lawn, shaded lawn

C Shaded lawn, sunlit lawn, concrete sidewalk, asphalt parking lot

D Sunlit lawn, shaded lawn, asphalt parking lot, concrete sidewalk

---

6 The trees in one acre of forest release enough oxygen each year for 18 people to breathe. Near Harlingen, Texas, the local Auduban Society has replanted a former landfill with native species of trees to create the 50-acre Hugh Ramsey Nature Park. When its trees mature, how many people could this park supply with oxygen in one year? Record and bubble in your answer below.

			.
⓪	⓪	⓪	
①	①	①	
②	②	②	
③	③	③	
④	④	④	
⑤	⑤	⑤	
⑥	⑥	⑥	
⑦	⑦	⑦	
⑧	⑧	⑧	
⑨	⑨	⑨	

TEKS Practice: Cumulative Review

7 Ellie uses a string to follow the path of light coming from a laser pointer. She experiments by pointing the light at a mirror and shining it through a glass of water. What will she find out about the path of light?

A It is hard to predict.

B It travels in straight lines.

C Once it passes through water, it becomes wavy.

D When it hits a mirror, its different colors separate.

---

8 Diagrams A and B show Earth at the same point in its orbit and seen from the same point in space.

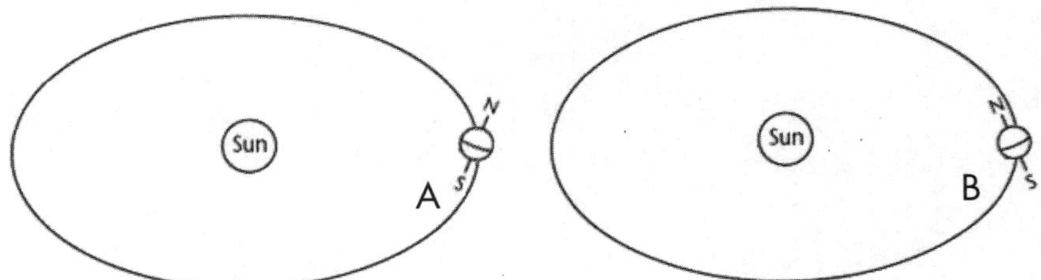

Diagram A shows the actual tilt of Earth's axis at that moment. What would happen if Earth tilted in the opposite direction, as shown in diagram B?

F There would be only two seasons on Earth.

G There would be only one season on Earth.

H There would still be four seasons in the Northern and Southern Hemispheres.

J The seasons in the Northern Hemisphere would no longer be the opposite of those in the Southern Hemisphere.

If you have trouble with . . .

Question	1	2	3	4	5	6	7	8
See chapter (lesson)	8 (1)	8 (2)	8 (2)	8 (2)	8 (3)	8 (4)	3 (3)	7 (2)
TEKS	9A	9A	9B	9A	9C	9D	6C	8C

WHAT
is this?

Growth and Survival

How do living organisms adapt and survive?

This scaly creature and other species in its family live in warm areas of Asia and Africa.

What do you think are some advantages of having scales?

....

....

....

Texas Essential Knowledge and Skills

Readiness TEKS: 10A Compare the structures and functions of different species that help them live and survive such as hooves on prairie animals or webbed feet in aquatic animals. **10B** Differentiate between inherited traits of plants and animals such as spines on a cactus or shape of a beak and learned behaviors such as an animal learning tricks or a child riding a bicycle.

Supporting TEKS: 10C Describe the differences between complete and incomplete metamorphosis of insects.

Process TEKS: 1A, 2A, 2B, 2C, 2D, 2F, 2G, 3A, 3C, 4A

PEARSON Texas.com

Lab zone® Inquiry Warm-Up

TEKS 10A, 1A, 2A, 2B, 2C, 2D, 2F, 2G

How can temperature affect seed growth?

1. Choose one type of seed to test. Use the cups and towels to grow the seeds.
2. Put one cup in a refrigerator. Put the other cup in a dark place in your classroom.
3. **Predict** how temperature will affect the seeds.

4. **Collect Data** Create a table to organize, examine, and evaluate your observations. Use a computer, if possible.

Materials

seeds (basil, pinto bean)
2 clear plastic cups
2 wet paper towels

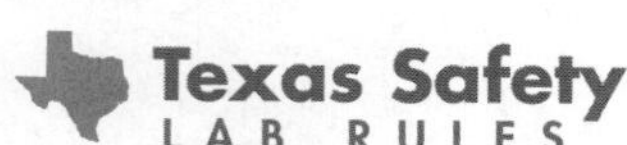

If any water spills, notify your teacher immediately. Wash your hands thoroughly upon completing the activity.

Inquiry Skill

You can **collect data** by drawing what you observe.

Seed Observations

Type of Seed ....

Temperature	Day 1	Day 2	Day 3	Day 4	Day 5
Cold					
Room temperature					

Explain Your Results

5. Compare your results with those of other groups. How did the seeds respond to temperature? **Infer** how this response might help a pinto-bean plant respond to changing seasons.

Focus on Compare and Contrast

You will practice the reading strategy of **compare and contrast.** You **compare** when you tell how things are alike. You **contrast** when you tell how things are different.

Connect to Reading

Gull and Eagle Feet

Feet are important structures for a bird's survival. Gulls find their food in and around water. Their feet are webbed. Webbed feet help gulls swim in the water as they search for food. Webbed feet also help gulls walk in the soft sand and mud that surrounds water. Eagles hunt animals for food. Their feet have large, sharp claws called talons. They use their talons to capture, kill, and carry their prey.

Practice It!

Complete the graphic organizer below to compare and contrast the feet of gulls and eagles.

Gulls

Eagles

Texas

LESSON 1

What are some physical structures in living things?

I will know TEKS 10A
I will explore how structures and functions help organisms live and survive in their environments.
(Also **1A**, **2A**, **2C**, **2D**, **2E**, **2F**, **3C**)

Vocabulary
exoskeleton

Connect to Math

Math TEKS 3A, 3B

Your lungs perform a very important function. They take in the oxygen you need to survive. You breathe in different amounts of air, depending on what you are doing. When you are running, you breathe in about 32 liters of air per minute. About how many liters of air would you breathe in if you ran for 15 minutes? Show your work.

When walking slowly, you breathe in about 14 liters of air. How many fewer liters of air would you breathe in if you were to walk instead of run for 15 minutes? Show your work.

PEARSON Texas.com

Quick Lab

TEKS 10A, 1A, 2A, 2C, 2D, 2E, 2F, 3C

Which bird beak can crush seeds?

Materials

glue
craft sticks
2 clothespins
4 pieces of straw

Texas Safety LAB RULES
Keep your work area clean. If any glue spills, notify your teacher immediately.

1. **Make a Model** of a heron's beak. Glue 2 craft sticks to a clothespin. Use the other clothespin as a model of a cardinal's beak. Use pieces of a straw as models of seeds.

2. Use the heron's beak. Pick up a seed. Does the beak crush the seed? Try 5 times. **Record.**

_____ _____ _____ _____ _____

3. Repeat with the cardinal's beak. Record.

_____ _____ _____ _____ _____

Explain Your Results

4. **Draw a Conclusion**
Which bird crushes seeds?

5. There are many seeds in a cardinal's environment. There are many fish, insects, and small animals in a heron's environment. **Infer** how the structure of each bird's beak helps the bird survive in its environment.

Physical Structures

Some trees shed their bark as a normal part of their growth. The tough outer covering of bark peels away so that new tree growth can expand outward. In a similar way, snakes shed their skins as they grow. All living organisms have structures that help them grow, get energy, and stay healthy. Sometimes structures can be very similar even though the organisms are different.

Other times, physical structures can be very different even if they do similar jobs. For example, an animal egg may be very delicate and may need to be hidden from predators. By contrast, many plant seeds have tough coverings and easily survive being swallowed by an animal. The seeds develop inside tasty fruits that animals like to eat. The seeds benefit because an animal can carry them to places where they may grow better.

paperbark maple tree

garter snake

1. **Compare and Contrast** Use the graphic organizer to compare the structures of different species that help them live and survive. Describe how the bark of a paperbark maple tree and the skin of a garter snake are alike and different in structure.

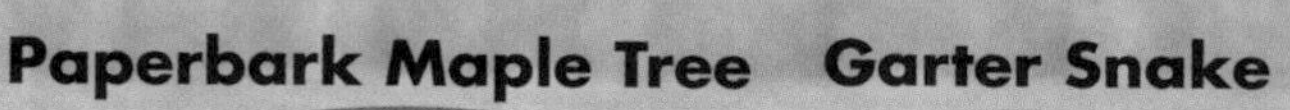

Paperbark Maple Tree **Garter Snake**

Life on the Prairie

Physical structures help animals adapt to different habitats. Deer and bison, for example, have physical structures that help them live in a prairie habitat and survive as herbivores. They have sharp teeth that break off the grasses and plants that make up their diet. They also have grooved flat teeth that grind the food, making it easier to digest. Their digestive systems have special structures that further break down the tough fibers in the grasses and plants.

Prairies are wide-open spaces. Deer and bison must move across the hard ground in search of grasses. To survive, they must also flee predators. Their long legs and hooves are physical structures that help them accomplish these tasks. Hooves cushion the animals' legs from the shock of the ground as they run. The hooves also increase the animals' speed by making their legs longer.

2. Cause and Effect **Underline** the physical structures that help herbivores survive on their diet of grasses and plants.

3. Main Idea and Details **Circle** the physical structures that help herbivores flee from predators.

4. Compare How are hooves and webbed feet similar in their functions?

Water birds, such as ducks, and some frogs have webbed feet to help them move through the water.

Structures for Support

Some animals, such as fish and humans, have internal skeletons. An internal skeleton supports the body. It also protects organs such as the brain and the heart.

Other animals have **exoskeletons,** which are hard skeletons on the outside of their bodies. Exoskeletons give structure and protection.

Plants have stems that stretch toward the sunlight and can hold the weight of leaves and fruit. Some plants, such as trees, have wood in their stems and branches for additional support.

5. Justify Many stems hold leaves high. Higher leaves are more likely to get sunlight. How is this helpful to a plant?

Insects, such as the cicada, have a hard exoskeleton. In order to grow, insects usually need to shed their old exoskeleton and grow a new one.

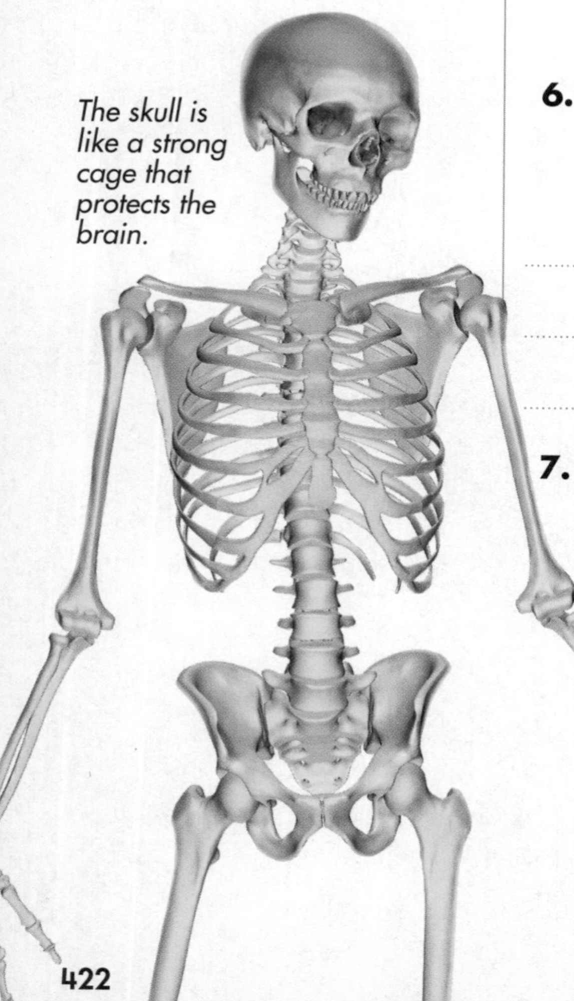

The skull is like a strong cage that protects the brain.

6. Compare Compare the structures of different species that help them live. How is an exoskeleton similar to an internal skeleton? How is it different?

7. Draw some organs that are protected by the rib cage.

Structures for Reproduction

Living things can make other living things similar to themselves. This process is called reproduction.

Many plants reproduce using flowers. For example, when pollen from a cherry flower is carried to another cherry flower, the receiving flower becomes fertilized. It grows into a cherry with a seed inside. The seed has a source of nutrition and a protective covering. If this seed lands on good soil, a new cherry plant may grow.

Animals reproduce in different ways. For example, some female fish lay eggs on underwater rocks, where the male fertilizes them. The fish grows within the egg, which has a source of nutrition and may also have a protective cover. In other animals, such as mammals, males have structures to fertilize eggs within the body of the female.

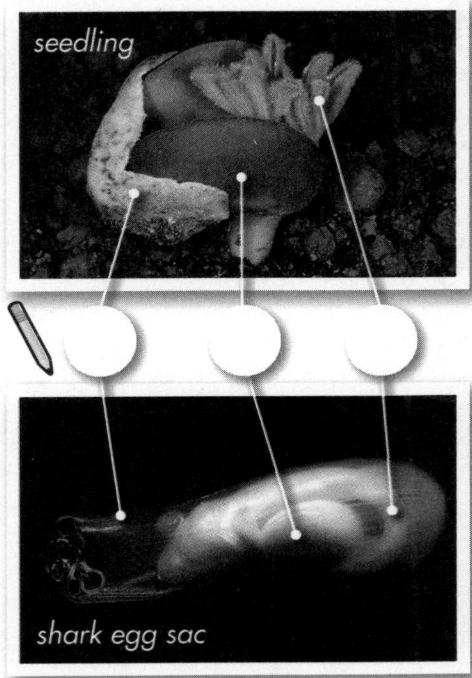

9. Label Write the correct letter in each circle above.

A organism

B protective cover

C nutrition source

8. Diagram Read the steps of Flower Fertilization below. Then, on the flower illustration, **circle** where a seed will develop.

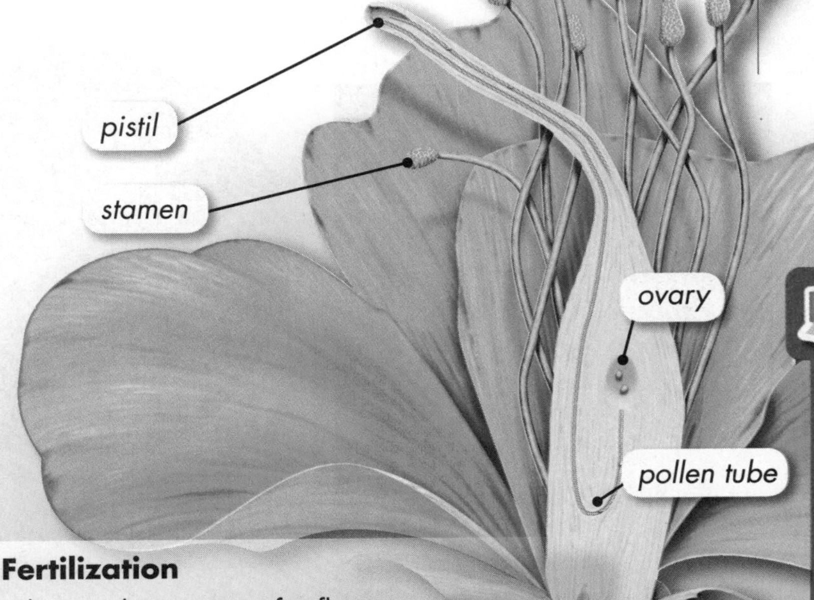

Flower Fertilization

1. Pollen leaves the stamen of a flower.
2. Pollen lands on the pistil of another flower.
3. A pollen tube grows from the pollen grain, and a sperm cell travels down the tube.
4. The sperm cell reaches an egg cell contained in the ovary. Fertilization occurs.
5. The fertilized egg goes on to become a seed.

Lab zone Quick Lab

Parts and the Whole

The bones in a skeleton make up a system. A system is a collection of parts that work together. Look at a bicycle. Is it a system? Explain. Think of 3 other systems that you can find in your home.

10. Draw a picture of one other animal that breathes using lungs and a picture of an animal that breathes with gills. Explain your choices.

Structures for Respiration and Circulation

In order for plants and animals to live, they need to exchange gases with their environments. Animals such as turtles and humans take in air through the mouth or nose and breathe using lungs. Some other animals, such as insects, take air in through structures called spiracles, which are holes in the insect's body. Most fish take in oxygen from water through their gills.

Lungs, spiracles, and gills are three ways animals can get oxygen. A spiracle often allows oxygen to go directly to body tissue. But with lungs and gills, oxygen entering the animal is transported through a circulatory system to the body's cells.

Plants have structures that are similar to spiracles on insects. These microscopic holes are called stomata and are located on the leaves of the plant. Carbon dioxide from the air enters the plant through the stomata. During photosynthesis, a plant uses energy from the sun and carbon dioxide to make sugar, or food. Oxygen is also produced and exits through the stomata.

Spiracles on the skin of a caterpillar open up to let gases in or out.

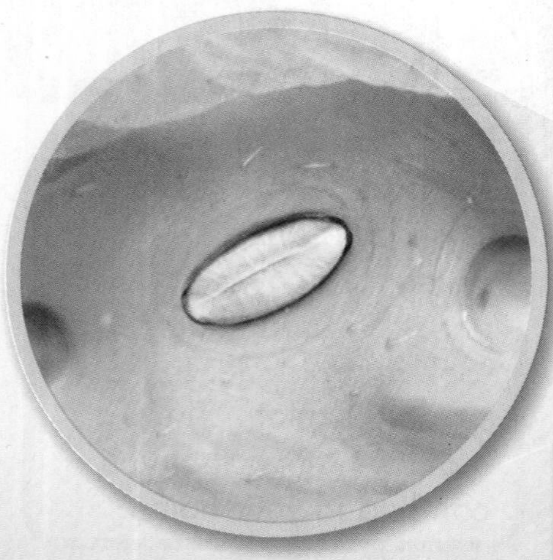

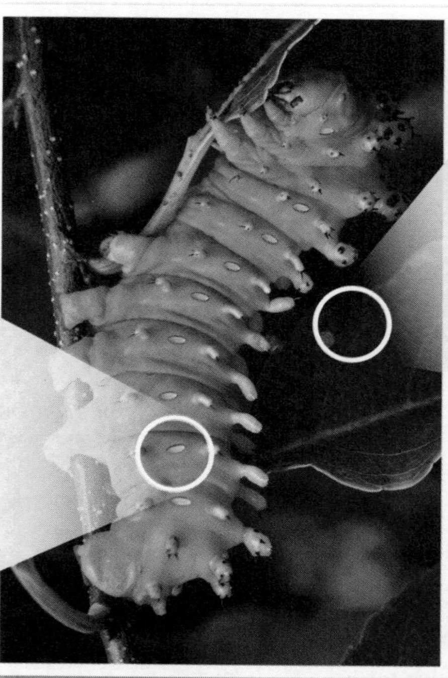

Like the spiracles of insects, stomata on the surface of a leaf open up to let gases in or out.

Some plants also have a circulatory system. These plants are called vascular plants. The tissues in the vascular system are similar to your blood vessels. The plant uses the vascular tissue to transport sugar made in the leaves to the roots for storage.

Tube structures within a plant stem transport water and nutrients to and from the leaves, roots, and rest of the plant.

11. Compare Blood travels through your body inside arteries and veins. Compare the function of a plant's vascular system to the function of your arteries and veins.

got it? TEKS 10A

12. Contrast List two structures that have similar functions in plants and animals. How are they different?

13. What are some structures in plants and animals that serve a similar purpose?

Stop! I need help with

Wait! I have a question about

Go! Now I know

How do adaptations help organisms survive?

I will know TEKS 10A, 10B
I will know about behavioral and structural adaptations. I will also know that some behaviors are inherited and some are learned. (Also **1A**, **2A**, **2D**, **2F**, **3A**, **3C**)

Vocabulary
behavioral adaptation
structural adaptation

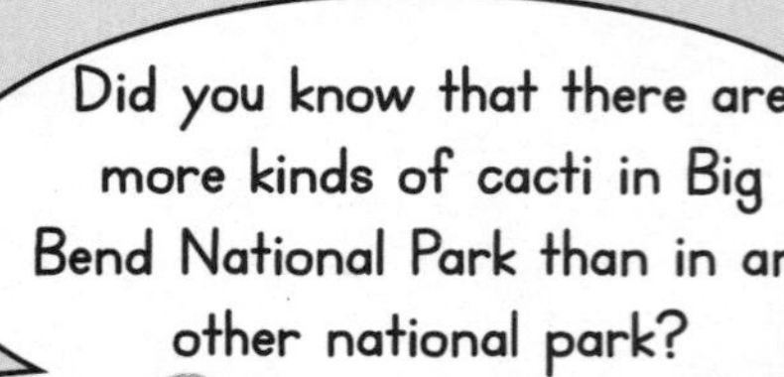

Did you know that there are more kinds of cacti in Big Bend National Park than in any other national park?

That's a lot of spines to look out for! The spines are adaptations that help a cactus keep water inside. They also protect it from being eaten!

Some cactus spines are 10 inches long!

Can you help us figure out how many centimeters of spines we would have if we collected 15 spines that are each 10 inches long?

Connect to Math

Show your work There are 2.54 centimeters in one inch. How many centimeters are in 10 inches? **Math TEKS 3E, 7**

....

How many centimeters would there be in the 15 spines?

....

PEARSON Texas.com

Quick Lab

TEKS 10A, 1A, 2A, 2D, 2F, 3A, 3C

How does shape affect bone strength?

Long bones are round like pipes, but filled with a soft material.

Materials

construction paper
tape
books

Texas Safety LAB RULES

Read the science activity thoroughly and understand its purpose.

Identify potential hazards and know which precautions to take.

1. Fold a piece of construction paper to make a square tube. Fasten completely with tape.
2. Roll another piece of paper to form a round tube. Fasten completely with tape.
3. Stand the tubes on a table. Place a book on top of each tube. Add books to each tube, one at a time, until a tube collapses.

Explain Your Results

4. Which tube held more books?

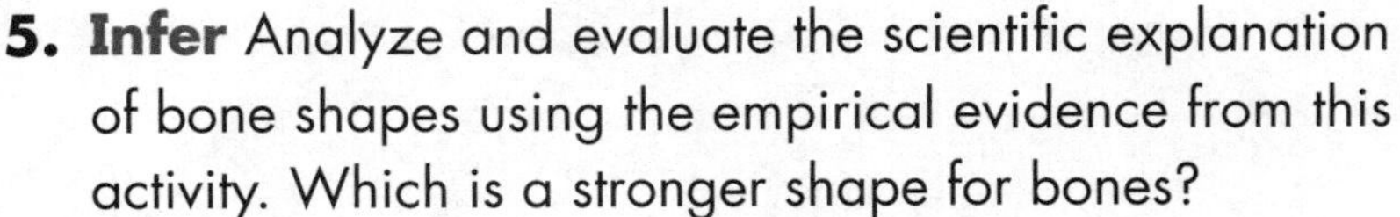

5. **Infer** Analyze and evaluate the scientific explanation of bone shapes using the empirical evidence from this activity. Which is a stronger shape for bones?

Adaptations

Organisms must compete for the same limited resources, such as food. Organisms that are best suited to their environment are more likely to survive and reproduce. An adaptation is a characteristic that increases an organism's ability to survive and reproduce. Adaptations do not happen quickly. They develop over many generations.

Different kinds of birds have adaptations that help them eat different foods. The type of beak that a bird has is an adaptation that helps the bird catch the types of food it relies on for survival. You can tell what type of food a bird eats by the shape of its beak.

Long and thin, for probing
Hummingbirds drink nectar from flowers; ibis probe in the mud for worms and insects.

1. Compare and Contrast How are the beaks of hummingbirds and ibis alike and different in their adaptations?

Short, thick, and cone-shaped, for cracking
Birds such as sparrows, finches, and cardinals eat seeds.

Pouch-like, for scooping
Pelicans scoop fish from the water.

Long and flat, for straining
Ducks strain small plants and animals from water.
Long and chisel-shaped, for drilling
Woodpeckers bore into wood for insects.
Sharp and curved, for tearing
Birds of prey such as hawks and owls eat meat.
Long and sharp, for spearing
Birds, such as herons and kingfishers, spear fish to eat them.

2. **Explain** What structural adaptation does a hawk have that helps it survive in its environment?

Like the birds on this page, mangrove trees have an adaptation that helps them survive. Mangrove trees grow in moist environments, where muddy soil does not supply enough oxygen to the trees. The roots of the mangrove trees are exposed to the air, so they can take in air, giving them the oxygen they need.

3. **Infer** How do you think the shape of mangrove roots might help the tree during a storm?

Inherited Traits

Organisms receive genes from their parents. Genes contain information that determines how the organism grows. Because of these genes, most organisms have the same traits, or characteristics, as their parents.

However, different combinations of genes may cause an organism to be a bit different from its parents. The color of a cat's fur may be different from its parents' color. An organism may also have a mutation, which is a random change in a gene. Mutations may be helpful, harmful, or neutral. If a mutation helps an organism survive in its environment, that organism will have a better chance to live and reproduce. The organism will pass on its genes to its offspring. If the mutation is harmful to the organism, the organism will be less likely to survive or reproduce.

Over many generations, small mutations can develop into adaptations. A process called natural selection favors useful mutations and reduces harmful mutations. Natural selection helps develop adaptations that allow organisms to survive in different environments. Natural selection affects all living things.

4. **Infer** The cat shown inherited the trait of having six toes on each front paw. How might the extra toes help the cat survive in a wild environment?

5. **Conclude** Do you think the cat's parents had six toes? Explain.

Behavioral Adaptations

Were you born knowing how to build a house? That is impossible! Atlantic ghost crabs, though, are born knowing how to dig deep holes in the sandy beaches where they live. This behavior is a behavioral adaptation. A **behavioral adaptation** is an inherited behavior that helps an animal survive. Behavioral adaptations are sometimes called instincts. They affect how an animal behaves around other animals. Some animals, such as the ghost crab, have an instinct to burrow into the ground to hide from predators.

Not all behaviors are instincts, though. Some behaviors are learned by trial and error or as a result of training. Just as you can learn to ride a bicycle, you can train a dog to do tricks. Animals learn in nature too. For example, lion cubs learn to hunt by watching their parents and other animals. A lion cub learns to pounce on its prey by pouncing on its mother's twitching tail. The cub learns these behaviors over time.

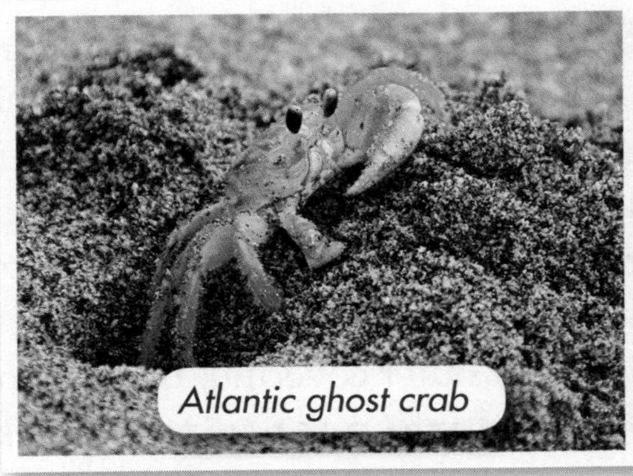

Atlantic ghost crab

7. Compare and Contrast How are the behaviors of a ghost crab and a lion cub similar? How are they different?

Seasonal Changes

In places with cold winters, there is little food for part of the year. Some animals deal with this food shortage by migrating, or moving. In spring and summer, Canada geese live in Canada and the northern United States. They migrate south to escape cold winter weather and to find food.

Another type of seasonal behavior is hibernation. Hibernation is a state of inactivity that occurs in some animals when it gets cold. These animals slow down or become inactive to conserve energy. Some mammals, reptiles, and amphibians hibernate.

6. Hypothesize What effect could less winter snow have on the fur of snowshoe hares over many generations?

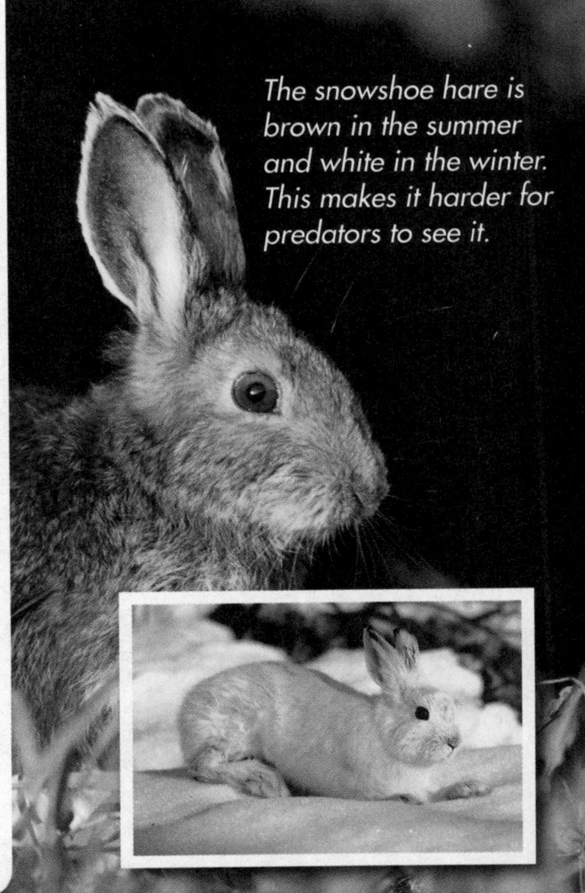

The snowshoe hare is brown in the summer and white in the winter. This makes it harder for predators to see it.

Structural Adaptations of Plants

Characteristics of a plant can help it survive in its environment. For example, coconuts are large seeds. If the coconuts from a particular palm tree can float a little better than the average, these coconuts will be more likely to stay afloat when they fall in the water. The floating husk, or outer covering, is a structural adaptation. A **structural adaptation** is a useful characteristic in a part of a plant or an animal. The floating husk is helpful when a plant has seeds that are dispersed by water. This type of husk might allow the coconut to travel farther in the ocean than a denser husk. If the seed travels farther than other seeds, it may have less competition for resources. The seed may then survive and grow into a mature palm tree.

Coconuts have a lightweight husk that allows them to float for months until they reach a beach where the seed can germinate.

8. Conclude Look at the leaves on the plants below. Each leaf is adapted to perform a function. What might be the function of each leaf?

Venus's-flytrap: ....

Prickly pear cactus: ....

Water lily: ....

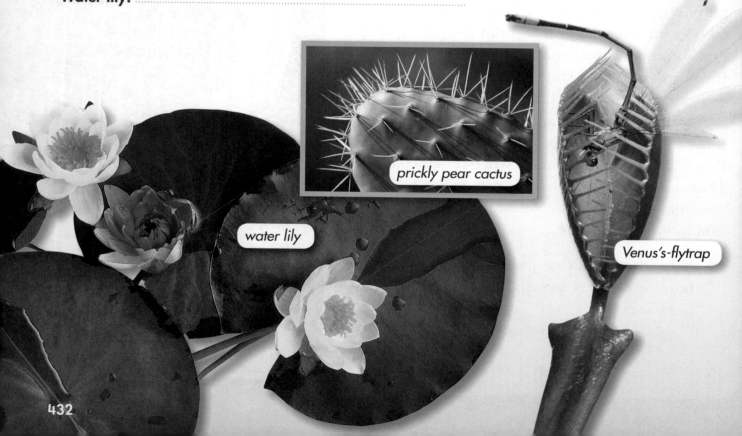

prickly pear cactus

water lily

Venus's-flytrap

Structural Adaptations of Animals

The body parts of animals have useful physical characteristics that help the animal survive. For example, animals that hunt tend to have eyes on the front of their heads. This placement makes them better at telling how far away their prey is. As a result, they can pounce or swoop with precision. Animals that are hunted often have eyes on the side of their heads, which helps them see where a predator might be coming from.

Individual animals do not develop structural adaptations. Instead, animal species develop their physical characteristics through the process of natural selection, just as plant species do.

Swimming Birds

With your fingers spread apart, move your hand through a tub full of water. With your fingers still spread apart, wrap plastic around your hand. Move it through the water again. Ducks have webbing on their feet. Infer how this adaptation helps a duck.

TEKS 10A, 2D, 3A, 3C

9. CHALLENGE A bird's bones are hollow. What advantage might this adaptation give the bird?

10. **Describe** The pictures below show three structural adaptations. Write the purpose of each.

okapi tongue

sea-urchin spines

gecko foot

Adaptations in Local Environments

Organisms have adaptations that enable them to survive and reproduce in different kinds of environments. Two Texas environments are a longleaf pine environment and a desert environment.

Longleaf Pine Environment

Organisms living in a longleaf pine environment have developed adaptations that allow them to survive forest fires. Forest fires from lightning strikes occur often in this environment. When a longleaf pine tree is just a seedling, it grows a moist tuft of needles. These needles help reflect heat from the stem and protect the plant from the fire. An adult longleaf pine tree is also protected from fire. Its thick bark protects the wood on the inside from heat. The bark is also scaly and flakes off as it burns.

Pine snakes live in longleaf pine environments too. They feed on pocket gophers, which build burrows in the ground. When there is a forest fire, pine snakes quickly find a gopher burrow and stay there until the fire is over. This adaptation helps them survive fires.

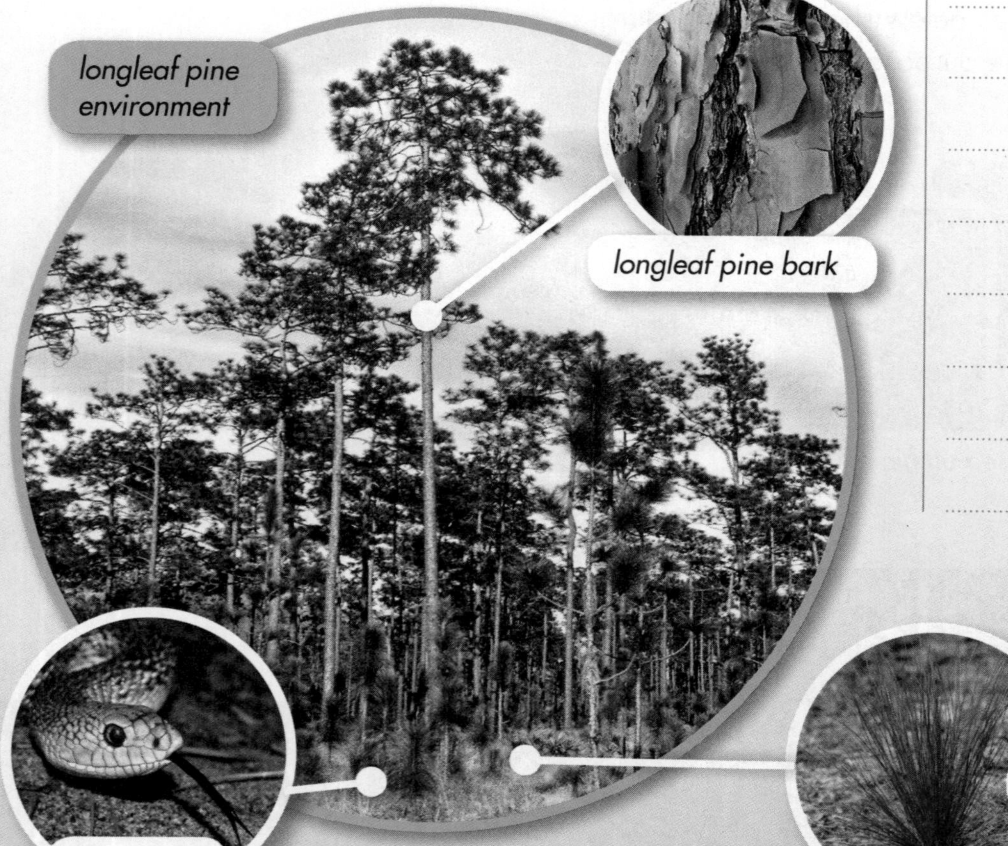

11. CHALLENGE How might bark that flakes off as it burns help the longleaf pine tree survive a forest fire?

12. Compare Differentiate between inherited traits of plants and animals by comparing and contrasting the adaptations of the longleaf pine and the pine snake.

Desert Environment

The Chihuahuan Desert in West Texas is home to many desert plants and animals. Among them are the yucca plant and yucca moth. The yucca plant and the yucca moth have a special relationship. The moth is the only insect that pollinates the yucca's flowers. The moth pollinates the plant in the process of laying its eggs. In return, the plant's seeds provide food for the growing moths.

13. Interpret What adaptations allow the yucca plant and yucca moth to survive in their environment?

got it? TEKS 10A, 10B

14. Identify Some animals instinctively play dead to avoid being eaten. Is playing dead a learned behavior or a behavioral adaptation? Explain.

15. Describe Describe three inherited traits that would help a plant to survive in a very windy environment.

Stop! I need help with

Wait! I have a question about

Go! Now I know

MEXICAN FREE-TAILED BATS

APPLY THE TEKS 10B

Each summer, some 20 million Mexican free-tailed bats set up a nursery in Bracken Cave near San Antonio! Mother bats are well adapted to cave life. They cling to the cave walls with their feet and thumbs while giving birth. Baby bats have a strong instinct to cling. Like their mothers, they use their feet and thumbs to cling to the cave's walls. They also use their sharp teeth to hold onto their mothers and other bats.

During the first hour of life, a baby bat and its mother learn each other's voices and smell. This is important because a mother bat needs to be able to locate her offspring among thousands of new babies in her area of the cave!

Mexican free-tailed bats are built to hunt in the air. Their very long, narrow wings help them fly fast and high. With a good tail wind, the bats can reach speeds of over 60 miles an hour!

Differentiate Differentiate between inherited traits of animals and learned behaviors. Use examples from the text above.

Roadrunners

TEKS 10A

Mexican free-tailed bats may be built for speed in the air, but roadrunners are built for speed on the ground. Unlike most birds, roadrunners do not like to fly. They prefer to race across open ground at speeds that can reach 15 miles an hour! When running at high speeds, the birds position their heads and tails parallel to the ground. They are aided in their running by their long legs and strong feet. Their speed and their oversized beaks help roadrunners catch their diet of insects, snakes, lizards, mice, and small mammals.

Analyze What structural adaptations help roadrunners catch their prey?

Texas Horned Lizards

TEKS 10A

It's not surprising that Texans refer to Texas horned lizards as horned toads. The animal's round, flat body and bumpy skin make it look more like a toad than a lizard. But a lizard it is—and a remarkable one at that! A tasty treat for roadrunners and other desert animals, the horned lizard has several adaptations that help it survive. When threatened it can flatten itself even further to blend into its desert surroundings. Or, if it prefers, it can blow itself up like a spiky balloon to ward off attack. If all else fails, the horned lizard can squirt blood from its eyes to scare away its attacker!

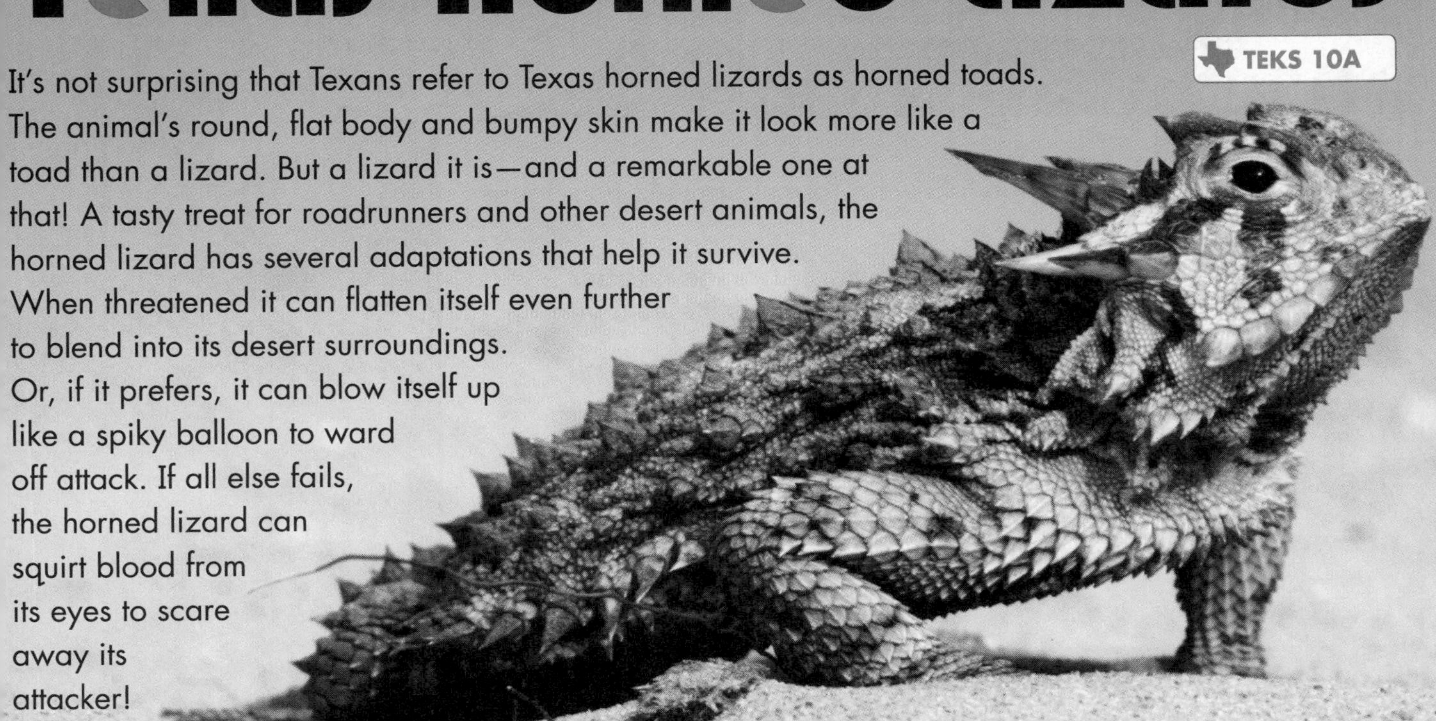

Texas

LESSON

3

What are the life cycles of some animals?

I will know TEKS 10C
I will explore the life cycles of some animals and know the differences between complete and incomplete metamorphosis. (Also **1A**, **2B**, **2C**, **2F**, **4A**)

Vocabulary
metamorphosis
larva
pupa

Have you ever heard the cicadas sing in the summer? Some summers they are very loud!

That's because some cicadas have a very long life cycle. Some remain underground for 13 years. Others remain underground for 17 years!

Help us figure out the cycles. If the 13-year cicadas appeared in Texas in 1972 and laid eggs that same year, when should they appear next?

Do the same calculation for 17-year cicadas. Use 1964 as your starting point.

Connect to Math

Math TEKS 4B

Show your work Use the following formula to help you figure out the answers:

$a + b = c$, where a is a year in the pattern, b is the number of years the cicadas stay underground, and c is the next year in the pattern.

13-year pattern

....

17-year pattern

....

Quick Lab

TEKS 10C, 1A, 2B, 2C, 4A

How does a milkweed bug grow and change?

Over several weeks you will observe the life cycle of a milkweed bug.

Materials

milkweed bug eggs
milkweed bug habitat or terrarium
hand lens

Texas Safety LAB RULES

Handle live animals with care.

Wash your hands thoroughly after completing the activity.

1. **Observe** a young milkweed bug. Use appropriate equipment. A hand lens might be more useful than a microscope, since milkweed bugs are not microscopic.
2. **Record** your observations. Describe the young milkweed bug in detail: How many legs does it have? How many antennae? What does it eat? What color is it? Does it have wings? Is it nocturnal?
3. Repeat Steps 1 and 2 with a milkweed bug that has reached the adult stage.
4. Using a computer, construct an appropriate chart to organize, examine, and evaluate your information. It can be a Venn diagram like the one shown here, a T-chart, or another chart you find useful. Plan ahead and make the chart large enough to fit all your data.

Explain Your Results

5. **Compare and Contrast** Use Internet or library resources to collect similar information about grasshoppers, dragonflies, or cockroaches. Construct another chart for the insect. Evaluate your information. How similar is the young insect to its adult form?

Metamorphosis

All animals have a life cycle that is a pattern of birth, growth, and death. Many animals, when they are born, look similar to their parents. Kittens look like small cats. Turtle hatchlings look like tiny turtles. As they grow, they get bigger. But some animals are born looking different from their parents. They develop in a series of stages. They have different forms in each stage. The process of an animal changing form during its life cycle is called **metamorphosis.** Amphibians and insects grow and develop through metamorphosis.

1. **Compare and Contrast** Use the graphic organizer to describe how a cat's growth and an insect's growth are alike and different.

Cat's Growth | **Insect's Growth**

2. **Identify** Do the young bees shown go through metamorphosis? Explain.

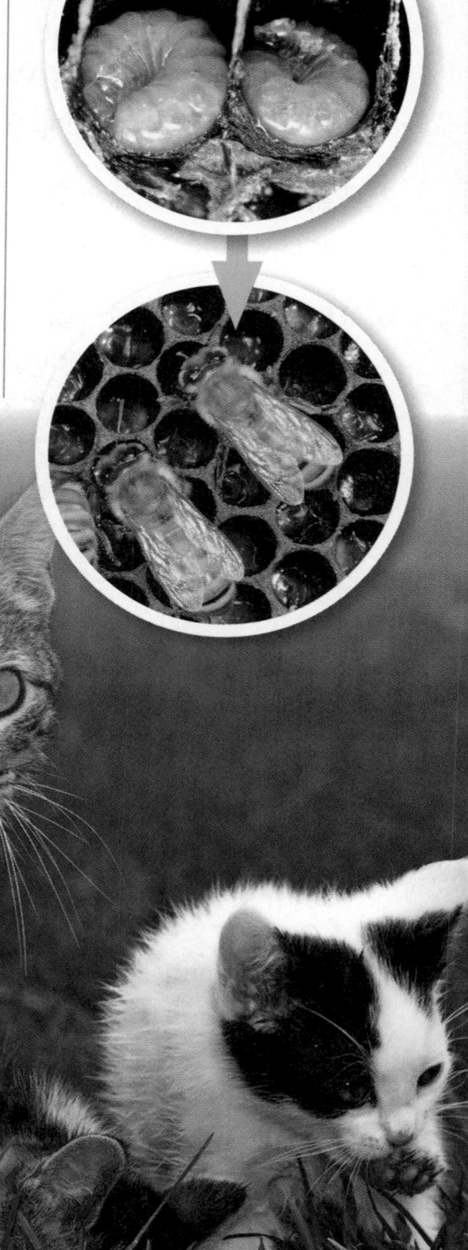

Dung Beetle
Dung beetles are common in Texas. They usually lay their eggs in cow and horse droppings. When the eggs hatch, the larvae eat the dung. A dung beetle larva does not look like an adult dung beetle. It must develop through stages before it takes its final form.

Milksnake
Milksnakes are like turtles and ducklings. They look like their parents when they hatch from their eggs. As they grow, they get bigger, but their general appearance does not change too much.

Great Green Bush Cricket
Not all insects develop and grow through metamorphosis in the same way. The very young great green bush cricket looks much like its parents.

3. **Compare and Contrast** How are great green bush crickets, dung beetles, and milksnakes alike and different in their life cycles?

Growing Up

Find one of your baby photos. Collect, record, and analyze information using a camera by asking a classmate to take your picture. For fun, you may want to mimic the expression you had in your baby picture. Compare your characteristics when you were a baby to how you look now. Write how you have changed.

TEKS 2C, 2F, 4A

Amphibian Metamorphosis

Frogs, toads, and salamanders develop through metamorphosis. You might be familiar with the stages of the life cycle of a frog. Frogs hatch as tadpoles from eggs laid in water. Tadpoles have gills and a tail. Slowly, the tadpoles grow legs, and their tails shorten. Soon they develop lungs and stop getting oxygen through gills. Then they begin to live on land. As adults, frogs look nothing like they did when they were young.

4. Describe How does a frog go through metamorphosis?

....

....

....

5 *adult*

bullfrog

The adult frog looks .... than it does in its tadpole stage.

5. Diagram The diagram numbers stages in a frog's metamorphosis. Fill in the captions to describe each stage.

1
egg
Eggs are laid in ....
2
tadpole
The tadpole has .... *and a tail.*
3
The young tadpole grows legs and its .... *shortens.*
4
The young tadpole develops lungs and stops getting oxygen through its ....

The diagram shows the four stages in a tiger swallowtail butterfly's metamorphosis.

egg

adult

Complete Metamorphosis

Some insects develop in four stages. This type of development is called complete metamorphosis because there is a complete change from one stage to the next stage. An insect begins its development as an egg. The egg develops into a **larva.** The larva is active, spending its time feeding and growing. It molts, or sheds, its outer covering a few times and then grows into a **pupa.** The pupa is inactive while many changes happen in its body. Once these changes are finished, the insect breaks out as an adult. It can now reproduce. Butterflies, ants, bees, flies, and beetles are some insects that go through complete metamorphosis.

6. Compare and Contrast How are a larva and a pupa similar? How are they different?

7. Identify Label the larva and the pupa in the diagram.

8. Infer During its development, a growing butterfly forms a cocoon called a chrysalis. A chrysalis is another name for the pupa of a butterfly. What does the chrysalis provide the growing butterfly?

Incomplete Metamorphosis

Insects that have three stages of development go through incomplete metamorphosis. The stages are egg, larva, and adult. In incomplete metamorphosis, the larva is called a nymph. The nymph looks similar to the adult but has no wings. Dragonflies, grasshoppers, and cockroaches go through incomplete metamorphosis.

The diagram shows the three stages in a broad-bodied chaser dragonfly's metamorphosis.

9. Explain Why is a dragonfly's metamorphosis considered incomplete?

10. Identify Circle a difference you see in the body of a nymph dragonfly and an adult dragonfly.

got it?

11. Describe How does a frog change during the stages in its metamorphosis?

12. How do insects such as butterflies grow and change?

Stop! I need help with

Wait! I have a question about

Go! Now I know

Lab Investigation

TEKS 10A, 1A, 2C, 2D, 2F

How do seeds grow?

Materials

paper towels
clear plastic cup
spray bottle with water
bean seeds

Texas Safety LAB RULES

If any water spills, notify your teacher immediately. Wash your hands thoroughly upon completing the activity.

Inquiry Skill

Observing a process in the classroom can help you understand what happens when the process occurs in nature.

Follow a Procedure

☐ **1.** Fold one paper towel. Place it in a cup. Crumple and push a second towel into the cup. Wet both towels.

☐ **2.** Place some bean seeds between the paper towels and the cup.

☐ **3.** **Observe** the seeds for 5 days.

4. Record Data Draw how the seeds look on each day. Use the chart to record your drawings.

Seed Changes				
Day 1	Day 2	Day 3	Day 4	Day 5

Analyze and Conclude

5. Draw Conclusions How did the seeds change as they grew?

6. What made it possible for the seeds to grow?

Science • Technology
Engineering • Math

TEKS 3D

Tracking Migrations

Each year, spring signals change for many living things. These signals include longer days and warmer temperatures. During spring, many species migrate. They migrate from their winter homes in the warmer southern areas to areas farther north.

The sandhill crane is one species of migrating birds. Scientists use NASA satellites to track different sandhill crane populations. They combine this information with data about plant growth along the migratory path. The green in the image shows areas where food is available. This information shows the health of the species, the route they take, and how long migration lasts. Scientists use this information to learn about sandhill cranes. This information may help scientists protect the sandhill cranes from extinction.

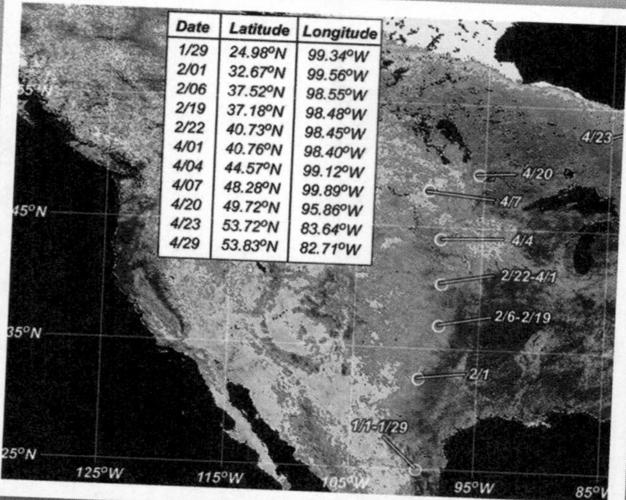

Date	Latitude	Longitude
1/29	24.98°N	99.34°W
2/01	32.67°N	99.56°W
2/06	37.52°N	98.55°W
2/19	37.18°N	98.48°W
2/22	40.73°N	98.45°W
4/01	40.76°N	98.40°W
4/04	44.57°N	99.12°W
4/07	48.28°N	99.89°W
4/20	49.72°N	95.86°W
4/23	53.72°N	83.64°W
4/29	53.83°N	82.71°W

In April, sandhill cranes migrate from their southern feeding grounds in Texas, New Mexico, Arizona, California, and Mexico to their northern breeding grounds.

Connect to Math

Solve Look at the map and table showing the migration of a group of sandhill cranes. How far in degrees of latitude did this group of sandhill cranes travel? Show your work. **Math TEKS 3A**

Vocabulary Smart Cards

exoskeleton
larva
pupa
behavioral adaptation
structural adaptation
metamorphosis

Play a Game!

Cut out the Vocabulary Smart Cards.

Work with a partner. Choose a Vocabulary Smart Card. Do not show the word to your partner.

Say clues to help your partner guess what your word is.

Have your partner repeat with another Vocabulary Smart Card.

metamorphosis

metamorfosis

exoskeleton

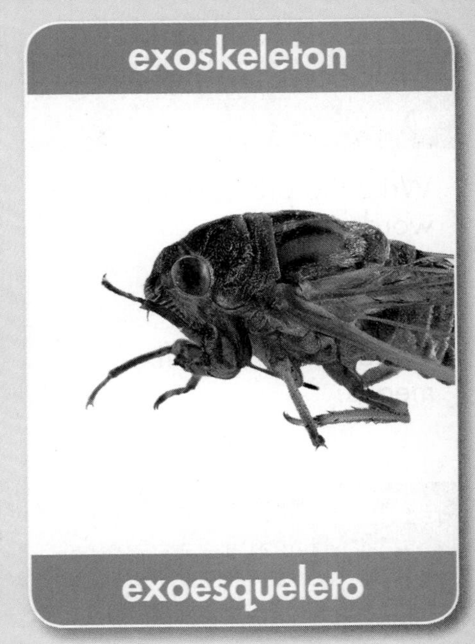

exoesqueleto

larva

larva

behavioral adaptation

adaptación de la conducta

pupa

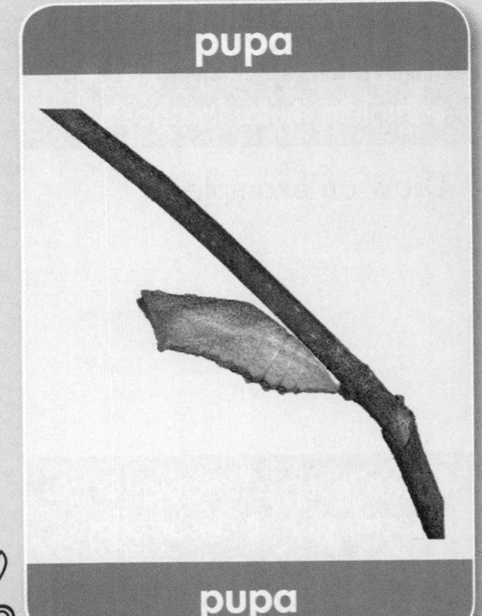

pupa

structural adaptation

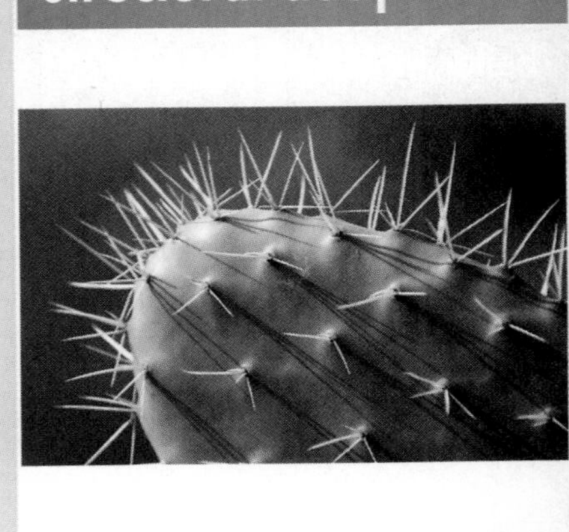

adaptación estructural

a hard skeleton on the outside of the body of some animals

Write the prefix of this word.

Write what the prefix means.

esqueleto duro en el exterior del cuerpo de algunos animales

the process of an animal changing form during its life cycle

What is the word root of this word?

proceso en el cual cambia la forma de un animal durante su ciclo de vida

an inherited behavior that helps an animal survive

Write a sentence using this word.

conducta heredada que le permite a un animal sobrevivir

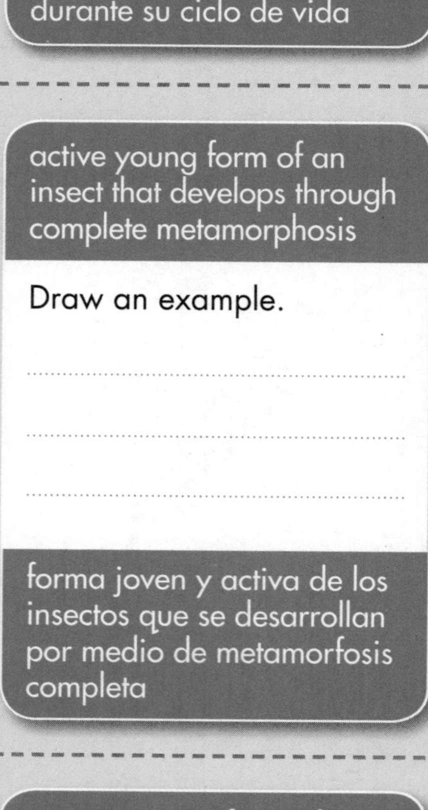

active young form of an insect that develops through complete metamorphosis

Draw an example.

forma joven y activa de los insectos que se desarrollan por medio de metamorfosis completa

a characteristic that allows an organism to survive better in its environment

Write an example.

característica que le permite a un organismo sobrevivir mejor en su medio ambiente

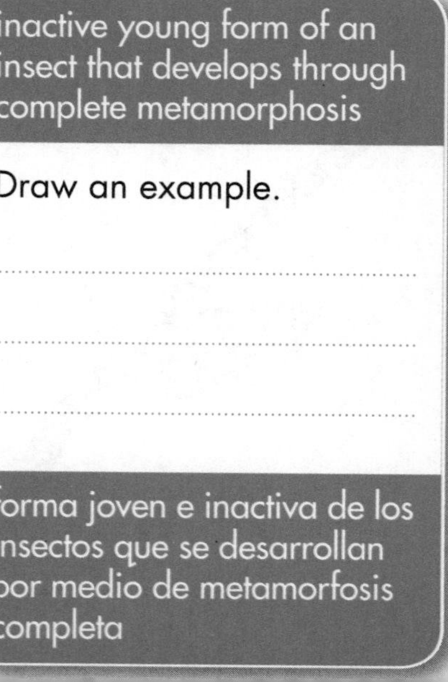

inactive young form of an insect that develops through complete metamorphosis

Draw an example.

forma joven e inactiva de los insectos que se desarrollan por medio de metamorfosis completa

Interactive Vocabulary

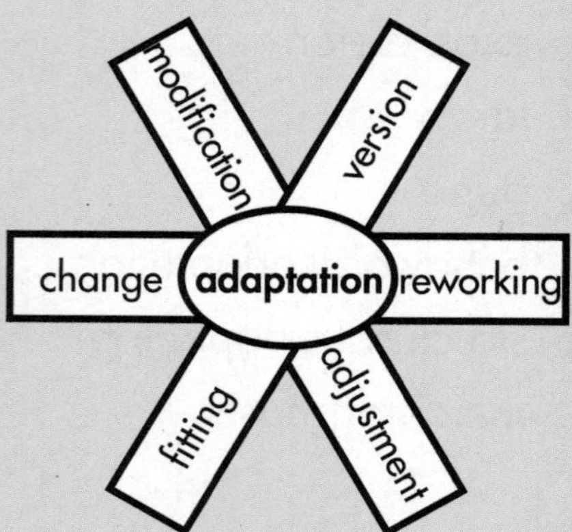

Make a Word Wheel!

Choose a vocabulary word and write it in the center of the Word Wheel graphic organizer. Write synonyms or related words on the wheel spokes.

TEKS Practice

Lesson 1 TEKS 10A

What are some physical structures in living things?

1. **Vocabulary** A(n) _____ is a hard skeleton on the outside of some animals that gives structure and protection.
   A. internal skeleton
   B. exoskeleton
   C. vascular tissue
   D. system

2. **Compare** Compare the function of structures of different species that help them survive. How are seeds and eggs similar in their structure and function?

3. **Explain** How do stems and branches help plants survive?

4. **Compare and Contrast** Compare the functions of structures of different species that help them live by explaining how lungs, spiracles, and gills are similar and different in their functions.

5. **Identify** Which structure in the flower below produces the pollen needed to fertilize another flower?

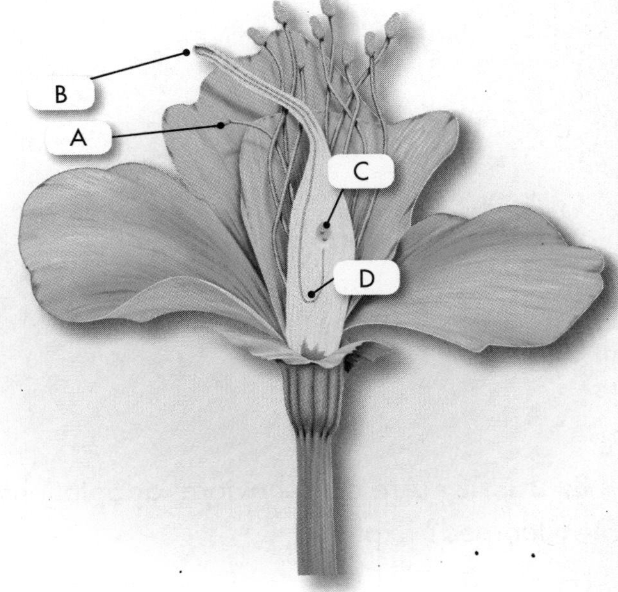

   A. stamen
   B. pistil
   C. ovary
   D. pollen tube

TEKS Practice

Lesson 2 TEKS 10A, 10B

How do adaptations help organisms survive?

6. **Vocabulary** A useful characteristic in a part of a plant or animal that helps it survive is a
   A. mutation.
   B. behavioral adaptation.
   C. natural selection.
   D. structural adaptation.

7. **Write About It** What role does natural selection play in some mutations developing into structural adaptations?

8. **Justify** Are all behavioral adaptations learned? Explain.

9. **Identify** Name a structural adaptation of the elephant in the picture below. List three functions you think it might serve.

10. **Differentiate** Differentiate between inherited traits of animals and learned behaviors. List one example of each.

TEKS Practice

Lesson 3 TEKS 10C

What are the life cycles of some animals?

11. Identify Which stage in a frog's metamorphosis does the picture show?

12. Contrast Read the paragraph below. Describe the differences between complete and incomplete metamorphosis of insects. Then describe how the processes are alike.

> Insects develop through metamorphosis. Some insects, such as butterflies, grow in four stages: egg, larva, pupa, and adult. Other insects, such as dragonflies, grow in three stages: egg, nymph, and adult.

Chapter 9

Lesson 1 What are some physical structures in living things?
In this lesson, you compared the structures and functions that help plants and animals live and survive in their environments.
Supporting TEKS 10A

Lesson 2 How do adaptations help organisms survive?
In this lesson, you learned about behavioral and structural adaptations. You also learned that some behaviors are based on inherited characteristics and others are learned.
Supporting TEKS 10A, 10B

Lesson 3 What are the life cycles of some animals?
In this lesson, you learned about the life cycles of some animals, including complete and incomplete metamorphosis.
Supporting TEKS 10C

★ TEKS Practice: Chapter Review

Read each question and circle the best answer.

1 Carlos puts a white carnation in a glass partially filled with water; then he adds 10 drops of red food coloring. He observes the color of the carnation once every 15 minutes for two hours. Then he notes any changes in his notebook. What function of the plant's system is Carlos testing?

A The life cycle of vascular plants

B The reproduction of flowering plants

C How plants take in air and give off carbon dioxide

D The movement of water and nutrients through the plant

2 The drawings show coconuts and dandelion seeds.

Compare coconuts and dandelion seeds. How do their structures help coconut and dandelion plants thrive?

F Their seeds taste good to animals that carry them to other places.

G Coconuts and dandelion seeds have structures that allow them to float on water or air to new areas.

H Coconuts and dandelion seeds have hooks that cling to passing animals, carrying the seeds to new areas.

J Coconuts and dandelion seeds grow where they fall, not far from the parent plant.

3 The picture shows a butterfly pupa.

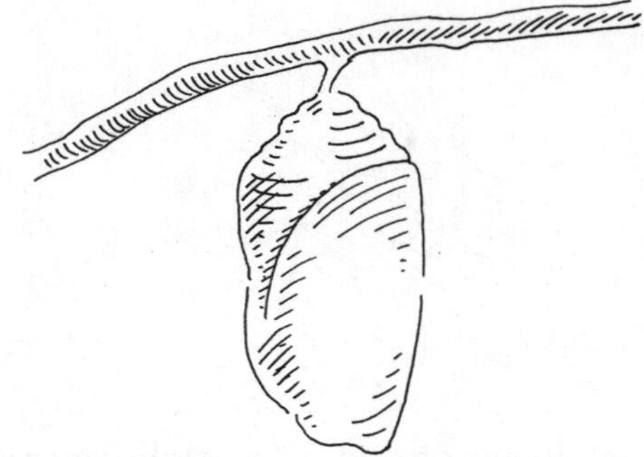

What is happening to the butterfly during the pupa stage?

A It is eating.

B It is getting ready to hatch.

C It is developing wings.

D It is going through an incomplete metamorphosis.

4 Many animals that live in desert ecosystems must adapt in some way to survive. Review the following adaptations, and determine which is a behavioral adaptation.

F Having fatty body tissue that stores water

G Having large ears with blood vessels near the skin to cool the body

H Having a cool burrow under the sand where the animal can escape the heat

J Having a light-colored body covering that absorbs less heat from the environment

5 The drawing shows some prairie grasses.

For plants in a windy environment, like a prairie, why might having stems that bend be a useful adaptation?

A Allows the plant to survive prairie wildfires

B Allows the plant to move with the wind and not be damaged

C Allows the plant to be eaten by grazing animals and survive

D Allows the plant to reproduce faster than plants with woody stems

---

6 Look at the pictures of a duck and a frog.

How does each animal use its feet in the same way to help it survive?

F They each use their feet as shovels to dig for food.

G They each use their feet as springs to jump for insects.

H They each use their feet as anchors to keep them in one place in the water.

J They each use their feet as paddles to push them through the water.

★ TEKS Practice: Cumulative Review

7 The drawing shows a weather map that predicts the weather for the next morning.

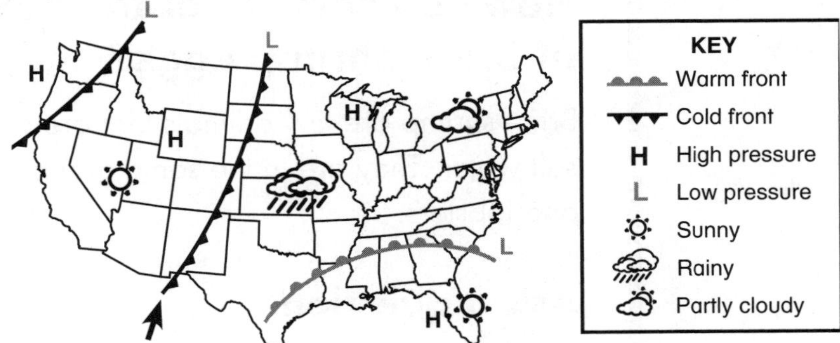

Look at the front with the triangles in the middle of the country. What will happen in western and northwestern Texas as the front passes over the area?

A Warm air will rise quickly as cold air pushes under it.

B Clouds will form.

C There may be storms.

D All of the above

---

8 Caitlyn and Olivia want to investigate what happens as Earth rotates. They use a classroom globe, and Caitlyn holds a flashlight to represent the sun. Olivia rotates the globe toward the east.

As Texas moves into the light, what will happen next in the states west of Texas as Olivia continues to rotate the globe?

F It will become nighttime in those areas.

G It will become daylight in those areas.

H It will become summer in those areas.

J It will become winter in those areas.

If you have trouble with . . .

Question	1	2	3	4	5	6	7	8
See chapter (lesson)	9 (1)	9 (2)	9 (3)	9 (2)	9 (2)	9 (1)	6 (p. 299)	7 (2)
TEKS	10A	10B	10C	10B	10B	10A	8A	8C

Lab zone® Open-Ended Inquiry

TEKS 9A, 1A, 2A, 2B, 2C, 2D, 2F, 2G, 3A, 4A

Materials

5 clear plastic cups
masking tape
pouring container with water
noniodized salt
measuring cup
flat toothpick
brine shrimp eggs
hand lens

Texas Safety LAB RULES

Demonstrate safe practices as described in the Texas Safety Standards during classroom investigations.

Handle live animals with care.

Never eat or drink in the lab area.

If any water spills, notify your teacher immediately.

Wash your hands thoroughly upon completing the activity.

Inquiry Skill
You **control variables** when you make sure the conditions you are not testing remain the same. Controlling variables helps you make sure your experiment is a fair test.

How can salt affect the hatching of brine shrimp eggs?

Brine shrimp are tiny animals that are adapted to live in salt water. They are in the same group of animals as crabs and lobsters.

Ask a question.

How does the amount of salt in the water affect how many brine shrimp eggs hatch?

State a hypothesis.

☐ **1.** Write a **hypothesis** by circling one choice and finishing the sentence.

If brine shrimp are put in water with different amounts of salt, then the most eggs will hatch in the cup with *(a) no salt, (b) a low salt level, (c) a medium salt level, (d) a high salt level, or (e) a very high salt level* because

Identify and control variables.

☐ **2.** When you conduct an **experiment,** you must change only one variable. The **variable** you change is the **independent variable.** What will you change?

☐ **3.** The **dependent variable** is the variable you observe or measure in an experiment. What will you observe?

☐ **4.** **Controlled variables** are the factors you must keep the same to have a fair test. List 3 of these factors.

Design your test.

5. Draw how you will set up your test.

6. List your steps in the order you will do them. Include any materials or equipment you will need.

Do your test.

☐ **7.** Follow the steps you wrote.

☐ **8.** Make sure to **record** your results in a table.

Collect and record your data.

☐ **9.** Create a table to organize, examine, and evaluate your observations. Use a computer, if possible.

Interpret your data.

☐ **10.** Analyze your data. Think about the level of salt. Think how many brine shrimp were moving after 4 days.

In which level of salt did you observe the most brine shrimp moving after 4 days?

State your conclusion.

11. Compare your **hypothesis** and your results. Analyze the scientific explanation about brine shrimp by using your results from experimental testing and your own logical reasoning. What is the relationship between salt levels and brine shrimp hatching?

12. Compare your results with those of other groups. Evaluate and critique their scientific explanations by using your results from the experiment and your own logical reasoning. Does the evidence support what you read about brine shrimp? Why or why not?

Measurements

Metric and Customary Measurements

The metric system is the measurement system most commonly used in science. Metric units are sometimes called SI units. SI stands for International System. It is called that because these units are used around the world.

These prefixes are used in the metric system:

kilo- means *thousand*
1 kilometer = 1,000 meters

milli- means *one thousandth*
1,000 millimeters = 1 meter, or 1 millimeter = 0.001 meter

centi- means *one hundredth*
100 centimeters = 1 meter, or 1 centimeter = 0.01 meter

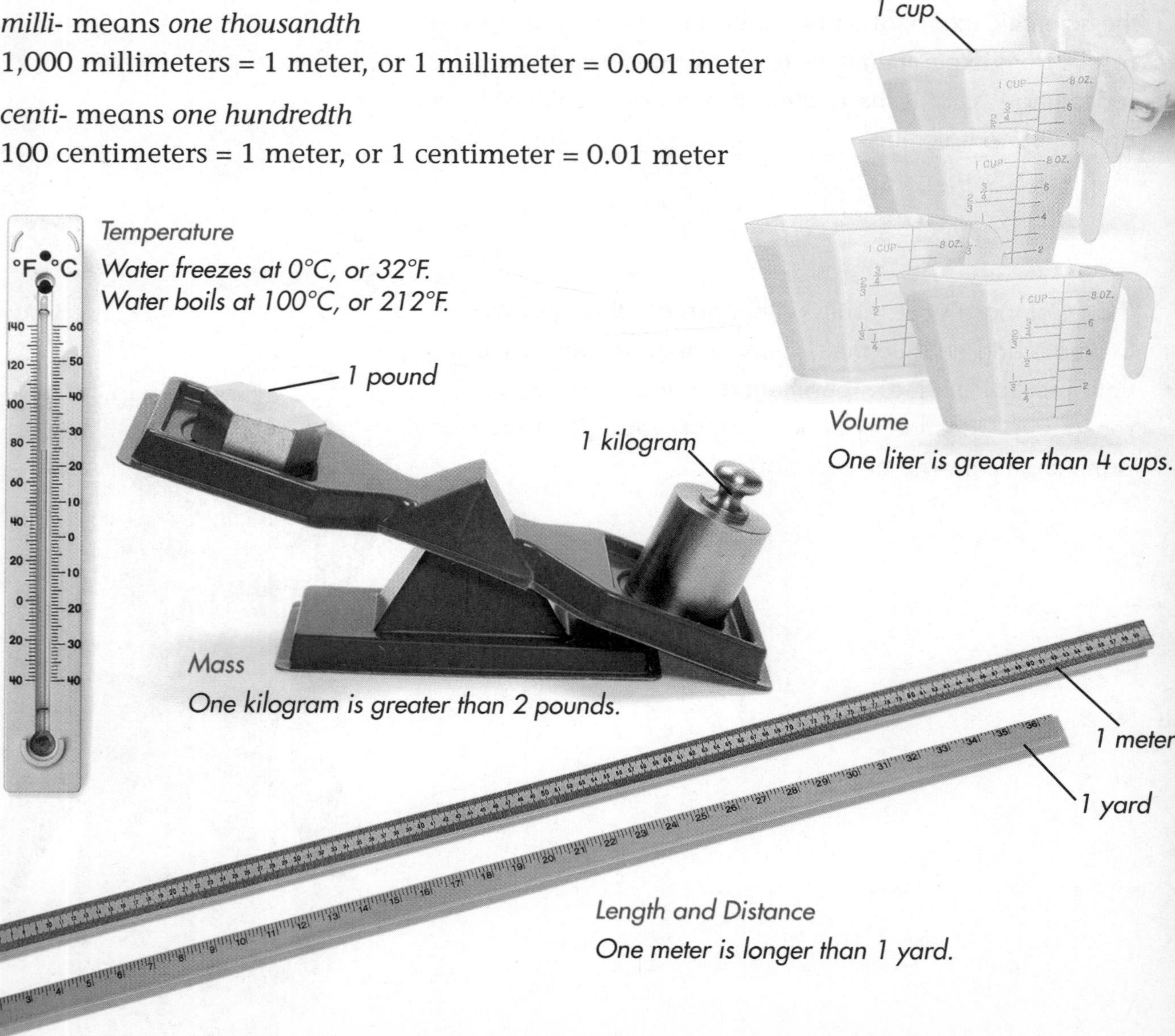

Temperature
Water freezes at 0°C, or 32°F.
Water boils at 100°C, or 212°F.

Volume
One liter is greater than 4 cups.

Mass
One kilogram is greater than 2 pounds.

Length and Distance
One meter is longer than 1 yard.

Glossary

The glossary uses letters and signs to show how words are pronounced. The mark ′ is placed after a syllable with a primary or heavy accent. The mark ′ is placed after a syllable with a secondary or lighter accent.

To hear these vocabulary words and definitions, go online to access the digital glossary.

Pronunciation Key

a	in hat	ō	in open	sh	in she
ā	in age	ȯ	in all	th	in thin
â	in care	ô	in order	ᴛʜ	in then
ä	in far	oi	in oil	zh	in measure
e	in let	ou	in out	ə	= a in about
ē	in equal	u	in cup	ə	= e in taken
ėr	in term	u̇	in put	ə	= i in pencil
i	in it	ü	in rule	ə	= o in lemon
ī	in ice	ch	in child	ə	= u in circus
o	in hot	ng	in long		

A

acceleration (ak sel′ ə rā′ shən) the rate at which the speed or direction of motion of an object changes over time

aceleración ritmo al cual cambia la rapidez o la dirección del movimiento de un objeto con el tiempo

atmosphere (at′ mə sfir) layer of gases wrapped around Earth that makes life possible

atmósfera capa de gases que envuelve la Tierra y hace posible la vida

axis (ak′ sis) an imaginary line around which an object spins

eje línea imaginaria en torno a la cual gira un objeto

B

barometric pressure (bar′ ə met′ rik presh′ ər) the pushing force of the atmosphere

presión atmosférica fuerza que ejerce la atmósfera

behavioral adaptation (bi hā′ vyər əl ad′ ap tā′ shən) an inherited behavior that helps an animal survive

adaptación de la conducta conducta heredada que le permite a un animal sobrevivir

boiling point (boi′ ling point) the temperature at which a substance changes from a liquid to a gas

punto de ebullición temperatura a la cual una sustancia cambia de líquido a gas

C

carbon cycle (kär′bən sī kəl) repeated movement of carbon through the enviroment in different forms

ciclo del carbono movimiento repetido del carbono en formas diferentes a través del medio ambiente

climate (klī′ mit) the average of weather conditions over a long time

clima promedio de las condiciones del tiempo durante un período largo

community (kə myü′nə tē) the group of all populations in an area

comunidad grupo de todas las poblaciones de un área

competition (kom′ pə tish′ ən) the struggle among organisms for the same limited resources

competencia lucha entre organismos por los mismos recursos limitados

condensation (kon′ den sā′ shən) the process in which a gas turns into a liquid

condensación proceso en el que un gas se convierte en líquido

conductor (kən duk′ tər) a material through which an electric charge can move easily

conductor material a través del cual fluye fácilmente una carga eléctrica

consumer (kən sü′ mər) organism that cannot make its own food

consumidor organismo que no puede hacer su propio alimento

contact force (kon′ takt fôrs) a force that requires two pieces of matter to touch

fuerza de contacto fuerza que requiere que dos porciones de materia se toquen

control group (kən trōl′ grüp) a standard against which change is measured

grupo de control estándar que se usa para medir un cambio

corona (kə rō′nə) the outer layer of the sun's atmosphere

corona capa más externa de la atmósfera del Sol

D

data (dā′ tə) information from which a conclusion can be drawn or a prediction can be made

datos información de la cual se puede sacar una conclusión o hacer una predicción

decomposer (dē′ kəm pō′ zər) organism that gets its energy by breaking down wastes and dead organisms

descomponedor organismo que obtiene su energía descomponiendo desechos y organismos muertos

density (den′ sə tē) the mass of an object divided by its volume

densidad masa de un objeto dividida por su volumen

dependent variable (di pen′ dənt vâr′ ē bəl) the variable that changes when the independent variable changes

variable dependiente variable que cambia cuando la variable independiente cambia

deposition (dep′ ə zish′ ən) process of laying down materials, such as rocks and soil

sedimentación proceso por el cual materiales como rocas y partículas de suelo se asientan

E

ecosystem (ē′ kō sis′ təm) all the living and nonliving things in an area and their interactions

ecosistema todos los seres vivos y los objetos inertes que hay en un área y sus interacciones

electric circuit (i lek′ trik ser′ kit) a circular path through which electricity can flow

circuito eléctrico camino circular por donde puede fluir electricidad

elevation (el′ ə vā′ shən) height above sea level

elevación altura sobre el nivel del mar

energy (en′ ər jē) ability to do work or cause change

energía capacidad de hacer trabajo o causar cambios

environment (en vī′ rən mənt) all of the conditions surrounding an organism

medio ambiente todas las condiciones que rodean a un ser vivo

erosion (i rō′ zhən) the movement of materials away from a place

erosión movimiento de materiales que se alejan de un lugar

evaporation (i vap′ ə rā′ shən) the changing of a liquid to a gas

evaporación cambio de líquido a gas

evidence (ev′ ə dəns) observations that make you believe something is true

evidencia observaciones que te hacen creer que algo es cierto

exoskeleton (ek′ sō skel′ ə tən) a hard skeleton on the outside of the body of some animals

exoesqueleto esqueleto duro en el exterior del cuerpo de algunos animales

experiment (ek sper′ ə mənt) the use of scientific investigation and reasoning to test a hypothesis

experimento uso de investigación y razonamiento científicos para poner a prueba una hipótesis

extinct (ek stingkt′) no longer existing as a species

extinto ya no existe más como especie

F

food chain (füd chān) a series of steps by which energy moves from one type of living thing to another

cadena alimenticia serie de pasos mediante los cuales la energía pasa de un ser vivo a otro

food web (füd web) a diagram that combines many food chains into one picture

red alimenticia diagrama que combina varias redes alimenticias en una sola imagen

force (fôrs) a push or pull that acts on an object

fuerza empujón o jalón que se le da a un objeto

fossil (fos′ əl) remains or mark of an animal or plant that lived long ago

fósil restos o marca de un ser vivo que existió hace mucho tiempo

friction (frik′ shən) the force that results when two materials rub against each other or when their contact prevents sliding

fricción fuerza que resulta al frotar un material contra otro o cuando el contacto entre ambos impide el deslizamiento

G

galaxy (gal′ ək sē) a large group of stars

galaxia enorme grupo de estrellas

---

gas (gas) a substance without a definite volume or shape

gas sustancia que no tiene ni volumen ni forma definidos

---

gravity (grav′ ə tē) the force of attraction between any two objects

gravedad fuerza de atracción entre dos cuerpos cualesquiera

H

habitat (hab′ ə tat) a place that provides all the things an organism needs to live

hábitat lugar que proporciona todas las cosas que necesita un organismo para vivir

---

hydrosphere (hī′ drə sfir) Earth's waters

hidrosfera toda el agua de la Tierra

---

hypothesis (hī poth′ ə sis) statement of what you think will happen during an investigation

hipótesis enunciado de lo que crees que ocurrirá en una investigación

I

igneous (ig′ nē əs) rocks that form when melted rock cools and hardens

ígnea rocas que se forman cuando la roca derretida se enfría y se endurece

---

independent variable (in′ di pen′ dənt vâr′ ē bəl) the variable that you control

variable independiente variable que tú controlas

---

inexhaustible resource (in′ ig zô′ stə bəl rē′ sôrs) a type of energy resource that will not run out

recurso inagotable tipo de recurso energético que nunca se agota

---

inference (in′ fər əns) a conclusion based on observations

inferencia conclusión basada en observaciones

insulator (in′sə lā t′ər) a strong resistor that can stop most electric currents

aislante resistencia fuerte que puede impedir el paso de casi cualquier corriente

K

kinetic energy (ki net′ ik en′ ər jē) energy due to motion

energía cinética energía que resulta del movimiento

L

larva (lär′ və) active young form of an insect that develops through complete metamorphosis

larva forma joven y activa de los insectos que se desarrollan por medio de metamorfosis completa

latitude (lat′ ə tüd) a measure of how far a place is from the equator

latitud medida de la distancia entre un objeto y el ecuador

liquid (lik′ wid) a substance that has a definite volume but no definite shape

líquido sustancia que tiene un volumen definido pero no una forma definida

M

magnetism (mag nə′ tiz′ əm) the ability of an object to attract certain metal objects

magnetismo capacidad de un objeto de atraer ciertos objetos de metal

mass (mas) the amount of matter in a solid, liquid, or gas

masa cantidad de materia que tiene un sólido, líquido o gas

melting point (mel′ ting point) the temperature at which a substance changes from a solid to a liquid

punto de fusión temperatura a la cual una sustancia cambia de sólido a líquido

metamorphic (met′ ə môr′ fik) rocks formed inside Earth from other rocks under heat and pressure

metamórfica rocas que se forman dentro de la Tierra a partir de otras rocas, bajo calor y presión

metamorphosis (met′ ə môr′ fə sis) the process of an animal changing form during its life cycle

metamorfosis proceso en el cual cambia la forma de un animal durante su ciclo de vida

meteorologist (mē/ tē or ol′ o gist) scientist who studies and predicts weather

meteorólogo científico que estudia y predice el estado del tiempo

mineral (min′ ər əl) a nonliving, naturally occurring solid that has its own regular arrangement of particles in it

mineral sólido natural, sin vida, cuyas partículas están regularmente organizadas

mixture (miks′ chər) different materials placed together, but each material keeps its own properties

mezcla unión de materiales diferentes en la cual cada material mantiene sus propiedades

model (mod′ l) object or idea that shows how something is constructed or how it works

modelo objeto o idea que muestra cómo algo está construido o cómo funciona

moon (mün) a natural object that revolves around a planet

luna satélite natural que orbita un planeta

N

nitrogen cycle (nī′ trə jen sī′ kəl) repeated movement of nitrogen through the environment in different forms

ciclo del nitrógeno movimiento repetido del nitrógeno en formas diferentes a través del medio ambiente

non-contact force (non kon′ takt fôrs) a force that acts at a distance

fuerza sin contacto fuerza que actúa a distancia

nonrenewable resource (non′ ri nü′ ə bəl rē′ sôrs) a type of energy resource that cannot be replaced at all or cannot be replaced as fast as people use it

recurso no renovable tipo de recurso energético que no se puede reemplazar o que no se puede reemplazar con la misma rapidez con que se lo usa

O

observation (ob′ zər vā′ shən) something you find out about objects, events, or living things using your senses

observación algo que descubres con tus sentidos sobre los objetos, sucesos o seres vivos

opaque (ō pāk′) describes materials that do not let any light pass through them

opaco describe materiales que no dejan pasar a través de ellos la luz

orbit (ôr′ bit) the path an object takes as it revolves around a star, planet, or moon

órbita el camino que sigue un objeto al girar alrededor de una estrella, un planeta o una luna

P

paleontologist (pā′ lē on tol′ ə jist) a scientist who studies fossils

paleontólogo científico que estudia los fósiles

photosphere (fō′ tə sfir) the surface of the sun visible from Earth

fotosfera superficie del Sol visible desde la Tierra

population (pop′ yə lā′ shən) a group of organisms of one species that live in an area at the same time

población grupo de organismos de la misma especie que viven en un área al mismo tiempo

potential energy (pə ten′ shəl en′ ər jē) energy that is not causing any changes now but could cause changes in the future

energía potencial energía que no está causando cambios actualmente pero que podría causarlos en el futuro

precipitation (pri sip′ ə tā′ shən) water that falls from clouds as rain, snow, sleet, or hail

precipitación agua que cae de las nubes en forma de lluvia, nieve, aguanieve o granizo

predator (pred′ ə tər) a consumer that hunts and eats another animal

predador consumidor que atrapa a otro animal y se lo come

prey (prā) any animal that is hunted by others for food

presa cualquier animal que es cazado por otros para alimentación

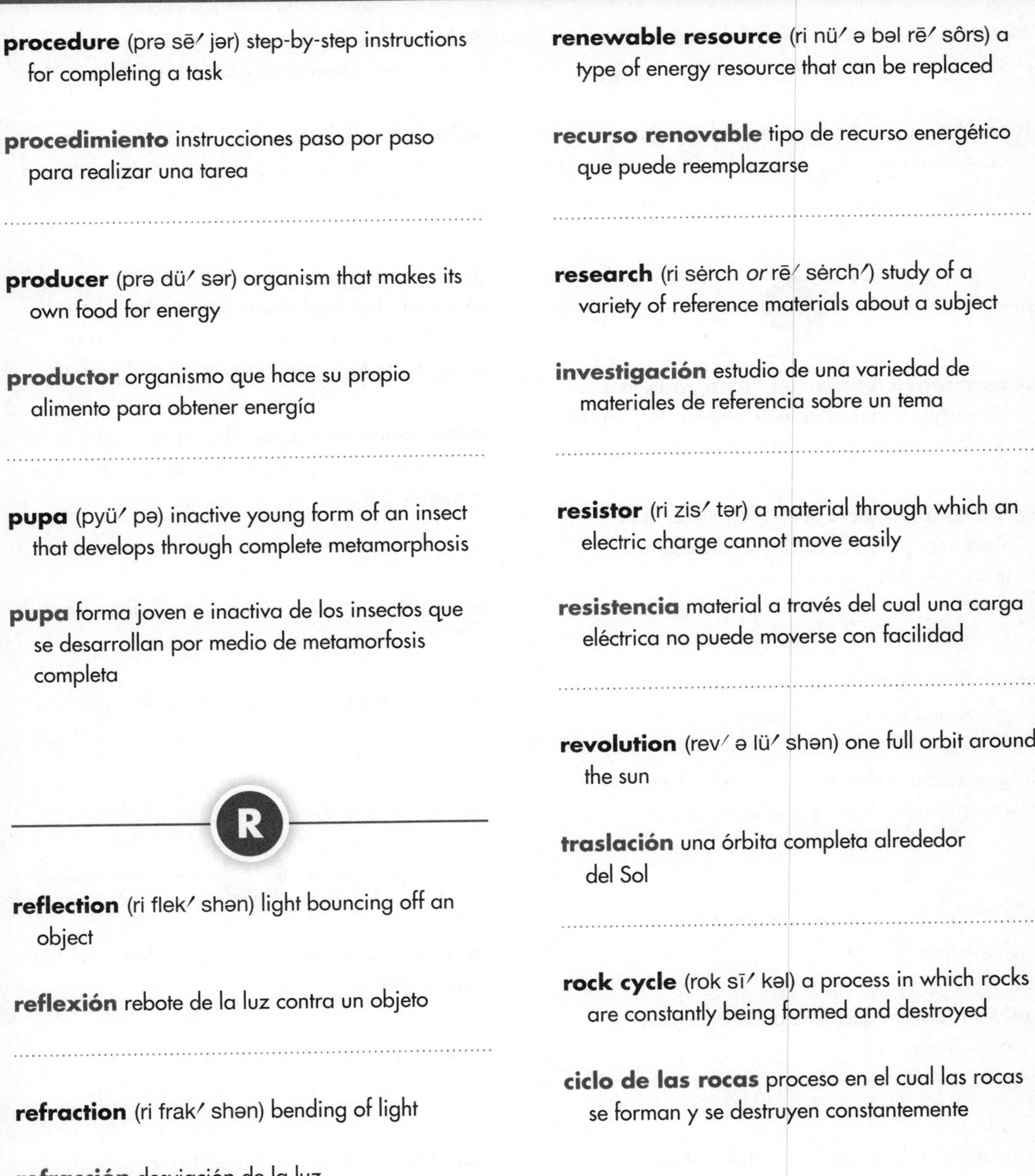

procedure (prə sē′ jər) step-by-step instructions for completing a task

procedimiento instrucciones paso por paso para realizar una tarea

producer (prə dü′ sər) organism that makes its own food for energy

productor organismo que hace su propio alimento para obtener energía

pupa (pyü′ pə) inactive young form of an insect that develops through complete metamorphosis

pupa forma joven e inactiva de los insectos que se desarrollan por medio de metamorfosis completa

R

reflection (ri flek′ shən) light bouncing off an object

reflexión rebote de la luz contra un objeto

refraction (ri frak′ shən) bending of light

refracción desviación de la luz

renewable resource (ri nü′ ə bəl rē′ sôrs) a type of energy resource that can be replaced

recurso renovable tipo de recurso energético que puede reemplazarse

research (ri sėrch *or* rē′ sėrch′) study of a variety of reference materials about a subject

investigación estudio de una variedad de materiales de referencia sobre un tema

resistor (ri zis′ tər) a material through which an electric charge cannot move easily

resistencia material a través del cual una carga eléctrica no puede moverse con facilidad

revolution (rev′ ə lü′ shən) one full orbit around the sun

traslación una órbita completa alrededor del Sol

rock cycle (rok sī′ kəl) a process in which rocks are constantly being formed and destroyed

ciclo de las rocas proceso en el cual las rocas se forman y se destruyen constantemente

rotation (rō tā′ shən) one whole spin of an object on its axis

rotación una vuelta completa de un objeto en torno a su eje

S

sedimentary (sed′ ə men′ tər ē) rocks that form when layers of materials and rock particles settle on top of each other and then harden

sedimentaria rocas que se forman cuando materiales y partículas de roca se asientan unos sobre los otros y se endurecen

solar flare (sō′ lər flâr) an explosive eruption of waves and particles into space

fulguración solar erupción explosiva de ondas y partículas emitidas hacia el espacio

solid (sol′ id) a substance that has a definite shape and volume

sólido sustancia que tiene una forma y un volumen definidos

solubility (sol′ yə bil′ ə tē) ability of one substance to dissolve in another

solubilidad capacidad de una sustancia de disolverse en otra

solution (sə lü′ shən) a mixture in which substances are spread out evenly and will not settle

solución mezcla en la cual una sustancia se dispersa de manera uniforme en otra sustancia y no se asienta

structural adaptation (struk′ chər əl ad′ ap tā′ shen) a characteristic that allows an organism to survive better in its environment

adaptación estructural característica que le permite a un organismo sobrevivir mejor en su medio ambiente

sunspot (sun′ spot′) dark spots on the surface of the sun

mancha solar mancha oscura en la superficie del Sol

transform (tran sfôrm) to change from one form into another

transformar cambiar de una forma a otra

translucent (tran slü′ snt *or* tranz lü′ snt) describes materials that let some light pass through, but not all

translúcido describe materiales que dejan pasar a través de ellos un poco de luz, pero no toda

transparent (tran spâr′ ənt) describes materials that let nearly all light pass through them

transparente describe materiales que dejan pasar a través de ellos casi toda la luz

variable (vâr′ ē ə bəl) something that can change in a test

variable algo que puede cambiar durante una prueba

vibration (vī brā′ shən) the back-and-forth motion of an object

vibración movimiento de un objeto hacia adelante y hacia atrás

volume (vol′ yəm) the amount of space an object takes up

volumen el espacio que ocupa un objeto

water cycle (wȯ′ tər sī′ kəl) repeated movement of water through the environment in different forms

ciclo del agua movimiento repetido del agua en formas distintas a través del medio ambiente

water vapor (wȯ′ tər vā′ pər) water in the form of an invisible gas

vapor de agua agua en forma de gas invisible

weather (weᴛʜ′ ər) the state of the atmosphere

estado del tiempo condición de la atmósfera

wind (wind) air movement caused by differences in air pressure

viento movimiento del aire debido a diferencias en la presión del aire

Index

Page numbers for pictures, charts, graphs, maps, and their associated text are printed in *italic type.*

B

D

G

H

I

Credits

Every effort has been made to secure permission and provide appropriate credit for photographic material. The publisher deeply regrets any omission and pledges to correct errors called to its attention in subsequent editions.

Unless otherwise acknowledged, all photographs are the property of Pearson Education, Inc.

COVER: Steve McKinzie/Getty Images

Title l Creatix/Fotolia; Title c jojje11/Fotolia; TitleBkgrd Larry Landolfi/Science Source/Photo Researchers, Inc.; Title plant Image Studio/Getty Images; iv HG Photography/Fotolia; v Radius Images/Alamy; vii Jamesbenet /iStockphoto; viii Q-Images/Alamy; ix Jim Parkin/Shutterstock; x Bernd Zoller/Imagebroker/Alamy; xi Corey Hochachka/Vibe Images/Alamy; xvii br iStockphoto; xix b Bloomau/Fotolia; 000 Banner TX flag Brandon Seidel/Fotolia; 000Bkgd Masterfile; 001Bkgrd Peter Essick/Aurora/SpecialistStock/Robert Harding World Imagery; 002Bkgrd ERproductions Ltd/Blend Images/GettyImages; 008b E Hickerson/FGBNMS/NOAA; 008Bkgrd Bill Heinsohn/Alamy; 008tr Emma Hickerson/FGBNMS/NOAA; 009BR FGBNMS/NOAA; 010b Ragnar Th Sigurdsson/ARCTIC IMAGES/Alamy; 011 Douglas Faulkner/Photo Researchers, Inc.; 012 James D Watt/Stephen Frink Collection/Alamy; 013 Getty Images/Jupiterimages; 014b Phillip Jones/Stocktrek Images/Alamy; 014Bkgrd Edvard76universe/Alamy; 015Bkgrd Tami Chappell/Reuters; 017 Vladimir Liverts/Fotolia; 018 Frank Herzog/Culture-Images GmbH/Alamy; 020L Jim West/Alamy; 020L Jim West/Alamy; 020R Royal Institute of Technology; 021 Masterfile; 024T JAUBERT IMAGES/Alamy; 026Bkgrd Lukethelake/Shutterstock; 028B Nssl/Noaa; 028Bkgrd Minerva Studio/Fotolia; 028T David R. Frazier/Photolibrary/Alamy; 029B Mike Coniglio/Nssl/Vortex2/Noaa; 029T J.J.Gourley/NOAA/NSSL/Vortex II; 031R Gary Kevin/DK Images; 032BCR Martin Shields/Alamy; 033B David Parker/Science Source/Photo Researchers, Inc; 034B Jerry Young/DK Images; 034CR Dave King/DK Images; 034T Karandaev/Fotolia; 035B Kanate/Fotolia; 035C Aaron Amat/Fotolia; 035TL Steve Gorton/DK Images; 035TR Dimedrol68/Fotolia; 037 Daniel Loretto; 038 Comstock/Jupiter Images; 039 Vicky Kasala/Photodisc/Getty Images; 040Bkgrd Jill Stephenson/Alamy; 042Bkgrd Gary Retherford/Photo Researchers; 042L Stanley Rippel/Fotolia; 042R Joel Sartore/National Geographic/Getty Images; 043B Joel Sartore/National Geographic/Getty Images; 043T George Lavendowski/U.S. Fish and Wildlife Service; 044 John Beatty/Science Source/Photo Researchers, Inc.; 045 Radius Images/Alamy; 048B Monika Bright/University of Vienna,Austria/NOAA; 048Bkgrd Noaa PMEL Vents Program; 049BR James D Watt/Stephen Frink Collection/Alamy; 049BR James D Watt/Stephen Frink Collection/Alamy; 049CR Douglas Faulkner/Photo Researchers; 049TL Frank Herzog/Culture-Images GmbH/Alamy; 049TR Ragnar Th Sigurdsson/ARCTIC IMAGES/Alamy; 051B Vicky Kasala/Photodisc/Getty Images; 051C David R. Frazier/Photolibrary/Alamy; 051TC JAUBERT IMAGES/Alamy; 051TL John Beatty/Science Source/Photo Researchers, Inc.; 051TR David R. Frazier/Science Source/Photo Researchers Inc; 064Bkgrd Jonasginter/Fotolia; 066Bkgrd Peter Carsten/National Geographic Stock; 069 Pls/Shutterstock; 070 Henryk Sadura/Fotolia; 072 Andy Crawford/DK Images; 073B Stuart Hannagan/Getty Images; 076 Clive Streeter/DK Images; 077T Clive Streeter/Courtesy of the Science Museum, London/DK Images; 078B Nasa; 078TL Nasa/Noaa/Gsfc/Suomi Npp/Viirs/Norman Kuring; 078TR CGEmapping/Elvele Images Ltd/Alamy; 079 Fabio Fersa/Shutterstock; 080Bkgrd Tom Fox/MCT/Newscom; 081 Blickwinkel/Alamy; 083 GlowImages/Alamy; 087 Ruta Saulyte/Fotolia; 090Bkgrd Nayashkova Olga/Shutterstock; 090R Steve Shott/DK Images; 091 JJAVA/Fotolia; 094T Mike Dunning/DK Images; 098 Shock/Fotolia; 098Bkgrd Carmela45/Fotolia; 099br Clive Streeter/DK Images; 099TL Clive Streeter/Courtesy of the Science Museum, London/DK Images; 101ct Steve Shott/Dorling Kindersle; 110Bkgrd Bruno De Hogues/Getty Images; 113 James Cavallini/Science Source/Photo Researchers; 116B Angel Vasilev/Fotolia; 116T Q-Images/Alamy; 117 Marjorie Kamys Cotera/Bob Daemmrich Photography/Alamy; 117Bkgrd VanHart/Shutterstock; 118br U.P.images_photo/Shutterstock; 118cr Jupiterimages/Getty Images; 118tr TebNad/Shutterstock; 119bl Michael Stokes/Shutterstock; 119cl Trutta/Shutterstock; 119tl Lawrence Roberg/Shutterstock; 122B Dave King/DK; 122Bkgrd Lijuan Guo/Fotolia; 122T Sheval/Fotolia; 124Bkgrd Oshchepkov Dmitry/Shutterstock; 126Bkgrd Handout/Reuters; 126bl Fuse/Jupiter Images; 127 Losevsky Pavel/Alamy; 130cl Trish Gant/DK Images; 131tl Arthur Tilley/Open Door Images/Jupiter Images; 134Bkgrd DeviantART/Fotolia; 134R Paulrommer/Shutterstock; 135 Paul Prescott/Fotolia; 136tl PhotoSky 4t com/Shutterstock; 137b Anya Levinson; 137T Don Farrall/Getty Images; 138tc D. Roberts/Science Source; 138tl Andy Crump/Photo Researchers, Inc.; 138tr Ted Kinsman/Science Source; 139R Mediacolor's/Alamy; 139TC Anthony Meshkinyar/Getty Images; 139tl Alfred Pasieka/Science Source; 139tr Mediacolor's/Alamy; 140 Roman Makhmutov/Flickr/Getty Images; 141 GIPhotoStock X/Alamy; 142 Popova Olga/Fotolia; 144Bkgrd Alexei Nikolaevich/Shutterstock; 146br Simon Lewis/Photo Researchers, Inc.; 146T Perry Mastrovito/All Canada Photos/Getty Images; 147b Ilker Canikligil/Shutterstock; 151 Terry Wild Studio, Inc.; 152B HO/Reuters/Newscom; 152Bkgrd Markus Gann/Shutterstock; 152T Tetra Images/Alamy; 153T Tanya Constantine/Blend Images/Alamy; 156 FB-Rose/Imagebroker/Alamy; 157bc Paulrommer/Shutterstock; 157br Michael Stokes/Shutterstock; 157c Paul Prescott/Fotolia; 157cr Lawrence Roberg/Shutterstock; 157ct Pearson Education; 157tr Angel Vasilev/Fotolia; 159cr PhotoSky 4t com/Shutterstock; 159tl Ilker Canikligil/Shutterstock; 162 Dan Suzio/Photo Researchers, Inc.; 168Bkgrd Sean Davey/Aurora Photos/Corbis; 171Bkgrd Tim Flach/Stone/Getty Images; 174B Ronald Manera/Fotolia; 174Bkgrd Tetra Images/SuperStock; 174T Robert J. Daveant/Shutterstock; 175B Neal and Molly Jansen/Alamy; 175T Ben Blankenburg/Corbis Premium RF/Alamy; 176b Marcel Jancovic/Shutterstock; 178l James Suger/Stock Photo/Black Star; 179R GIPhotoStock/Science Source/Photo Researchers; 179t Science Source/GIPhotoStock; 180Bkgrd Rolf Nussbaumer Photography/Alamy; 182B Brigette Sullivan/Outer Focus Photos/Alamy; 182Bkgrd Christopher Alan Selby/Alamy; 182T Toni L Bailey/AP Images; 183B Sue Ogrocki/AP Images; 183C ZUMA Press Inc/Alamy; 183cb ZUMA Press Inc/Alamy; 183T

Garry Gay Photography/Alamy; 190 Stockbyte/Getty Images; 191 Santiago Cornejo/Shutterstock; 198B Joggie Botma/Shutterstock; 198T NASA; 199bc Harry Taylor/Natural History Museum, London/DK Images; 199br Joel Arem/Photo Researchers, Inc; 199c James Suger/Stock Photo/Black Star; 199cr Susan E. Degginger/Alamy; 199tc Andreas Einsiedel/DK Images; 199tc GIPhotoStock/Science Source/Photo Researchers; 199tl Ronald Manera/Fotolia; 199tr Carbonbrain/Fotolia; 201L Randy Faris/Corbis Super RF/Alamy; 201R Bob Daemmrich/Alamy; 202 Stockbyte/Getty Images; 214Bkgrd Gerhard Zwerger-Schoner/Imagebroker/Alamy; 216B Volker Steger/Photo Researchers; 216T Frank Greenaway/DK Images; 217c Psamtik/Shutterstock; 218Bkgrd H. Armstrong Roberts/ClassicStock/Alamy; 220B Maxximmm/Fotolia; 220 vilax/Shutterstock; 220T Carbonbrain/Fotolia; 221? Radius Images/Alamy; 221Bkgrd Radius Images/Alamy; 221cl Joel Arem/Photo Researchers, Inc; 221l Colin Keates/Courtesy of the Naturel History Museum; 222b Marcel/Fotolia; 222BL RF Company/Alamy; 222BR Marcel/Fotolia; 222cl Mike Dunning/DK Images; 222T Andreas Einsiedel/DK Images; 223bl Harry Taylor/DK Images; 223br Harry Taylor/DK Images; 223c Harry Taylor/DK Images; 223cr Andy Crawford/DK Images; 223tl U.S. Geological Survey; 224B Harry Taylor/Natural History Museum, London/DK Images; 224Bkgrd David J. Phillip/AP Images; 224C Harry Taylor/Natural History Museum, London/DK Images; 224T Matthew Ward/DK Image; 225tr Getty Images; 226Bkgrd Jim Parkin/Fotolia; 228Bkgrd John E. Marriott/Alamy; 229B Mike Norton/Shutterstock; 229T RIRF Stock/Shutterstock; 230b Peter Arnold, Inc./Alamy; 231b Apply pictures/Alamy; 231tr Mountainpix/Shutterstock; 232b Frans Lemmens/Alamy; 233tr Ian Bracegirdle/Shutterstock; 234 John Holsenbeck/Noaa; 235 Witold Skrypczak/Alamy; 235Bkgrd Jason Langley/Alamy; 237cr VanHart/Shutterstock; 238b Corbis; 240B Theodore Clutter/Photo Researchers, Inc.; 240BC John Dickey/Alamy; 240T Szfei/Shutterstock; 240TC Thinkstock/Jupiter Images; 241 Q-Images/Alamy; 244b Colin Keates/DK Images; 245b Pierre-Philippe Marcou/AFP/Getty Images; 246tl EIGHTFISH/Alamy; 247cr Psamtik/Shutterstock; 247tl Pylypenko/Shutterstock; 247tr Andrew N. Ilyasov/Shutterstock; 248bl John Cancalosi/Alamy; 248br Emilio Ereza/Alamy; 248tr Dorling Kindersley; 249Bkgrd American Museum of Natural History; 249c Jamie York/iStock; 254 Kevin Ebi/Alamy; 257br Szfei/Shutterstock; 257c Psamtik/Shutterstock; 257cr Mike Norton/Shutterstock; 257tc Corbis; 257tr John E. Marriott/Alamy; 259L Joel Arem/Photo Researchers, Inc.; 260 Christopher and Sally Gable/DK Images; 266Bkgrd Martin Amm; 269 Inga Spence/Alamy; 270Bkgrd Timothy Lee Lantgen/Shutterstock; 272b Mike Timo/Getty Images; 272Bkgrd Elena Petrova/Fotolia; 273B Dmitry Shishov/Fotolia; 273TL Discpicture/Shutterstock; 273TR Kated/Shutterstock; 280Bkgrd Pavel Blagoveshchens/Fotolia; 281B David R. Frazier Photolibrary, Inc./Alamy; 281T Imac/Alamy; 282 Paul Seheult/Eye Ubiquitous/Corbis; 284c David Philips/Shutterstock; 284t Stephen Oliver/DK; 286Bkgrd RIRF Stock/Shutterstock; 287Bkgrd RIRF Stock/Shutterstock; 288B Radius Images/Alamy; 288Bkgrd Randall Stevens/Shutterstock; 288T ZUMA Wire Service/Alamy; 289B Nathan Lambrecht/The Monitor/AP Images; 289Bkgrd Randall Stevens/Shutterstock; 289T Zerega/Alamy; 291b Antonio Jorge Nunes/Shutterstock; 291C Les Polders/Alamy; 291t Yadid Levy/Alamy Image; 292b NASA; 293c NASA; 294 Luc Novovitch/Danita Delimont Photography/Newscom; 295 TLF Design/Alamy; 295Bkgrd Design Pics Inc/Alamy; 300Bkgrd Comstock/Thinkstock; 301BL David R. Frazier Photolibrary, Inc./Alamy; 301TR Discpicture/Shutterstock; 303bc NASA; 303br Stephen Oliver/DK; 303cr Paul Seheult/Eye Ubiquitous/Corbis; 303TR Imac/Alamy; 306br Clint Farlinger/Alamy; 312Bkgrd Aaron Favila/ASSOCIATED PRESS; 315 NASA Charles Conrad, Jr./Johnson Space Center/NASA; 316Bkgrd NIX/NASA; 317 Jim Hughes/Shutterstock; 318Bkgrd John A Davis/Shutterstock; 322 Digital Wisdom Inc; 322 Digital Wisdom, Inc.; 324B Procy/Shutterstock; 326 Brandon Laufenberg/iStock Vectors/Getty Images; 327 Roman Gorielov/Fotolia; 328Bkgrd Kim Taylor/Photoshot; 329 Hulton Archive/Getty Images; 334 Human Space Flight/NASA; 338B Gary Hincks/Science Source/Photo Researchers; 338Bkgrd Danshutter/Shutterstock; 338C Dmitry Kosterev/Shutterstock; 339tr John A Davis/Shutterstock; 354 Exactostock/SuperStock; 356 Michael Kienetsky/Shutterstock; 359Bkgrd Robert Francis/Alamy; 359t John Cancalosi/Alamy; 362B Ragnar Th. Sigurdsson/Age fotostock/SuperStock; 362Bkgrd Matt Jones/Shutterstock; 362T Imagebroker/SuperStock; 363B Krys Bailey/Alamy; 363C Robert Pickett/Papilio/Alamy; 363T Blickwinkel/Hecker/Alamy; 364 Martin Strmiska/Alamy; 364Bkgrd Mark Conlin/Alamy; 365bl Rod Planck/Photo Researchers, Inc.; 365cb Blickwinkel/Hecker/Alamy; 365CL Rick & Nora Bowers/Alamy; 365CR Jerry L. Ferrara/Photo Researchers, Inc.; 365TL Michael Dwyer/Alamy; 365TR Buddy Mays/Alamy; 366cr Anthony Mercieca/Photo Researchers, Inc.; 368 Wolfgang Pölzer/Alamy; 370B Bill Draker/Rolf Nussbaumer Photography/Alamy; 370Bkgrd Rolf Nussbaumer Photography/Alamy; 370T David Cole/Alamy; 371B Rolf Nussbaumer Photography/Alamy; 371T David Davis/Fotolia; 372bl Photoshot Holdings Ltd./Alamy; 372cl Rob Crandall/Alamy; 372tl Michael P. Gadomski/Photo Researcher; 374cr Jack Milchanowski/AgeFotostock/Photolibrary; 374ct Jack Milchanowski/AgeFotostock/Photolibrary; 376cl Inga Spence/Photo Researcher; 376tl Jim Strawser/Alamy; 377tr Wolfgang Pölzer/Alamy; 378 Nature's Images/Photo Researchers; 379B Alan & Sandy Carey/Photo Researchers; 379T Kletr/Fotolia; 382 Art Wolfe/The Image Bank/Getty Images; 383Bkgrd A.CollectionRF/Image Source; 383BL Lee Prince/Shutterstock; 383BR Paul Buck/EPA/Newscom; 383T David Frazier/Corbis Super RF/Alamy; 384b Carsten Peter/Getty Images; 384tl Jupiterimages/Getty Images/Thinkstock; 385B Nigel Cattlin/Alamy; 385Bkgrd Lemmiu/Fotolia; 385CL Natika/Fotolia; 385CR Nigel Cattlin/Photo Researchers, Inc.; 386Bkgrd Chad Ehlers/Stock Connection; 388cl Cordelia Molloy/Photo Researcher.inc; 389t JM Storey, Carleton University; 390Bkgrd Otto Bathurst/Jon Arnold Images/SuperStock; 392Bkgrd NASA Archive/Alamy; 393B Eye Ubiquitous/SuperStock; 393T Masterfile; 403BR Martin Strmiska/Alamy; 403C Mark Conlin/Alamy; 403c Rolf Nussbaumer Photography/Alamy; 403cb Bill Draker/Rolf Nussbaumer Photography/Alamy; 403cr Matt Jones/Shutterstock; 403tr Imagebroker/SuperStock; 405cb Art Wolfe/The Image Bank/Getty Images; 405tr Bill Coster/Alamy; 414Bkgrd Jen & Des Bartlett/OSF/Photolibrary; 417 Magnus Elander/Johner Images/Alamy; 418Bkgrd Jim Lane/Alamy; 419B JupiterImages; 419T JupiterImages; 420cr

Cosmos Blank/Photo Researcher.inc; 420tr Blickwinkel/Alamy; 421B Tim Zurowski/All Canada Photos/Alamy; 421Bkgrd Tomaz Kunst/Fotolia; 421T Dr Ajay Kumar Singh/Shutterstock; 422c Dole/Shutterstock; 422tl ImageDJ/Jupiterimages; 423cr Xavier Safont- V&W/Bruce Coleman Inc./Photoshot; 423tr Photographed by Ori Fragman-Sapir, Jerusalem Botanical Gardens; 428B Nagel Photography/Shutterstock; 428Bkgrd Grady Harrison/Alamy; 428C Bill Draker/Rolf Nussbaumer Photography/Alamy; 428T Jack Milchanowski/Papilio/Alamy; 429C Fred J. Lord/Jaynes Gallery/Danita Delimont/Alamy; 429TL Deb Campbell/Shutterstock; 429TR Tammy Camp/Alamy; 430br Alex Gore/Alamy; 431Bkgrd Getty Images; 431bl Photos.com/Jupiterimages; 431br Mark Conlin/Alamy; 432c Photos To Go/Photo library; 433bc Joze Maucec/Shutterstock; 433bl William Munoz/Photo Researcher.inc; 433br Audrey Snider-Bell/Shutterstock; 434bc John Serrao/Photo Researchers, Inc.; 434br Gilbert S. Grant/Photo Researcher.inc; 434tr Inga Spence/Alamy; 434bl Michael Dye/Fotolia; 435 Gilbert S. Grant/Science Source/Photo Researchers; 436 NHPA/SuperStock; 437B Derrick Hamrick/Rolf Nussbaumer Photography/Alamy; 437T Marvin Dembinsky Photo Associates/Alamy; 439 Edward L. Snow/Photoshot; 440Bkgrd Gengirl/Shutterstock; 440C Scott Camazine/Photo Researchers, Inc.; 440T Scott Camazine/Photo Researchers, Inc.; 441B Clément Philippe/Arterra Picture Library/Alamy; 441C Matt Jeppson/Shutterstock; 441CL FLPA/Alamy; 441CR Juniors Bildarchiv GmbH/Alamy; 441TL Bill Gozansky/Alamy; 441TR Blickwinkel/Alamy; 442bc Dan Suzio/Photo Researchers, Inc.; 443bl Gary Meszaros/Photo Researcher.inc; 443br George Bernard/Photo Researcher.inc; 443tl Dr. Keith Wheeler/Photo Researchers, Inc.; 443tr Stephen Dalton/Photo Researchers, Inc.; 445C Marko König/Imagebroker/Alamy; 445L Jan Taylor/Bruce Coleman Inc/Alamy; 445R Heinz Kühbauch/Imagebroker/Alamy; 448bkgrd Mike Briner/Alamy; 448br Huetter C/Arco Images GmbH/Alamy; 449BR Photos To Go/Photo library; 449cr Mark Conlin/Alamy; 449tr Dole/Shutterstock; 452 Jupiter Images; 453 Jupiter Images

Take Note

This space is yours. It is great for drawing diagrams and making notes.

This is your book. You can write in it.